MW01046394

BUFFETT'S TIPS

A GUIDE TO FINANCIAL LITERACY AND LIFE

JOHN M. LONGO

AND

TYLER J. LONGO

WILEY

Copyright © 2021 by John M. Longo and Tyler J. Longo. All rights reserved.

Published by John Wiley & Sons, Inc., Hoboken, New Jersey.

Published simultaneously in Canada.

No part of this publication may be reproduced, stored in a retrieval system, or transmitted in any form or by any means, electronic, mechanical, photocopying, recording, scanning, or otherwise, except as permitted under Section 107 or 108 of the 1976 United States Copyright Act, without either the prior written permission of the Publisher, or authorization through payment of the appropriate per-copy fee to the Copyright Clearance Center, Inc., 222 Rosewood Drive, Danvers, MA 01923, (978) 750–8400, fax (978) 646–8600, or on the Web at www.copyright.com. Requests to the Publisher for permission should be addressed to the Permissions Department, John Wiley & Sons, Inc., 111 River Street, Hoboken, NJ 07030, (201) 748–6011, fax (201) 748–6008, or online at www.wiley.com/go/permissions.

Limit of Liability/Disclaimer of Warranty: While the publisher and author have used their best efforts in preparing this book, they make no representations or warranties with respect to the accuracy or completeness of the contents of this book and specifically disclaim any implied warranties of merchantability or fitness for a particular purpose. No warranty may be created or extended by sales representatives or written sales materials. The advice and strategies contained herein may not be suitable for your situation. You should consult with a professional where appropriate. Neither the publisher nor author shall be liable for any loss of profit or any other commercial damages, including but not limited to special, incidental, consequential, or other damages.

For general information on our other products and services or for technical support, please contact our Customer Care Department within the United States at (800) 762–2974, outside the United States at (317) 572–3993, or fax (317) 572–4002.

Wiley publishes in a variety of print and electronic formats and by print-on-demand. Some material included with standard print versions of this book may not be included in e-books or in print-on-demand. If this book refers to media such as a CD or DVD that is not included in the version you purchased, you may download this material at http://booksupport.wiley.com. For more information about Wiley products, visit www.wiley.com.

Library of Congress Cataloging-in-Publication Data

Names: Longo, John M., author. | Longo, Tyler J., author. | John Wiley & Sons, Inc., publisher.
Title: Buffett's tips : a guide to financial literacy and life / by John M. Longo, Tyler Longo.
Description: Hoboken, New Jersey : Wiley, [2021] | Includes bibliographical references and index.
Identifiers: LCCN 2020041943 (print) | LCCN 2020041944 (ebook) | ISBN 9781119763918 (cloth) | ISBN 9781119763727 (adobe pdf) | ISBN 9781119763710 (epub)
Subjects: LCSH: Buffett, Warren—Anecdotes. | Financial literacy. | Investments.
Classification: LCC HG179 .L5729 2021 (print) | LCC HG179 (ebook) | DDC 332.67/8—dc23
LC record available at https://lccn.loc.gov/2020041943
LC ebook record available at https://lccn.loc.gov/2020041944

Cover image: Eyeglasses: © bubaone/Getty Images
Hair: Wiley
Cover design: Wiley

SKY10022403_111120

To my wife Kim and son/co-author, Tyler, the two most important people in my life.
—J.L.

To my grandfather for providing me with the seed capital to make my first million.
—T.L.

Contents

Preface

Many surveys have found that a large percentage of households would struggle to come up with $400 in the event of an emergency. The COVID-19 pandemic has turned this conceptual question into a very real one with potentially devastating human consequences. Financial literacy, and ultimately, financial independence are goals that everyone should aspire to. Beyond the knowledge gained, we believe that those who take the lessons of this book to heart will experience a sense of confidence and freedom in financial matters. The confidence to make good financial decisions. Freedom from the stress that comes from living paycheck to paycheck. Ultimately, the freedom to live the life you want to live and to help the people and causes that you care deeply about.

What better way to become financially literate than to use a framework inspired by perhaps the greatest financial mind that ever existed—Warren Buffett's? That's the concept and desired outcome of this book. No one reading this book will become as rich as Warren Buffett, but we do aim to teach you to become financially literate, with the backbone of the book being 100 "tips" or strategies that are largely quotes and anecdotes from Warren Buffett. We're two of his biggest fans and Berkshire Hathaway shareholders.

For decades Buffett met with groups of college students several Fridays each year for a two-plus hour Q&A session, followed by a lunch at a local Omaha restaurant. Gorat's Steakhouse and Piccolo Pete's Restaurant (now closed) were two of Buffett's favorite places to take the students. The students also received a management-guided tour of several of Berkshire's subsidiaries, such as Nebraska Furniture Mart, Borsheims, and the Oriental Trading Company. John, a Finance Professor and money manager, led four trips with Rutgers students to meet with Buffett at Berkshire's headquarters in Omaha, Nebraska. In case you're curious, Buffett did pay for the students' lunch, and a root beer float, Buffett's favorite, was often a dessert. He often also generously posed for selfies and group photos and autographed books. It seemed like Buffett had as good a time on these visits as the students and faculty in attendance.

One thing that struck John about these meetings was Buffett's wisdom on non-financial-related topics, such as the importance of communication skills, having a group of friends that would inspire you, and the significance of helping others. So, although this book is primarily focused on financially related topics, the "life" part of the book contains many equally valuable lessons.

A confluence of events resulted in the creation of this book. Professors are required to do research, so John is always thinking about some type of research activity. He has also taught investment-related courses for roughly 20 years, with an emphasis on value investing, which is Buffett's specialty. Over the past few years, John was teaching his teenage son, Tyler, about financial-related topics in real time. For example, they opened several financial accounts specifically geared towards minors, such as a savings account, checking account, debit card, credit card, college savings plan, and brokerage account. Additionally, Tyler had completed enough coursework in financial-related topics that he was able to make meaningful contributions to this book. Specifically, he has completed coursework in Financial Literacy, AP Economics, AP Statistics, and the Introduction to Business, Finance, and Economics program for high school students at Columbia University. There are a lot of books on Buffett and even more on the topic of financial literacy. But we believe this is the *only* book that effectively combines the two topics.

Part of Buffett's charm is his plain-spoken language, pop culture references, and wonderful sense of humor. You will see many examples of these characteristics in our book. We tried to incorporate those elements into our writing as well. To illustrate this point, here's one example from Chapter 6. "You might find it amazing that Berkshire Hathaway has almost 400,000 employees, but there are only 25 people in Berkshire's corporate headquarters in Omaha. How can he manage so many people with a staff slimmer than Snoop Dogg's waistline?" We want this book to be understandable to all readers, so the emphasis of any conceptual topic is on intuition. Any (non-trivial) formulas are relegated to an endnote or appendix.

Financial literacy is a vast topic, so we considered a number of approaches to deciding on the content for this book. There are some basic building blocks for being financially literate, such as having the right mindset, living within your means, starting early, paying off credit cards, and investing in stocks for the long term. All of these topics receive detailed coverage, peppered with Buffett quotes to drive these points home.

Chapter 1 begins by talking about the incredible life of Warren Buffett. Many people unfamiliar with his story will be surprised at the financial success Buffett experienced at a very young age. We then move on in Chapter 2 to discussing some of the fundamentals of investing, such as the "miracle" of compound interest and how supply and demand interact to determine price. Chapter 3 takes some baby steps into financial products offered by banks and other firms. Things such as a bank account, checking account, and credit cards. It also covers newer apps, such as Venmo and Zelle, as well as your credit score.

Chapters 4 through 6 cover the bond market and stock market, the two most important financial markets for most people. Stocks are clearly at the heart of how Buffett generated his enormous wealth, so they are given detailed coverage. We discuss what a stock is, how it trades, and how it is valued by investors, as well as the features Buffett looks at when he buys part of a company, or a firm in its entirety. Chapter 7 discusses the fundamentals of accounting, which is the language of business. We'll try to make it painless by looking the essence of the financial statements of Apple and drum roll. . .Berkshire Hathaway.

Very few people put all their assets in a single investment. Therefore, it is crucial to discuss risk and how to create a portfolio of investments. We'll discuss two main approaches espoused by Buffett in Chapter 8. First is an index fund, an investment product that aims to own a broad cross section of investments. The second, which we refer to "expert mode," is concentrating your assets in less than 10 firms that you thoroughly understand, or what Buffett refers to as in "your circle of competence."

Part of being financially literate is knowing what is going on in the world of business. So Chapters 9 and 10 discuss the "who's who" of industry, both with respect to people and firms. Regardless of how much money you make, you won't build any wealth if you can't live within your means. We've all read articles about famous celebrities or athletes who were once multimillionaires but eventually went bust. Therefore, Chapter 10 is focused on being thrifty like Buffett. It basically covers ways to save money. Saving money in some respects is more important that making money, since you pay taxes on the latter approach and not the former. The two biggest purchases for most individuals are their homes or cars. Given the importance of these big-ticket purchases, we decided to devote a whole chapter to it, Chapter 12.

Buffett said taking a Dale Carnegie course in communications and dealing with people literally changed his life for the better. Chapter 13 discusses some of the key concepts espoused by Carnegie, as well as a newer topic developed by author Dan Goleman, emotional intelligence. Another big-ticket item for young people, or their parents, is college. It is more of an investment than a purchase; hence, we give the topic its own chapter. Chapter 14 discusses the ins and outs of college, especially with respect to financing it. Buffett has had an enormously successful business career, even separate from his legendary investment prowess. Chapter 15 focuses on career-related issues, such as maxing out your retirement plans and filling out the inevitable paperwork that comes with most jobs. We end the book with Buffett's tips for philanthropy. In case you don't know, Buffett is giving virtually all of his wealth away, proving that he did it for the love of the game, rather than trying to build the biggest pile of money.

We hope you read this book more than once. Even so, it's easy to forget some of the terms or concepts. To aid your life-long learning process, we've included a detailed glossary and summarize each chapter with a handy list of Buffett's tips. If you find this book helpful, don't thank us. Rather, thank Buffett by paying it forward and doing something kind for a person in need. We know he would approve!

Reference

Nova, Annie. "Many Americans Who Can't Afford a $400 Emergency Blame Debt." CNBC, July 21, 2019. https://www.cnbc.com/2019/07/20/heres-why-so-many-americans-cant-handle-a-400-unexpected-expense.html.

Acknowledgments

We would like to thank Joseph Gasparro, Joshua Pearl, and Joshua Rosenbaum for introducing us to the Wiley family and for impressing upon us the need to create a full business plan for the book. Publishing any book today is truly a multimedia endeavor, and Joe, Josh, and Josh helped us see the light on this issue. We also greatly appreciate the work of Bill Falloon, executive editor of finance and investment at Wiley, especially for championing our book within his firm. We thank Purvi Patel of Wiley and her fine staff for their invaluable comments and for shepherding this book from first draft to final production in an impressively quick fashion, without sacrificing quality. We also thank S. Indirakumari of Wiley and Lori Martinsek at Adept Content Solutions for their editorial assistance.

Of course, we were greatly inspired by Warren Buffett. We view him as the greatest investor ever and perhaps an even better person. Although he didn't contribute directly to the writing of this book, his "fingerprints" are all over it through his numerous writings, speeches, media appearances, and homespun wisdom. Buffett is a role model for young and old alike.

We thank Dr. Kimberly Morel, the other central part of our family, for her love, encouragement, enthusiasm, and understanding. Completing a work of this magnitude took a lot of time away from our family activities that would certainly have been more enjoyable. But Kim steadfastly saw the short-term and long-term benefits of this book.

We thank the faculty and student communities of Rutgers University and Global EMBA-Asia (Columbia University, London Business School, and The University of Hong Kong) for encouragement and conversations that ultimately improved this book and its ancillary materials. In particular, we thank Columbia alums Calvin Shueh and JoJo Zou, for helping to promote the book in Asia. We also thank Beacon Trust and Provident Bank for their support of financial literacy and related issues, a cause obviously near and dear to our hearts.

1

Who Is Warren Buffett?

"I tap dance to work, and when I get there I think I'm supposed to lie on my back and paint the ceiling. It's tremendous fun."

—Warren Buffett, *Tap Dancing to Work: Warren Buffett on Practically Everything, 1966–2012*

Introduction

Everyone wants to be financially literate and, ultimately, financially independent. What better way to become financially literate than to use the mindset of Warren Buffett, likely the greatest and richest investor who ever lived? That's the premise of this book. Through his decades of writings, interviews, and speeches, Buffett has provided reams of advice, but he has never written a book on financial literacy. This book takes much of that material and rearranges it in a way to make you financially literate and puts you on the path to becoming financially independent. It may be the next best thing to having Buffett on speed dial!

Buffett's **net worth**—the amount of money he would have after paying off any debts—was recently pegged at about $80 *billion*. But minting money just scratches the surface of Buffett's accomplishments. He'll also go down in history as one of the greatest philanthropists ever. He's giving away virtually all of his money to charitable organizations. If that's not enough, he and Bill Gates—the co-founder of Microsoft—set up the Giving Pledge, an organization where many of the world's billionaires have pledged to give at least half of their wealth to philanthropy.

Buffett's also a great guy, a genuine down-to-earth person who enjoys life on his own terms. He also has an amazing sense of humor.

Here's a sample. When asked why he has a diet filled with junk food, Buffett replied, "I checked the actuarial tables, and the lowest death rate is among six-year-olds. So I decided to eat like a six-year-old." In short, Buffett's a great role model for all people, regardless of age—if you can get past his diet.

In this book, we take some of the experiences, quotes, wit, and wisdom of Warren Buffett and apply them not only to issues related to financial literacy, but also to lessons on having a successful life. It's a boot camp on personal finance and life, with the backbone of the book constructed by the lessons of Warren Buffett from his many writings, interviews, and external biographies. Although the topic of financial literacy may be of greatest benefit to teens and young adults, since they are often starting with a clean slate, the concepts are really applicable to people of all ages, especially those without a financial background. You're probably thinking, "What can I learn from a 90-year-old?" A lot! At least in our view. And we promise to make it painless for you and, hopefully, fun!

Buffett the Teen

Buffett wasn't born rich, and he didn't turn into a financial superstar when he was an older adult. The foundation to his success was laid during his *pre-teen* years. When Buffett was in elementary school, in Omaha, Nebraska, he sold Wrigley's chewing gum and bottles of Coca-Cola—both future investments for him—to make money. He bought his first **stock** at the age of 11! We'll devote two whole chapters in this book to the stock market, but for now you can think of stock as something that makes you part owner of a business. He filed his first tax return at the age of 13, deducting the costs of his watch and bicycle as business expenses, resulting in a net payment to the U.S. Treasury of $7. Paying taxes is about as exciting as watching paint dry, but they're something you *won't* be able to avoid down the road, especially if, make that when, you get richer. One of America's Founding Fathers, Benjamin Franklin, once wrote, "In this world nothing can be said to be certain, except death and taxes."

Buffett's father, Howard, was a United States Congressman for 6 years, and Warren moved with his family to Washington, DC, during the 1940s. Buffett got a newspaper route in DC delivering *The Washington*

Post (another future stock investment). By the age of 15 he had used the profits from his business ventures to buy 40 acres of farmland in Nebraska. As a teenager, he and a friend also bought pinball machines and put them in barbershops, splitting the profits with the shop owners. Thus, we hope you can see that the experiences of the young Warren Buffett played an important role, making him the man that he is today.

Who Are We to Write This Book?

Well, first we think there's a gap in the teachings of Warren Buffett. He participated in a cartoon series, *Secret Millionaires Club*, over the 2011–2013 period that provided some simple tips on financial literacy, but not enough to make someone financially competent. Buffett also writes a detailed letter to the **stockholders** of his firm, Berkshire Hathaway, each year. Stockholders own stock and, therefore, are part owners of a business. You can find Buffett's Berkshire letters going back to 1977 on the web at http://www.berkshirehathaway.com/letters/letters.html.

You may not have heard of Berkshire Hathaway, but you've almost certainly come across some of its businesses. It owns Dairy Queen, GEICO Insurance (the car insurance company with the funny commercials), Duracell batteries, See's Candy, and dozens of other businesses. It's also one of the biggest stockholders in several of the companies that you likely know, such as Coca Cola, Kraft Heinz (maker of ketchup and mac & cheese), American Express, Wells Fargo, Bank of America, Amazon.com, Apple, and many others.

We're guessing you may not want to read a bunch of annual reports and letters to shareholders, even ones as insightful and often humorous as Berkshire's. But we've read them and extracted many nuggets of information that apply to financial literacy and life. There've been several excellent books written about Buffett, such as Alice Schroeder's *The Snowball: Warren Buffett and the Business of Life*. It's the only book on Buffett that had his explicit cooperation, but at 832 pages, it's almost the size of *War and Peace*! Plus, these and other excellent Buffett-oriented books and websites assume you know a fair amount about business and finance. This book doesn't take that knowledge for granted and teaches you financial literacy concepts along the way. So one way to think of this book is that it's like a *CliffsNotes* on the life of Buffett that makes you financially literate and gives you some life skills to boot—but don't sign up just yet for the reality TV show *Survivor*. :-)

John is a finance professor and investment manager who has met Buffett on four separate occasions. He also teaches graduate college classes on Value Investing, a style of making investments that Buffett follows. He teaches mostly at Rutgers University but also on a part-time basis in the global Executive MBA Program at Columbia University—the same university where Buffett got his master's degree. More precisely, it's a joint Executive MBA program among Columbia, London Business School, and the University Hong Kong, one of the most highly ranked in the world. He's also served as chief investment officer for two billion-dollar-plus investment firms for more than 15 years in total.

Younger people may not want to hear advice from a middle-aged college professor and money manager any more than they want to hear it from their parents. Enter Tyler, a teenage high school student who is learning about personal finance issues in real time. He's completed coursework in financial literacy, economics, statistics, and the Introduction to Business, Finance, and Economics Program for high school students at Columbia University. He is co-author of this book, having written portions of the book, and has his finger on the pulse of teens and young adults to a much greater extent than any college professor. And, perhaps most importantly, his understanding of the concepts in this book acts as an important filter to make sure the book is understandable to teens, young adults, and people new to finance of all ages. Plus, if you see slang words, such as savage, lit, and take the L, used to make the book more readable and less stuffy, that's probably Tyler's influence too. You can also thank him for the handy glossary near the end of this book, so you can brush up on your vocab when you hear a financial term that you don't know. He also contributed some important stories, such as the one related to the Patagonian toothfish that we'll get to in **Chapter 11**.

What Is Financial Literacy and Why Does It Matter?

Literacy means being able to read and write. The President's Advisory Council on Financial Literacy defines **personal financial literacy** as "the ability to use knowledge and skills to manage financial resources effectively for a lifetime of financial well-being." In plain English, it means understanding things related to money and being able to make good financial decisions.

In this book, we'll examine a bunch of concepts related to financial literacy including bank accounts, credit cards, credit scores, balancing a checkbook, the stock market, the bond market, mutual funds, real estate, car loans, student loans, mortgage loans, financial websites, financial apps, retirement accounts, and tips for saving money. But we'll do a lot more than that. We'll also discuss other skills that may be useful in your growth and personal development including communication skills, dealing with adversity, learning from mistakes, and ultimately, helping others.

Some Fundamental Buffett "Tips"

Let's start with some core lessons from Buffett's life, or what we'll call "tips." We'll start with 10 tips in the first chapter, but we'll cover 100 in total by the time we're done with this book. Some of the tips are direct quotes from Buffett, while others are implied from his actions or words. And we'll make it easy for you, summarizing a list of the "tips" at the end of each chapter, just in case someone forced you to read this book. :-) (You can just skip to the tips and be done with it!) Here's our first tip for building wealth based on the life of the young Warren Buffett.

Imagine having—through your own hard work and *not* by gift—the equivalent of roughly $60,000 by the time you finished high school. That's some serious coin! Well, that's about what Buffett had, adjusted for **inflation**, back in the late 1940s.

Inflation refers to rising prices. We'll cover how it's measured in some more detail later in the book, but for now you can assume that the prices of most things rise over time. College tuition is a biggie for most people under the age of 30, or for someone paying the bill. Tuition, room, board/food, fees, and books at top private colleges can run more than $75,000 a *year* today. But around 30 years ago, the number was closer to $17,000 for these same "name brand" schools. The same dynamic—rising prices—is usually true if you look at the prices of cars, homes, doctor's visits, and a broad mix of products and services that make up the economy.

The sooner you start saving, the more time your money is able to work for you. The **interest rate** is the rate at which your money grows if you are saving. Or the rate at which your debt grows if you borrow money. We'll cover more on this topic in **Chapter 2** and **Chapter 3**. For now, you can think of interest as a snowball rolling downhill. That's sort of how the book by Alice Schroeder we mentioned earlier,

The Snowball: Warren Buffett and the Business of Life, got its title. There's a quote from Buffett on the back book jacket, which says, "Life is like a snowball. The important thing is finding wet snow and a really long hill." A really long hill is the equivalent of starting early.

One more point on the importance of interest before we move on. A journalist reportedly once asked Albert Einstein, perhaps the most brilliant physicist ever, what he thought was the greatest invention of all time. Einstein purportedly responded, "Compound interest." Compound interest refers to the interest earned on interest. The "miracle of compound interest," as it's sometimes referred to in financial circles, explains how small sums of money can grow into gigantic sums of money over long periods of time. It also explains how small debts can snowball into huge debts. Better yet, stay out of debt, if you can avoid it.

Getting back to the young Buffett, his first known business enterprise started when he was only 6 years old! Buffett bought packs of gum—Juicy Fruit, Spearmint, Doublemint, and so forth—from his grandfather's grocery store, and he would go around door to door in his neighborhood selling them at a higher price. A little bit later he set up a lemonade stand near his friend's house, since it had more traffic, and therefore more potential customers. Sharp thinking for someone still in elementary school!

Other early ventures included finding stray golf balls at a local golf course and then reselling them later for a **profit**. Profit is the money you make from selling an item (also known as **revenue**), minus any expenses involved in selling the item. In this case, Buffett had no expenses since he got the stray golf balls for nothing, so his profit was equal to his sales, or revenue. This brings to mind a quote that dates back to at least 1860, "One man's trash is another man's treasure." While we're on the topic of trash, the young Buffett would often go to the horse racetrack and look for tickets thrown on the ground. Once in a while he would find a winning ticket that someone mistakenly threw away and cash it in. For a short while he also made money at the track selling a "tip sheet"—a list of predictions of which horses would win each race. That is, until the people running the racetrack shut his tip sheet business down. Bummer!

Buffett eventually got a "real" job as a caddy, carrying golf clubs for adults playing golf, at a wage of $3 a day, or about $50 today, adjusted for inflation. And we previously mentioned his paper route and pinball machine businesses that were still ongoing at the time that had him minting money. Needless to say, Buffett got an early start in business in route to becoming a billionaire. If you don't have much money right now, don't worry. Time is on your side, as long as you get started soon, like that snowball rolling downhill. Need more motivation? Consider the words of Lao-Tzu, an ancient Chinese philosopher, who once said, "A journey of a thousand miles begins with a single step." The previous discussion gets us to our first Tip.

Buffett Tip 1:

Start building wealth early.

Buffett's Work Ethic

John once asked Buffett if he thought a great investor was born or made. Buffett said it was a combination of both. He gave the example of the champion golfer, Tiger Woods, in his prime. Buffett said that Tiger was born with an aptitude for golf, but he also put in an insane amount of practice by often hitting 500 golf balls a day. Practicing hard each day, when combined with his huge natural talent, turned Tiger Woods from a good golfer into a *great* golfer.

The first part of working hard is simply showing up on time, *all the time*. Not just when you feel like it, or when it's easy. Woody Allen, the comedian and film director, once said, "Eighty percent of success is just showing up." In other words, many people aren't responsible and reliable. You can get ahead of 80% of people just by being responsible and doing what is expected of you. That goes for school, work, relationships, and many other activities.

Thomas Edison, inventor of the modern lightbulb, record player (the ancient way we listened to music before we had streaming and downloadable music), and movie camera, said, "Ninety percent of a man's success in business is perspiration." And, of course, success in business applies to women too. By the way, Buffett is a huge proponent of women in business, as we'll discuss later in this book.

A quote often (incorrectly) attributed to Thomas Jefferson says, "The harder I work, the more luck I have." According to our research, this quote, or something similar, first came from writer Coleman Cox. Regardless of who first said it, it's good advice. Hard work often gives rise to new opportunities and the skill set to make the most of them, bringing to mind the expression, "Make your own luck."

We discussed several of the jobs that Buffett had, even before he graduated from high school. Although he liked most of his jobs, clearly they involved some hard work. He had three paper routes when he was in high school, making him the equivalent of $28,000 a year, adjusted for inflation. Buffett estimated that he delivered almost 600,000 newspapers when he was a teenager. With all that throwing, we're surprised he didn't become a professional baseball player. Buffett usually had to wake up before 5:00 a.m. to deliver his papers before school. His family would often return to Omaha during the summers. One summer job for Buffett in his teen years involved him carrying 50-pound bags of animal feed from a railroad freight car to a warehouse. Later, when he became interested in dating girls, he would read about books to develop big arm muscles. Suns out, guns out!

Ashton Kutcher, a hugely successful actor perhaps best known for his roles in TV shows *That 70's Show*, *Punk'd*, and *Two and a Half Men*, said in a 2013 speech at the Teen Choice Awards, "I never had a job that was better than me." Before Kutcher was a big TV and movie star, he had menial jobs such as sweeping Cheerios dust off the factory floor. And it might surprise you to learn that Kutcher has made many millions of dollars outside of acting, from his investments. For example, he made extremely successful investments in Uber and Airbnb.

Let's turn that advice from Buffett, Edison, Jefferson, and others into our second Tip.

Buffett Tip 2:

Work hard.

Buffett Has Spent a Lifetime Learning

Many of the *Secret Millionaires Club* episodes ended with Buffett's cartoon character saying, "The more you learn, the more you earn." It's true, and we'll show you some data to support that quote. Right off the bat, let's turn that Buffett quote into a Tip.

Buffett Tip 3:

The more you learn, the more you earn.

Income, or the amount of money you make from your job and other sources, generally goes up with educational level. A 2019 study by a unit of the US government, The Bureau of Labor Statistics (BLS), examined weekly income levels and **unemployment rates** by educational levels. Someone is considered unemployed if they are not able to find work *and* are looking for a job.

The study found that in 2019, someone with a four-year college degree (bachelor's) earned $1,248 a week on average, more than twice the amount ($592 a week) earned by a high school dropout. Not only did the college graduates earn more, they also had significantly lower unemployment rates, making it easier for them to get a job if they needed one. The college graduates had a 2.2% unemployment rate, while the high school dropouts had a 5.4% unemployment rate.

But wait, it gets better for those more educated. People who attended graduate school (college beyond a four-year degree), made even more money and also had lower unemployment rates. The best paid and most likely to find jobs were people who went to professional graduate schools, including doctors, lawyers, and businesspeople. Those holding a graduate professional degree earned an average of $1,861 a week and had an unemployment rate of only 1.6%. If you see someone cruising by you in a Tesla, Mercedes, BMW, or Porsche, odds are they have a professional degree! **Table 1.1** provides a summary of the study's results.

https://www.bls.gov/emp/tables/unemployment-earnings-education.htm

Buffett was a strong student, although he had a little bit of trouble with his grades when he first moved to DC, getting a bunch of Cs. He was a bookworm and estimated he read about 100 books, outside of what was required by school, by the time he graduated from high school. He read most of the financial-related books in his library twice! One of his favorites, *One Thousand Ways to Make $1,000*, was tied to his interest in business. Buffett skipped a grade and was born in August, so he was younger than most of his classmates and graduated high school at the ripe old age of 16.

Buffett graduated from his high school ranked 16th out of a class of 374. His businesses were doing well, and he wasn't keen on attending college but took his father's advice and entered the business school of the University of Pennsylvania—The Wharton School. It's often ranked as the top business school in the US, if not the entire world.

The University of Pennsylvania is one of eight Ivy League schools, which are among the best and most prestigious colleges in the world.

Table 1.1 Unemployment rates and earnings by educational attainment, 2019

Educational attainment	Unemployment Rate (%)	Median Usual Weekly Earnings ($)
Doctoral degree	1.1	1883
Professional degree	1.6	1861
Master's degree	2.0	1497
Bachelor's degree	2.2	1248
Associate's degree	2.7	887
Some college, no degree	3.3	833
High school diploma	3.7	746
Less than a high school diploma	5.4	592
Total	**3.0**	**969**

Source: "Employment Projections", U.S. Bureau of Labor Statistics.

The eight Ivy League schools ordered by the year they were founded are Harvard University, Yale University, University of Pennsylvania, Princeton University, Columbia University, Brown University, Dartmouth College, and Cornell University. Buffett spent two years at the University of Pennsylvania but got homesick and wanted to focus on his business ventures in Nebraska. So he finished his undergraduate degree in business administration from The University of Nebraska–Lincoln at the age of 19. He had roughly $100,000, when adjusted for inflation, by the time he finished college. Today, sadly, many college students end up more than $100,000 in debt. In **Chapter 14**, we'll give you some advice on how to avoid, or at least reduce, this.

A year after finishing his undergraduate degree, Buffett attended Columbia University, another Ivy League university, in New York City. He graduated with a master's degree in economics from Columbia at the age of 20. By that time, Buffett was a budding financial superstar. He received the only A+ in a graduate school class at Columbia taught by his eventual mentor, investment legend Benjamin Graham.

Why Is Buffett Happy?

Buffett is a happy guy, in large part because he loves what he does for a living. He said, "I can certainly define happiness, because happy is what

I am. I get to do what I like to do every single day of the year. I get to do it with people I like, and I don't have to associate with anybody who causes my stomach to churn. I tap dance to work, and when I get there I think I'm supposed to lie on my back and paint the ceiling. It's tremendous fun." We'll simplify that quote for our fourth tip.

Buffett Tip 4:

Do what you love for a living.

Despite the success of the TV show *Dancing with the Stars*, most young people don't tap dance anymore. For you, it might be doing the Floss Dance, Nae Nae, or Gangnam Style Dance on the way to work. :-) Needless to say, Buffett loves his job, running and making investments for Berkshire Hathaway. That's why he didn't retire even after he became enormously wealthy. He also likes the people he works with, especially his business partner, Charlie Munger. You can view Charlie as Buffett's BFF, using today's hip language. Munger, another billionaire investor, is 96 and still works too! We'll be hearing a lot more about Charlie over the course of this book, so you may want to remember his name.

One of Berkshire Hathaway's companies is Nebraska Furniture Mart. Its Omaha, Nebraska, store is the biggest furniture store in North America. Yes, they sell furniture, but also a bunch of other items, such as TVs, computers, and refrigerators. They basically sell anything that you might need to furnish your home. Berkshire bought the company in 1983 from its owner, Rose Blumkin, affectionately known as "Mrs. B." Even though she was wealthy, Mrs. B worked at the Furniture Mart until shortly before her death at the age of 104! For nearly her entire business career, Mrs. B exhibited a tremendous work ethic, often working 7 days a week, 10 hours a day. In her later years, she still worked extremely long hours and used a motor scooter to get around. Now that's commitment!

In one of John's meetings with Buffett, someone asked Buffett what was his favorite place to go. Buffett replied, "The office." He went on to say that he has vacationed in some nice places around the world, but he'd rather be working than traveling to some distant land. The bottom line is this. If you do what you love for a job, you will enjoy going to work. You're more likely to be successful at your job since you'll probably be very good at it, which will ultimately lead not only to more money but also to greater happiness. We're going to devote **Chapter 15** to career-related issues, through the lens of Buffett, of course.

Improve Your Communication Skills and See Your Lifetime Earnings Increase 50%

In another of John's meetings with Buffett, a student asked what skills would be most valuable for having a successful career. Buffett's response? Communication skills. He said, if you have a good idea and can't communicate it well, it's similar to "liking a girl and winking at her in the dark." Of course, in the dark no one could see if you're winking and, therefore, it would have no effect. He also estimated that having strong communication skills, over time, could increase your earnings power by 50%—an awesome return on your time investment and one that merits a Tip.

Buffett Tip 5:

Develop strong communication skills.

Communication skills include speaking, writing, listening, and interpersonal skills. That is, skills helpful in getting along with, influencing, and leading other people. Buffett said the biggest thing that improved his communication skills was taking a Dale Carnegie course. Dale Carnegie was a self-help guru active during the first half of the 20th century, perhaps best known for his book, *How to Win Friends and Influence People*. At last count, the book has sold 30 million copies worldwide, so it must be pretty good! We'll devote an entire chapter, **Chapter 13**, to communication and interpersonal skills, including a large section devoted to techniques taught by Dale Carnegie.

Buffett claims he was a "basket case" before taking the Dale Carnegie course. Although he attended some excellent colleges, such as the University of Pennsylvania, University of Nebraska, and Columbia University, the only diploma he hangs on his office wall is from his Dale Carnegie program.

It might not be fair, but people often form an impression of your intelligence based on the way you speak and write. If you act like a jerk or bully, people won't want to be around you. They won't want work with or for you. Or date you. So take Buffett's word for it. Polishing up and improving your communications skills is one of the most important things you can do to improve not only your wealth but also virtually all other aspects of your life.

Acting with Integrity Is the Right Thing to Do and Good for Business

Integrity means being honest and acting in an honorable and ethical manner. Being a person of your word. Being trustworthy. Being principled. Buffett was never perfect and got into a bit of trouble when he was a teen. But today, Buffett's known for his integrity almost as much as he is known for his wealth and philanthropy. Let's look at a few examples.

In the late 1960s Buffett was investing money for some family, friends, and acquaintances with spectacular results. He was making the equivalent of more than a million dollars a year, adjusted for inflation. However, he decided to shut down his investment business and give investors their money back. Why? He thought the stock market was expensive and that his style of investing was out of favor. In other words, if he didn't think he could do a good job for his investors, he would pass up the chance to earn millions of dollars a year!

Buffett tells his employees to act in a manner such that they wouldn't be embarrassed if they saw their actions written up by a reporter in their local newspaper for all to see. Today, you might substitute "newspaper" for Facebook, Instagram, or Snapchat.

In Berkshire's 1990 Letter to Shareholders, Buffett wrote, "We will behave exactly as promised, both because we have so promised, and because we need to in order to achieve the best business results." That is, behaving with integrity isn't only the right thing to do morally, it makes for good business.

In the 1990s, Buffett invested in a Wall Street investment bank by the name of Salomon Brothers. Among other things, investment banks trade stocks and bonds. Some of the firm's biggest traders broke some securities laws, and the firm was on the verge of failing. Buffett agreed to step in and run the firm, in an effort to prevent it from going under. He was asked to testify before Congress, which was conducting a hearing on the trading scandal. In his opening remarks, Buffett uttered one of his most famous phrases, "Lose money for the firm and I will be understanding. Lose a shred of reputation for the firm and I will be ruthless."

More recently, in early 2017, a person running a local Dairy Queen business in Zion, Illinois, made some racist remarks directed at a customer. Recall, Dairy Queen is owned by Buffett's Berkshire Hathaway. Dairy Queen promptly fired the operator of the Zion Dairy Queen that made the racist remark and shut down the location. A Dairy Queen spokesperson said, "The recent actions of this franchisee are inexcusable, reprehensible, unacceptable, and do not represent the values of the Dairy Queen family, our employees, fans, and other independent franchises around the world. We expect our franchisees and their employees to treat every single person who walks through their doors with the utmost dignity and respect. Nothing less is acceptable." Although Buffett likely let Dairy Queen's senior management handle this particular case, there is no denying that Berkshire's culture required the firm to respond with a swift and severe punishment. All of these stories have the concept of integrity at their core and merits a Tip.

Buffett Tip 6:

Act with integrity.

Buy Low, Sell High

If you buy something online or in person at a great price you probably feel good. Make that great. We've all seen some "buy one, get one free" or 70% off sales. And who doesn't love free stuff? The investment advice "Buy low and sell high" is as old as the hills. One of Walmart's most famous slogans is "Save money, live better."

In Buffett's case, he buys stocks or entire companies. He follows a style of investment called **Value Investing**. Value investors try to buy things at deep discounts. The lower you buy, the greater the profit when you sell, assuming the thing you're selling rises in price.

Buffett's most famous investment is Berkshire Hathaway. He first started buying the stock way back in December 1962 at $7.65 a share. Looking at its books and records, or what investment analysts term **financial statements**, Buffett thought it should have been worth at least $20.00 a share. So he thought he was getting it at about a 62% discount. He eventually bought enough shares to acquire full control of the company in 1965. And today? The stock is worth about $300,000 a share! Yes, for a single share!

Buffett's investment successes are almost too numerous to mention. He first gained attention on **Wall Street,** a term which refers not only to the physical street in downtown Manhattan but also to the firms at the center of the US financial system, buying stock in American Express. You probably know American Express for their credit cards.

In 1963, American Express helped finance a firm called Allied Crude Vegetable Oil Refining Company. It was a fancy name for a company that sold salad oil or dressing. The main problem was that the company committed fraud, lying about their business. They stored their salad oil in huge barrels filled with water with salad oil sprinkled on the top, when they told everyone the barrels were full of only salad oil. Oops!

Eventually, someone blew the whistle on the scam, and the jig was up. American Express lent the company money before the fraud was uncovered, and its stock took a huge hit when the scam was revealed. Enter Warren Buffett. He thought the scandal was a bad but not insurmountable problem for American Express. Their other businesses, such as credit cards and **traveler's checks** (a substitute for cash when spending money overseas), were doing well. Buffett called several people to make sure that was still the case. American Express's stock plunged from $65 a share, before the scandal, to $37 in January 1964. Buffett started buying it around the time the stock cratered. When he sold, about 5 years later, the stock had gone up more than five-fold! Buffett has hit many other investment "grand slams" that we'll cover throughout this book. Let's turn the common thread of these stories into a Tip.

Buffett Tip 7:

Buy things at attractive prices.

Buffett Doesn't Succumb to Peer Pressure: The Inner Scorecard

Peer pressure is one of the hardest things for young people, and even adults, to deal with. It's hard to say no when your friends are asking you to do things, even when you think they might be wrong. Buffett developed a response for dealing with peer pressure. It's something he learned from his father, Howard Buffett. He calls it an **Inner Scorecard**. It basically means living your life on your own terms, according to your own self-judgment. If you are influenced more by what others think, then you have an **Outer Scorecard**.

Buffett said, "The big question about how people behave is whether they've got an Inner Scorecard or an Outer Scorecard. It helps if you can be satisfied with an Inner Scorecard." That is, try not to worry too much about what other people think. Do what you think is right. Buffett went on to say, "In teaching your kids, I think the lesson they're learning at a very, very early age is what their parents put the emphasis on. If all the emphasis is on what the world's going to think about you, forgetting about how you really behave, you'll end up with an Outer Scorecard."

We're keeping this book PG rated. Here's one of the more risqué Buffett quotes, relating to the Inner Scorecard concept. He said, "I always pose it this way. I say: 'Lookit. Would you rather be the world's greatest lover, but have everyone think you're the world's worst lover? Or would you rather be the world's worst lover but have everyone think you're the world's greatest lover?'" Of course, someone following the Inner Scorecard mentality wouldn't care much for what the outside world thought, secure in their own truth.

Buffett applies an Inner Scorecard to all areas of his life, despite his multi-billionaire status. He lives a fairly modest existence, residing in the same house—***not*** a mansion—since 1958. His diet is terrible, healthwise, often consisting of McDonald's and a bunch of junk food like hamburgers, fudge, peanut brittle, and Cherry Coke. From an investment standpoint, he is not afraid to go against the crowd. In fact, that's where you can make the most money if you're right. Buffett said, "Be fearful when others are greedy and greedy when others are fearful." We'll come back to this point in more detail in **Chapter 5**, but here's a quick example.

He put this famous saying into action during **The Great Recession** of 2007–2009, which was the one of the biggest downturns in the economy we've had since World War II. Financial firms, such as Citibank, Lehman Brothers, Bear Stearns, Merrill Lynch, Morgan Stanley, and American International Group (AIG), were among the most affected during The Great Recession.

In the midst of The Great Recession, while it looked like the financial markets were collapsing, Buffett bought stock in Goldman Sachs and General Electric, which had a big financial division. Later, he bought stock in Bank of America. And when the economy recovered—you guessed it—he made a killing, pocketing billions of dollars on each investment!

As we are writing this book the world is grappling with the fallout from the coronavirus, COVID 19. Berkshire is sitting on a pile of more than $125 billion in cash as the COVID-19 crisis unfolds. We're more than willing to bet on the end financial result for Buffett and Berkshire. Another series of purchases of great companies at great prices and another multibillion-dollar profit for Berkshire. Let's turn Buffett's thoughts on the Inner Scorecard into a Tip.

Buffett Tip 8:

Don't be swayed by the crowd—have an Inner Scorecard.

Buffett's Fallback Career—Comedian

Anyone over the age of five realizes that life is like a rollercoaster, with lots of ups and downs. As Apple co-founder Steve Jobs once said in a terrific commencement speech at Stanford University, "Sometimes life's going to hit you in the head with a brick. Don't lose faith." Jobs dealt with many highs and lows over the course of his incredible life. He was once fired by Apple's **Board of Directors**, the group with the ultimate responsibility for running a company. You might be thinking, "How can you get fired from a company you started?" Well, Jobs didn't own all of the company, and he clashed with the board on how to best run the company. They sided with another manager, and Jobs was kicked out of Apple in 1985. He eventually made a triumphant return in 1997, turning Apple into the most valuable stock in the world at the time of his passing.

Steve Jobs also experienced a long-term battle with cancer. He was first diagnosed with pancreatic cancer in 2003 and bravely fought the disease over the course of many years. He ultimately died of cancer in October 2011 but not before changing the world.

If Buffett didn't turn out to be a great investor, he may have had a second career as a comedian. He often pokes fun at himself, telling students that they dress and eat better than him. People that poke fun at themselves have what's known as a self-deprecating sense of humor. Buffett has it in spades, and it's a technique that's strongly encouraged by those running Dale Carnegie seminars today. Few people like a show-off, "hot dog," or simply a jerk. So back to Buffett and his cool sense of humor. Check out his (PG-rated) response when asked about career advice:

"There comes a time when you ought to start doing what you want. Take a job that you love. You will jump out of bed in the morning. I think you are out of your mind if you keep taking jobs that you don't like because you think it will look good on your resume. Isn't that a little like saving up sex for your old age?"

A resume, as you probably know, is a document that describes your education, work experience, and skills. You usually give a print or electronic copy to people when you're looking for a job. We'll get back to that topic in **Chapter 15** on careers.

Here's another self-deprecating Buffett quote from his 1987 Chairman's Letter to Berkshire Shareholders:

"It must be noted that your Chairman, always a quick study, required only 20 years to recognize how important it was to buy good businesses. In the interim, I searched for 'bargains'—and had the misfortune to find some. My punishment was an education in the economics of short-line farm implement manufacturers, third-place department stores, and New England textile manufacturers."

You get the point(s). Buffett is a funny guy who doesn't take himself too seriously, despite his almost unfathomable success, and that's one of the reasons why people like him so much. This gets us to our ninth Tip.

Buffett Tip 9:

Be able to laugh at yourself.

Buffett's Lasting Legacy: Philanthropy

Buffett is donating more than 99% of his money to philanthropic organizations. To us, at least, that proves that his quest for becoming the richest person in the world was about the love of his work and not about the money. A generation or two from now, people may remember him more for his philanthropic work than for his investment prowess. It may sound hard to believe, but many people know Bill Gates today as a person who runs the Gates foundation, rather than as the co-founder of Microsoft.

The point is Buffett didn't become rich to purchase a lot of bling. That's not how he rolls. Buffett said, "If you're in the luckiest 1% of humanity, you owe it to the rest of humanity to think about the other 99%." Buffett gives credit to his father and his first wife, Susan or Susie, for having the biggest impacts on his character and ethics. Howard Buffett was a man of such high integrity that when he served in Congress, he refused to accept an increase in his pay, since he claimed he was voted in at the lower rate.

Buffett's wife Susan was involved in numerous charities and supported the civil rights movement in the 1960s, which fought for equal rights for all Americans. In one of Buffett's best-known charity activities, he auctions off a lunch each year for the Glide Foundation of San Francisco. People bid in an auction with the winning prize resulting in a lunch date with Buffett. The winning bid has sometimes exceeded $4.5 million! That is one expensive lunch! Susan Buffett was the one who brought the Glide Foundation to Buffett's attention. And we mentioned Buffett working with Bill Gates on the Giving Pledge, whereby trillions of dollars will eventually be donated to philanthropic activities.

If you are not financially rich, there are still many things you can do for charity that don't involve money. They might involve giving your time, labor, or heart (not literally!). On one of John's trips with college students to see Buffett, he presented Buffett with a card where each person pledged to do something for charity. It was a "thank you" gift for Buffett, for taking the time to host them. His response after getting the card? "That was the best thing you could have done for me." We'll cover the topics of charity and philanthropy in our last chapter, **Chapter 16,** but let's begin to close this chapter with its final Tip.

Buffett Tip 10:

Give back to society.

So that's an intro to Warren Buffett and some fundamental tips on financial literacy and life to get the ball, or book, rolling. Welcome aboard!

Buffett's Tips from Chapter 1

Buffett Tip 1: Start building wealth early.
Buffett Tip 2: Work hard.
Buffett Tip 3: The more you learn, the more you earn.
Buffett Tip 4: Do what you love for a living.
Buffett Tip 5: Develop strong communication skills.
Buffett Tip 6: Act with integrity.
Buffett Tip 7: Buy things at attractive prices.
Buffett Tip 8: Don't be swayed by the crowd—have an Inner Scorecard.
Buffett Tip 9: Be able to laugh at yourself.
Buffett Tip 10: Give back to society.

References

"Bloomberg Billionaires Index." Bloomberg.com, *Bloomberg News.* Accessed June 10, 2020. http://www.bloomberg.com/billionaires/.

Brownlee, Adam P. "Warren Buffett: Be Fearful When Others Are Greedy." *Investopedia,* April 5, 2019. https://www.investopedia.com/articles/investing/012116/warren-buffett-be-fearful-when-others-are-greedy.asp.

Buffett, Warren. "Berkshire Hathaway Inc. Shareholder Letters." Accessed June 10, 2020. https://www.berkshirehathaway.com/letters/letters.html.

Buffett, Warren. "Letter to Shareholders of Berkshire Hathaway Inc." Berkshire Hathaway, Inc., 1990. https://www.berkshirehathaway.com/letters/1990.html.

Buffett, Warren. "My Philanthropic Pledge." *The Giving Pledge.* Accessed June 27, 2020. https://givingpledge.org/Pledger.aspx?id=177.

Buffett, Warren. *Secret Millionaires Club: Volume 1.* A Squared, 2013. https://www.smckids.com/.

Carnegie, Dale. *How to Win Friends and Influence People.* New York: Simon & Schuster, 1936.

Close, Kerry. "Warren Buffett Documentary to Air on HBO | Fortune." Fortune, December 7, 2016. https://fortune.com/2016/12/07/warren-buffett-documentary-hbo/.

"Cryptocurrency Pioneer Bids $4.5 Million to Have Lunch with Warren Buffett." MarketWatch, June 3, 2019. https://www.marketwatch.com/story/cryptocurrency-pioneer-bids-45-million-to-have-lunch-with-warren-buffett-2019-06-03.

Dillon. "Why Warren Buffett Decided to Close His Investment Partnership in 1969." *Vintage Value Investing,* September 21, 2016. https://www.vintagevalueinvesting.com/warren-buffett-decided-to-close-his-buffett-partnership/.

Duke, Phil La. "If 80 Percent of Success Is Showing Up Then 20 Percent Is Following Up." *Entrepreneur,* November 8, 2016. http://www.entrepreneur.com/article/282745.

FINN. "Warren Buffett on Reputation: Lose a Shred and I Will Be Ruthless (1991)." YouTube Video, 1:00, February 22, 2016. https://www.youtube.com/watch?v=7u7-UNSkr4o.

Garnett, Laura. "27 Quotes That Will Inspire You to Have Work You Love." *Inc.,* November 4, 2019. https://www.inc.com/laura-garnett/27-quotes-that-will-inspire-you-to-have-work-you-love.html.

Gonzales, Sara. "Dairy Queen Closes Franchise after Owner's Racist Tirade against a Biracial Customer." *TheBlaze,* January 9, 2017. http://www.theblaze.com/news/2017/01/09/dairy-queen-closes-franchise-after-owners-racist-tirade-against-a-biracial-customer/.

Green, William. "I've Followed Warren Buffett for Decades and Keep Coming Back to These 10 Quotes." *Observer*, May 4, 2015. https://observer.com/2015/05/ive-followed-warren-buffett-for-decades-and-keep-coming-back-to-these-10-quotes/.

Greenburg, Zack O'Malley. "How Ashton Kutcher and Guy Oseary Built a $250 Million Portfolio with Startups like Uber and Airbnb." *Forbes* magazine, August 9, 2016. http://www.forbes.com/sites/zackomalleygreenburg/2016/03/23/how-ashton-kutcher-and-guy-oseary-built-a-250-million-portfolio-with-startups-like-uber-and-airbnb/.

Hilimire, Jeff. "The Inner Scorecard vs Outer Scorecard." *Begin the Begin,* July 28, 2016. https://jeffhilimire.com/2016/07/the-inner-scorecard-vs-outer-scorecard/.

History.com Editors. "Great Recession." History.com. A&E Television Networks, October 11, 2019. https://www.history.com/topics/21st-century/recession.

Kennon, Joshua. "Warren Buffet: One of the Wealthiest People in America." *The Balance,* March 19, 2020. http://www.thebalance.com/warren-buffett-timeline-356439.

Langlois, Shawn. "From $6,000 to $73 Billion: Warren Buffett's Wealth through the Ages." *MarketWatch,* January 6, 2017. http://www.marketwatch.com/story/from-6000-to-67-billion-warren-buffetts-wealth-through-the-ages-2015-08-17.

Loomis, Carol. *Tap Dancing to Work: Warren Buffett on Practically Everything, 1966–2012.* London: Portfolio Penguin, 2014.

Lowenstein, Roger. *Buffett the Making of an American Capitalist.* New York: Random House Trade, 2008.

Mikkelson, David. "Einstein and Compound Interest." Snopes.com, April 19, 2011. https://www.snopes.com/fact-check/compound-interest/.

Miller, Jeremy. "This Is Warren Buffett's Top Investment Rule." *Time,* April 21, 2016. https://time.com/4286850/warren-buffetts-ground-rules/.

Minaker, Frances C. *One Thousand Ways to Make $1000: Practical Suggestions, Based on Actual Experience, for Starting a Business of Your Own and Making Money in Your Spare Time.* Austin, TX: The Greenleaf Groups, 2016.

Myers, Brandon. "Ashton Kutcher Speech—Teen Choice Awards (HQ)." YouTube Video, 4:40, August 13, 2013, https://www.youtube.com/watch?v=FNXwKGZHmDc&t=4s.

O'Toole, Garson. "I'm a Great Believer in Luck. The Harder I Work, the More Luck I Have" *Quote Investigator,* July 21, 2012. https://quoteinvestigator.com/2012/07/21/luck-hard-work/.

O'Toole, Garson. "Showing Up Is 80 Percent of Life." *Quote Investigator,* June 10, 2013. https://quoteinvestigator.com/2013/06/10/showing-up/.

Schroeder, Alice. *The Snowball: Warren Buffett and the Business of Life.* New York: Bantam Books, 2009.

Sellers, Patricia. "Warren Buffett's Secret to Staying Young: 'I Eat Like a Six-Year-Old'" *Fortune,* February 25, 2015. https://fortune.com/2015/02/25/warren-buffett-diet-coke/.

Smith, Robert. "Buffett Gift Sends $31 Billion to Gates Foundation." NPR, *June* 26, 2006. http://www.npr.org/templates/story/story.php?storyId=5512893.

Stanford. "Steve Jobs' 2005 Stanford Commencement Address." YouTube Video, 15:04, March, 7 2008. https://www.youtube.com/watch?v=UF8uR6Z6KLc.

Taylor, Bryan. "How the Salad Oil Swindle of 1963 Nearly Crippled the NYSE." *Business Insider,* November 23, 2013. http://www.businessinsider.com/the-great-salad-oil-scandal-of-1963-2013-11.

Tian, Charlie. "Jokes in Warren Buffett's Shareholder Letters." *GuruFocus,* November 22, 2016. http://www.gurufocus.com/news/459932/jokes-in-warren-buffetts-shareholder-letters.

Todd, Susan. "Graduate Students Spend a Day with Warren Buffett." *Rutgers Business School-Newark and New Brunswick,* October 17, 2016. https://www.business.rutgers.edu/news/graduate-students-spend-day-warren-buffett.

Tolstoy, Leo. *War and Peace*. New York: New American Library, 2007.

"Unemployment Rates and Earnings by Educational Attainment." US Bureau of Labor Statistics, September 4, 2019. https://www.bls.gov/emp/chart-unemployment-earnings-education.htm.

"What Is Financial Literacy—Your Life Your Money." Public Broadcasting Service. Accessed June 13, 2020. http://www.pbs.org/your-life-your-money/more/what_is_financial_literacy.php.

2

Investment Fundamentals According to Buffett

"The most important quality for an investor is temperament, not intellect."
—Warren Buffett, *Rules That Warren Buffett Lives By*

Introduction

When you first started school, you were taught the "3 Rs"—reading, 'riting, and 'rithmetic. Okay, for those grammatical purists out there (i.e., "grammandos"), let's relabel them as reading, writing, and arithmetic (math). These three subjects were the foundation for most of the subjects you learned from elementary school on. Most public schools and many private schools use what's known as the Common Core, a more detailed framework on what should be taught in math and language arts/English classes. Well, there's a core set of concepts in financial literacy, and we're going to tackle some of them in this chapter. And by the end of this book, we think you should consider yourselves financially literate, if you didn't just skim the summary sections. :-)

You've probably heard the expression "Time is money." Financial folks twist this around a bit, saying, "There is a time value to money." One easy way to understand this concept is that if you have some cash, let's say $100, you could put it in the bank and earn interest, a concept we mentioned in **Chapter 1**. The $100 will grow to something more than $100 over time. The exact amount depends on the interest rate. The bank takes the money you deposited and lends out most of it to people who need money, known as **borrowers**. The borrower might need the money for a car loan, student loan, home loan, or a whole host of other reasons. Borrowers could also be companies or governments. A loan on a home or building is known as a **mortgage**.

The interest rate is one form of what is called the **return on an investment**. The return is the amount at which your money grows if you make money or falls if you lose money. So a return could be computed when you put your money in the bank, to buy a stock, house, or many other things. It's the number that is one of the main drivers of your net worth. But let's just stick with the notion of interest rates for now.

The "Miracle of Compound Interest" Explained

Let's go back to the fictional $100 you deposited in your local bank. Assume the annual interest rate is 3%. One year later, if you look at your account balance, it will be $103. And one year after that, assuming you kept your money in the bank, it would grow another 3% to $106.09. For those not comfortable with math, we'll keep any equations in this book to a minimum. Any equations that can't be explained in plain English will be relegated to a endnote or Appendix. The general equation, known as a **Future Value** formula, is that the value a year from now equals today's value times one plus the return on investment raised to the T power. T refers to time and is one year in our example.

One of our Tips from **Chapter 1** was "Start early." Let's see the dramatic effect of how money can grow into the future using the Future Value formula, especially over *long* periods of time, with the "miracle of compound interest" we referred to in **Chapter 1**. Due to advances in medicine, one study finds that about a third of people born today will live to be at least 100. So, even though it might be the furthest thing from your mind, you should plan on living into the triple digits!

Let's see what happens if you put aside $10,000 when you're 20 (or 20 at heart) and look at what you'll wind up with when you're 100.

For those over 20, we'll assume in this example that you are part vampire (spoiler alert), like Kristen Stewart's character in the *Twilight* series of films. Yeah, we know $10k is a decent amount of cash to have at 20, but it's possible if you work hard and save early. We have the starting value, $10,000. We have the time period, 80 years. All we need is the rate at which your money will grow, or compound.

Let's do the calculation for two strategies. First, we'll put it in a basket of smaller stocks selling at a discount, known as **small cap value stocks** in the financial world, and assume it gives us its historical return of 14% a year. We'll go into more detail on small cap and value in **Chapter 5**, but let's continue with our example. For the second strategy, we'll give it to Buffett to invest, or a clone of Buffett, which earns his historical return of 20% a year.

What do you think you'll wind up with at the end of 80 years? A few million dollars? Try almost $357 million for the first strategy of small stocks! And the Buffett strategy? How about $21.6 billion! **Figure 2.1** shows the amazing results. The picture illustrates that the bulk of the money made occurs near the later years. That's why it's really important to start early. What's that saying? The early bird gets the worm? Indeed!

Another issue related to the time value of money is that you often receive money in the future and must decide how much to pay for it *today*. For example, in **Chapter 4** we'll talk about **US Savings Bonds** issued by the federal government. With a savings bond, you purchase it at a discount to its face value and it accrues or gathers interest monthly. If you purchase the most common savings bond, known as EE, the US government guarantees it will at least double over a 20-year time period. You can think of it as a loan you give to the government.

Let's look at the reverse of the example we did a bit earlier. If someone will give you $100 one year from today, how much would you pay them now? We hope you're thinking something less than $100 to account for the time value of money concept that we just discussed. The exact amount depends on the interest rate, also known as the **discount rate** in this type of problem, since you are applying a discount to something that you expect to receive in the future. When we flip around our Future Value formula and solve for the amount we'd pay for something *today*, it's known as the **Present Value** formula. Using the same 3% interest rate, to get the Present Value we divide the Future Value by one plus the interest rate raised to the T power. Once again, T stands for time, or 1 year in our example. Crunching these numbers, we calculate you should

Figure 2.1 $10,000 Invested With Buffett or in a Small Cap Value Index Fund Over 80 Years.

be willing to pay a *maximum* of $97.23 today to receive $100 a year from now. Anything less than $97.23 might be considered a good deal.

Trade-Offs: A Fundamental Principle of Life

When you were a little kid perhaps your parents or a teacher read to you some of Aesop's Fables such as *The Hare and the Tortoise*, *The Fox and the Grapes*, or *The Wolf in Sheep's Clothing*. Aesop was around a long time ago, and we mean ancient. Like more than 2,400 years ago! As you can imagine, recordkeeping wasn't that great at the time, so one version of Aesop's bio is that he was a slave who lived in ancient Greece from 620–564 B.C. He was apparently freed due to his magnificent storytelling abilities, which eventually turned into the more than 600 fables that he is today credited with creating.

One of Aesop's Fables, *The Hawk and the Nightingale*, has the famous quote "A bird in the hand is worth two in the bush." This trade-off, a certain meal today versus the prospect of a bigger meal in the future, is the essence of investing. Buffett said, "The formula for value was handed down from 600 BC by a guy named Aesop. A bird in the hand is worth two in the bush. Investing is about laying out a bird now to get two or more out of the bush."

Of course, Buffett wants us to think about dollars rather than birds. He said something similar in another one of his shareholder letters, using the important term *inflation*, which we mentioned in **Chapter 1** and will discuss in more detail in **Chapter 3**. He said, "Investing is laying out money now to get more money back in the future—more money in real terms, after taking inflation into account." Investing is a core financial literacy skill, so let's put that as one of our Tips.

Buffett (and Aesop) Tip 11:

Investing is laying out money now to get more money back in the future—more money in real terms, after taking inflation into account.

A famous study, known in academic circles as The Marshmallow Experiment, showed the enormous effect delayed gratification, or waiting for something good, can have on your life. In the 1960s Professor Walter Mischel of Stanford University (a university on par with, if not better than, the Ivy League schools) tested hundreds of 4- to 5-year-old kids and tracked how they turned out decades later.

Here's the experiment Professor Mischel tried on the kids. He, or a member of his research staff, had a kid come into a room and offered them a marshmallow. We'd prefer a Snickers or Twix bar, but let's continue with the story. He said he had to leave the room for a little while but that if the marshmallow was still there when he came back, he'd give the kid *two* marshmallows. Sort of like a marshmallow in the hand versus two in the bush, or in the waiting room.

He left the room for about 15 minutes and then came back. Some of the kids couldn't resist and ate the marshmallow right away. Others waited a bit but couldn't last the full 15 minutes. And yes, some of the kids were able to wait the full 15 minutes. Let's assume these kids liked marshmallows too but had greater self-control and what we termed as a delayed gratification element of their personality.

The key to the story isn't what happened with the marshmallow but what Professor Mischel found after he tracked how the kids turned out *decades* later. The kids who were able to wait the full 15 minutes (i.e., those who exhibited delayed gratification skills) wound up with better SAT scores, lower levels of substance abuse, and better social skills and scored better on a number of other positive life measures. The results held true over 40 years later!

You've probably heard the expression "Patience is a virtue." Well, that concept certainly holds true for being a successful investor as well. Buffett said, "The most important quality for an investor is temperament, not intellect." Temperament is one of those SAT/ACT words that means your nature, makeup, or disposition. And being patient and not being swayed by the crowd are two characteristics often associated with financial success. Buffett's comments on temperament merit a Tip.

Buffett Tip 12:

The most important quality for an investor is temperament, not intellect.

Tying this Tip back to the time value of money graph: The longer you wait to spend your money, the more money you'll have down the road because it's able to grow or compound over a longer time period. That snowball rolling downhill that we mentioned in **Chapter** 1. And, of course, if you didn't save anything, you would have ***no*** money down the road. So the trade-off is between something good today and the likelihood of something even better down the road, be it tomorrow, or next month/year/decade.

The Saint Petersburg Paradox: A Lesson on Risk and Return

Saint Petersburg is a city in Russia located near the Baltic Sea. In 1713 a famous mathematician by the name of Nicolaus Bernoulli created an example similar to the one we'll discuss below. Stick with it—it has a real punch at the end!

Bernoulli said, let's flip a fair coin until the first head appears. A fair coin has heads on one side and tails on the other, each with a 50% chance of appearing. If a head appears on the first flip you get $2. If the first head appears on the second flip (which means the first flip was a tail and second flip was a head) you get $4. If the first head appears on the third flip you get $8. The general formula is that if the first head appears on the nth flip, you get $\$2^n$. In theory, you could flip the coin forever, even though the likelihood is that a head would appear on the first handful of coin flips. So how much would you pay to participate in this coin flipping game?

There is no exact answer, but most people say something between $2 and $10. But let's compute the expected return or value on this game. The probability of a head appearing on the first flip is 50%. If you multiply that by the payoff in the first case, $2, you get $1. The probability of the first head appearing on the second flip is ½ times ½, or 25%. If you multiply that by the payoff in the second case, $4, you get $1. The probability of the first head appearing on the third flip is, ½ times ½ times ½, that is 1/8th, or 12.5%. If you multiply that by the payoff in the third case, $8, you get $1. Hopefully, you can see the pattern here. You get $1 in each case and since theoretically you can flip the coin forever until the first head appears, you get $1 added to each case stretching out to infinity! In other words, the expected value or return is infinite!

But most people are willing to pay less than $10 for this game. How can we reconcile the two values—infinity versus less than $10? Well, the **risk** of the game is also infinite, if risk is calculated by a measure of dispersion, known as **variance**, or its square root, **standard deviation**. There are a lot of ways to measure risk, including Buffett's definition that we'll get to in a moment. Intuitively, in this game there is a good chance a head will appear on the first few flips, so that's why most people are willing to pay less than $10 for the game. But there is a very small chance you could go dozens if not hundreds of flips before the first head appeared, resulting in a potentially huge payoff.

So the point of the St. Petersburg paradox is that potential risk is just as important as return when you're picking investments—and with many other things in life as well.

Risk and Return: The Evidence

The notion of investing has been around since the beginning of time. You'd think we'd all agree on how to measure or define risk. Well, we don't. Just like we can't agree on the best musician of all time, the best movie, best athlete, and so forth. If you talk to the average person on the street—that means you—most people define risk as the chance of losing money or the chance of not meeting an important goal, such as going to college or paying their rent. Buffett, using the definition from the dictionary, describes risk as "The possibility of loss or injury." Let's put that as our lucky Tip number 13.

Buffett Tip 13:

Risk is "the possibility of loss or injury." ***(Buffett's and the dictionary's definition)***

We don't disagree with him, or with the dictionary definition, but examples like that are hard to pin down numerically, so economists typically focus on something they can measure more precisely, such as the standard deviation term from statistics we mentioned a few moments ago. Something with small dispersion or variation has little risk according to the standard deviation measure. Like the change in the temperature across seasons in Hawaii or San Diego. Nearly always nice and sunny. Something with wide dispersion has a lot of risk according to the standard deviation measure, like the change in the temperature across seasons in Canada. Often it's either freezing cold—for much of the year—or warm and sunny, during the summer.

There's a whole range of investments, but let's consider the three biggies: stocks, bonds, and cash. Of course, there is no guarantee that the past will be exactly like the future, but using data that spans about

100 years, researchers have found that there is a long-term relationship between risk and return. And we mean looooong. Sometimes it takes more than 10 years for the relationship to work! By "work" we mean that over long periods of time low-risk investments deliver the lowest returns, while high-risk investments deliver the highest returns. Buffett has somewhat of an issue with this viewpoint when you take inflation and taxes into account, but we'll leave that story for another chapter.

In the short run, the exact opposite often occurs! That is, in the short run, it's possible for low-risk investments to have the highest returns and for high-risk investments to have the lowest returns. Therefore, you need patience to be successful at investing.

And Buffett has a lot of quotes on patience, besides our **Tip 12** on temperament. Here're a couple of our favorites, including one that's PG rated. "The stock market is a device for transferring money from the impatient to the patient." Another is "Successful investing takes time, discipline, and patience. No matter how great the talent or effort, some things just take time: You can't produce a baby in one month by getting nine women pregnant." Let's put a shortened version of this quote as Tip 14.

Tip 14:

Successful investing takes time, discipline, and patience.

Let's get back to those three broad investment categories: stocks, bonds, and cash. Cash not only refers to cash in your hand or in the bank but also cash-like investments, such as short-term income securities issued by the US government, known as **US Treasury Bills**, or **T-Bills** for short. These investments are incredibly safe since they are backed by the government and pay off in less than a year. The government can always raise taxes or run the printing press to pay its bills. **Table 2.1** shows that T-Bills historically had the lowest return (3.3%) of the three categories but also the lowest risk as measured by standard deviation (3.1%). Of course, recently the returns have been a lot lower, close to zero in fact.

Next up is bonds. Bonds are issued when a company or a government borrows money from investors. They have an expiration date lasting from more than 1 year to up to 30 years. Very rarely will you see a bond that lasts more than 30 years in the US, although the US Treasury periodically floats the idea of issuing a 50- or 100-year bond.

Due in part to the long period of time you have to wait to get your money back, these bonds are riskier than T-Bills, even when issued

Table 2.1 Risk and Return in the US: 1926–2019

Investment	Annual Return	Annual Standard Deviation
Treasury Bills	3.3%	3.1%
Government bonds	5.1%	5.6%
US stocks	10.2%	19.8%

Source: Morningstar.

by the same entity (i.e., a government or company). As can be seen in **Table 2.1**, US government bonds of intermediate maturity (i.e., 5–10 years) historically provide higher returns than T-Bills (5.1% vs. 3.3%), but also higher volatility (a standard deviation of 5.6% vs. 3.1%).

Saving the best for last, we get to stocks, specifically, US common stocks. Stocks have the highest volatility (standard deviation of 19.8%), but they also have the highest historical return (10.0%). Stocks can be insanely volatile but, if you have the patience to stay the course, a basket of them usually turns out well in the long run.

Diversification: One of the Few Free Lunches in Life

Who doesn't like a free lunch? Well, there's a free lunch in finance, and it's called **diversification**. Diversification means spreading your money across many investments and not just one or a limited few. It reduces your risk, while not necessarily reducing your return. People have known intuitively about the benefits of diversification for a long time. You've likely heard the expression "Don't put all your eggs in one basket." It means that if you have everything riding on a single stock, piece of real estate, farm, and so forth, and something goes wrong, you're in big trouble—if not wiped out. However, if your investments are diversified across many assets, a disaster for one investment doesn't mean your entire portfolio is ruined.

One early person who said not to put all your eggs in one basket was the renowned author Miguel de Cervantes in his classic book, *Don Quijote de la Mancha. Don Quijote* (or *Don Quixote*) is on the required reading list in most high school programs and is considered by many literary scholars to be one of the greatest books ever written. Cervantes wrote (translated from Spanish to English), "It is the part of a wise man to keep himself today for tomorrow, and not venture all his eggs in one basket."

Speaking of great writers, another staple of high school English or language arts programs is William Shakespeare. Shakespeare was also down with the importance of diversification. In *The Merchant of Venice* he wrote, "My ventures are not in one bottom trusted, nor to one place, nor is my whole estate upon the fortune of this present year. Therefore, my merchandise makes me not sad."

Yeah, we know Shakespeare's writing sounds weird. That's how people in England spoke in the late 1500s. Fortunately, we'll stick to conversational English in this book. In *The Merchant of Venice*, Shakespeare's character Antonio basically said his business interests are diversified across many places, as well as across time. This diversified portfolio of investments, or business activities, allowed him to not worry too much in case something went wrong with one of his businesses.

Diversification can provide you with peace of mind. You've probably seen a Chase Bank branch near your home. It's a division of JPMorgan Chase & Co., one of the largest banks in the world. We'll come back to J.P. Morgan in **Chapter 9** in our discussion of some of the most important businesses today. Anyway, there was a real person, J.P. Morgan, who was the most famous banker in the world in the early 1900s. He looked kind of like the banker in the game Monopoly. One story says that a friend of Morgan's approached the banking legend in a distressed mood. He said the ups and downs in the stock market didn't let him sleep well at night. J.P. Morgan supposedly uttered the famous phrase, "Sell down to the sleeping point." That is, make changes to your portfolio so its ups and downs will allow you to sleep easy at night. The changes usually entail a plan for dialing down the portfolio's risk.

In practice, this plan might include diversifying your money across different types of investments, such as stocks, bonds, cash, and real estate, as well as diversifying within each segment. For example, owning a basket of stocks spread across different sectors, such as technology, financials, energy, health care, and others, may result in less risk than owning all technology stocks. Industries don't always move in the same direction with each other since they are affected by many factors, such as government policies and consumer demand. And speaking of demand . . .

Supply and Demand Determine Price

What determines the price of something you buy? A lot of things factor into it, but it can be succinctly summed up in two words, **supply** and

demand. Supply is the amount produced of the product or service. It could be the amount of cars, cell phones, houses, shoes, or a raft of other things that are produced. Demand is the willingness and ability to pay for a good or service. So you might want to buy a new Ferrari, but it wouldn't count toward demand if you couldn't afford it. A more realistic example is the price you would be willing to pay for a Taylor Swift, Drake, or U2 concert ticket.

Let's consider four possibilities. First, if something is in high demand and the supply is constant or lower, its price will usually go up. Going back to the concert ticket example, the number of seats in the arena are fixed, so, in order to snag a ticket, you're probably going to have to pay up. Bummer!

Second, if something is in low demand and its supply is constant or higher, its price will usually go down. Think about unpopular clothes, bought out of season. Let's say a sports jersey or hat for a team that won't exist for much longer. Like the Oakland Raiders of the National Football League (NFL), which recently moved to Las Vegas. You could probably get a good price searching the bargain bin for these items if you still wanted to wear them this season. Yeah, we know, some people might consider them vintage or throwback jerseys, but most won't want them.

In the other two cases, high demand and high supply or low demand and low supply, it's hard to tell what the effect on the price will be. It could be higher or lower than its historical price. A simple diagram can give us a feel if the price of an item will go up or down. Drum roll . . . it's called a supply-demand diagram. A sample one is shown in **Figure 2.2**.

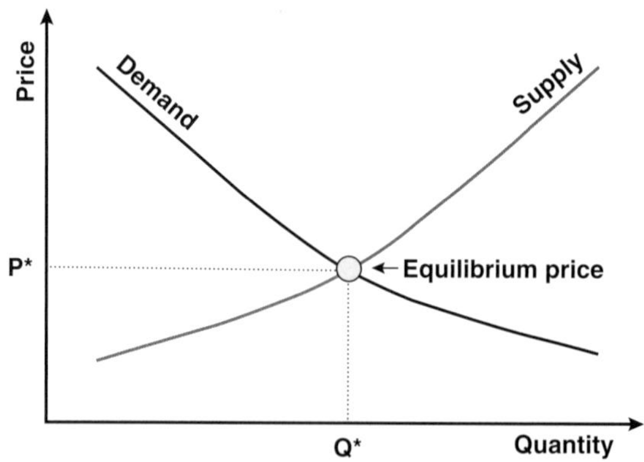

Figure 2.2 Supply-Demand Diagram

There's a simple way to remember which way each part of the diagram flows. Demand starts with a D, and the line (or sometimes curve) goes downward. This means that with most products and services, if the price falls, you would want more of it. Let's say a pair of LeBron's Nike sneakers were selling for only $20. Sign us up for a dozen pair! Conversely, if those Nike sneakers were selling for $500 a pair, we'd move to the sidelines. Sorry, LeBron. Maybe we'd scout out a pair of Steph Curry Under Armours at a much lower price instead.

The slope of the supply line moves up and to the right, in a northeast direction. There isn't a trick (or mnemonic) as catchy as D for demand, but we'll give you something. How about S for stars. Stars are in the sky and most people are right-handed (sorry, lefties) so if you point to the stars, you are probably pointing up and to the right. If the price for selling a product or service is high, especially relative to the cost of producing it, companies will try to crank out a bunch of the stuff. Like someone selling snow shovels and salt during a snowstorm. Or an umbrella in a rainstorm, if you're not from an area where it snows. Or a mask during the COVID-19 pandemic. On the flip side, if you can't receive a price for your product or service that is higher than its cost, you wouldn't supply much of it, if any, since you'd be forcing your firm to incur losses.

It's the intersection between the upward sloping supply curve and downward sloping demand curve that determines the price of a good or service and amount supplied in the end. By "the end" we mean a term economists call **equilibrium**. It means that there is a state of balance between those demanding a good and those supplying it. Equilibrium doesn't last forever, since the world changes.

A simple way to think about the intersection of supply and demand determining price is to visualize scissors. Which blade of the scissors does the cutting? It's sort of a trick question. It's not one blade that does the cutting, but rather both working together. So, there you have it; the only way to for something to have a stable price is to simultaneously consider supply and demand in equilibrium.

Summary on Financial Fundamentals

Let's wrap this chapter up. In it we covered a lot of the fundamentals of financial literacy. Things like compound interest, diversification, supply and demand, and the relationship between risk and return. We'll come back to these concepts throughout the book and—sorry to break it to you—you'll run into them for the rest of your life when you make financial decisions. But armed with some of Buffett's tips, such as the importance of having the right temperament and patience, you should wind up on the right side of the financial scorecard. And you can take that to the bank!

Buffett's Tips from Chapter 2

Buffett Tip 11: Investing is laying out money now to get more money back in the future—more money in real terms, after taking inflation into account. (Buffett and Aesop)
Buffett Tip 12: The most important quality for an investor is temperament, not intellect.
Buffett Tip 13: Risk is "the possibility of loss or injury." (Buffett's and the dictionary's definition)
Buffett Tip 14: Successful investing takes time, discipline, and patience.

References

Aesop. *Aesop Fables*. Franklin Center, PA: Franklin Library, 1984.

Bernoulli, Daniel. "Exposition of a New Theory on the Measurement of Risk." *Econometrica* 22, no. 1 (1954): 23–36. https://doi.org/10.2307/1909829.

Bingham, John. "Two Thirds of Today's Babies Could Live to 100," December 12, 2013. http://www.telegraph.co.uk/news/health/news/10511865/Two-thirds-of-todays-babies-could-live-to-100.html.

"Buffett on Aesop's Formula for Value." *The Investment Blog,* November 12, 2009. http://theinvestmentsblog.blogspot.com/2009/11/aesops-formula-for-value.html.

Chen, James. "Time Value of Money (TVM) Definition." *Investopedia,* April 21, 2020. https://www.investopedia.com/terms/t/timevalueofmoney.asp.

Clear, James. "The Marshmallow Experiment and the Power of Delayed Gratification." JamesClear.com. Accessed June 14, 2020. http://jamesclear.com/delayed-gratification.

Dzombak, Dan. "25 Best Warren Buffett Quotes." *The Motley Fool,* September 28, 2014. https://www.fool.com/investing/general/2014/09/28/25-best-warren-buffett-quotes.aspx.

Herbison, B.J. "Notes on the Translation of Don Quixote." Herbison Consulting, March 28, 2009. https://herbison.com/herbison/broken_eggs_quixote.html.

Kaplan, M. *Lindsay. William Shakespeare, Merchant of Venice: Texts and Contexts.* Boston: Bedford/St. Martin's, 2002.

Loomis, Carol. *Tap Dancing to Work: Warren Buffett on Practically Everything, 1966-2012.* London: Portfolio Penguin, 2014.

Popik, Barry. "Sell Down to the Sleeping Point." *The Big Apple, October* 2, 2008. http://www.barrypopik.com/index.php/new_york_city/entry/sell_down_to_the_sleeping_point_wall_street_proverb.

Rose, Autumn. "10 Billionaires Give Their Best Advice on Getting—and Staying—Rich." *Business Insider,* April 20, 2016. https://www.businessinsider.com/10-billionaires-give-their-best-advice-on-getting-and-staying-rich-2016-4.

3

Bank Accounts, Debit Cards, Credit Cards, and Your Credit Score

"We will never become dependent on the kindness of strangers."

—Warren Buffett, *2009 Letter to Berkshire Hathaway Shareholders*

Introduction

Okay, by now you should know who Buffett is and why you should care, as well as some of the fundamentals of how the financial markets operate. Now let's move on to the actual menu of investments and how they work. In this chapter, we'll tackle most of the things you can find at your local bank and how they affect your life. In the next chapter we'll talk about the different types of **bonds** and how you can estimate their value. A bond is a loan taken out by a company or government with the money provided from investors.

Insured Bank Deposits

You've probably heard the expressions "You can take that to the bank" or "You can bank on it." It means that something is rock solid, like the Rock of Gibraltar or movie star Dwayne "The Rock" Johnson's biceps. But it wasn't always that way. Many reforms were enacted after the **Great Depression** of 1929–1933, the biggest economic downturn in modern history. At its worst point, more than 20% of people in the US were unemployed. During the Great Depression thousands of banks failed, resulting in many customers losing their money due to no fault of their own. In the aftermath of The Great Depression, and even today, some people keep their money "**under the mattress**," which means in a safe place in their home or somewhere that is readily accessible and perceived as safe.

One of the good things that resulted from the tragedy of the Great Depression was the creation of the **Federal Deposit Insurance Company (FDIC)** and their deposit insurance program. It means that your bank account is guaranteed by the US government for up to $250,000. So if your bank goes under, your money is safe since the federal government will step in and make sure any losses are recovered to your account. For most people, there is no good reason to keep your money "under the mattress." You're probably better served keeping it in the bank and earning some interest on it. If you keep a lot of cash home, it might get lost, stolen, damaged in a fire, flood, earthquake, or some other natural disaster. (Let's not go down the road where people are keeping money in cash from ill-gotten gains or to avoid taxes.)

To show you why it is usually exceptionally safe to keep your money in an FDIC-insured savings account, let's look at what happened during a more recent downturn, the Great Recession of 2008–2009. The epicenter of this economic calamity was with the financial services sector and especially real estate. Many banks failed and others, such as Citi, had to be bailed out or else they would have failed. How did bank account holders in FDIC-insured accounts held at perilous banks fare? Just fine, thank you. No one in an FDIC-insured account with a balance less than $250,000 lost money. It wasn't a walk in the park for all customers, since in some cases there may have been a delay or stress involved, but they got their money.

You may be thinking, "What happens if you have more than $250,000 in a bank?" Good question. Buffett would probably like the way you think! There are a few things you can do. First, the $250,000 limit is for each category. So one category can be you as an individual. If you are married, another category can be you and a spouse. There are other categories as well, including **trusts**, which are financial documents or structures set up by wealthy people to pass on their wealth across generations or to minimize taxes. But there is another simple solution. You can open up a second, third, fourth, and so forth, account at another bank. It gets back to the concept of diversification that we mentioned in **Chapter 2**. Lastly, many banks maintain insurance in excess of the $250,000 limit in case you want to keep everything in one place.

Savings Accounts and Certificates of Deposit (CD)

What do we mean when we say, "Putting your money in the bank"? To answer that question, we'll need to look at some of the different types of accounts you can open at a bank. There are a bunch of different accounts that your bank offers. Let's start with two of the most popular, **savings accounts** and **certificates of deposit (CD)**. Most people over the age of 30 think about compact discs when they hear the acronym CD, but today most people listen to their music wirelessly or through an mp3 file. So if we mention CDs in this book, we're referring to the bank product and not the musical storage device. And no, there aren't any financial products that you will get confused with albums, cassettes, or 8-track tapes.

A savings account is just what it sounds like. You put your money in the bank to save, and it earns interest. The amount of interest varies on a daily basis according to market rates, but the numbers are generally low, currently around 1% per year or less. They are nearly all covered by FDIC insurance, so they're safe. And you can get access to your money during banking hours and outside regular banking hours through an **automated teller machine (ATM)**. Today, most savings accounts are tracked online, but in the past, it was common to get a booklet, known as a **passbook** savings account, that would allow you to track additions (**deposits**) to and subtractions (**withdrawals**) from the account.

If the prospect of getting 1% or less on your savings account gives you a case of the blahs, you can often get a slightly higher interest rate through a CD. The only catch is your money is "locked up" for a period of your choice, spanning from three months to 10 years. By locked up, we mean that if you want to get your money back sooner, you'll have to pay a penalty that will usually wipe out much of the interest that you've earned. So we'd suggest using a CD if you know you won't need that money until the CD matures over that three-month to 10-year period. The interest rates on a CD depend on how long you're willing to have your money locked up and the amount of money you have. Generally, larger amounts invested get you higher interest rates. Recently CDs have been giving you interest rates, also known as **yields**, of roughly 1%. A couple of nifty little websites that track interest rates for many financial-related items we're going to talk about are BankRate.com and NerdWallet.com. You might want to bookmark these sites and come back to them over the years, since there is no need to leave money on the table, or in your bank's pocket, rather than your own.

Savings accounts are not a great way to build wealth over the long term since they pay low interest rates and often fail to keep up with inflation, but they play an important role in the financial world. First, if you have an important expense coming up, such as a college tuition payment, car payment, or mortgage payment, or even cell phone payment, you don't want to risk it in the stock market, or other potentially volatile investment that might lose money in the short run. You should place the money for those important purchases in something safe, such as a savings account. Someday you might have unexpected things happen to you, such as the loss of a job or medical illness that affects your ability to work. The fallout from the COVID-19 pandemic literally shutdown entire industries for months at a time. Having money for important expenses or unexpected events is often called a "**rainy-day fund**." Buffett has a rainy-day fund at Berkshire, but it is to the tune of $20 billion! He keeps that huge pile of cash at Berkshire because he doesn't want to be at the mercy of anyone, especially during times of distress. In Berkshire's 2009 Letter to Shareholders Buffett wrote:

> We will never become dependent on the kindness of strangers. Too-big-to-fail is not a fallback position at Berkshire. Instead, we will always arrange our affairs so that any requirements for cash we may conceivably have will be dwarfed by our own liquidity. Moreover, that liquidity will be constantly refreshed by a gusher of earnings from our many and diverse businesses.

A summary of that quote merits a Tip.

Buffett Tip 15:

Never get into a position where you become dependent on the kindness of strangers.

Checking Accounts and Electronic Bill Payment

A **checking account** is another very popular type of banking product. You can view it as a savings account with a checkbook attached to it. Some checking accounts pay interest, while others don't. Most come with FDIC insurance, so you usually don't have to worry about the safety of the bank sponsoring your checking account. The main reason for having a checking account is to pay **bills**, which is payment for a product or service that you purchased. Of course, the good aspect of a checking account is when someone gives you a check, such as for a birthday or for a graduation present. In that case, money goes into your account. Ka-ching! Both savings and checking accounts are considered **demand deposits**. It's your money, and you can "demand" it, or have access to it, at virtually anytime.

In the past, checking accounts were always pieces of paper that were part of a checkbook. A sample check is shown in **Figure 3.1 below**. We'll cover its different parts in a minute. Today, a lot of "checks" are written electronically. These electronic checks are usually considered to be part of the electronic bill presentment and payment system. **Automated Clearing House (ACH)** payments are the equivalent of electronic checks, taking money from your checking account and giving the funds to another person or organization. To make an analogy, paper checks are to regular mail as electronic checks are to email. The electronic version is faster, easier to track, and saves you a stamp. Most banks offer free electronic bill payment today.

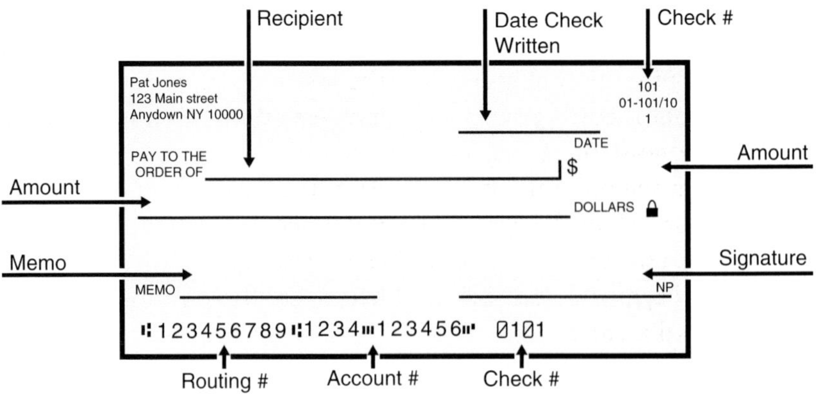

Figure 3.1 A Sample Check

Parts of a Check

Let's go over the different parts of the check in **Figure 3.1**. The first part, usually in the upper left-hand corner, has your name and address. Across that to the right is the check number (each one is unique) and the date. The person who receives your check is not supposed to deposit it until the date on the check, or later. But sometimes it slips through the cracks and the check is often deposited as soon as someone receives it. So you should only send out a check when you are sure there's enough money in your checking account to cover the check. If you write a check and there isn't enough money in the checking account to pay the amount on the check, it's called a **bounced check**. This is something you really don't want to do. And we really mean *really*! The person on the receiving end of the check will be p.o.'d. They'll get hit with a fee, usually around $20 and you might also get hit with a similar fee. If you purposely bounce checks, you may have committed a crime (fraud) and can go to jail. Most banks offer **overdraft protection**, which will prevent checks from being accidently bounced, up to a limit, such as $500. Once the overdraft protection kicks in, you then owe that amount to the bank.

We hope we scared you about not bouncing checks, so let's get back to the different parts of the check. The next part of the check, still near the top, is the "Pay to the Order of" section. It could be anyone, but is usually paid to a person, place, or thing. Oops, that's the definition of a noun. The check is usually paid to a person, business, government, charity, or religious organization. Basically, any entity that you want to send money to.

To the right of the "Pay to the Order of" section is the amount of the check in dollars and cents, in numbers. Right below that is the same thing, the amount of the check, except written out in words. This might seem redundant to write it both in letters and numbers, but it is an important way for the computer (or in the past, person) to double-check that the amount is correct. If the two numbers don't match up then the check may be **void**, or cancelled.

Next, near the bottom left-hand part of the check there is a section called "For" or "Memo." It's optional, but it acts as a reminder of what the check was used for. Examples could be anything, but "Birthday Gift," "Cell Phone Payment," and "School Tuition" are three common examples in personal finance.

At the bottom of the check you'll notice three strings of numbers, separated by a colon or some other strange symbol designed to signify that the three numbers are distinct. The first 9-digit number is called the

American Banking Association (ABA) Routing Transit Number. This is a fancy name for identifying the bank holding your checking account funds, such as Wells Fargo, Bank of America, or Chase. Some large banks may have more than one ABA Routing Transit Number, but most have one. The second number identifies your specific checking account. It may be nice to have your bank mix up your checking account with Buffett's, but it's not going to happen. Sigh! The last number identifies the check number. It must match the number at the top that we mentioned, although sometimes you'll see an extra zero or two in front of the check number at the bottom.

If you are sending (or receiving) money internationally, there's another number you have to worry about called a **SWIFT code**. SWIFT is the acronym for the Society for Worldwide Interbank Financial Telecommunication. Yeah, now you know why we call it SWIFT.

Last, but not least, at the bottom right-hand part of the check is the space for your signature. Your "John Hancock" (the fancy signer of the Declaration of Independence) that is written in cursive or script writing. When you first get a checking account, the bank asks for your signature, and the electronic system examining your check should ensure there is a reasonable match. If there is no match or no signature, the check should be rejected as being invalid.

If you notice there's something wrong with a check you have written (e.g., incorrect amount) or have second thoughts (e.g., feeling pressured to write a check to someone) you can call your bank to **stop payment** or cancel a check. If you sent a **certified check** or made a **wire transfer**, transactions which are guaranteed by the bank, it is extremely difficult, if not impossible, to cancel them. Certified checks or wire transfers are checks where the bank verifies that the funds are in your account. They are often used in important transactions, such as a down payment for a home or for the purchase of a business. So we suggest you use "regular" checks from your checking account unless you are 100% certain you want to make a transaction.

Balancing a Checkbook

We hope we made it clear that you don't want to bounce a check. Remember, the checks could be of the paper or electronic kind. Let's work through an example of balancing your checkbook. Suppose you get $200 in birthday gift money from various friends and relatives and

Table 3.1

Checking Account Transaction	Starting Balance	Change in Balance	Ending Balance
Deposit $200 of birthday gift money	$0	$200	$200
Pay $100 for cell phone bill	$200	–$100	$100
Deposit $50 from tutoring job	$100	$50	$150
Pay $100 for used Beats headphones	$150	–$100	$50

deposit the funds in your checking account. Assuming this is the first transaction in the account, your balance would start at $0 and then increase to $200. Next, let's say you have to pay your cell phone bill for $100. Your balance is now $100, or $200 minus $100. Then let's say you received $50 for tutoring someone (in financial literacy!). Your balance is now $150. Lastly, let's say you snag a pair of used Beats headphones from your friend for $100. Your ending balance is now $150 minus $100, or $50. The sequence of transactions, and the corresponding balances, are shown in **Table 3.1.**

Balancing a checkbook is essentially addition and subtraction. Piece of cake! You can access your bank account online, so you don't even have to do the math. You can also deposit checks at most banks with an app on your smartphone that takes a picture of the check, so you don't even have to set foot in the bank branch. Most people who have problems balancing their checkbook don't follow its balance closely. Also, when you deposit cash in your checking account, you have access to the money right away. When you deposit a check in the account, it takes some time for you to get access to the funds. The length of time for you to have access to the funds is related to the **clearing process**. It takes most checks about 2 days to clear after depositing, but in some cases, it might take up to a week. So you should look at your account online and see what you have in **available funds**, which is the maximum amount you may write checks for, before writing a check.

Debit Cards and Automated Teller Machines (ATM)

Debit cards are tied to either your savings or checking account and allow you to access your money without having to carry around the physical cash. Carrying around a piece of plastic, or in some cases metal, provides some protection against having your cash being lost or stolen. Imagine if you were as rich as Buffett, carrying around billions of dollars in cash. You'd need a truck to do it! When you purchase something from a store, such as Walmart or the Apple Store, you can pay for it with your debit card. The money is deducted from your account, just like in the checking examples we discussed.

One advantage of a debit card is that you can't spend more than you have in the bank. If you try—let's say by attempting to purchase a $300,000 Ferrari with only 100 bucks in your savings account—the transaction will be cancelled. No dice! But do give us a call when you're really able to afford a Ferrari, since we'd love to take a spin. :-) Most banks will give someone a debit card as soon as age 13. Some vendors don't accept debit cards, so you'll have to pay them in cash. You can get cash by putting your debit card in an automated teller machine (ATM), also known as a "cash machine," and withdrawing funds from your checking or savings account.

There are a few points that you should be aware of related to ATM machines. First, almost always you pay no fees when withdrawing money from at ATM machine owned by your bank (e.g., Chase, Wells Fargo, Citi, or Bank of America). However, if you have an account at Chase and try to get money from a different ATM machine, say one operated by Wells Fargo, then you'll usually get hit with a fee in the neighborhood of $1 to $3. Second, you can make deposits of cash or check into the ATM. This may come in handy when the bank is closed. As noted above, we think it's easier to deposit a check using your smartphone, but we want you to be aware of this option. Third, in order to access an ATM, you need to have a **personal identification number (PIN)**. A PIN is set up when you open your checking or savings account and reduces the risk of theft in case someone finds or steals your debit card. The PIN is usually a 4-digit number but sometimes longer. Select a PIN that you'll remember but not something that's obvious, such as numbers related to your birthday or address.

Credit Cards and Charge Cards

A **credit card** looks like a debit card, but it's a lot different in how it works. It allows you to purchase things in advance of having the money leave your checking or savings account. It is basically an advance or loan from the credit card company. On paper it's good—IF you pay off your credit card bill in full each month. Why can a credit card be good? First, it is an interest-free loan if you pay your bill promptly. Second, like with a debit card, it allows you to avoid the need of holding a lot of cash. Third, with nearly all credit cards, you are not responsible for purchases if the card is lost or stolen. Fourth, *most* have no annual fee.

Plus, there are all sorts of **reward programs**, which give you things such as cash back, free airline tickets, and discounts on purchases. For example, Amazon.com has their own credit card, through Chase bank, which provides you with a 5% discount when buying things on Amazon.com. Sweet! There are a bunch of websites out there that will recommend specific credit cards for you based on your goals and spending patterns. Four popular ones are WalletHub.com, CreditCards.com, ThePointsGuy.com, and ConsumerReports.org. For some people, having a credit card can actually *pay* you with either cash or discounts on things that you like to buy.

So what's the problem and why do a lot of people say credit cards are bad? They can be bad for your financial future if you are not able to pay the bill off in *full* each month. One recent study found that 65% of Americans don't pay their bill off in full each month.

The problem with not paying your bill in full is that the credit card company charges you interest on the unpaid balance. And most cards charge a high rate of interest, to the tune of 15% or more each year. Occasionally, you'll see a credit card company offer a very low, temporary interest rate, called a **teaser rate**. But it will eventually revert to something much higher.

At the 2020 Berkshire Hathaway Annual Meeting, which was held virtually due to COVID-19, Buffett relayed an insightful story about the importance of paying credit cards in full each month. A friend approached him looking for investment advice. She was hoping for a stock tip, but she was disappointed when Buffett told her the first thing she should do is pay off any credit card balances. The interest rate she was paying on her credit card was a not uncommon 18%. Buffett told her he didn't know of any investment that would pay her 18% per year, looking ahead. He then dispensed some tip-worthy advice saying, "Avoid using credit cards as a piggy bank to be raided."

Buffett Tip 16:

Avoid using credit cards as a piggy bank to be raided.

Remember, Berkshire's stock has historically increased 20% per year, and Buffett is likely the greatest investor ever. It's extremely unlikely that what you purchased with the credit card will go up in value more than the interest rate the bank charges. Most people use their credit cards to buy goods or services that they consume, such as clothes, food, vacations, electronics, and the like, that don't increase in value over time. In fact, they usually decrease in value quite rapidly, if not disappear, such as a Starbucks latte or a snack of avocado toast. The bottom line is that credit card debt that is rolled over from month to month will be destructive to the wealth of nearly everyone that has it. To explain this rollover concept, we have to go into some of the details on how a credit card works.

First, you have to apply to get a credit card, usually from a bank. For most people, you need to be at least 16 years old, often with a parent or guardian personally guaranteeing payments. If you're 18 years or older you can apply for a card without permission from someone else. Frankly, for most people, it's not hard to get approved for a credit card, even if you have no credit history. Let's say you're approved. They bank will mail you a credit card, and you'll have to activate it by calling a toll free number or by going to their website. The credit card will come with a limit, unless you're super rich. Like Kylie Jenner or Jay-Z rich. For people with little to no credit card history, the limit is usually in the $500 to $2,000 range.

Continuing with our example, you can go crazy and buy $2,000 worth of stuff, even if you have only 5 bucks in your checking account. Obviously, we don't recommend it, but some people are swayed by their peers to buy things or simply aren't responsible with their money. The trouble starts when you get the bill, usually within 30 to 45 days of your first purchase. The credit card company will send you a bill that says what your **required minimum payment** is, as well as the payment if you want to pay the bill in full ($2,000 in our example). The required minimum payment varies by credit card company but is typically 3% to 5% of what you owe the credit card company, sometimes referred to as the balance or amount outstanding**.** In our example, if you pay 3% of $2,000, or $60, the remaining amount, $1,940, would incur interest costs.

As long as you pay the required minimum payment each month, your credit card is kept "on." This is the "rollover" strategy we alluded to earlier. You are basically kicking the (debt) can down the road. But paying the minimum isn't a winning strategy since your debt can really snowball out of control. Using some round numbers, if you have $2,000 in debt and compound that for 10 years at an interest rate of 20%, you'd owe $ 12,383. Ouch! That's a tough hole to dig out of, so the best way to avoid it is to pay the balance in full each month. If you don't have the discipline to do it, then you should just stick with the debit card.

Buffett's character in *Secret Millionaires Club* weighed in on the topic of just paying the minimum on your credit card in colorful fashion. He said, "Making those minimum payments while you continue to charge is like bailing out a sinking ship with a teaspoon. Pretty soon, you are in way over your head."

Before we move on, there is also something similar to a credit card, called a **charge card**. The charge card requires you to pay your balance in full each month. If you don't pay in full, then the card may be turned "off," and you'll incur (usually high) interest rate charges. American Express became famous in part for issuing charge cards but now offers a range of credit cards too.

Apps to Send Money: PayPal, Venmo, Zelle, Apple Pay, Android Pay, and so forth

Sending money to pay for things or giving money to people, such as friends and family, is a pretty common occurrence. Let's say you're buying something, such as a used game of Monopoly, from another person on eBay, the most popular auction website. You can send the person selling you the Monopoly game a check in the mail, but it will take awhile for them to get their check and for the check to clear. The seller also may not be in a position to accept credit cards. To accept a credit card, you need to be approved by one of the credit card companies, such as Visa, Mastercard, American Express, and Discover.

Not surprisingly, some products were developed to fill these gaps. One of the first solutions is PayPal. And also not surprisingly, PayPal was once owned by eBay but now exists as a separate company. PayPal allows you to pay for something or send money by taking the money from your checking account or by making a charge to your debit or credit card. PayPal isn't a charity, it does this for a small fee. The fee, typically 2.9% of the transaction price plus 30 cents, is taken from the seller of the good—the Monopoly game in our example. The buyer typically pays no transaction fees.

As smartphones developed, techniques were used to send or receive money through apps on your phone. The most popular one currently is Venmo. PayPal owns that too. You may view Venmo as a digital wallet that allows people to send money directly to each other. One thing that's cool about Venmo is you can send a person money just by having their phone number or email address, assuming they also have a Venmo account. There's also a window of time, usually from a day to a week, where you can cancel the transaction if you suffered from a bout of temporary insanity.

The Venmo app works behind the scenes to send the money to the person's bank account without having you know their information. If you use a credit card to send money, Venmo charges a 3% fee. For most other transactions, it's free. Venmo also has a social media component, somewhat like Facebook. It has news feeds, comments, and other features as well, such as the part of its app that helps you quickly split a bill. Venmo has caught on like wildfire and has more than 40 million active users. Not surprisingly, other firms wanted a piece of the action and came out with similar apps. Google/Alphabet offers Android Pay. Apple offers Apple Pay. A group of large banks combined resources to form Zelle, which is now running neck and neck with Venmo.

Let us tell you about one more resource for sending money. There has been a company doing it for more than 150 years. Western Union was founded in 1851 and is famous for their slogan, "The fastest way to send money." That slogan doesn't resonate as much today with apps such as Venmo, but Western Union has over 500,000 locations in more than 200 countries around the world. They have various businesses that facilitate the transfer and receipt of money, including cold hard cash.

Although it's very easy to send money to people, including friends and family, it doesn't mean you should do it without careful thought. During one episode of *Secret Millionaire's Club*, Buffett's character said, "You have to think carefully before you loan money to anyone, especially a friend." The reason is that if they don't pay you back, either willfully or due to difficult circumstances they are facing, it may create problems in your relationship. In some cases, it might end the relationship. And if you're dealing with relatively small amounts of money, that's probably not a good trade-off (i.e., loss of a friend over a loss of a relatively small amount of money). So we and Buffett aren't saying you should never do it but just that you should think long and hard about it.

Your Credit Score: A Report Card of Your Financial Responsibility

You might be done with receiving a report card when you finish college. Sorry to break it to you, but there's something similar to a financial report card that you'll have for the rest of your life, called a **credit**

score. A credit score measures how responsible you are when borrowing money. Borrowing money could take many forms, including credit cards, student loans, car loans, home mortgages, and even utility bills. You should check your credit report at least once a year. It may contain some errors that you will want to get corrected. Buffett once checked his credit score and found it to be 718, modestly above average, even though he is one of the richest people in the world! He found he had an imposter who opened a credit card in his name and didn't pay the bills. He eventually got things fixed, and presumably his credit score is near the top of the upper range. If having an error on a credit report can happen to Buffett, it can happen to anyone, so let's create a new Tip.

Buffett Tip 17:

Check your credit report on a regular basis—it may include errors, which you should fix as soon as possible.

Your credit score is a number that ranges from 300 (worst) to 850 (best). The average credit score in America is about 700, although it changes a bit every year. There are a few firms that compute credit scores. The most popular credit score is called a **FICO score**, named after the financial firm that created it, Fair, Isaac, and Company. Credit scores differ somewhat by age. Younger people tend not to have much of a credit history and so usually wind up with lower credit scores. Why is a credit score such a big deal? Well, if you have a high credit score, you often will pay a lower interest rate when you borrow money for "big ticket" purchases, such as a car or home. And that will save you a lot of money, especially with a mortgage that might last 30 years. So you want to get the best credit score that you can, just like you wanted to get an A on important exams.

How is a credit score calculated? The exact formula is somewhat of a secret, but Fair Isaac has given out some information that suggests your FICO score has five categories, as shown in **Figure 3.2**. Your payment history counts for about 35% of the score. The amount of money that you owe counts for another 30%. The length of your credit history accounts for 15%. The number of new credit applications accounts for 10%, and the type of credit used (e.g., credit card or student loan) counts for another 10%. Young people are less likely to have a long credit history and have more new credit applications than someone that is over 30. However, you can pay your bills in full on time every month, which would give a nice boost to the two biggest weights that go into computing your credit score.

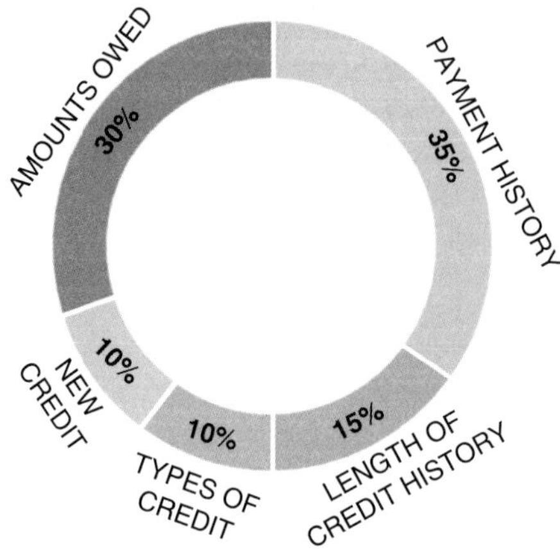

Figure 3.2 Components of a Credit Score

Borrowers with the strongest credit scores—generally 740 and above—are put in the **prime** category. They nearly always pay their bills on time and don't carry much debt. They also typically have a long credit history of a decade or more. Occasionally, you'll read about a **super-prime** category. These individuals typically have credit scores of at least 800 and may pay even lower rates than prime borrowers.

The second of the four major credit categories is called **Alt-A**. Alt-A means that you have a good credit score but perhaps are not strong in one or two categories, such as length of credit history. Many younger borrowers fall into this category. The typical FICO range for the Alt-A category is 670 to 739. The third-lowest credit rating category is called **subprime**. Borrowers with a subprime credit score typically score poorly on many of the credit factors, such as not paying their bills on time or having too much debt relative to their income. The lowest credit category is simply called **poor**. These borrowers don't have a good record of paying their bills on time, or at all. In some cases, they have declared **bankruptcy**.

Personal Bankruptcy: Try to Avoid at all Costs

Bankruptcy refers to a legal process that is pursued when you have significantly more debts than assets and you want to try to get some of your debts reduced or eliminated. Individuals, companies, and some governments may declare bankruptcy. Individuals may declare bankruptcy for many reasons but among the most common are medical debt, loss of a job, losing a lawsuit, business losses, and purchasing items (e.g., home, car, or jewelry) that they couldn't afford. Buffett's own sister, Doris, had a brush with bankruptcy in the 1980s due to some bad and risky investments, so it's not just a problem for those with lower income.

On the surface, you might think having some of your debt erased sounds good. But bankruptcy can be very bad since your credit will be tarnished for a very long time, typically seven years or more. Declaring bankruptcy might make it very difficult to get a mortgage or other loan in the future. And if you do, you will likely pay a much higher interest rate than someone with a good credit rating. Declaring bankruptcy kills your credit score, putting you firmly in the poor or subprime categories.

A bankruptcy court may eliminate some, or all, of your credit card debt, but it won't get rid of student loan debt and some other types of debt. Up until the mid-1800s in the US, bankrupt persons were often placed in a **debtors' prison** where they were required to work to pay off their debts. Today, those who declare bankruptcy are put in the equivalent of a "financial penalty box" but not prison. However, some state laws do provide for the equivalent of prison sentences for individuals unable to pay debts. In some cases, you can negotiate with your lenders and voluntarily have them take less than what they are owed. This negotiated reduction in debt might hit your credit score but not nearly as much as a formal declaration of bankruptcy. The best way to avoid bankruptcy is to purchase only things you can afford and to have the discipline to invest on a regular basis. In short, try to avoid bankruptcy at all costs.

A Word on Bitcoin from Buffett

This might surprise you, but it used to be possible to exchange currency (e.g., a $20 bill) in the US for gold coins or bars, known as **bullion**. And the reverse trade worked too, swapping gold for paper money. The ability for individuals to make this trade ended to a great extent in 1934 when the **Gold Reserve Act** was enacted. The point of this discussion is that there used to be an *explicit* link between gold and money, which, in aggregate, is known as the **money supply**. There are different definitions of what constitutes the money supply, but the most conservative definition (known as **M1**) consists of physical currency/bills, coins, demand deposits, and traveler's checks. Basically, M1 consists of cash or something that may be converted to cash very quickly.

In theory, if enough gold wasn't held at Fort Knox, or some other federal depository, the printing or coin press couldn't be run. That all changed in 1971 when the US went off the gold standard, meaning that currency could no longer be exchanged for gold, even for the institutions that were previously permitted to do so after the enactment of the Gold Reserve Act. Nearly all countries around the world followed suit, ending their gold standards. The reasons for going off the gold standard are beyond the scope of our book, but many government leaders felt that being tied to a gold standard restricted the ability of the economy to grow.

Today, most money printed is called "**fiat**." No, not the Italian car, but the currency is declared to have value by government decree. So in theory, the government could crank the printing press at full steam and not worry about anything. Also in theory, the more money printed, the more inflation that would occur. We'll cover inflation in more detail in **Chapter 4.** If money was printed like it was going out of style, it should push the prices of most things up, resulting in inflation.

So what does all this have to do with **Bitcoin**? Well, the (still unknown) creator(s) of Bitcoin wanted to create a currency that couldn't be arbitrarily devalued by running the printing press. The creator of Bitcoin also wanted a way of **transmitting** (i.e., sending and receiving) money that was anonymous, beyond government control, and could be used for all types of business and personal transactions. Even for **black market,** or illegal transactions beyond government oversight or taxation. For example, writers of **ransomware**, software that "hijacks" someone's computer, often demand to be paid in Bitcoin.

The details of how Bitcoin works is also well beyond the scope of this book, but you can think of it as an alternative digital currency, known in some circles as **cryptocurrency.** Today, you can even see a Bitcoin machine in some locations, which looks a lot like an ATM machine. It might sound like science fiction, but Bitcoin is accepted as money by many firms today, including Dell, Microsoft, PayPal, and the Wikimedia Foundation, operator of the famous Wikipedia website. They think of Bitcoins in the same way as you might think of a US dollar, euro, British pound, Japanese yen, or Chinese renminbi. Basically, as money.

The price of Bitcoin has skyrocketed, going from less than a penny a "coin," shortly after its creation in 2008–2009, to almost $20,000 in 2018 and now roughly $11,000 as we are writing this book. That's a peak return of about 100 million percent! A feat that even Buffett can't match! While on the topic of astronomical returns, we'll tell you a Wall Street expression about the difficulty of having perfect timing. "The only person that buys at the bottom and sells at the top is a liar." So what does the Oracle of Omaha have to say about Bitcoin? It's a controversial topic, so we'll include Buffett's full quote and then make some comments afterward. Buffett said:

> Stay away. Bitcoin is a mirage. It's a method of transmitting money. It's a very effective way of transmitting money and you can do it anonymously and all that. A check is a way of transmitting money, too. Are checks worth a whole lot of money just because they can transmit money? Are money orders? You can transmit money by money orders. People do it. I hope Bitcoin becomes a better way of doing it, but you can replicate it a bunch of different ways and it will be. The idea that it has some huge intrinsic value is just a joke in my view.

Buffett's feelings on Bitcoin are pretty clear, so we're going to put that as a Tip. There are a couple of words in Buffett's response that may require an explanation. We'll define "**intrinsic value**" in more detail in **Chapter 6**, but for now, you can think of it as a reasoned measure of what something is worth. For example, the intrinsic value of a house includes the land, materials, and benefits of living in a certain community, such as its school system or proximity to work. **Money orders** are a way of sending money, other than physical cash, if you don't have a checking account. It's rarely a good idea to send cold, hard cash in the mail. You can get a money order from the post office or most banks (as two examples), swapping cash for the money order, for a fee. The fee is usually less than 1 percent of the size of the transaction (e.g., the fee is less than \$5 for a \$500 money order), although the fee may be a bit higher on a percentage basis for small transactions.

Buffett Tip 18:

Bitcoin is a mirage. It may be a better way of transmitting money, but it doesn't have an intrinsic value.

Our job here is to educate and not pontificate. At this point, we can objectively say that Bitcoin as an *investment* is speculative or risky. Its volatility has been incredible, often moving hundreds of dollars in price in a single day. There have been people who have had their Bitcoins stolen by cyberattacks. But the notion of an anonymous currency that is not based on fiat and not tied to a specific government has some appeal and we expect the cryptocurrency industry to continue to evolve. We talked about Buffett's belief of staying within your "circle of competence." Cryptocurrencies are not within our circle of competence, so we will be like most observers today and just wait and see what happens with Bitcoin.

Buffett's Tips from Chapter 3

Buffett Tip 15: Never get into a position where you become dependent on the kindness of strangers.
Buffett Tip 16: Avoid using credit cards as a piggy bank to be raided.
Buffett Tip 17: Check your credit report on a regular basis—it may include errors, which you should fix as soon as possible.
Buffett Tip 18: Bitcoin is a mirage. It may be a better way of transmitting money, but it doesn't have an intrinsic value.

References

Akin, Jim. "What Are the Different Credit Score Ranges?" *Experian,* January 7, 2019. http://www.experian.com/blogs/ask-experian/infographic-what-are-the-different-scoring-ranges/.

Buffett, Warren. "Letter to Shareholders of Berkshire Hathaway Inc." Berkshire Hathaway, Inc., 2009. https://www.berkshirehathaway.com/letters/2009.html.

Buffett, Warren. *Secret Millionaires Club: Volume 1.* A Squared, 2013. https://www.smckids.com/.

"Great Depression." History.com. A&E Television Networks. Accessed June 27, 2020. https://www.history.com/topics/great-depression.

Hill, Kashmir. "Bitcoin Battle: Warren Buffett vs. Marc Andreessen," March 27, 2014. https://www.forbes.com/sites/kashmirhill/2014/03/26/warren-buffett-says-bitcoin-is-a-mirage-why-marc-andreessen-thinks-hes-wrong/.

Langager, Chad. "How Is My Credit Score Calculated?" *Investopedia,* February 12, 2020. http://www.investopedia.com/ask/answers/05/creditscorecalculation.asp.

Loomis, Carol. *Tap Dancing to Work: Warren Buffett on Practically Everything, 1966–2012.* London: Portfolio Penguin, 2014.

Steverman, Ben. "The Credit Card Rewards War Rages. Are You the Loser?" *Bloomberg,* June 26, 2017. https://www.bloomberg.com/news/articles/2017-06-26/the-credit-card-rewards-war-rages-are-you-the-loser.

"Warren Buffett: People Should Avoid Using Credit Cards as a Piggy Bank to Be Raided." Yahoo! News. Yahoo!, May 3, 2020. https://www.yahoo.com/news/warren-buffett-people-avoid-using-011209713.html?bcmt=1.

Wolff-Mann, Ethan. "The Average American Is in Credit Card Debt, No Matter the Economy." *Money*, February 9, 2016. https://money.com/average-american-credit-card-debt/.

4

Bonds and Inflation

"In economics, interest rates act as gravity behaves in the physical world."
—Warren Buffett, *Warren Buffett on the Stock Market*

Introduction

In the prior chapter, we took some "baby steps" into the world of investing, discussing investment products available at most banks, things such as savings accounts and CDs. In this chapter, we'll expand into other types of investments, mostly bonds, a term introduced in the last chapter that we will expand upon here. A bond is a loan, or an IOU. Bonds don't result in the company giving up a piece of ownership in itself, which occurs when they sell stock. Why do companies or governments issue bonds? Mainly to raise money to pay for things such as recurring operations or to expand.

Bonds don't necessarily have to be boring. For example, later in this chapter, we'll discuss bonds that were issued by the late rock star David Bowie. Not surprisingly, they're called Bowie Bonds. Bonds usually fall under the heading of **fixed income securities**. This name is derived from the fact that the amount and timing of the cash or income you get from owning most bonds are fixed. Of course, there are exceptions, and we'll cover some of them too.

Although stocks get all the hype, bonds will probably play a bigger role in the lives of most people. The global bond market is also bigger than the stock market, so it's of enormous importance to how the world runs. You've probably heard the Dunkin' Donuts slogan, "America runs on Dunkin." Well, the global financial markets to a great extent run on bonds, which are a form of debt, or borrowed money. Most people own their home with the help of a mortgage, where you pay cash for part of the purchase price and borrow the rest. That's debt, and that's a bond. If you have a student loan, it's valued like a bond. A car loan is the same thing. Basically, anything that has regular cash payments attached to it can be turned into a bond.

US Savings Bonds

A type of bond that you've most likely seen is a US Savings Bond issued by the **United States Treasury**—the branch of the federal government that is responsible for its finances and collecting taxes. Maybe you received a savings bond as a gift at some point in your life. In the past, the buyer typically paid half the **face value** of the savings bond, and the holder eventually got to cash it in for the full amount. The face value is literally the amount that it says on the paper or physical bond. For example, perhaps you received a $50 US savings bonds as a gift in the past. The person who gave you the gift probably paid $25 for it. Maybe you were fooled into thinking they paid $50 for it, but any gift is a nice gift, regardless of how much was paid for it.

However, in 2012 the US Treasury ditched the paper bonds. Now, they are all virtual or electronic. One reason why the US Treasury did this is that the new electronic ones are easier to track. The reason for buying a bond, of course, is the interest that you'll earn. Both the old paper bonds and newer electronic bonds pay interest. Not a lot, but it's another one of those rock-solid investments that you can "take to the bank." The bonds are backed by the "full faith and credit of the US government." That means you're virtually guaranteed to get paid. The US government can always run the money printing press or tax its citizens to pay its bills.

The most common type of US savings bonds are called Series EE Savings Bonds. There is a less popular US Savings Bond, called Series I, which we'll discuss later in this chapter. As you might have guessed, the I stands for inflation. The minimum purchase amount for a US Savings Bond is $25, and the maximum purchase is $10,000 per calendar year for each Social Security number. You can buy them, without paying any commission or transaction fees, directly from the US Treasury at TreasuryDirect.gov.

As with a CD, your money is "locked up" for a while, or else you have to pay a penalty. You can cash them in after 1 year, but if you cash them in before 5 years, you lose the last 3 months of interest. For example, if you cash a Series EE bond after 2 years, you get the first 1 year and 9 months' worth of interest. You can hold them as long you want, but they stop paying interest after 30 years. The US Treasury determines the interest rates offered on its EE Savings Bonds semi-annually, on May 1 and November 1.

There are some modest tax advantages to buying US savings bonds, at least when you make enough money to be required to pay taxes. You have to pay federal government taxes on the interest earned on savings bonds, but they are exempt from state and local taxes. Some lucky people living in states such as Florida, Texas, and Washington have no state income tax. Others, living in states such as California, Oregon, Minnesota, New York, New Jersey, and Iowa have a top state income tax rate of 8% or more. Some cities, such as New York City, charge additional income taxes to their residents. So paying taxes on Series EE bonds may not be a big concern for you for a while, but it may be someday, especially if you heed Buffett's advice for building long-term wealth.

Other US Treasury Fixed Income Securities

Some people who hear the words "interest rate" think it's a single number that applies to all fixed income securities. It's not. There's a whole range of interest rates ranging from short-term (usually about 1 month) to long-term (usually up to 30 years) maturity dates. In addition, riskier borrowers will have to pay higher rates across this maturity spectrum. Historically, long-term interest rates are higher than short-term rates because long-term bonds usually have a greater chance of a loss, but it's not always the case. The relationship between time to maturity and the interest rate, known as the **yield to maturity** in bond lingo, is called the **yield curve**. Sometimes it goes by the fancier academic term, **the term structure of interest rates**, especially when listed in a tabular format. We'll stick with yield curve. A picture is shown in **Figure 4.1**.

The shortest term issued US Treasury securities are called US Treasury Bills, or T-bills for short. They mature or expire in one year or less. T-bills are issued for periods of 28, 91, 182, and 364 days. You can hold them beyond their maturity date, but they won't gain any additional income or **accrued interest**, a term which also refers to interest that gathers between payment dates. They are sold below or at a discount to

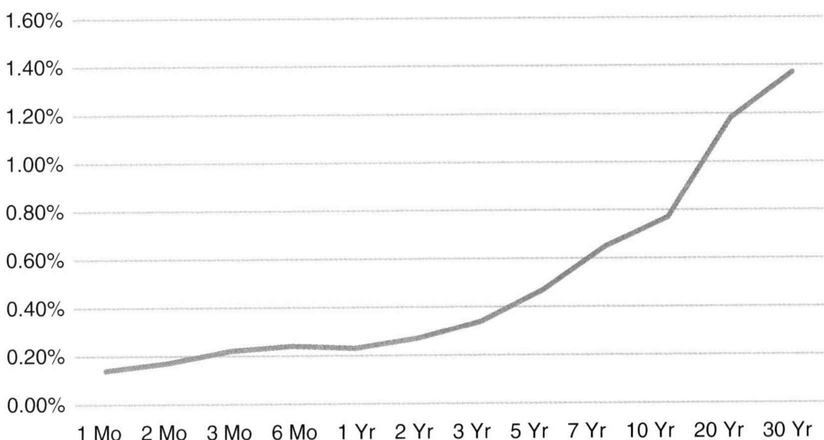

Figure 4.1 The U.S. Treasury Yield Curve, April 2020
Source: From DOT, U.S. Treasury Yield Curve, April 2020, U.S Department of Treasury

their face values, typically $1,000. For example, if the interest rate is 1%, a 364 day T-bill, using our Present Value formula from **Chapter 2**, would sell for about $990.10, when it's issued. You can collect the money when the T-bill matures: $1,000 in our example. T-bills are usually the safest and most liquid of all fixed income securities. As we mentioned in the last chapter, it's what Buffett uses for his rainy-day fund.

US Treasury notes (T-note for short) are fixed income securities issued by the US government that mature, when issued, between 1 and 10 years. The most common ones issued are the 2-year and 10-year US Treasury notes. US Treasury bonds are securities issued by the US government that mature, when issued, in more than 10 years. The most common ones issued are 20-year and 30-year US Treasury notes. There isn't a meaningful difference between a Treasury note and Treasury bond, other than the maturity dates. They both pay interest semi-annually, or twice a year, and usually have a face value of $1,000. The amount of interest paid on a bond (e.g., $50) is known as the **coupon**. If it's expressed as a percentage (e.g., 5%), it's called the **coupon rate**. Most bonds have a coupon rate that is fixed for the life of a bond and a face value of $1,000. These are often called "plain vanilla" bonds since they are the most common, like vanilla ice cream within the ice cream universe.

The last major type of US Treasury security aims to protect its holders from inflation. They're called **Treasury Inflation Protected Securities**, or **TIPS** for short. We previously discussed inflation as having a negative effect on your **purchasing power,** or ability to buy things. For example, today $10 might be enough to get you a decent meal at Chipotle, Shake Shack, or your favorite fast casual restaurant. But 20 years from now, the odds are that $10 might only be enough to pay for your drink at the same restaurant. TIPS are tied to inflation. When inflation goes up, your interest payment from the TIPS bond goes up too. When the interest payment or coupon on a bond changes, it's known as a **floating-rate bond**. Most bonds have fixed coupon payments, but floating-rate bonds are out there as well. The most common floating-rate benchmark is called London Inter-bank Offered Rate (LIBOR), which is determined as an average of interest rates posted daily by a group of banks in London.

In essence, TIPS protect you to a great extent from the ravages of inflation. TIPS are currently offered in 5-year, 10-year, and 30-year maturities. You might think, "If these bonds protect you from inflation, why don't all investors buy them?" Since it is close to a risk-free rate of return, they pay low rates of interest. For example, a 5-year TIP was recently yielding a paltry 0.16% annual rate of interest. No one is going to get rich earning less than 1% a year, even after inflation. Since inflation is such an important topic, according to Buffett, we'll give it its own section in this chapter.

Inflation and the Consumer Price Index (CPI)

The prices of most new things go up in value over time, historically about 2% or 3% per year. We call this process inflation (**Chapter 1**). In some cases, prices fall, and when they do, it's called **deflation**. Deflation might occur due to oversupply or falling demand for something, or because it becomes cheaper to manufacture. For example, Tesla's early cars often cost more than $80,000 each. However, after their "gigafactory" was up and running, they were able to sell their Model 3 car starting at $35,000. Still a lot of money, but by producing batteries in bulk, they were able to drive down the cost of some of their cars.

We can say inflation means rising prices, but we need to measure it more precisely in order to make good financial decisions. The most common way is by calculating a **Consumer Price Index (CPI)**. The CPI represents a basket of goods and services purchased by the *typical* American household and is calculated by a unit of the US government, the Bureau of Labor and Statistics (BLS). Different countries will have their own inflation measures. There are different parts to the US basket, as shown in **Figure 4.2**.

The biggest part of CPI for most households is where you live, or housing. That's typically about 40% of someone's spending. Other big parts are transportation, such as the cost of having a car or commuting to work, and medical care. But your own personal CPI may differ dramatically from the BLS's calculation. For example, many young people live at home or at college, where part or all of the expenses are paid for by their parents. Their biggest current spending items are probably related to food, clothing, and entertainment. However, as people age and move out on their own, housing, health care, and transportation will probably occupy the bulk of their spending.

The BLS publishes the CPI monthly and periodically updates the components of the CPI basket and its weights. For example, there were no cell phones 50 years ago, and very few people had their own computers. Typewriters and the buggy whip have largely disappeared from today's modern economy. So the CPI changes represent the ebb and flow of the economy and what is purchased by its survey of thousands of US households.

Bond Ratings and Corporate Bankruptcy

Companies such as Apple, Disney, and Nike also issue bonds. Unlike the US government, however, they can't run the money printing press to pay their bills. There's a chance that they won't pay what's promised in terms of the interest payments or principal. The chance they don't pay on time or in full is called **default risk**. The percentage of bonds that default is called the **default rate**. Just as with individuals (e.g., Buffett vs. you) companies differ widely in terms of their wealth and ability to pay their debts.

Fortunately, you don't have to be a bond guru to get an estimate of a company's ability to pay its bills. There are companies, called **rating agencies**, that do it for many companies and governments on a global basis. The largest bond rating agencies in the US are Standard & Poor's (S&P), Moody's, and Fitch. We'll see the S&P name again in the context of stocks, so file it away for now. They rate bonds with a combination of letters. They differ slightly in their nomenclature, so we'll stick with the one S&P uses. The best rating is AAA. It might surprise you that there are only two companies in the US with a AAA rating today (Microsoft

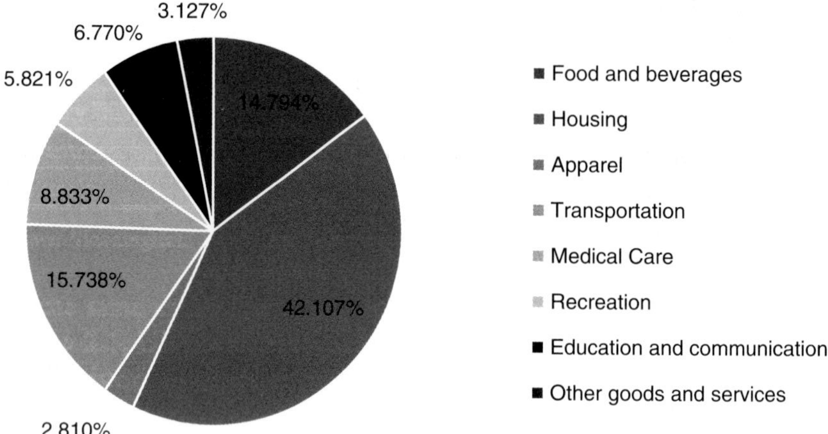

Figure 4.2 Consumer Price Index Components
Source: Data from Relative importance of components in the Consumer Price Indexes: U.S. city average, December 2019.

and Johnson & Johnson). Below AAA is AA+, then AA, AA–, A+, A, A–, BBB+, BBB, and BBB–, plus some others. Bonds rated BBB– and higher are called **investment grade bonds**. Bonds rated below that, BB+ all the way through D, are called **high yield** or **junk bonds**. Why would someone buy junk bonds? They offer higher rates of interest, convincing some investors that they're worth the risk.

Why do investment analysts make the distinction between investment grade and junk bonds? Some investors are prevented from owning junk bonds, so they aren't for everyone. If fact, Buffett would say they rarely make sense for anyone. Buffett is not a fan of newly issued junk bonds but will occasionally buy some when they get really, really cheap. In his 1990 letter to shareholders, Buffett wrote, "Junk bonds remain a minefield, even at prices that today are often a small fraction of issue price. As we said last year, we have never bought a new issue of a junk bond. (The only time to buy these is on a day with no "y" in it.) We are, however, willing to look at the field, now that it is in disarray."

The default rate for all bonds historically averages around 1.5% per year. But the number is higher during recessionary periods in the economy and lower during expansionary periods. And, as you might guess, the default rates differ for investment grade bonds versus junk bonds. If the overall default rate is 1.5% in any given year, roughly

4% of junk bonds default and less than ½ of 1% of investment grade bonds default.

A D rating means **default**, which means the company didn't pay what it promised. In many cases the firm is, or will be, in bankruptcy. Bankruptcy can apply to corporations and even some governments, just like we discussed with individuals in the last chapter. It might surprise you, but some companies can still operate while they are in bankruptcy. There are two major types of corporate bankruptcy, **Chapter 7** and **Chapter 11**.

In Chapter 7, the firm sells whatever it can and gives the net amount to its creditors (i.e., the investors that purchased the firm's bonds and, rarely, stockholders) and then ceases to exist. The Chapter 7 process is known as **liquidation**. You may recall the electronics store Circuit City or the online music download service Napster. These companies have disappeared.

A Chapter 11 bankruptcy allows the firm to continue to operate. Some of its debt is usually eliminated, while other parts are restructured. In most cases the old stockholders are wiped out and the new shareholders are often the original bondholders who didn't get paid in full. The **recovery rate** is the amount of money (e.g., 70 cents on the dollar) that the old bondholders receive during the Chapter 11 process. Since they are usually taking a significant loss or haircut, they are often given stock in the new, reorganized firm. You've certainly come across companies that went through the Chapter 11 process, even if you weren't familiar with the term. Examples include General Motors (GM), Chrysler, Macy's, Aéropostale, Sears, and Delta Airlines.

Corporate Bonds, Municipal Bonds, and Bowie Bonds

Corporate bonds are issued when companies borrow money from investors. They can also borrow money from banks, which is often called a **term loan**. Both types are debt obligations of the firm. We mentioned Apple, Disney, and Nike in the last section, but literally thousands of companies sell bonds to investors. Just as with US Treasuries, the borrowings may be short term in nature (i.e., less than 1 year) or long term (i.e., up to 30 years). It's often the cheapest way for them to fund their businesses, pay for the development of new products and services, or buy other companies. In **Chapter 7**, we'll cover the basics on accounting, but for now, we'll tell you that there is a tax advantage for companies issuing debt. The interest they pay on their bonds is tax deductible, meaning it lowers their tax bill.

State and local governments may also issue bonds, which are known as **municipal bonds**, or **munis**. For example, the government of the state that you live in likely sells debt to investors and uses the money to help pay for various things, such as schools, roads, the state police, health care services, and many other items. Your local school district may issue municipal bonds that help pay for the building of schools and teacher salaries. State colleges and universities often issue municipal bonds. Municipal bonds are usually very safe, but occasionally, there are bankruptcies, as once occurred with the city of Detroit and the US territory of Puerto Rico.

There is also a big tax benefit to municipal bonds. Buyers pay no federal income taxes on the interest they receive from the bonds, unlike US Treasuries, which are taxable to individuals. This is one of the few legal ways you can avoid Ben Franklin's quote on the inevitability of death and taxes. And if you live in the place where the bonds are issued, you are also exempt from paying taxes on the interest to state and local governments. For example, if you live in New York City and purchase a New York City school bond, the interest is exempt from federal, state of New York, and New York City income taxes. The tax deductibility of municipal bonds is also a great benefit to the issuer of the bonds (e.g., a school district) since they can pay their investors lower interest rates than would be the case if the bonds were fully taxable.

Bowie Bonds and Other Asset-Backed Securities

We mentioned that almost anything that has a cash flow tied to it can be turned into a bond. When a song is played on the radio, or through some other broadcast mechanism, the composer of the song is entitled to a small **royalty.** If you are a best-selling recording artist, like Taylor Swift, U2, Drake, Beyoncé, The Beatles, or David Bowie, these royalties can add up to millions of dollars per year. David Bowie was the first recording artist to monetize his music royalties by issuing a bond, with what became known as Bowie bonds.

The bonds were issued back in 1997 and were based on the royalties from 25 David Bowie albums recorded before 1990. The bonds raised $55 million and had a life of 10 years at an interest rate of 7.9%. Later, other artists followed suit with their own bonds, including James Brown, the "Godfather of Soul." Marvel, now owned by Disney, once issued bonds backed by the rights to some of its comic book characters, such as Captain America. Bonds backed by specific things, such as music royalties, comic book characters, auto loans, and many other items, are known as **asset-backed securities**.

The Federal Reserve: The Central Bank of the United States

To better understand what drives interest rates and bond prices, we need to discuss a country's **central bank**. A central bank may be viewed as the "banker's bank." It can provide money for banks when they get in trouble and it also oversees, or regulates, banks. It also determines how much money a country should print. **The Federal Reserve**, or "**The Fed**," is the central bank of the US. Most other countries, or economic regions, also have their own central bank. For example, there is the Bank of Japan (BOJ), People's Bank of China (PBOC), Bank of England (BOE), and the European Central Bank (ECB). The ECB helps manage the money supply for those countries that are part of the euro currency.

The Fed is a quasi-independent unit of the US government, meaning they are a part of the government but run independently. The leadership of the Federal Reserve is known as **Federal Reserve Board of Governors**. But they don't run for election. They are appointed by the president for terms of 14 years and confirmed by the US Senate, with the chance of renewal. The long-term nature of their appointments provides them with some independence, since the US president cannot be elected for more than two 4-year terms. The head of the Fed's Board of Governors is its chairperson, currently Jerome Powell. The chair is appointed for 4 years, but the term may be renewed at the president's discretion. Some Fed chairpersons have served for almost 20 years.

The Fed has two main goals. The first is to maximize employment, or alternatively, to minimize unemployment. The unemployment rate can never be zero due to a mismatch of skills between the job openings and the skillset of those applying for jobs, as well as the unawareness of job openings or candidates, and the difficulty of relocating to the areas where the jobs are available. Full employment varies by country, but in the US it is estimated to be about 97%, or 3% unemployed.

The second main goal is to have stable prices, generally believed to have inflation average about 2% per year. You might ask, "Why should there be any desired inflation?" You can view money as the lubrication of the economic system. Just like a gasoline-powered engine needs oil to run smoothly, an economy needs money to be clicking on all cylinders. A little bit of extra money helps take into account things such as population growth and helps avoid the fear that money is "tight" or scarce. These two main goals, maximum employment and stable prices, are known as the Fed's **dual mandate**. It has other lesser goals as well, such as a strong economy and stable interest rates, but they are closely related to the dual mandate.

The Fed tries to achieve its goals through three main techniques. The first is related to a bank's **reserve requirements**. This term refers to how much money a bank has to keep in the vault, either literally or electronically on reserve with the Fed. It might surprise you, but if you deposit, let's say, $100 in the bank, the bank doesn't put all of it in the vault. It puts about 5% to 10% in the vault and then lends out the rest to companies or individuals seeking loans. This is why there is no bank that can survive **a run on the bank**, which means many of the bank's customers simultaneously request their money back. The Fed will step in during any run on a bank to help stabilize it. Occasionally, like in the Great Recession of 2008–2009, the Fed will allow some banks to fail, but it will make sure that all FDIC-insured deposits are safe, as we mentioned in the last chapter.

The second main tool that the Fed uses is to change short-term interest rates. Specifically, it sets the rate for what's known as the **federal discount rate**. The federal discount rate is the interest rate charged when banks borrow from the Fed. Since banks lend money to their customers, it's often used as a base rate of interest for short-term loans. When the Fed raises or lowers the federal discount rate, banks usually promptly follow suit with the interest rates they give to their customers. Bank customers usually are charged a rate higher than the federal discount rate due to the credit risk (i.e., chance of not making payments on time), a term we mentioned earlier in the chapter. The best customers of the bank pay what's known as the **prime rate**. Other customers pay higher rates. In short, the Fed helps control short-term interest rates through its changes to the federal discount rate. In the aftermath of the COVID-19 pandemic, the Fed slashed the discount rate to 0% in an effort to spur economic growth.

The Fed's third tool is called **open market operations**, which means its policy of buying and selling securities. It usually buys or sells US government bonds, or bonds indirectly backed by the US government, such as mortgage-backed securities. The act of buying injects money into the economy and generally lowers interest rates, especially those of the intermediate- to long-term part of the yield curve. It goes back to our supply and demand diagram discussed in **Chapter 2**. If there is additional demand buying bonds and the supply is roughly fixed, it winds up lowering interest rates and pushing up the price of bonds.

We'll cover this concept more in the next section, but one factoid to remember is that when interest rates go down, the price of most bonds go up. The reverse is also true (i.e., when rates go up, bond prices go down). When the Fed buys a lot of bonds, it's generally referred to in the financial press as **quantitative easing**, or **QE**. QE generally results in lower interest rates and is often used by central banks when short-term rates are close to zero. To fight off the recession triggered by the COVID-19 panic, the Fed is literally buying trillions of dollars of securities over the 2020–2021 period through its QE program.

Lower interest rates generally speed up economic growth, while higher interest rates generally put the brakes on economic growth. You might be thinking, "Why would a central bank want to put the brakes on economic growth?" To avoid too much inflation, which means the economy is in danger of overheating and heading into a recession.

What Determines Interest Rates?

There are several factors behind the level of interest rates. The behavior of The Fed, or the central bank of a country, is a big influence. But there are other factors as well. Economic growth is generally tied to the level of interest rates. During strong periods of growth, both companies and individuals often need access to funds. Companies might need money to pay for new projects they have planned. Individuals might need money for homes, cars, and other spending plans. So during strong periods of economic growth, interest rates are usually higher since demand is high. During weak periods of economic growth, rates are usually lower since demand is low.

The financial markets are global, so interest rates in another country, adjusted for currency conversion rates (e.g., US dollars for euros), also affect the level of interest rates. For example, if the rates on bonds of similar riskiness are higher in the US than in Europe, European investors would move money out of Europe and into the US. Using the supply and demand dynamics we previously discussed, this behavior would generally result in slightly lower US interest rates and slightly higher rates of interest for economies using the euro. Investor sentiment or market psychology also plays a role in interest rates and prices. Usually, when there is a lot of fear, due to some financial crisis or shock to the economic system, people gravitate toward safe securities, such as US government bonds. This "**flight to quality**" behavior generally lowers interest rates in most countries with strong credit ratings.

We can explain after the fact what moved bond prices. Forecasting them in advance is a hard task and almost impossible over the short term. In his 1980 letter to shareholders, Buffett wrote, "We believe that short-term forecasts of stock or bond prices are useless. The forecasts may tell you a great deal about the forecaster; they tell you nothing about the future." A pretty harsh but likely accurate criticism. We've waited a while in this chapter for a Tip, so this quote will be our first for the chapter.

Buffett Tip 19:

Short-term forecasts of stock or bond prices are useless.

Intuition on Estimating the Price of a Bond

As mentioned previously, we're going to keep the math to a minimum, with any equations put in the Appendix or endnote if they can't be explained in plain English. We'll give you the intuition for valuing a bond in this section and put the specific formula for bond valuation in the Appendix. Recall, from **Chapter 2**, the Present Value formula says how much you would pay today to receive a cash flow, such as $100, in the future. Well, with a bond, there are two types of cash flows. The coupon (aka interest) payment and the face value (aka principal). The price of the bond is simply the present value of these two groups of cash flows (i.e., coupon payments and face value).

As noted earlier in the chapter, the discount rate on a bond is called the yield to maturity. It's a market-determined rate that changes slightly each day. The difference between the (fixed) coupon rate and (floating or market-based) yield to maturity helps explain why the price of the bond isn't always $1,000, or its face value.

When a bond is first sold to investors, the coupon rate is usually close to the yield to maturity. But it can drift over time since the yield to maturity is determined by market forces, while the coupon rate is always fixed, unless it is a floating-rate bond. We can give you some good rules of thumb for bond valuation without any equations.

If the coupon rate equals the yield to maturity, the price estimate for a bond always equals its face value. That is, $1,000 in most cases, which is known as **at par** in bond lingo. If the coupon rate is higher than the yield to maturity, then the price of the bond will sell for more than its face value and is known as a **premium bond**. The intuition is that the coupon rate is higher than the market rate, therefore the bond should be more valuable since it gives you more interest than is expected and therefore should sell for a higher price. If the coupon rate is lower than the yield to maturity, then the price of the bond will sell for less than its face value, or what's known as a **discount bond**. The intuition is that the coupon rate is lower than the market rate, so it should sell at a discount.

A key aspect to plain vanilla bond prices is that they move in the opposite direction of interest rates. That is, when interest rates go up, plain vanilla bond prices go down. And when interest rates go down, the prices of plain vanilla bonds go up in value, other things equal. Or as Buffett said, "In economics, interest rates act as gravity behaves in the physical world." It's a play on the old expression, "What goes up must come down." Buffett's point is an important one, so we'll add it to our growing pile of tips.

Buffett Tip 20:

In economics, interest rates act as gravity behaves in the physical world.

When interest rates fall (rise), it means the bond is less (more) risky. If it's less (more) risky, you should be willing to pay more (less) for it. Sorry for all those parentheses! We know certain things about bonds can be really boring, like an opera concert for a heavy metal fan!

Another point to be aware of is that bonds that have high coupons are generally less risky than bonds with low or no coupons. The coupons act as sort of a "cushion" to help offset changes in interest rates. And, as we mentioned earlier in the chapter, long-term bonds are generally riskier than short-term bonds. They move around a lot more when interest rates change. It doesn't mean that you wouldn't own them, but rather, you'd want them at a good price or when you think interest rates are going to go down. Putting these two concepts together, long-term low or no coupon bonds are the riskiest, and short-term high coupon bonds are the safest.

So Are Bonds Good Investments?

We're almost to the end of this chapter, so let's talk about the role of bonds in your financial portfolio. If you need the money for short-term purchases and can't afford to lose money, then yes, bonds, CDs, and savings accounts are probably good investments. They would fall into the "**safe haven**" category of investments that *usually* hold up, when the stock market or economy are having problems. However, according to Buffett, if you are trying to build wealth and have a long-term horizon, bonds are generally *not* good long-term investments. In fact, they may destroy your wealth, after taking inflation and taxes into account. We cite a fairly long quote from Buffett's 2011 Chairman's Letter to Berkshire Shareholders to prove our point:

> Investments that are denominated in a given currency include money-market funds, bonds, mortgages, bank deposits, and other instruments. Most of these currency-based investments are thought of as "safe." In truth, they are among the most dangerous of assets. . . . Over the past century these instruments have destroyed the purchasing power of investors in many countries, even as the holders continued to receive timely payments of interest and principal. This ugly result, moreover, will forever recur.
>
> Governments determine the ultimate value of money, and systemic forces will sometimes cause them to gravitate to policies that produce inflation. From time to time such policies spin out of control. Even in the US, where the wish for a stable currency is strong, the dollar has fallen a staggering 86% in value since 1965, when I took over management of Berkshire. It takes no less than $7 today to buy what $1 did at that time. Consequently, a tax-free institution would have needed 4.3% interest annually from bond investments over that period to simply maintain its purchasing power. Its managers would have been kidding themselves if they thought of any portion of that interest as "income."
>
> For tax-paying investors like you and me, the picture has been far worse. During the same 47-year period, continuous rolling of US

> Treasury bills produced 5.7% annually. That sounds satisfactory. But if an individual investor paid personal income taxes at a rate averaging 25%, this 5.7% return would have yielded nothing in the way of real income. This investor's visible income tax would have stripped him of 1.4 points of the stated yield, and the invisible inflation tax would have devoured the remaining 4.3 points.

A summary of this quote merits a Tip.

Buffett Tip 21:

Bonds may be a good "safe haven" investment but will destroy wealth for many investors over the long term, after taking into account inflation and taxes.

This Tip is a fairly controversial point among investors, but we think he's right. There may be select periods of time, as in the early 1980s when interest rates were in the teens, when owning bonds may make great financial sense over the *long term*. Recall, one of our lessons in this chapter is that when interest rates fall (like they are apt to do when they're very high), bond prices go up. But the greatest investor ever knows what he's talking about when it comes to the Benjamins. As you might guess, Buffett is a big fan of stocks as a way of building long-term wealth, and we'll talk about them over the next two chapters.

A Note on Negative Bond Yields

It's been a crazy decade or so for the bond market, especially when you look on a global basis. The yields on debt from many sovereign nations, such as Switzerland, Japan, Germany, and Denmark, have been negative in recent years! That means you are guaranteed to lose money on the investment if you hold them until the maturity date. What is going on here? Why would anyone buy an investment that is guaranteed to lose money if held to maturity?

First, the negative yield comes from buying a bond at a price greater than its face value. The coupon rate paid on the bond is often too small to overcome paying such a high price to start. The two parts together, coupon plus the difference between the purchase price and sale price help determine your total return. Investors may buy bonds with a negative yield since it is a safe, liquid place to park money. By safe, we mean that the prices won't fluctuate much, unlike a stock or something like Bitcoin. The modest loss incurred by buying these bonds may be viewed as akin to a small tax for these investors. In the US, T-bills were briefly, slightly negative during the Great Recession and during the peak of the COVID-19 pandemic. However, it's a peculiar footnote in the investing world that is slightly more common than a Loch Ness Monster sighting, at least in the US. We and Buffett certainly wouldn't recommend putting a lot of your wealth in something poised to lose money over the long term, regardless of the perceived safety.

Appendix: Bond Valuation

In this Appendix, we'll cover a quantitative formula for valuing bonds. As we discussed in the main body of the chapter, we're simply going to value the bond as the present value of the coupon payments and the present value of the face value. Most bonds pay interest semi-annually, but to simplify the calculation, we'll assume interest is paid once a year. Let's assume our bond matures in 3 years, its coupon rate is 5%, and its face value is $1,000.

We need the discount rate for the bond, which we mentioned is called the yield to maturity. As a reminder, the coupon rate is fixed for "plain vanilla" bonds for the entire life of the bond. However, the yield to maturity is a market rate that changes a bit virtually every day. The difference between the (fixed) coupon rate and the changing yield to maturity helps explain why the price of the bond isn't always equal to $1,000, or its face value.

Getting back to our numerical example, let's assume the yield to maturity on the bond is 4%. In practice you can get this number by looking at bonds from the same industry with a similar credit rating. We'll do a simple example that is possible to do by hand or with a basic calculator, but in practice most analysts use Excel or a financial calculator.

Recall, our Present Value formula takes the cash flow we expect in the future and discounts it by $(1 + r)^T$, where r is the discount rate (yield to maturity for a bond) and T is the time in years for the bond to mature. In our example, we have four cash flows. The first three cash flows are the coupon payments, $50 a year, or 5% of the $1,000 principal. And then at the end of 3 years we get back the $1,000 principal. Since, in year

3 we get the $50 coupon and $1,000 principal value, we'll add the two numbers in our example. The yield to maturity is 4% and the number of years to maturity, T, is 3.

$$\text{PV(Bond)} = \frac{\$50}{1.04^1} + \frac{\$50}{1.04^2} + \frac{\$1,050}{1.04^3} = \$1,027.75$$

Presto! We have our estimate for the price of this specific bond, which is $1,027.75. If the price of the bond is selling in the market for less than this price, we'd think it's a good buy and purchase it. If the price of the bond is selling in the market for more than this price, we'd think its overvalued and likely sell it if we already owned it or avoid it, if we had no prior position.

Buffett's Tips from Chapter 4

Buffett Tip 19: Short-term forecasts of stock or bond prices are useless.
Buffett Tip 20: In economics, interest rates act as gravity behaves in the physical world.
Buffett Tip 21: Bonds may be a good "safe haven" investment but will destroy wealth for many investors over the long term, after taking into account inflation and taxes.

References

Buffett, Warren. "Letter to Shareholders of Berkshire Hathaway Inc." Berkshire Hathaway, Inc., 1980. https://www.berkshirehathaway.com/letters/1980.html.

Buffett, Warren. "Letter to Shareholders of Berkshire Hathaway Inc." Berkshire Hathaway, Inc., 1990. https://www.berkshirehathaway.com/letters/1990.html.

Buffett, Warren. "Letter to Shareholders of Berkshire Hathaway Inc." Berkshire Hathaway, Inc., 2011. https://www.berkshirehathaway.com/letters/2011.html.

"Comparing Series EE and Series I Savings Bonds." Treasury Direct. Accessed June 14, 2020. https://www.treasurydirect.gov/indiv/research/indepth/ebonds/res_e_bonds_eecomparison.htm.

Espiner, Tom. "'Bowie Bonds'—the Singer's Financial Innovation." BBC News. BBC, January 11, 2016. https://www.bbc.com/news/business-35280945.

Kaeding, Nicole. "State Individual Income Tax Rates and Brackets for 2016." Tax Foundation, February 8, 2016. https://taxfoundation.org/state-individual-income-tax-rates-and-brackets-2016/.

Kenny, Thomas. "How Likely Is It That a Bond Will Default?" The Balance, January 27, 2020. https://www.thebalance.com/what-is-the-default-rate-416917.

Leinfuss, Nancy. "Entertainment Royalty ABS Seen Gaining Momentum." Thomson Reuters, January 19, 2007. https://www.reuters.com/article/financial-assetbackeds-entertainment/entertainment-royalty-abs-seen-gaining-momentum-idUSN0845429320061109.

Mislinski, Jill. "Inside the Consumer Price Index: May 2020." *Advisor Perspectives*, June 10, 2020. https://www.advisorperspectives.com/dshort/updates/2017/06/14/what-inflation-means-to-you-inside-the-consumer-price-index.

5

Stock Market Fundamentals

"Be fearful when others are greedy. Be greedy only when others are fearful."
—Warren Buffett, "2004 Letter to Berkshire Hathaway Shareholders"

Introduction

What is a stock? As we noted in **Chapter 1**, stock (also known as **equity** in the singular or **equities** in the plural) represents part ownership of a business. Buffett learned this point from his mentor, Benjamin Graham, and never forgot it. It's such an important point according to both Graham and Buffett that we'll put it as a Tip.

Buffett Tip 22

Stock equals ownership in a business. ***(Courtesy of Benjamin Graham)***

If you own all of the **shares outstanding**, you own 100% of the business. If you own 1% of the shares outstanding, you own 1% of the business. Shares outstanding are the amount of shares held by all investors of a firm. The number of shares outstanding is determined by policies set forth by the board of directors (BOD), which we previously noted is the group formally in charge of a firm. Sometimes there is a lag, typically ranging from a few months to a year, between when the shares are authorized by the BOD and when they are purchased by investors. This gets at the heart of how stocks are "born." It's probably not as exciting as your first "birds and bees talk." But we won't tell you stocks come from the stork. :-)

Initial Public Offerings (IPOs): The Birth of a Stock

Regarding the birth of stocks, we're going to focus on **publicly traded stocks**. The type that trades on a stock exchange and that anyone with enough money can own. We made the distinction between publicly traded stocks, such as Berkshire Hathaway and Apple, and privately held firms, such as the New York Yankees, the Dallas Cowboys, and Fidelity Investments.

Why do some firms go public and list their shares on a stock exchange? First, they get money for selling a piece (usually starting at 10–20%) of themselves. This money can be used to help the firm grow by developing new products, entering new markets, and many other approaches. Second, it gives existing shareholders a chance to cash out by selling their existing shares to new shareholders. It's harder for shareholders of a private firm to turn their shares into cash. Why? Shares trading on an exchange are more liquid (a term we introduced in **Chapter 3**) than shares of private firms since they trade every weekday, minus holidays. Third, it may make it easier to buy other companies, most of which have a preference to be acquired by public firms. Fourth, public firms generally attract more publicity than private firms. They are also more closely followed by Wall Street. Other than perhaps sports teams, can you think of any private company that gets more attention than public firms such as Apple, Alphabet, Facebook, Amazon.com, and the like?

Investment Banks and Investment Bankers

Okay, so let's say your firm, let's call it TJL Industries, wants to go public. The next step is to hire a firm to help you accomplish this goal. The firms that handle this task are called **investment banking firms**, and the people who work for them are called **investment bankers**. Some of the leading firms active in the investment banking business include

Goldman Sachs, Morgan Stanley, and J.P. Morgan. If your firm is in great demand, like Uber was in 2019, the investment banking firms will compete for your firm's business, telling you why they will do a great job for your firm. This process of competition for raising money for a firm is called on Wall Street a "**beauty contest**" or "**bake-off**." Maybe not as exciting as the Miss America or Miss Universe pageants, but it's also important. Let's say TJL Industries picks Goldman Sachs as the winner. Goldman would be called the lead **underwriter** in this instance. It's a term we'll flesh out in a moment since other investment banking firms may help out as well but in a lesser capacity.

The next step is called a **roadshow**, where Goldman's investment banking team takes the senior management of the firm (TJL Industries) to meet with potential investors. These investors may be large financial firms, such as BlackRock, Fidelity Investments, and Prudential Investments, as well as individual investors. Large firms and rich investors, often called **high net worth (HNW) investors**, typically receive the lion's share of new stock offered by the firm (TJL Industries).

Goldman gathers information from these investor meetings regarding the demand by investors for the stock. Goldman also looks at the prices of similar stocks in the same industry trading on the exchange, known as **comparable firms**, to get an idea regarding how to set the initial price the stock. (After it begins trading on the exchange, its price will be determined by the market forces of supply and demand.) The investment bankers and the firm set a price for TJL's stock that will be sold to (mostly) institutions and HNW investors. Let's say it's $20 a share and that the firm has 50 million shares outstanding. This values the firm at $1 billion, or $20 per share times the 50 million shares outstanding. But remember, the firm usually sells just a small part of itself when it goes public. Let's assume it's 10%. So Goldman helped TJL Industries raise $100 million in our example. The investment bank earns a fee of about 7% of the money raised in deals, which comes out to $7 million. For larger deals, the investment bank earns a smaller fee on a percentage basis (e.g., 2–5%).

For large deals, and occasionally smaller deals, the investment banks become sort of frenemies and combine to take the firms public. When they join forces, like in *The Avengers*, *X-Men*, or *Suicide Squad* movies, this group of underwriters is called a **syndicate**, and they share in the fees and work. The basic idea behind the syndicate is twofold. First, in a **firm commitment offering**, the investment bank (Goldman Sachs) guarantees it will raise the full amount ($100 million). If it significantly overestimates the demand for TJL Industries' stock, it "takes the L" and is on the hook for $100 million. Ouch!

Second, if several investment banks promote TJL to their clients or customers, it may increase demand for the stock. Two, or many, hands are usually better than one when trying to complete an important task. The investment banks sometimes put an advertisement, called a **tombstone,** in a financial newspaper to help drum up demand in the offering. It's nothing to freak out about, like seeing Jason from *Friday the 13th* in a cemetery. The name comes from the rectangular shape of the ad, similar to most gravestones.

The Main Event: The Stock Begins Trading on the Exchange

Now we're ready for the main event, the **initial public offering**, or **IPO** for short. In our example, 5 million shares of TJL Industries were sold primarily to various "connected" investors, such as big investment firms and rich individuals, at $20 a share. The $100 million raised, minus the $7 million fees paid to the investment bankers, goes to the firm doing the IPO (TJL Industries). The firm will use this money to support its future growth plans.

What about everyone else? Can't they get a piece of the action? Let's call them John and Jane Public. They can buy the stock when it starts trading on the exchange, typically a few weeks after the roadshow. But the catch is they won't likely be able to get it at the $20 a share price that the connected investors got it at. Since anyone can now buy it the morning it trades on the stock exchange, there is usually a big jump in price. Let's say to $25. Bummer. A 25% jump in price on day 1 of the IPO is fairly common, but during periods of investor craziness or euphoria, jumps of more than 100% in a *single day* are not unheard of! Investors often rush to get in on the "ground floor" of something they think will be big. They are hoping for the next Apple, Google, Starbucks, or Berkshire. Of course, very few firms meet these lofty expectations.

You might be thinking, "Who sells the shares to John and Jane Public?" Some of the connected investors sell, even though it may slightly anger the investment banks and the firm that just did the IPO. These investors who sell quickly after the IPO occurs are called **flippers**. Maybe you've seen a show on TV about flipping houses or cars. Well, it's the same concept, except with stocks. Investors that flip a lot may be cut out of the next deal by the investment bankers, since companies prefer stable, long-term investors.

Another question you might have is, "How do companies raise money after an IPO?" The process is very similar to what happened with the IPO and also involves the help of investment bankers. The term **secondary** or **seasoned offering** refers to the sale of securities by a firm that is already public. The process is a little more straightforward, and the fees are lesser on a percentage basis since the firm is already well known by investors.

There's also a special group of traders at the exchange called **market makers**, who always have shares available to buy or sell—at a price. You may not like the price ($25 in our example), but they are like 911—always there when you call or, in our case, trade. Most trading is done online these days, but they still have telephones. Let's talk a bit more about the stock exchange. How it works is not that much different than trading football cards, Beanie Babies, Hot Wheels cars, or anything else you traded with your friends as a kid.

The Stock Exchange

The stock exchange is a place for trading shares of a firm that have already been issued, such as after an IPO or seasoned offering. When the firm raises money from investors with an IPO or seasoned offering, it's called a **primary market transaction**. The trading of shares on an exchange after these primary market transactions have occurred is called **secondary market transactions**. So, as we said a minute ago, it's like investors trading the equivalent of football cards or Beanie Babies that were purchased in the past. If you think in these terms, it's easy to see that the firm gets *no money* in these secondary market transactions. Just like Apple gets no money if you resell your iPhone to another person. It's simply people trading on the side. Except there is a lot of trading on the exchanges—often over a billion shares in a single day!

There are two main stock exchanges in the US, the **New York Stock Exchange (NYSE)** and the **National Association of Security Dealers Automated Quotation System (NASDAQ)**. There is also a third, smaller stock exchange, the **NYSE American**, previously known as the **American Stock Exchange (AMEX).** All three of these stock exchanges are headquartered in Manhattan.

The exchanges are open for business Monday through Friday from 9:30 a.m. to 4:00 p.m., Eastern Standard Time (EST), except for holidays. This typically results in 252 trading days a year. One factoid that may interest you is that the stock exchange typically closes for one day, soon after a former US President dies. There's also a bit of trading outside these normal hours in what is known as **after-hours trading**. The only thing is that this after-hours trading may occur before the market opens (4:00 a.m.–9:30 a.m. EST) and after it closes (4:00 p.m.–8:00 p.m. EST). The bulk of these after-hour trades occur two hours before the market formally opens and two hours after the market closes. It should really be called "outside of regular market hours trading," but the term after-hours has stuck. Occasionally, it's called **extended hours trading** to better reflect the times available for trading.

Today, it doesn't make much difference on what exchange a stock trades. In the past, it was sort of a big deal for a company where your stock traded. Kind of like the difference between the coolness factor of driving a sleek Mercedes and a plain Chevy (not a Corvette!). Historically, it was prestigious if your stock traded on the New York Stock Exchange, which went by the nickname "**the Big Board**." The name refers to a time before computers where stock prices were written on a chalkboard or came out of a **ticker tape machine**.

You might get a kick out of seeing a picture of a ticker tape machine. A ticker tape machine built by Thomas Edison's firm is shown in **Figure 5.1**. (Thomas Edison, of course, was the inventor of the modern-day lightbulb.) Perhaps you've heard the term **ticker tape parade**. For example, when the Yankees win the World Series in baseball, New York City holds a parade for them. The players and coaches are driven down Broadway in Manhattan, and people throw bits of paper at them in celebration, similar to confetti. In the past, the paper was mostly ticker tape. Today, it's mostly shredded paper. A ticker tape machine looks sort of like a big lightbulb that would spit out thin strips of paper. On the strip of paper would be the stock symbol (T for AT&T, as an example), the stock price ($45 a share, for example), and perhaps the number of shares traded (100 shares, for example).

The requirements to be listed or traded on the NYSE are stricter than what are needed to be listed on NASDAQ or AMEX. By requirements we refer to minimum standards of revenues and profits of the firm, and its **total capital**, which is the amount of a firm's debt and equity. Berkshire first listed on NASDAQ but eventually moved its listing to the NYSE. NASDAQ used to be known as an **over-the-counter (OTC)**

Figure 5.1 Edison Stock Ticker Machine
Source: H.Zimmer, https://commons.wikimedia.org/wiki/File:Edison_Stock_Telegraph_Ticker.jpg. Licensed under CC BY 3.0

market since, before computers became widespread, its trades were literally entered over the counter at a brokerage office.

A lot of big technology stocks, such as Apple, Intel, and Microsoft, listed on NASDAQ in the 1970s and 1980s and have chosen to remain there. Since some of the biggest firms in the world are listed on NASDAQ, the distinction isn't that big of a deal anymore. And speaking of computers, there is a relatively new type of stock exchange called an **Electronic Communication Network (ECN)**. If you visit the floor of the NYSE on Wall Street in Manhattan, you will see traders working there. With an ECN, it is mostly a bunch of computer servers doing the work, whose job is to simply match buy and sell orders.

A Sidebar on Stock and Mutual Fund Symbols

Did you ever wonder how a company picks its stock symbol? In some cases, the symbol is similar to what the name sounds like. For example, the stock symbol for the construction equipment firm Caterpillar is, not surprisingly, CAT. If a firm trades on AMEX or NYSE, its ticker symbol usually has 3 letters or less. For example, IBM has the ticker symbol IBM. The financial firm J.P. Morgan Chase, has the symbol (JPM). AT&T has the symbol T. If a firm, like AT&T, has only a single letter for its ticker symbol, it's supposed to be prestigious, like a personalized license plate, or a rock star or rapper wearing a lot of bling. Some firms with a single letter symbol that you may have come across include Citi (C), Macy's (M), and U.S. Steel (X).

If the stock has 4 letters in its ticker symbol, it usually trades on NASDAQ. For example, Apple is AAPL. Intel is INTC. Amazon.com is AMZN. Starbucks is SBUX. There are some rare exceptions. For example, Facebook trades on NASDAQ and has the symbol FB.

A **mutual fund** is an investment product where a bunch of people pool their money together and have it invested by a **fund manager**, a person who manages investments for others. The investments may include a bunch of things such as stocks, bonds, and cash. We'll talk about them more throughout this book, but for now, we'll mention that mutual funds have a ticker symbol with 5 letters and the last one ends in X. For example, the ticker symbol for the Fidelity Magellan mutual fund is FMAGX. F is for the parent company, Fidelity Investments. MAG is for the Magellan Fund, and X is because it is a mutual fund.

Dividends

A dividend is cash paid by the company to its stockholders. It's similar to a bond coupon paid to bondholders of a firm. A dividend is a check in the mail so to speak, but the money is usually deposited in your brokerage account, which holds your stocks. Who doesn't like getting a check in the mail? The richest person in modern times (i.e., since the Industrial Revolution) was John D. Rockefeller, an oil industry tycoon. You are probably familiar with a company he founded that still exists today, ExxonMobil. He was worth the equivalent of $340 billion today! That amount even leaves Buffett's net worth in the dust!

Anyway, here is an epic quote from Rockefeller on dividends. "Do you know the only thing that gives me pleasure? It's to see my dividends coming in." Rockefeller thought dividends were the bomb! To give you some perspective, the average dividend paid in percentage terms for the stock market as a whole in recent years, known as the **dividend yield**, has been roughly 2%. Thus, if a company had a stock price of $100, it would typically pay a dividend of $2 a year. How often are dividends paid? For most companies, they are paid on a quarterly basis.

There is an exception. Sometimes companies pay a one-time, or non-recurring, dividend, known as a **special dividend**. Perhaps it was because a company got a one-time windfall such as the sale of a building or business. Or maybe there were special tax reasons that made paying the dividend worthwhile. In any event, the company makes it clear when it's paying a regular or special dividend.

Most companies that pay dividends take the money from their quarterly profits or earnings. If a company misses or cuts its dividend payment, its stock will usually get crushed. The company's management knows this, so sometimes it pays out dividends from its equivalent of a piggy bank, or "rainy day fund," known as retained earnings. More formally, **retained earnings** is the sum of the company's profits since it started minus any dividend payments over its history. When the company pays dividends from its retained earnings—or worse, borrows the money to pay its dividends—it's like robbing Peter to pay Paul. It can't continue for too long or else the company will crash and burn, like the Falcons blowing a 25-point lead to the Patriots in Super Bowl 51. Sorry, Falcons fans.

There is a whole group of investors who seek out dividends. They often view the dividends as part of their income and use them to help pay living expenses. Some companies make it especially convenient for these dividend-seeking investors and set up what's called **Dividend Reinvestment Programs**, or **DRIPs** for short. These programs usually enable investors who don't need the income to use the dividends to buy more shares of stock in the company. In some cases, they let you buy the stock at a slight discount, such as 5% or less. In almost all cases they let you buy the additional shares without paying transaction costs, such as brokerage commissions or record-keeping fees. The company does this since the DRIP investors are often long-term investors, with their actions resulting in less volatility for the company's stock, a feature that is attractive from the perspective of the company's management.

The percentage of earnings paid out each year is called the **payout ratio**. The remaining portion of the earnings is called the **plowback,** or **retention, ratio**. For example, if a company had $10 in annual earnings and paid out $4 in annual dividends, its payout ratio would be 40%, and its retention ratio (or plowback ratio) would be 60%. Of course, the sum of the payout ratio and retention ratio must equal 100%.

Payout ratios vary widely by industry. It could be more than 80% for many electric and gas utilities. For most companies, it's less than 50%. A lot of companies don't pay any dividends since they think they can use the money that would be sent out as a dividend to invest in good projects, which will result in even more profits down the road. Facebook would fall into this category as well as Alphabet, whose stock was previously known as Google. Google is now a unit of Alphabet. Here's how Buffett said it in his 1981 letter to Berkshire shareholders:

> Logically, a company with historic and prospective high returns on equity should retain much or all of its earnings so that shareholders can earn premium returns on enhanced capital. Conversely, low returns on corporate equity would suggest a very high dividend payout so that owners could direct capital toward more attractive areas.

One way of estimating "high profits down the road" is through a financial ratio called return on equity (ROE). It's the profit a firm earns divided by the amount of the firm's equity on its books. We'll discuss some accounting terms Buffett mentioned in his quote, as well as others, when we get to **Chapter 7**. So don't worry if you don't have a strong grasp of these concepts yet. Let's summarize Buffett's quote into a Tip.

Buffett Tip 23:

Companies with strong new profit opportunities should wait to pay dividends, while companies without many attractive new profit opportunities should pay most of their earnings out as dividends.

Berkshire hasn't paid a dividend in many decades, since Buffett believes he can invest the money wisely resulting in even more growth in his firm's stock price than if he paid it out as dividends. And historically he has been right. For example, Berkshire paid $44 billion for the transnational railroad Burlington Northern back in 2009. Since that time Burlington has generated tens of billions of dollars in profits, and Berkshire owns the railroad until the end of time. Clearly it takes a lot of dough to do a deal like that, and if Berkshire paid out a lot of its earnings as dividends, it probably wouldn't have had the cash to do it.

You may be wondering why someone might invest in a company that has no short- to intermediate-term chance of paying dividends. The answer is you hope to sell the stock at a higher price than what you bought it for. When you do make a profit in this way, it's called a

capital gain. When the opposite occurs, that is, you sell it for a price lower than what you paid for it, it's called a **capital loss.** You've taken the L in that case. We've all been there, including Buffett. Nobody bats a thousand in investing. An all-star investor is right roughly 60% of the time. Intense competition makes it hard to make a lot of money quickly and easily.

There's actually a way to make money from a fall in a stock's price. It's called **selling short**, and we don't recommend it for nearly all investors because it's riskier than a buy-and-hold strategy. Similar to "a don't try this stunt at home" disclaimer you might see on TV. Buffett also advises against selling short, so we're including it as a Tip. Timing when to get in and out of an investment is very difficult. Here's his quote, "We probably had a hundred ideas of things that would be good short sales. Probably 95% of them at least turned out to be, and I don't think we would have made a dime out of it if we had been engaged in the activity. It's too difficult."

Buffett Tip 24:

Don't sell short. It's too difficult.

We've included a brief discussion of selling short in the Appendix, in case you wind up as a professional investor and want to learn more about the technique. We know most people don't read appendices, so that gives you yet another reason not to sell short.:-)

Large Cap vs. Small Cap

Analysts often classify stocks by certain characteristics. You can think of it as placing stocks in certain buckets. The main buckets we'll focus on are small cap, large cap, growth, value, domestic, and international. Let's define each of these terms.

In baseball, they make a distinction between the minor leagues and major leagues. With stocks, investors often make a distinction between big and small firms. Recall the term market capitalization, or market cap for short, is the amount of money that represents owning 100% of the company's stock. It equals the stock price times the number of shares outstanding. Companies with a market cap of less than $1 billion are often characterized as **small cap**, a term we briefly touched upon in **Chapter 2**. Firms with a market cap of at least $1 billion are considered **large cap**. It's a big category since some firms, such as Microsoft and Apple, are valued at more than a *trillion* dollars!

In this book, we're going to focus mainly on the distinction between large cap and small cap, but there are finer distinctions in size. Sticking with our baseball analogy, there are different levels of minor leagues, like A, AA, and AAA. **Micro cap** is a term used for the smallest firms, usually those with a market cap of less than $100 million. And if that's not small enough for you, a company with a market cap of less than $50 million is called a **nano cap** (which means very small).

Mid cap is a term used for companies with a market cap between 1 and 10 billion dollars. The term **mega cap** is often used for firms valued at more than $100 billion. Those are the rock stars of the stock market. Most investors know their names: Microsoft, Disney, Amazon.com, Berkshire, and the like. We're going to cover some of these firms in more detail in **Chapter 9**.

Growth vs. Value

Another distinction investors make is between growth and value stocks. Value stocks are less expensive relative to some metric, such as the profits they earn each year. They're often beaten down in price. Not much is expected of these firms. **Growth stocks** are usually growing quickly and are more expensive. They are often emerging all-stars or existing all-stars. Market participants, as a whole, expect big things of these companies, in terms of future rapidly growing sales and earnings. It's usually a case of buying high and expecting to sell higher. For example, it might be a younger version of Amazon.com or even the large and still strongly growing Amazon.com that exists today.

There are many ways to differentiate between growth and value stocks or expensive versus inexpensive. A common approach is to compare their **price-to-earnings**, or **P/E ratios**. The P/E ratio for a firm is the market cap of the stock divided by its earnings. Remember, earnings are the same thing as profits and are measured by taking the sales of the firm and then subtracting all of its expenses. The time horizon for this measurement period is typically one year. You get the same P/E ratio if you do this calculation for the entire firm or a single share of its stock.

The companies with the highest P/E ratios (50th percentile or higher) are usually considered to be growth stocks. The companies with the lowest P/E ratios (less than 50th percentile) are considered value stocks. To give you some perspective, historically the P/E of the market as a whole has averaged about 15. Thus, under this barometer, a stock with a P/E less than 15 would be considered a value stock. A stock with a P/E of 15 or higher would be considered a growth stock. In recent years, the P/E for the market has averaged about 16 or 17, so that may be a more accurate cutoff value today.

One important takeaway from this discussion is that the price of a stock alone doesn't tell you if it is expensive or inexpensive. You need to look at the P/E, or other valuation metrics that we'll discuss later. For example, Berkshire Hathaway (Class A) recently sold for about $300,000 for a single share! And because the firm had a P/E less than the market, you could argue the stock is a good value. If you want to blow someone's mind, tell them you know of a stock that costs more than a quarter of a million dollars and that you think it's inexpensive or cheap! Prepare for some blank stares, or worse, but with the knowledge that you're likely correct. This may be a small example of Buffett's Inner Scorecard belief system that we mentioned in **Chapter 1**.

Many mutual funds have some combination of the words "large," "small," "growth," and "value" in their names, such as the BlackRock Large Cap Value Fund. Investment analysts have coined the term "style box" to explain where they fall on the size and style spectrum. A box has two dimensions. Instead of length and width, we have size and style. The traditional way of showing the style box is in **Figure 5.2** for the mutual fund Fidelity Magellan.

Style boxes are well entrenched in Wall Street jargon, but Buffett isn't a fan of the term. He believes growth is really just part of the equation of estimating the value of a stock and that all investors are value oriented since they all want to buy undervalued investments. In his 2000 Letter to Berkshire's Shareholders, Buffett wrote, "Market commentators and investment managers who glibly refer to 'growth' and 'value' styles as contrasting approaches to investment are displaying their ignorance, not their sophistication. Growth is simply a component—usually a plus, sometimes a minus—in the value equation."

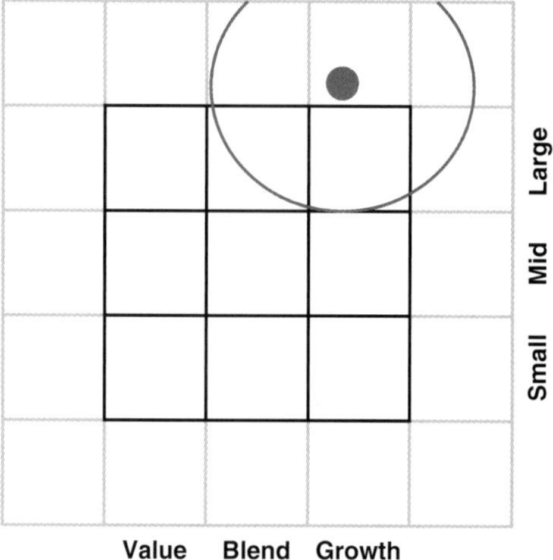

Figure 5.2 The Style Box

Source: © 2020 Morningstar, Inc. All Rights Reserved. Reproduced with permission.

Domestic vs. International

There are stock markets in most countries around the world. If you invest in companies with their headquarters in your home country (the US in our case) it's called **investing domestically**. If you invest in companies headquartered outside your home country, it's called **investing internationally**. If your portfolio or basket of investments consists of both domestic and international stocks, it's called a **global portfolio**.

Why invest internationally? We can give you several reasons, but it was perhaps said best by Sir John Templeton, an investor who was as famous as Buffett during his day. Sir John said, "If you search worldwide you will find more bargains and better bargains than by searching one nation."

Buffett invests mostly in the US but has made some international investments. For example, in 2013 Berkshire purchased the Israeli-based tool company Iscar for $2.05 billion. He also invested in a large Chinese oil firm called PetroChina at one point and still maintains a position in the Chinese auto firm BYD.

An Index Fund: A Great "Set It and Forget It" Long-Run Investment

All right. Now that you have some basic fluency concerning the stock market, let's get to the topic of investing in stocks. The first type of investment is simple, but surprisingly effective, and called an **index fund**. You've probably heard of the **Dow Jones Industrial Average (DJIA)**. That's an index of 30 of the leading, or "blue chip," stocks headquartered in the US. We'll cover "The Dow" further in **Chapter 9**. An index fund tries to track the performance of a specific index, such as the DJIA. It's something that's investible, as opposed to being theoretical or conceptual.

You've probably heard of the term **blue chip** in the context of sports. It means the athlete is almost "can't miss" in terms of being a star. Like Zion Williamson coming out of Duke University or Tiger Woods shortly after he started college. Not all blue-chip athletes pan out, and neither do all stocks with the blue-chip label, at least on a forward-looking basis.

An index with only 30 stocks is kind of narrow. After all, not every athlete or stock can be considered a blue chip. Perhaps the most widely followed index in the US is the **Standard and Poor's 500 (S&P 500)**. We came across the S&P name in **Chapter 4** in the context of bond ratings, such as AAA, AA, and so forth. The S&P 500 consists of 500 large cap stocks headquartered in the US. There's an index called the **Wilshire 5000**, which tries to measure the performance of all publicly traded stocks in the US. When the index was first created, it had about 5,000 stocks in it. Today the number is closer to 4,000.

Sometimes stocks leave an index because they get taken over and no longer trade independently. In other cases, they go out of business or are bankrupt. In that case, their values are virtually zero and wouldn't register on the index.

Buying a diversified stock index fund, such as the S&P 500, is basically a bet on the (American) economy. Over long periods of time, if the economy does well, the index should do well. And Buffett has said something similar many times. For example, in his 2013 Letter to Berkshire Shareholders he wrote, "The 21st century will witness further gains, almost certain to be substantial. The goal of the non-professional should not be to pick winners—neither he nor his 'helpers' can do that—but should rather be to own a cross-section of businesses that in aggregate are bound to do well. A low-cost S&P 500 index fund will achieve this goal." He said it more succinctly in another of his writings, "A low-cost fund is the most sensible equity investment for the great majority of investors." That's a good Tip to remember.

Buffett Tip 25:

A low-cost fund is the most sensible equity investment for the great majority of investors.

Of course, there are index funds available on pretty much every stock market around the world.

We mentioned that index funds perform surprisingly well over the long term (e.g., 10+ years). What is surprisingly well? How about that this simple buy-and-hold strategy that requires minimal effort beats about 90% of active managers over the long term. Say what? Ninety percent? How can this be possible? There are two main reasons: low costs and competition.

Buying an index fund usually isn't free, but its cost is extremely low. The typical cost of an index fund is a tiny fraction of 1% per year, something like 0.1% or 0.2%. With low numbers, such as fractions of 1 percent, analysts often use some other terms. One percent equals 100 **basis points**. So, 1/10 of 1% equals 10 basis points. Let's tie those numbers to an example. Let's say you invest $1,000 in an index fund on the S&P 500. Your fee would be about $1 a year. Not bad for an investment that historically rises about 10% a year, or $100 in our sample investment. In contrast, if you pay to have someone manage your money, they typically charge you more, often more than 100 basis points a year.

Beating the Market and the Efficient Market Hypothesis

Now let's look at our second reason why it's extremely hard to produce returns higher than a market index, or what's usually called "**beating the market**" in the financial press. We're not saying it can't be done. Obviously, Buffett has done it over many decades, and we're going to sketch out his approach in the next chapter. We're just giving you the argument why an index fund approach may make sense for the vast majority of investors.

We mentioned intense competition as the second reason why it's difficult to consistently beat the market. We'll provide a bit more detail and start our explanation with a story. There's a story in the most popular college investments textbook that goes something like this.

Two college professors are walking down the street, and there appears to be a $20 bill lying in the middle of the street. Let's say the first professor teaches finance, and the second professor teaches history. The finance professor walks by the $20 bill, and the history professor stoops down to pick it up and says, "Why didn't you try to pick up the money on the ground?" The finance professor replies, "Well, if it was real, someone would have picked it up beforehand."

Not funny? Well, you can't expect too much in the way of comedy from a textbook. :-) The moral of the story is that investors aren't going to leave free money on the ground. When they see it, they pick it up very quickly. When important information comes out about a stock, such as its earnings report, a merger, new product, and so forth, investors interpret this information very quickly. If the news is good and better than what is expected, the stock will quickly go up. If the news is bad and worse than expected, the stock will quickly go down. For example, when it became apparent that the COVID-19 pandemic would shut down entire segments of the economy, stock prices quickly plummeted about 30%!

A market that quickly *and* appropriately reacts to information is called **efficient**. Sometimes it goes by its theoretical name, the **Efficient Market Hypothesis** (**EMH**). The financial press often uses another name—the **Random Walk Hypothesis**. This latter term has a colorful history. One story says the name is derived from a drunk person looking for his keys that fell on the ground at night. He'd take a step in one direction and then another and then another and wind up where he started, without the keys!

Since there will always be intense competition on Wall Street and new information is usually quickly reflected in stock prices, it's mainly *new* information or news that moves stock prices. Almost by definition, new information is virtually impossible to predict; therefore, most investors have no advantage versus a simple buy-and-hold index fund strategy.

If your mind is spinning from the Random Walk Hypothesis, we have a cool way of thinking about this concept that is easy to understand. If the market is always efficient, you could throw darts at the stock pages of *The Wall Street Journal* and a basket of the stocks that were hit with the darts would, on average, perform about the same as the market or a portfolio picked by a *professional* investor!

Meet Mr. Market, the Manic-Depressive Stock Market

But there is a glimmer of hope for those who want to engage in active stock selection in order to try to beat the market. Buffett said that some expert investors, or those who study to become experts, have a chance of beating the market. He criticized academics who say the market is always efficient. In his 1988 Letter to Berkshire Shareholders he wrote, "Observing correctly that the market was frequently efficient, they went on to conclude incorrectly that it was *always* efficient." Let's spin that quote into a Tip.

Buffett Tip 26:

The stock market is usually efficient but not always efficient. Therefore, there is room to beat the market.

Benjamin Graham used a widely cited analogy to explain how the stock market works. He said imagine being in business with a manic-depressive business partner by the name of **Mr. Market**. Sometimes he's extremely happy and generous and offers you a great price for your share of the business, if you want to sell. Other times he is extremely depressed and offers you a very low price for your share of the business, also in the event that you want to sell.

In other cases, he'd offer you a fair price for your share of the business if, yet again, you want to sell. In this latter case, you can view the market as being efficient. Graham's point is don't try to change Mr. Market's mind since it can't be done. Just try to take advantage of his irrational behavior, by buying (low) when he is depressed and by selling (high) when he is euphoric.

You might be wondering what causes Mr. Market, or the market as a whole, to be occasionally out of whack. Well, it basically boils down to two words about human nature that have been around since the beginning of time: fear and greed.

Benjamin Graham had another analogy to describe the market that uses a pendulum instead of a moody business partner. He said, "The market is a pendulum that forever swings between unsustainable optimism (which makes stocks too expensive) and unjustified pessimism (which makes them too cheap). The Intelligent Investor is a realist who sells to optimists and buys from pessimists." Buffett said it more succinctly when he wrote in his 1986 letter to shareholders, "We simply attempt to be fearful when others are greedy and to be greedy only when others are fearful." We mentioned this quote back in **Chapter** 1. It's one of his most famous sayings, so let's put it as an official Tip here.

Buffett Tip 27:

Be fearful when others are greedy. Be greedy only when others are fearful.

When prices get really out of whack, it's called a **bubble**—similar to blowing a bubble with a piece of bubble gum. It slowly inflates, due to hope, excitement, and, eventually, greed. At some point more rational thinking prevails, and then the bubble pops, driven by fear. There have been many investment bubbles throughout history. Not only with stocks but with all kinds of things. One of the most famous bubbles occurred in Holland during the late 1630s with, of all things, tulips. Yes, we mean the pretty-looking flowers. We'll skip the details, but during the peak of "Tulip mania," in around 1637, the price of a single prized tulip sold for the equivalent of four tons of beer, two tons of butter, one thousand pounds of cheese, four fat oxen, eight fat swine, twelve fat sheep, four lasts of rye, two hogsheads of wine, a complete bed, a suit of clothes, and a silver drinking-cup! Or for the price of a house in many parts of America.

Buffett, and most rational investors, know that bubbles can't last forever. In his 2000 Letter to Berkshire Shareholders he wrote, "But a pin lies in wait for every bubble. And when the two eventually meet, a new wave of investors learns some very old lessons: First, many in Wall Street—a community in which quality control is not prized—will sell investors anything they will buy. Second, speculation is most dangerous when it looks easiest." Let's include the key lesson as a Tip.

Buffett Tip 28:

A pin lies in wait for every bubble.

You might think only fools or ignorant people get caught up in bubbles. On the contrary, Buffett wrote about one of the smartest people who ever lived, Sir Isaac Newton, getting caught up in a bubble related to a stock called the South Sea Company. Sir Isaac lost roughly the equivalent of $4 million today. Buffett wrote in his 1993 Letter to Berkshire Shareholders, "Long ago, Sir Isaac Newton gave us three laws of motion, which were the work of genius. But Sir Isaac's talents didn't extend to investing: He lost a bundle in the South Sea Bubble, explaining later, 'I can calculate the movement of the stars, but not the madness of men.' If he had not been traumatized by this loss, Sir Isaac might well have gone on to discover the Fourth Law of Motion: For investors as a whole, returns decrease as motion increases." In other words, don't try to chase the latest hot thing when a frenzy or bubble is building up around an investment. Be patient, and always look for value.

Buffett's Tips from Chapter 5

Buffett Tip 22: Stock equals ownership in a business. (Courtesy of Benjamin Graham)

Buffett Tip 23: Companies with strong new profit opportunities should wait to pay dividends, while companies without many attractive new profit opportunities should pay most of their earnings out as dividends.

Buffett Tip 24: Don't sell short. It's too difficult.

Buffett Tip 25: A low-cost fund is the most sensible equity investment for the great majority of investors.

Buffett Tip 26: The stock market is usually efficient but not always efficient. Therefore, there is room to beat the market.

Buffett Tip 27: Be fearful when others are greedy. Be greedy only when others are fearful.

Buffett Tip 28: A pin lies in wait for every bubble.

Appendix: Selling Short (or the "Don't Try This at Home" Area of Investing)

You've probably heard the expression "Buy low and sell high." It's the way most investors try to make money. For example, you might buy a stock for $10 a share and hope to sell it sometime down the road for $20. This traditional way of investing is called **buying long**.

As we mentioned in the main body of this chapter, there's a way of profiting from a *drop* in a stock's price. It's called **selling short**. The emphasis is on the word *short* to differentiate it from plain old selling. The traditional order is first buying a stock and then selling, when you are ready to close out the investment. For example, you may buy a stock at $15 and hopefully sell it at a higher price—let's say $20 a share—for a profit of $5 a share.

With selling short you first sell and then buy back later, hopefully at a lower price. You have *no* position in the stock prior to the short sale. For example, if you sell short a stock at $20 and later buy it back for $15, you've made a profit of $5. Once again, notice the order of selling first and buying back later, as well as the $5 positive profit earned after the stock dropped from $20 to $15.

We're sure you're thinking, "How can you sell something that you don't own?" The answer is that the stock is borrowed from another investor at the firm. This other investor is usually clueless as to what is going on. As far as they are concerned, they still own the stock. And they do from a legal perspective. But the information technology system of the brokerage firm keeps track of everything behind the scenes.

Instead of borrowing a pencil, ruler, or calculator from someone, you've borrowed a stock. And just like with a physical good, you can get in trouble if you don't return something that you borrowed. In this case you've made a promise to buy the same amount of shares that you borrowed, at some point in the future.

Another question you may have is, "When does the short seller have to buy back the stock and return the borrowed shares?" The answer is slightly complicated. Here goes. If there are a lot of shares available for borrowing, then you can keep your short position open for many years—almost indefinitely. However, if a lot of investors are trying to short the company, shares to borrow might be in tight supply. In that case, the brokerage firm may force you to buy back shares from the market even if you are not ready. When the broker forces you to return the shares when you're not ready, it's called a **short squeeze**. The brokerage firm maintains a list of hard-to-borrow stocks each day. These are the stocks that are susceptible to being the subject of a short squeeze, providing the short seller with at least some warning.

So why do most people recommend not selling short? First, the stock market usually goes up over long periods of time. Historically it has risen about 10% a year. Therefore, by selling short you are basically swimming against the tide since you are betting a stock is going to fall in price while the general tide of the market is to rise in price. Second, if a stock pays dividends, the short seller is obligated to pay the dividends to the original lender of the shares. Third, small investors may have to pay extra money, in the form of interest to the brokerage firm, in order to get the shares. And last but not least, your risk of loss on the downside is virtually unlimited.

For example, if you sell a stock short at $10 and it goes to zero you've made $10. But what if the stock goes up in value, to say $50 a share. Here you've lost $40 a share (bought at $50 and sold at $10). Imagine if someone sold Berkshire Hathaway short when Buffett took over the company and somehow they were able to maintain their position through the end of 2019. A $1,000 short sale investment would have resulted in a loss of more than $20 million!

References

Belludi, Nagesh. "The Drunkard's Search or the Streetlight Effect [Cognitive Bias]." Right Attitudes, *February* 26, 2016. https://www.rightattitudes.com/2016/02/26/drunkard-search-streetlight-effect/.

Bodie, Zvi, Alex Kane, and Alan J. Marcus. *Investments,* 10th edition. New York: McGraw-Hill Education, 2013.

Buffett, Warren. "Letter to Shareholders of Berkshire Hathaway Inc." Berkshire Hathaway, Inc., 1981. https://www.berkshirehathaway.com/letters/1981.html.

Buffett, Warren. "Letter to Shareholders of Berkshire Hathaway Inc." Berkshire Hathaway, Inc., 1988. https://www.berkshirehathaway.com/letters/1988.html.

Buffett, Warren. "Letter to Shareholders of Berkshire Hathaway Inc." Berkshire Hathaway, Inc., 1993. https://www.berkshirehathaway.com/letters/1993.html.

Buffett, Warren. "Letter to Shareholders of Berkshire Hathaway Inc." Berkshire Hathaway, Inc., 2000. https://www.berkshirehathaway.com/letters/2000.html.

Buffett, Warren. "Letter to Shareholders of Berkshire Hathaway Inc." Berkshire Hathaway, Inc., 2004. https://www.berkshirehathaway.com/letters/2004.html.

Buffett, Warren. "Letter to Shareholders of Berkshire Hathaway Inc." Berkshire Hathaway, Inc., 2013. https://www.berkshirehathaway.com/letters/2013.html.

Chiglinsky, Katherine. "Buffett's Railroad Aims to Sustain Its Profit Streak as Rivals Grow Wary." *Bloomberg*, August 1, 2019. https://www.bloomberg.com/news/articles/2019-08-01/buffett-s-bnsf-aims-to-sustain-profit-streak-as-rivals-grow-wary.

Fama, Eugene F. "The Behavior of Stock-Market Prices." *Journal of Business* 38, no. 1 (1965): 34. https://doi.org/10.1086/294743.

Graham, Benjamin, and Jason Zweig. *The Intelligent Investor: The Definitive Book on Value Investing*. New York: Harper Business, 2006.

Hargreaves, Rupert. "Warren Buffett Explains Why He No Longer Shorts Stocks." GuruFocus.com. Yahoo!, March 13, 2019. https://finance.yahoo.com/news/warren-buffett-explains-why-no-204005627.html.

"John D. Rockefeller Quotes." Accessed June 14, 2020. https://www.brainyquote.com/quotes/quotes/j/johndrock129792.html.

Jun, Jae. "3 Of the Most Overpriced Stocks with Real Downside Risk." Old School Value, March 3, 2020. https://www.oldschoolvalue.com/stock-analysis/3-most-overpriced-stocks-with-real-downside-risk/.

Levine, Matt. "Warren Buffett Quadrupled His Ketchup Investment." *Bloomberg, March* 25, 2015. https://www.bloomberg.com/view/articles/2015-03-25/warren-buffett-quadrupled-his-ketchup-investment.

Malkiel, Burton Gordon. *A Random Walk down Wall Street: Including a Life-Cycle Guide to Personal Investing*. New York: Norton, 2000.

"Morningstar Style Box." Morningstar. Accessed June 27, 2020. https://www.morningstar.com/InvGlossary/morningstar_style_box.aspx.

Proctor, William, and Scott Phillips. *The Templeton Touch*. West Conshohocken, PA: Templeton Press, 2012.

Tuchman, Mitch. "5 Warren Buffett Quotes for Anyone Who Thinks They Can Pick Stocks and Get Rich like He Did." *MarketWatch,* August 11, 2017. http://www.marketwatch.com/story/the-5-times-warren-buffett-talked-about-index-fund-investing-2017-04-28.

6

Buffett's Approach to Stocks

"You only have to be able to evaluate companies within your circle of competence."
—Warren Buffett, 1996 Letter to Berkshire Hathaway Shareholders

Introduction

In the last chapter, we went over the basics of the stock market. Things such as how a stock is "born" and winds up on an exchange, what a dividend is, what an index fund is, and why it's hard to "beat the market." This chapter will make additional inroads into getting a better understanding of the stock market. We'll discuss two important topics. First, how to estimate the true value of a stock—what's known as a **price target** on Wall Street. As we'll see, there can be a huge difference between your price target and the current price of a stock. The second key part of the chapter is that we'll provide some more detail on Buffett's approach to the stock market. The stock market is Buffett's bread and butter, so you'll see a heavy dose of Tips in this chapter. Let's get started.

Estimating the Value of a Stock

Estimating the value of a stock, or any other investment, really gets into the heart of investing. Unlike the laws of physics, which work 99.9999% of the time (weird cases of quantum mechanics aside), there are no magic formulas that will enable you to value a stock with a *high degree of precision*. Most investment classes teach techniques that might be right, on average, over long periods of time. Using a baseball or softball expression, nobody bats a thousand in the world of investing. Even Buffett. Let's go over two approaches investment analysts commonly use to estimate what should be the price target of a stock. One approach is related to the "time value of money" concept we covered in **Chapters 2** and **4**. The other technique will be as easy as pie, since it simply multiplies two numbers together to get a price target.

As usual, we'll do our best to avoid any formulas or relegate them to a endnote or appendix. A formula can give you a precise number, but if the formula is wrong, it doesn't matter if you get an answer to the tenth decimal point. In Buffett's 2008 Letter to Berkshire Shareholders, he essentially said the same thing, summing it up with the quote "Beware of geeks bearing formulas." Let's put that quote as our first Tip for the chapter.

Buffett Tip 29:

Beware of geeks bearing formulas.

Getting a Price Target with the Discounted Cash Flow Model

Let's tackle the first approach we alluded to, which is called a **discounted cash flow (DCF)** model. It basically involves applying the time value of money, a concept we previously covered to valuing a company. The DCF approach says the price of the stock is equal to what we called the present value of future cash flows. Buffett calls this approach the intrinsic value, a term we briefly came across in **Chapter** 3. In his 1993 Letter to Shareholders, he wrote, "We define intrinsic value as the discounted value of the cash that can be taken out of a business during its remaining life. Anyone calculating intrinsic value necessarily comes up with a highly subjective figure that will change both as estimates of future cash flows are revised and as interest rates move. Despite its fuzziness, however, intrinsic value is all-important and is the only logical way to evaluate the relative attractiveness of investments and businesses."

There's a lot going on in that Buffett quote, but it's of huge importance. We'll summarize it by saying that intrinsic value is the best way to think about valuing an investment, even though there will be some debate about the cash flows and discount rate. That's certainly worthy of a Tip.

Buffett Tip 30:

Intrinsic value is the best way to think about valuing an investment.

For a bond, it is a piece of cake to determine the cash flow. It's just the coupon payments and the face value, or principal. It's usually a finite period lasting from less than one year to up to 30 years. However, a stock has no expiration date. That is, it exists forever or in perpetuity unless it goes out of business or is bought out by another company. For example, The Bank of New York Mellon was founded in 1784 by Alexander Hamilton and is still thriving today. We wouldn't be surprised to see it around another 230 years from now!

How do you value something that goes on to infinity? Good question. Fortunately, there is a handy formula, known as the **Gordon growth model**, that involves only simple algebra. All we need are three things: the discount rate, next year's dividend, and the long-term, or steady-state, growth rate.

We've covered the basics of the discount rate in Chapters 2 and 4. For bonds, we said the appropriate discount rate is the yield to maturity (YTM) on the firm's debt. YTM can be approximated for a firm by taking the US Treasury Bond yield at the same maturity and then adding an extra amount for credit risk. For stocks, it's related to how risky they are. The discount rate for the stock market as a whole is roughly 10% per year. It's not a coincidence that this discount rate of 10% is close to the US stock market's historical average annual return. Of course, with any given average, some firms will have a discount rate less than 10%, and others will have a discount rate greater than 10%. A beverage company such as Coca-Cola may have a discount rate of 7%. A more volatile technology-oriented stock such as Amazon.com might have a discount rate closer to 12%. The discount rate for stocks is often obtained from the Capital Asset Pricing Model (CAPM), which is covered in **Chapter 8**.

A pretty good estimate for next year's dividend is equal to this year's dividend times one plus the long-term growth rate. What if the firm doesn't pay dividends? No problemo. We can use a term called **free cash flow** as an estimate. It's basically the cash the firm generated during the year minus what the firm needs to reinvest in itself so it doesn't fall apart down the road.

The long-term growth rate is typically close to the rate the economy grows net of inflation—usually around 2% to 4% per year. Let's try out this handy little formula with a real stock, AT&T, a large telecommunications firm. You may know AT&T since it's one of the largest cell phone carriers, the owner of DirecTV, and owner of Time Warner. Time Warner is famous for its *Batman*, *Superman*, *Wonder Woman*, and *Harry Potter* movies, among other things.

Let's assume a growth rate of 2%, the average growth of the US economy in recent years. It has a current dividend of $2.05 a share. So next year's dividend is simply $2.05 times one plus 2%, or $2.09. AT&T has been around a long time and has a history of stable earnings, so its discount rate should be less than 10%. Let's say it's 8%.

Putting it all together, we get our price target for AT&T as next year's estimated dividend of $2.09 divided by the difference between its discount rate of 8% and growth rate of 2%, or $34.83 a share. Now let's compare this number to the current price of the stock, as of the time we're writing this book. It's about $31 a share. Since the upside is about 12%, and there's another 6% in dividends, we'd say AT&T is a buy. If a forecasted return is between 0% and 10%, including the return from the dividend, Wall Street analysts typically would rate it a hold. If a price target is less than the current price, Wall Street analysts would typically rate it a sell and try to avoid the stock, especially since we mentioned in the last chapter that Buffett thinks it is dangerous to sell short a stock. Of course, if you already own the stock, a sell rating means sell it.

Getting a Price Target with the Wall Street P/E Model

We prefer multiplication to division, so we'll give you an even easier approach to getting a price target. We're just going to multiply two numbers. The first is our estimate of the company's earnings per share next year. Professional analysts often build a detailed financial model to do this. In the interest of time and simplicity we're going to ditch that approach and use something like *CliffsNotes* or Shmoop for Finance. Not ideal, but often good enough.

One handy approach is to use the average of professional analysts' estimates, formally known as a **consensus estimate**. Another simple approach is to use the company's own estimate, which it gives to professional analysts, formally known as management's **earnings guidance**. Management's numbers tend to be a lowball estimate, since they want to underpromise and overdeliver; otherwise, the stock will often get crushed. In practice they'll say they are being prudent or conservative with their estimates. If the actual reported earnings number is higher than the consensus estimates, it's called an **earnings surprise**. The second number we need to get our price target is the long-run, or sustainable, P/E ratio that the firm should trade at. If the firm has been around a long time, such as AT&T, taking its 10-year average or median value is usually a pretty good estimate.

To get our price target we just multiply the two numbers, the one-year-ahead earnings estimate and the long-run P/E ratio estimate. This approach is known as the **P/E relative valuation model**. We prefer the term Wall Street P/E model, since it's the most common way professional analysts come up with a price target. When Buffett does a similar calculation, he likes to look at least five years ahead rather than just one, since he focuses on the long term.

Let's compute a price target using the Wall Street P/E model for AT&T. The consensus analyst earnings estimate for AT&T next year is $3.70. Its median P/E over the past 10 years has been about 10. Multiplying these two numbers together we get $37. Since the number plus the dividends is more than 10% greater than the current price of $31, we'd put it in the buy territory.

It's okay if the DCF model and Wall Street P/E model give different stock price estimates. In fact, it's pretty common. One approach to getting a final price target is to simply take the average of the two techniques. Buffett prefers the DCF approach, which he calls intrinsic value, but the P/E approach is more common in Wall Street since it's less subject to **sensitivity analysis errors**, which means that a small change in the inputs to the model may result in wild changes to the output (price target). Kind of like the analogy of a butterfly flapping its wings in South America ultimately setting off a hurricane in North America.

Buffett's Approach to Stocks

Now, for the moment you have been waiting for! You can't boil Buffett's approach to investing down to a simple equation, like the two approaches we just discussed. It can't even be discussed in a single chapter. However, he has laid out a number of principles that he looks for when making a purchase. We'll discuss many of these principles for the remainder of this chapter and include them in our growing Tip list.

The word "purchase," for Berkshire, may be an entire company or a big chunk of a company's stock. The fact that Buffett is investing billions shouldn't concern you too much. Remember, both he and his mentor Ben Graham said you shouldn't purchase a single share of stock if you aren't willing to buy the entire company, if you have enough money. One of Graham's and Buffett's fundamental principles is stock equals ownership in a business. We previously labeled it as Tip 22 in this book. We also discussed a key aspect of Buffett's investment approach back in **Chapter 1** with Tip 7: Buy things at attractive prices. But these tips merely scratch the surface of Buffett's awesome investment skills.

Yes, Buffett has a framework for investing, but he gets a lot of his investment ideas from just reading. Reading is part of the learning process and harkens back to his quote (Tip 3) in **Chapter 1**, "The more you learn, the more you earn." When one interviewer asked him about the source of his investment ideas, he said, "I just read. I read all day. I mean, we put $500 million in PetroChina. All I did was read the annual report."

To make this chapter more digestible, we're going to organize Buffett's investing approach according to three broad categories: (1) Getting into the Buffett mindset on investing; (2) the types of businesses Buffett likes, and (3) Buffett's thoughts on when to sell.

Getting into the Buffett Mindset on Investing

Having the proper mindset is essential for success in investing and almost all other fields. Maybe you've seen or read about athletes having a case of the "yips," which refers to a loss of fine motor skills due to mental, rather than physical, reasons. For example, there have been professional baseball pitchers (e.g., Steve Blass and Rick Ankiel) who couldn't consistently throw the ball over home plate, infielders that couldn't consistently throw the ball to first base (e.g., Steve Sax and Chuck Knoblauch), or kickers (e.g., Blair Walsh) who couldn't consistently kick the football through the goal posts. There was a slightly happy ending in Rick Ankiel's case as he went from being a wild pitcher to a moderately successful outfielder and batter.

Remember our Buffett Tip 12, "The most important quality for an investor is temperament, not intellect." This gets the ball rolling on the importance of the proper mindset to help drive success. Although this book is mostly about financial literacy and Buffett, the most successful self-help or motivational speaker today is Tony Robbins. Robbins has sold tens of millions of books on the topic, and millions more have participated in his live seminars. A key part of Robbins's motivational philosophy is having the proper mindset.

Stay within Your Circle of Competence

Everyone knows a lot about *something*. It could be sports, music, fashion, video games, apps, or tons of other things. Buffett applies the same concept to investing. He knows a lot about certain industries, such as insurance, banking, food, beverages, shoes, and airlines, to name a few. However, he doesn't know a lot about many other industries. He has famously shied away from investing in technology firms since he believes the industry changes rapidly, giving him less confidence in a tech firm's ability to succeed in the future. However, in recent years Berkshire has made investments in Apple and Amazon.com. Whether these investments were made by Buffett or his two junior investment managers, Todd Combs or Ted Weschler, is unknown. Our sense is the junior guys made the case to Buffett, who then "supersized" the positions. Apple is currently Berkshire's largest stock holding.

Just because technology is out of Buffett's circle of competence, it doesn't mean it will be outside of *your* circle of competence. Many young people can run circles around their parents and grandparents when it comes to technology-related things. Buffett refers to sticking to areas that you know well as staying within your circle of competence. If you understand the product and the firm's business, you're less likely to make a mistake.

In Buffett's 1996 Letter to Berkshire Shareholders, he wrote, "Intelligent investing is not complex, though that is far from saying that it is easy. What an investor needs is the ability to correctly evaluate selected businesses. Note that word 'selected': You don't have to be an expert on every company, or even many. You only have to be able to evaluate companies within your circle of competence. The size of that circle is not very important; knowing its boundaries, however, is vital." Let's summarize that with a fundamental Tip.

Buffett Tip 31:

Invest within your circle of competence.

The Importance of Being Patient

Staying within your circle of competence is important for long-term investment success. However, what if everything in your circle of competence seems expensive? Buffett has advice in that case too. He says wait for a "fat pitch." For those not familiar with baseball or softball terminology, it means wait until the timing is right. Buffett provides further detail on this thought by telling a story about Hall of Fame baseball player Ted Williams. Props to Mike Trout, Aaron Judge, and Bryce Harper, but Ted Williams was perhaps the greatest hitter ever to play major league baseball. He was the last major leaguer to hit over .400, back in 1941. He also hit 521 homeruns in his career, despite missing three years of his prime due to military service as a fighter pilot in World War II.

In his 1997 Letter to Berkshire Shareholders, Buffett wrote, "In his book *The Science of Hitting*, Ted explains that he carved the strike zone into 77 cells, each the size of a baseball. Swinging only at balls in his "best" cell, he knew, would allow him to bat .400; reaching for balls in his "worst" spot, the low outside corner of the strike zone, would reduce him to .230. In other words, waiting for the fat pitch would mean a trip to the Hall of Fame; swinging indiscriminately would mean a ticket to the minors." So don't feel compelled to buy a particular investment. Be patient. Wait until the price is right and for the investment to be within your circle of competence. It's great advice and similar to Tip 14 on being patient, so we won't duplicate it here.

Good vs. Bad Companies and the Passage of Time

Buffett had a lot of success early in his career by strictly following the techniques of his mentor, Benjamin Graham. Graham would focus mostly on quantitative measures of value, hoping to buy companies at a very cheap price, even if he wasn't optimistic about the company's long-term future. He called these companies "cigar butts." Smoking cigars is a pretty disgusting habit, especially if you pick up someone's mostly smoked cigar off the street and try to get a few free puffs out of it. Graham looked for the equivalent of these cigar butts in the investment world. He held on to them for awhile and then looked to get out. One way Buffett eventually diverged from his mentor is that Buffett liked to buy high-quality companies even if he had to pay more for them. He learned this approach from Charlie Munger and another well-regarded growth investor, Philip Fisher. This new philosophy for Buffett became even more important as he started to manage large sums of money, since "cigar butt" stocks tend to be small in market cap. However, even using this new approach, Buffett would still stay disciplined and not overpay.

Here's how Buffett described it in his 1989 Letter to Berkshire Shareholders:

> If you buy a stock at a sufficiently low price, there will usually be some hiccup in the fortunes of the business that gives you a chance to unload at a decent profit, even though the long-term performance of the business may be terrible. I call this the "cigar butt" approach to investing. A cigar butt found on the street that has only one puff left in it may not offer much of a smoke, but the "bargain purchase" will make that puff all profit.
>
> Unless you are a liquidator, that kind of approach to buying businesses is foolish. First, the original "bargain" price probably will not turn out to be such a steal after all. In a difficult business, no sooner is one problem solved than another surfaces—never is there just one cockroach in the kitchen. Second, any initial advantage you secure will be quickly eroded by the low return that the business earns. . . . Time is the friend of the wonderful business, the enemy of the mediocre.

Let's use the last sentence of that quote as a Tip, especially since it implies holding onto stock in a good company, despite short-term problems.

Buffett Tip 32:

Time is the friend of the wonderful business, the enemy of the mediocre.

One last thought on this Tip using a Buffett quote to further illustrate the point. In his 2014 Letter to Berkshire Shareholders, he wrote, "It's better to have a partial interest in the Hope Diamond than to own all of a rhinestone." To save you a minute searching Wikipedia or asking your smart speaker, the Hope Diamond is one of the largest and most valuable diamonds in the world. It's bluish in color and currently resides at the Smithsonian Institute in Washington, DC.

How Buffett Thinks About Change in an Industry

Perhaps you've heard the quote, attributed to the ancient philosopher Heraclitus, "The only thing constant is change." Well, change is a constant in the investment world too, but industries change at different rates. Wrigley's chewing gum and Oreo cookies haven't changed much in the past 100 years, but the cell phone industry has changed dramatically. In the past, the phone was used mostly to talk to someone. Today, your smartphone is the equivalent of a phone plus a supercomputer in your pocket. Not surprisingly, Buffett has weighed in on how to think about change in an industry.

In his 1991 Letter to Berkshire Shareholders, he said, "While investors and managers must place their feet in the future, their memories and nervous systems often remain plugged into the past. It is much easier for investors to utilize historic P/E ratios or for managers to utilize historic business valuation yardsticks than it is for either group to rethink their premises daily. When change is slow, constant rethinking is actually undesirable; it achieves little and slows response time. But when change is great, yesterday's assumptions can be retained only at great cost."

Now you can see why he prefers industries that don't change a lot. It's harder to invest in industries that change since you have the difficult task of trying to predict the future. That's not to say it can't be done with more than a coin flip of accuracy, but it's just not Buffett's cup of tea. Let's combine these thoughts into another Tip.

Buffett Tip 33:

When change is slow, constant rethinking is actually undesirable. When change is great, yesterday's assumptions can be retained only at great cost.

Types of Businesses Buffett Likes

A Moat Around a Business Is a Recipe for Success

It's not easy being in business. If you're a profitable firm, other competitors will be gunning for your business. Amazon's Jeff Bezos famously said, "Your [profit] margin is my opportunity." Companies with consistent earnings, profit margins, and growth over time, according to Buffett, have **moats** around their businesses. They have found ways to fend off their competition. You've almost certainly seen a picture of a moat around a castle. For those just arriving from Mars, a moat is a body of water around a castle, often with dangerous animals, such as crocodiles, swimming within to discourage an enemy invasion. Typically, the only way to enter the castle is by having the drawbridge opened from the inside.

In his 2005 Letter to Berkshire Shareholders, Buffett described in some detail how he hopes Berkshire Hathaway widens its moat. He wrote:

> Every day, in countless ways, the competitive position of each of our businesses grows either weaker or stronger. If we are delighting customers, eliminating unnecessary costs, and improving our products and services, we gain strength. But if we treat customers with indifference or tolerate bloat, our businesses will wither. On a daily basis, the effects of our actions are imperceptible; cumulatively, though, their consequences are enormous. When our long-term competitive position improves as a result of these almost unnoticeable actions, we describe the phenomenon as "widening the moat." And doing that is essential if we are to have the kind of business we want a decade or two from now.

Since the concept of a moat is essential in the types of businesses and stocks that Buffett loves, let's summarize it with a Tip.

Buffet Tip 34:

A wide moat is essential for long-term business success.

A moat around a business can come from many sources, some of which were mentioned in Buffett's quote. For example, "Delighting the customer" is an example of great customer service. It's one of Jeff Bezos's philosophies for Amazon.com. Some companies have great marketing, while others have a great distribution network. Others have **patents**, or legal protection, for their products lasting up to 20 years. And others produce their goods or services at the lowest price among the competitors in the industry, what is known as the **low-cost producer**. Let's look at some examples of a moat in the context of a favorite Buffett investment, Coca-Cola.

Coca-Cola is an example of a firm that Buffett often cites as having a moat. Almost anyone can make soda. It's basically fizzy water plus sugar and some flavoring. Yet, Coca-Cola has remained a dominant beverage firm for about 100 years. Their moat comes from not just a good product, but also their great brand name and exceptionally strong marketing and distribution network.

Coca-Cola beverages are distributed in more than 200 countries around the world. Almost everyone recognizes the Coca-Cola logo, which is a sign of effective marketing. They sell a consumable product, which means repeat business if their customers like the product. In contrast, if you buy a pair of scissors or a piece of furniture, it can often last for decades without replacement. Coke also has a great distribution network with supermarkets and restaurants, such as McDonald's. There's practically no way a start-up firm can supplant them.

It's true that people are consuming less carbonated and sugary beverages today than in years past. That's okay with Coca-Cola. It also owns Vitamin Water, Dasani bottled water, Minute Maid juices, and big chunks of Monster Energy and Keurig, the single-serving coffee company. As long as you're drinking liquid, Coca-Cola, the company, will be fine. Lastly it benefits from population growth—more customers around the world are born each day.

On Coca-Cola Buffett once remarked, "If you gave me $100 billion and said to take away the soft drink leadership of Coca-Cola in the world, I'd give it back to you and say it can't be done." Really, with $100 billion? Now that's a savage moat!

Demonstrated Consistent Earnings Power

If the company hasn't survived the ups (known as an **expansion**) and downs (known as a **recession**) of the economy, you can't tell how durable it is. Or, as Buffett said more colorfully, "You can't tell who is swimming naked until the tide comes out." Coca-Cola certainly falls in this category as well Dairy Queen and perhaps Kraft Heinz, despite some recent missteps. People need to eat regardless of how the economy is doing. Even GEICO would fit the bill here as well. Anyone with a car needs to drive, Uber and Lyft aside, and GEICO is one of the more inexpensive sellers of auto insurance.

Look for Companies with Good Management

You might find it amazing that Berkshire Hathaway has almost 400,000 employees, yet there are only 25 people in Berkshire's corporate headquarters in Omaha. How can he manage so many people with a staff slimmer than Snoop Dogg's waistline? The trick is when he buys a company, he largely leaves it alone. He plays a role in big-picture things, such as how to invest the firm's money, a term that goes by the formal name of **capital allocation**. He likes it when there is good management in place. Buffett lets them do their thing. That's how he likes to roll at Berkshire. The lean, not-so-mean approach of Buffett and Berkshire merits a Tip.

Buffett Tip 35:

Invest in companies with good management in place.

You may ask, "What is good management?" It's hard to define precisely, but good management increases sales, earnings, and **market share** (i.e., a firm's revenues as a percentage of total industry revenues) over time. If the stock is publicly traded, it should have historically outperformed the market and its industry peers. Good management usually is able to underpromise and overdeliver on earnings expectations, as we noted earlier. In other words, they consistently exceed expectations when reporting their quarterly financial statements. In recent years, Apple, Facebook, Microsoft, Amazon.com, JPMorgan Chase, and Google/Alphabet would fall into this category.

The retail industry (i.e., stores in your local strip mall or shopping mall) is one area where good management can make a big difference. In Buffett's 1995 Letter to Berkshire Shareholders, he joked, "Buying a retailer without good management is like buying the Eiffel Tower without an elevator." With this quip, Buffett implies that many retailers sell the same stuff, so the point of differentiation is *how* the firm is run by its management.

But good management *can't* help sinking industries.

Sometimes Superman, Iron Man (Tony Stark), or [insert your favorite superhero here] cannot overcome a business saddled by poor profitability. Some industries have intense competition and require large and continual expenditures to survive. The airline industry is one that Buffett likes to cite that would fall into this category. Few airline firms have consistently made profits (Southwest Airlines is the main exception), despite strong overall revenue growth for the industry over the past roughly 100 years.

In Buffett's 2007 Letter to Berkshire Shareholders, he wrote, "The worst sort of business is one that grows rapidly, requires significant capital to engender the growth, and then earns little or no money. Think airlines. Here a durable competitive advantage has proven elusive ever since the days of the Wright Brothers. Indeed, if a farsighted capitalist had been present at Kitty Hawk, he would have done his successors a huge favor by shooting Orville down."

The Wright brothers joke is one of Buffett's most widely cited. Let's put the first sentence down as a Tip. Speaking of jokes, he has another on management that is also Tip worthy. Let's round out our discussion of management with Tip 37 on the limits of management's powers.

Buffett Tip 36:

The worst sort of business is one that grows rapidly, requires significant capital to engender the growth, and then earns little or no money.

Buffett Tip 37:

When a management with a reputation for brilliance tackles a business with bad economics, it is the reputation of the business that remains intact.

Buy Companies That Have the Power to Overcome Inflation

We've discussed inflation at various times in this book. It's a measure of rising prices, or how much your standard of living is falling if your income is flat. Investors like it when companies show rising profits. However, if a firm struggles to raise prices, especially during periods of high inflation, the company's earnings will probably take a hit, and that can't be good for its stock price.

In his 1980 Letter to Berkshire Shareholders, Buffett wrote, "A disproportionate number of the great business fortunes built up during the inflationary years arose from ownership of operations that combined intangibles of lasting value with relatively minor requirements for tangible assets. In such cases earnings have bounded upward in nominal dollars, and these dollars have been largely available for the acquisition of additional businesses."

We'll simplify this quote for you since it's heavy in accounting speak. According to Buffett, two types of firms are particularly well suited to survive, or even thrive, during inflationary periods. The first type is comprised of firms that have strong intangibles or brand names. The second is comprised of firms that are among the lowest-cost producers or sellers in their industries. The first type is fairly obvious. A company selling a product protected by a patent is one example of an intangible asset. It usually has the power to raise prices, since there may not be a good substitute. For example, if someone needed a certain patented medicine to remain healthy, they'd probably have to pay the higher price.

People often will pay up for a brand name, preferring, for example, an Oreo or Chips Ahoy! cookie over a "no name" similar cookie sold in their local supermarket. Buffett places Berkshire subsidiary See's Candy in the strong brand category. They are known for their scrumptious chocolates and candies. See's has been able to raise prices virtually every year since Berkshire purchased the firm in 1971. Plus, See's doesn't require a ton of cash to invent new products. Popular flavors may change, but chocolate has stood the test of time.

GEICO is a good example of a low-cost producer or seller of car insurance. Historically, most car insurance was sold through a network of branch offices. It's fairly costly to operate this branch network since you have to pay rent or buy real estate for the office and pay for a bunch of insurance agents, as well as many other expenses. GEICO sold auto insurance mostly through the mail, and in later years, over the Internet, largely avoiding the cost of building a branch network. This lower-cost structure enables GEICO to offer lower prices to its customers, providing it with an edge. In the event it has to raise prices, it would still be among the lowest-cost choices for purchasers of car insurance. Let's summarize the concepts in this section with a Tip.

Buffett Tip 38:

Prefer companies that have the power to overcome inflation.

Focus on Firms with Favorable Long-Term Prospects

Products and industries come and go over time. Before there were cars, the buggy was the main mode of personal transportation, especially if you didn't live near a railroad. It was basically a carriage or stagecoach pulled by some horses. Someone over the age of 40 probably learned how to type on a typewriter, rather than on a computer or tablet. Car phones used to be popular until the business was supplanted by a cell phone you could carry in your pocket that could be hooked up "hands free" to your car.

Kodak became one of the most powerful firms in the world through its creation of film used in many cameras, until the advent of digital photography. The film that turned Kodak into a powerhouse was largely made of chemicals and plastic. Digital film is a totally different business; it's a type of computer chip called flash memory. The evolution of the film business and Kodak's inability to effectively adapt to a new world for its core product resulted in the once iconic firm's bankruptcy in 2012.

Joseph Schumpeter, a Harvard economist during the first half of the 20th century, called the tendency of certain industries to supplant or destroy old industries "**creative destruction**." Usually, the firm that creates the new product or service benefits. The consumer also usually benefits. But the firm that relies on the older product or service is harmed and sometimes mortally wounded. For example, Walmart's **business model** (i.e., the way it tries to make money) of having huge stores selling at low prices and backed by a very sophisticated computerized inventory management system, negatively affected retail stores such as Sears and Kmart from the 1980s through 2000. Sears and Kmart eventually merged but declared bankruptcy in 2018. Since the mid to late1990s, Amazon.com's business model of selling a huge range of goods online at low prices has negatively affected not only Walmart but virtually all other retail stores. The "**retail apocalypse**" is a phrase used to describe a long list of firms that have gone bankrupt due to the inability to compete with Amazon and Walmart. This graveyard of firms includes Toys "R" Us, Forever 21, Payless ShoeSource, Fred's, Barneys New York, Gymboree, Claire's Stores, RadioShack, HH Greg, and many others. The closing of many retail stores in the aftermath of the COVID-19 pandemic may accelerate the retail apocalypse.

In more recent years, Clayton Christensen, also a former Harvard economist, adapted Schumpeter's theory to the rapidly evolving world of technology. Christensen used the term "disruptive technology" or "**disruptive innovation**" to describe better, faster, or cheaper products or services that make it likely a firm will overtake the current market leader. For example, Tesla's pioneering development of the electric car has given it a larger market cap than Ford and GM combined, companies that have been around for more than 100 years!

You might be thinking, "Why does the government allow companies to be negatively affected, if not destroyed?" The government generally allows such behavior to occur since the consumer usually benefits by lower prices and a wider selection of goods. Most economies around the world are based on the economic system of **capitalism**. Capitalism is an ideology, or set of beliefs, based on the private ownership of resources and the pursuit of profit. It is analogous to Charles Darwin's "**survival of the fittest**" theory that describes the process which occurs in many areas of nature. In recent years, there has been momentum to add **environmental, social, and governance** (**ESG**) factors to the goal of the firm and not to single-mindedly focus on profits.

Thus, the ability to think carefully about the changing factors facing firms and industries is an important topic. Not surprisingly, Buffett has weighed in on the subject. In his 1987 Letter to Berkshire Shareholders, he wrote:

> Severe change and exceptional returns usually don't mix. Most investors, of course, behave as if just the opposite were true. That is, they usually confer the highest price-earnings ratios on exotic-sounding businesses that hold out the promise of feverish change. That prospect lets investors fantasize about future profitability rather than face today's business realities.

What kind of firms offer a better chance for exceptional returns? In one interview, he said, "I look for businesses in which I think I can predict what they're going to look like in 10 or 15 or 20 years. That means buying businesses that will look more or less as they do today, except that they'll be larger and doing more business internationally. . . . So I focus on absence of change. . . . That doesn't mean I don't think there's a lot of money to be made from that change, I just don't think I'm the one to make a lot of money out of it." Let's also put the first sentence in this quote as a Tip.

Buffett Tip 39:

Look for businesses where you can predict what they're going to look like in 10–20 years.

When to Sell

Much of what you might read about on investing focuses on which securities to buy. Very little has been written on when to sell. Not surprisingly, Buffett has made some comments on the topic. Some investors say to sell after you've made a profit. Buffett disagrees, saying, "Of Wall Street maxims the most foolish may be 'You can't go broke taking a profit.'" Buffett says don't sell simply because an investment has gone up in value, especially if it's a strong firm.

In his 1987 Letter to Berkshire Shareholders, Buffett expounded on when to sell in more detail, writing, "We need to emphasize, however, that we do not sell holdings just because they have appreciated or because we have held them for a long time. We are quite content to hold any security indefinitely, so long as the prospective return on equity capital of the underlying business is satisfactory, management is competent and honest, and the market does not overvalue the business." Let's summarize these thoughts with a Tip.

Buffett Tip 40:

Sell when the fundamentals of a business change for the worse, not simply because it has gone up in price or you've owned it for a long time.

The fundamentals of the business changed for Kodak when digital photography became popular. The fundamentals changed for Sears and Kmart when they first had to deal with the threat of Walmart, and now they also have to deal with the threat from Amazon.com and other online competitors. Kodak, Sears, and Kmart lost their "moats" in Buffett speak. Sometimes Buffett will sell if he needs the money for another investment that he thinks has more upside. For example, in 2017 he sold his stock in IBM and used some of the proceeds to add to his position in Apple. So far, that swap has paid off big time for Berkshire!

Summarizing Buffett's Approach

We covered a lot of ground in this chapter, but it's crucial to building wealth because it lays out many of the core principles that Buffett considers in his investment approach. If it seems overwhelming, don't worry, we'll end with a couple of tips that summarize Buffett's overall investment approach. In his 1978 Letter to Berkshire Shareholders, Buffett wrote, "We get excited enough to commit a big percentage of insurance company net worth to equities only when we find (1) businesses we can understand, (2) with favorable long-term prospects, (3) operated by honest and competent people, and (4) priced very attractively."

He said something similar, and more succinctly, in his 1994 Letter to Berkshire Shareholders, writing, "We believe that our formula—the purchase at sensible prices of businesses that have good underlying economics and are run by honest and able people—is certain to produce reasonable success."

Charlie Munger, we noted earlier, convinced him of the value of buying great businesses rather than just fair ones. In his 1997 Letter to Berkshire Shareholders, Buffett wrote, "More than 50 years ago, Charlie told me that it was far better to buy a wonderful business at a fair price than to buy a fair business at a wonderful price."

Let's end this chapter by summarizing this section with two important Tips.

Buffett Tip 41:

The purchase at sensible prices of businesses that have good underlying economics and are run by honest and able people is certain to produce reasonable success.

Buffett Tip 42:

It is far better to buy a wonderful business at a fair price than to buy a fair business at a wonderful price. ***(Courtesy of Charlie Munger)***

Buffett's Tips from Chapter 6

Buffett Tip 29: Beware of geeks bearing formulas.
Buffett Tip 30: Intrinsic value is the best way to think about valuing an investment.
Buffett Tip 31: Invest within your circle of competence.
Buffett Tip 32: Time is the friend of the wonderful business, the enemy of the mediocre.
Buffett Tip 33: When change is slow, constant rethinking is actually undesirable. When change is great, yesterday's assumptions can be retained only at great cost.
Buffet Tip 34: A wide moat is essential for long-term business success.
Buffett Tip 35: Invest in companies with good management in place.
Buffett Tip 36: The worst sort of business is one that grows rapidly, requires significant capitai to engender the growth, and then earns little or no money.
Buffett Tip 37: When a management with a reputation for brilliance tackles a business with bad economics, it is the reputation of the business that remains intact.
Buffett Tip 38: Prefer companies that have the power to overcome inflation.
Buffett Tip 39: Look for businesses that you can predict what they're going to look like in 10–20 years.
Buffett Tip 40: Sell when the fundamentals of a business change for the worse, not simply because it has gone up in price or you've owned it for a long time.
Buffett Tip 41: The purchase at sensible prices of businesses that have good underlying economics and are run by honest and able people is certain to produce reasonable success.
Buffett Tip 42: It is far better to buy a wonderful business at a fair price than to buy a fair business at a wonderful price. *(Courtesy of Charlie Munger)*

References

"107 Best Warren Buffett Quotes on Life, Wealth, & Investing." Sure Dividend, January 10, 2019. http://www.suredividend.com/warren-buffett-quotes/.

Bodie, Zvi, Alex Kane, and Alan J. Marcus. *Investments,* 10th edition. New York: McGraw-Hill Education, 2013.

Buffett, Mary, and David Clark. *Buffettology: The Previously Unexplained Techniques That Have Made Warren Buffett the World's Most Famous Investor*. London: Pocket Books, 1999.

Buffett, Warren. "Letter to Shareholders of Berkshire Hathaway Inc." Berkshire Hathaway, Inc., 1978. https://www.berkshirehathaway.com/letters/1978.html.

Buffett, Warren. "Letter to Shareholders of Berkshire Hathaway Inc." Berkshire Hathaway, Inc., 1980. https://www.berkshirehathaway.com/letters/1980.html.

Buffett, Warren. "Letter to Shareholders of Berkshire Hathaway Inc." Berkshire Hathaway, Inc., 1987. https://www.berkshirehathaway.com/letters/1987.html.

Buffett, Warren. "Letter to Shareholders of Berkshire Hathaway Inc." Berkshire Hathaway, Inc., 1991. https://www.berkshirehathaway.com/letters/1991.html.

Buffett, Warren. "Letter to Shareholders of Berkshire Hathaway Inc." Berkshire Hathaway, Inc., 1993. https://www.berkshirehathaway.com/letters/1993.html.

Buffett, Warren. "Letter to Shareholders of Berkshire Hathaway Inc." Berkshire Hathaway, Inc., 1994. https://www.berkshirehathaway.com/letters/1994.html.

Buffett, Warren. "Letter to Shareholders of Berkshire Hathaway Inc." Berkshire Hathaway, Inc., 1995. https://www.berkshirehathaway.com/letters/1995.html.

Buffett, Warren. "Letter to Shareholders of Berkshire Hathaway Inc." Berkshire Hathaway, Inc., 1996. https://www.berkshirehathaway.com/letters/1996.html.

Buffett, Warren. "Letter to Shareholders of Berkshire Hathaway Inc." Berkshire Hathaway, Inc., 1997. https://www.berkshirehathaway.com/letters/1997.html.

Buffett, Warren. "Letter to Shareholders of Berkshire Hathaway Inc." Berkshire Hathaway, Inc., 2007. https://www.berkshirehathaway.com/letters/2007.html.

Buffett, Warren. "Letter to Shareholders of Berkshire Hathaway Inc." Berkshire Hathaway, Inc., 2008. https://www.berkshirehathaway.com/letters/2008.html.

Buffett, Warren. "Letter to Shareholders of Berkshire Hathaway Inc." Berkshire Hathaway, Inc., 2014. https://www.berkshirehathaway.com/letters/2014.html.

Buffett, Warren. "Letter to Shareholders of Berkshire Hathaway Inc." Berkshire Hathaway, Inc., 2015. https://www.berkshirehathaway.com/letters/2015.html.

Fisher, Philip A. *Common Stocks and Uncommon Profits and Other Writings*. Hoboken, NJ: Wiley, 2003.

Frankel, Matthew. "What Percentage of Coca-Cola Does Warren Buffett Own?" *The Motley Fool,* March 10, 2017. https://www.fool.com/investing/2017/03/10/what-percentage-of-coca-cola-does-warren-buffett-o.aspx.

Gordon, M. J. "Dividends, Earnings, and Stock Prices." *The Review of Economics and Statistics* 41, no. 2 (1959): 99–105. https://doi.org/10.2307/1927792.

Hagstrom, Robert G. *The Warren Buffett Way*. Hoboken, NJ: Wiley, 2014.

Graham, Benjamin, and Jason Zweig. *The Intelligent Investor: The Definitive Book on Value Investing*. New York: Harper Business, 2006.

Loomis, Carol. *Tap Dancing to Work: Warren Buffett on Practically Everything, 1966–2012*. London: Portfolio Penguin, 2014.

Lowenstein, Roger. *Buffett the Making of an American Capitalist*. New York: Random House Trade, 2008.

Schroeder, Alice. *The Snowball: Warren Buffett and the Business of Life*. New York: Bantam Books, 2009.

Team Tony. "The Mindset of a Champion." Tony Robbins, December 12, 2018. https://www.tonyrobbins.com/mind-meaning/the-mindset-of-a-champion/.

The Wealth Acquirer. "Warren Buffett Gives the Best Advice in Just Three Minutes!" YouTube Video, 4:40, April 14, 2017. https://www.youtube.com/watch?v=7Qo_f7Gzqds.

Witzel, Morgan. "Darwin Is More than Survival of the Fittest." *Financial Times*, November 3, 2010. https://www.ft.com/content/99d59478-e797-11df-8ade-00144feab49a.

7

Accounting Fundamentals: The Report Card for Businesses

"Accounting numbers, of course, are the language of business and as such are of enormous help to anyone evaluating the worth of a business and tracking its progress."
—Warren Buffett, 1986 Letter to Berkshire Hathaway Shareholders

Introduction

Students get a report card. It's a measure of how you performed in your classes over the course of the marking period. In business, companies have their own type of report card. They're called financial statements, a term we introduced in **Chapter 1**. Understanding the "report card" of a business is an important part of financial literacy. It provides you with insights related to how companies act and how they've performed. And who knows? Maybe you'll have your own business someday, and then you'll have to understand this stuff in even greater detail, since it's what you'll have to show to *your* investors.

It's worth your time to grasp the basics of accounting and financial statements now. In fact, when one teen asked Buffett for financial advice, Buffett suggested, "Take all the accounting courses you can." In his 1986 Letter to Berkshire Shareholders, Buffett called accounting the "language of business" and said he and his business partner, Charlie Munger, use it as the basis for evaluating businesses. Here's the full quote.

"Accounting numbers, of course, are the language of business and as such are of enormous help to anyone evaluating the worth of a business and tracking its progress. Charlie and I would be lost without these numbers: They invariably are the starting point for us in evaluating our own businesses and those of others. Managers and owners need to remember, however, that accounting is but an aid to business thinking, never a substitute for it." Let's summarize these points with a Tip.

Buffett Tip 43:

Take all the accounting courses you can. Accounting is the language of business.

There are two types of companies, for profit and nonprofit. Nonprofit institutions include governments, charities, and most schools and religious organizations. Their goals are often not related to making money. For example, schools mainly exist to educate their students. However, nonprofit doesn't necessarily mean no profit. If these nonprofits do generate profits, they are reinvested in the institution.

We're going to discuss charity later in the book since it's a big part of Buffett's character and the ultimate destination for his money, but for now, we're going to focus on firms that try to make money. These are for-profit firms, such as Apple, Facebook, Disney, and—of course—Berkshire Hathaway. Both types of groups have financial statements, but we'll get a better feel for them when talking about profit-seeking firms.

Businesses sell something—usually a product or a service. Let's start with a firm selling a product since it's a bit easier to visualize. Warren Buffett's first business was buying packs of gum from the supermarket (through his grandfather) and selling them to his friends and neighbors at a higher price. As mentioned in **Chapter 1**, the difference between the price at which something is sold and all the costs involved in selling it is usually called either profit or earnings. If the number is negative, that is, the firm sells a product at a price less than what it costs to make it, it's called a **loss**. The notion of profit and loss and the current financial condition of a firm are what financial statements are mostly about.

The Income Statement: A Company's Report Card for One Period

Most companies produce financial statements on a quarterly basis, typically at the end of March, June, September, and December. These quarterly statements, or **quarterly reports,** roll up into an annual statement, or **annual report**. The reports include other things besides financial statements. For example, we have often referred to the letters Buffett writes to Berkshire Hathaway's shareholders. But we'll put those non-financial things aside for now. The watchdog of the US financial markets, known as the **Securities and Exchange Commission (SEC)**, requires companies trading on stock exchanges to file these reports. The SEC calls the quarterly report a **10-Q** and the Annual Report a **10-K.**

Most company's annual reports cover the period January 1 to December 31, the **calendar year**, but there are some exceptions. The year used when computing financial statements is called the **fiscal year**. For most firms, the calendar year equals the fiscal year. But here's a common exception: colleges. Colleges usually have a fiscal year that goes from July 1 to June 30, to align it with the academic year.

The financial statements are produced by the people running the firm, its management, but they are **audited** by accountants. Audited means to check out, or to try to verify that the numbers are accurate and prepared according to the rules. The rules for companies that trade on a US stock exchange are called **Generally Accepted Accounting Principles (GAAP)**. Many international firms follow a slightly different set of rules, called **International Financial Reporting Standards (IFRS)**. Technically, only a special type of accountant is able to conduct an audit. These "black belt" accountants are called **Certified Public Accountants,** or **CPAs** for short. They have to pass a range of exams and must have taken a certain amount of accounting and college courses in order to call themselves CPAs.

There are thousands of accounting firms, but four huge ones do most of the audits for big, publicly traded companies. Not surprisingly, in business they are known as the "**Big Four**." In case you wind up on

Jeopardy, we'll tell you their names: Deloitte, Ernst & Young (E&Y), KPMG, and PricewaterhouseCoopers (PwC).

Apple's Income Statement

The first financial statement that we're going to tackle is called the **income statement**. It measures the profit or loss for a firm over a specified period of time. Sometimes it's called the **profit and loss statement**, or **P&L** for short. You can think of the income statement as the report card of a firm for one period, typically a quarter or a full year. Let's look at a simplified income statement for Apple, one of the most valuable, profitable, and coolest firms in the world. It's simplified since we don't want you to need a degree in accounting to read this book. We'll examine its income statement for the 2019 fiscal year, shown in **Figure 7.1.**

We'll start with the **top line** number known as revenue. Revenue also goes by other names, such as **sales** or **net sales,** if you make adjustments for things such as returns, discounts, and other allowances. We're sure you've stood in a line at some point in your life to return a gift you didn't want from the holiday season, such as the proverbial ugly sweater or fruitcake. If so, your actions have been included in the net sales of some firm even if you didn't realize it.

In Apple's case its revenue comes from the sale of its products and services. It comes mostly from the sales of its hugely popular iPhone but

Apple Income Statement (Simplified)	
Fiscal Year 2019 ($ billions)	
Revenue	$267.68
Less: cost of goods sold (COGS)	166.10
Gross profit	101.58
Less: selling, general & administrative	35.43
Operating income	66.15
Plus: other	1.60
Less: income taxes (15.08%)	10.22
Net Income	**$57.53**

Figure 7.1

also from its other products and services such as Macs, iTunes songs, iPads, apps, Beats headphones, and many other things. Apple had immense revenue of $267.68 billion in fiscal year 2019. That's bigger than the sales generated by some entire countries!

Well, it costs something to run a business. We're going to look at the two main cost items. The first is the cost of producing the item, such as the iPhone. Accountants call that term by the formal name of **cost of goods sold**. Cost of goods sold often goes by the acronym **COGS**. Apple had COGS of $166.10 billion in fiscal year 2019. Accountants know when to add or subtract something on a financial statement, but we're going to try to make it easy for you. If we put the word "Less" next to an item, that means you subtract it from the number above. We'll also occasionally put an underline symbol too, known in accounting speak as single accounting underline. So in our mini Apple income statement you'll see "Less: cost of goods sold." The difference between net revenue and cost of goods sold is called **gross profit**.

Sticking with our iPhone example, Apple might charge $1,000 for a phone that costs them $500 to make, resulting in a gross profit of $500 per phone. Is that a good number? It is, but to answer it more precisely you should compare Apple's numbers to its competitors', such as Samsung and Alphabet (the parent company of Google). You should also compare the current values of Apple for any statistic to its values in prior years. If the gross profit is increasing per phone sold, it tells you the company is getting stronger and building up its moat, in Buffett speak. A lean, mean fighting machine!

Analysts sometimes use another technique to determine if a specific number is good or bad. They often divide a specific item, such as gross profit, by sales. These **financial ratios** (dividing one financial variable by another) make it easy to make comparisons across firms, and across time for the same firm, since everything is expressed by a percentage. Thus, in this instance, if Apple had a higher gross profit-to-sales ratio, known as a **gross margin ratio**, than Samsung, it would be considered to have done better in this aspect of its financial report card. The term "**common-sizing**" a financial statement refers to dividing items on the income statement by sales (i.e., creating ratios that express things as a percentage of sales) and dividing items on the balance sheet (covered in the next section) by total assets.

But Apple has other costs too, such as wages. You wouldn't work full-time for a company for free, would you? At least not for too long. Apple also has to pay other expenses, such as the cost to set up shop in the mall, typically called **rent** or a **lease obligation**. Apple also has to put money aside to invent new products. That iPhone, iPad, or Apple Watch that you love was once just a glimmer in someone's eye more than a decade ago. Funds put aside to invent new products and services go toward **research and development**, or **R&D** for short. We'll put all of these costs into a term informally known as **overhead.** The formal name that accountants use for overhead is **selling, general, and administrative**, or **SG&A** for short. This is the second main cost of running a business that we alluded to earlier.

Apple had SG&A expense of $35.43 billion in fiscal year 2019. Once again, you can get a feel if the number is "good" by comparing it, both in dollar terms and on a percentage basis (i.e., as a percentage of revenues), to the values of its competitors' and Apple's own prior values. Gross profit minus (or less) selling, general, and administrative expenses is called **operating income.** It's what the company makes before paying taxes and other items that we'll briefly discuss. Accountants sometimes use a wordy substitute for operating income called **earnings before interest and taxes**, or **EBIT** for short. We'll stick with operating income. (You can thank us later.) Operating income is what the company makes on a regular basis, before taxes it pays to the government(s) and interest to its debtholders, from its regular course of business.

Hang in there, we're almost to the bottom line, and we mean that literally. We've included another item called "other" that is a catch-all term for anything outside the firm's regular course of business. It might include payments made to or received from business disputes, known as **lawsuits** or **litigation**. It might include **interest income** related to a firm's investments. It might include **interest expense** owed on a firm's loans or bonds. In Apple's case, it has a huge amount of cash and investments, more than $200 billion in fiscal year 2019, so the interest income item overwhelms everything else, and its "other" item is $1.60 billion in fiscal year 2019.

We mentioned the dreaded term "taxes" back in **Chapter 1**. They're basically payments to help fund the government. Taxes not only pay politicians' salaries, but they are also used for arguably more important items such as the armed forces (Army, Navy, Air Force, Marines, Coast Guard, etc.), maintaining the highway system, and for police and fire departments, plus thousands of other items. Even companies can't avoid taxes, at least most of the time, if they turn a profit.

The **tax rate** is the percentage of your income that you owe to the government. So if you make a $1,000 and you owe $100 to the government in taxes, your tax rate is \$100 divided by \$1,000, or 10%. Taxes are paid at the federal (e.g., Washington, DC) level and often at the state (e.g., New York) and occasionally at the local (e.g., New York City) level. We're just going to call it **taxes** and won't bore you with the details.

How much in taxes does a company pay? There are **tax tables** or **tax schedules** created by the government that provide specific information. The department of the federal government responsible for handling tax issues is the **Internal Revenue Service (IRS).** There are different levels or **tax brackets** for each amount of income that you or a company might earn. In general, as you make more money, you pay a higher tax rate. When tax brackets increase as you make more money, they are called **progressive tax rates**. Tax rates differ not only by state but also by country. Some territories or countries, such as Bermuda, charge no or minimal income taxes! Apple sells its products in many countries around the word, and its fiscal 2019 tax rate turned out to be a little bit more than 15%. In dollar terms, it amounted to a huge \$10.22 billion. With those kinds of payments, many governments around the world should be huge fans of Apple too!

By taking operating income, adding other income, and subtracting income taxes, we finally arrive at **net income,** known as the "bottom line" in finance and accounting circles. Apple earned \$57.53 billion in net income during fiscal year 2019. Way to go, Apple. That's a savage A+ grade!

Buffett suggests that one year of earnings is not too meaningful, especially for **cyclical firms**, or firms whose earnings vary widely with the business cycle. The analysis of a firm's financial earnings over a full business cycle, which typically lasts five-plus years, is called **normalized earnings**. In his 1983 Letter to Berkshire Shareholders Buffett wrote, "We never take the one-year figure very seriously. After all, why should the time required for a planet to circle the sun synchronize precisely with the time required for business actions to pay off? Instead, we recommend not less than a five-year test as a rough yardstick of economic performance."

In his 1998 Letter to Berkshire Shareholders, he expressed even longer-term thinking, writing:

> We give each a simple mission: Just run your business as if: (1) you own 100% of it; (2) it is the only asset in the world that you and your family have or will ever have; and (3) you can't sell or merge it for at least a century.

Let's wrap those thoughts up with a Tip and move on to the second major financial statement of a firm, the **balance sheet**, which is like a picture of the firm at a specific point in time.

Buffett Tip 44:

Don't take one year of accounting figures very seriously. Focus on periods of five or more years in your analysis.

The Balance Sheet: A Picture of a Company's Report Card Since Inception

Perhaps you or your friends like to take a lot of selfies and post them on Instagram, Snap, Facebook, or some other site. Well, a company has sort of a selfie. It's called a balance sheet. It's a snapshot or picture of what the company looks like at a certain point in time. Like with the income statement, the balance sheet is prepared by management on a quarterly basis and audited by an external CPA firm on an annual basis. Sometimes you'll see the balance sheet referred to as a **statement of financial position** or **statement of financial condition**. We're going to stick with balance sheet since it's the term used most often and also conveys some important information. That is, a balance sheet *must* balance. This is an important point to remember. We'll define what we mean by balance in a bit, so hang on.

A second way to view the balance sheet is that it is a sum of what the firm has become from its birth, or formation, to the present. In some respects, it's how the firm started, plus the results from all of its income statements. In this manner, it can be viewed like the sum total of all your grades since you started school. In college and most high schools, the sum of your grades is called a cumulative grade point average, or simply GPA. Most colleges compute your GPA on a 4-point scale. Thus, a 4.0 GPA means you got As in all of your classes since you entered school. Sweet!

Let's mix it up a bit and look at the December 31, 2019, balance sheet of Warren Buffett's firm, Berkshire Hathaway. Berkshire's calendar and fiscal year is the same, going from January 1 to December 31 of each year. Unlike the income statement, there are two sides to a balance sheet, a left side and a right side. This arrangement might seem a bit weird to you, but it has a long history. It actually goes back to the end of the 13th century! Man, that's old!

Way back then, a Florentine merchant named Amatino Manucci developed the notion of the balance sheet. The way the balance sheet is set up—that is, having the two sides—is also known as a **double-entry form of bookkeeping**. If something affects one side of the balance sheet, it usually has a corresponding effect on the other side of the balance sheet. Let's now describe what we mean by "sides."

The items on the left-hand side of the balance sheet add up to an accounting term called **assets** or **total assets**. You can think of assets as the "stuff" the firm owns. Its cash, buildings, real estate, products, and so forth. The right-hand side of the balance sheet tells you who has claim to the "stuff." Sometimes it's people or banks that lent the firm money. Other times it could be the owners of the business, what we referred to as stockholders. The total of the left-hand side of the balance sheet has to equal the total of the right-hand side of the balance sheet. Always! If they don't, it would be like getting a 0 on an exam for the person or firm that prepared the balance sheet. Let's not even think about it!

So, getting back to Berkshire's balance sheet, we can see a simplified version of it in **Figure 7.2**. It has two sides to it, so it's a little more complex than the income statement. Let's start with the left-hand side,

Berkshire Hathaway Balance Sheet (Simplified)			
Period Ending December 31, 2019			
Figures in $ millions			
Current assets		**Current liabilities**	
Cash and short-term investments	127,997	Accounts payable	36,437
Accounts receivable	53,362		
Inventory	19,852	**Long-term liabilities**	
		Long-term debt	99,425
Long-term assets			
Property, plant & equipment	180,282	Other liabilities	257,076
Long-term investments	284,674	**Stockholders' equity**	424,791
Other	151,562		
Total assets	817,729	**Total liabilities plus stockholders' equity**	817,729

Figure 7.2

which we know is called total assets. Total assets are made up of two sections, current assets and long-term assets. **Current assets** are cash or things that are expected to turn into cash within one year (365 days). Long-term assets are things that have value but are unlikely to be converted into cash within one year. Let's get into some specifics related to Berkshire's business or, more accurately, businesses.

Current Assets

Looking at the current assets section you'll notice three items. **Cash and short-term investments, accounts receivable**, and **inventory**. You know what cash is. It's cash in your wallet, cash in a cash register, cash in a checking account, as well as some other things. The main thing to remember is that it's very safe. You can rely on it, at least as much as Steph Curry making a free-throw in a basketball game. "Cash is king" is a popular saying in the financial world. It means if you're cash rich, you have a lot of power, especially during economic downturns. Short-term investments are those that are about to expire or mature within one year, things such as US Treasury bills or **commercial paper,** which is short-term debt issued by corporations with a strong credit rating. These things are almost always considered very safe as well.

Accounts receivable is our next item under current assets. It might sound kind of strange, but you do have some familiarity with it, even if you don't know it yet. Sometimes is known as **net receivables**. Accounts receivable are sales made on credit, as from a credit card. Let's say you purchase from Dairy Queen a huge Oreo Cookies Blizzard® Treat. Yum! Assume the ice cream treat was paid for with a credit card. It will take a little bit of time, usually less than a month, for the credit card vendor, such as Visa, MasterCard, Discover, or American Express, to give Dairy Queen/Berkshire the cash. But it's a pretty safe asset in most cases, unless the company goes bankrupt. Not gonna happen in Berkshire's case!

The last item under current assets is **inventory**. Inventory is easy to visualize as the "stuff" the company has for sale before it's purchased by a customer. In Berkshire's case, it could be the ice cream in a Dairy Queen that has yet to be sold, it could be cans of paint in its Benjamin Moore stores, as well as thousands of other items. Inventory could also be raw material or work in progress, but it's easier to think about finished products. They can probably be sold for something within a year and likely have some value.

Long-Term Assets

Moseying on down to the left-hand side of the balance sheet we get to **long-term assets**. They refer to something that the firm owns that is of lasting value. These items are unlikely to turn into cash within a year. **Property, plant, and equipment,** or **PP&E** for short, is pretty much what it sounds like. First, it consists of land. Berkshire owns a lot of land, perhaps most noticeably in its railroad unit, Burlington Northern Santa Fe (BNSF). Berkshire bought the railroad for $26.5 billion back in 2010. It's easy to see why there is a moat around the business. They aren't building too many new railroads in the US, especially those that span much of the country.

BNSF is huge! It operates 32,500 miles of track across 28 states and has over 8,000 locomotives. For many items, such as barrels of oil found in the mid-continental United States, it is often cheaper to send them over rail rather than loading them on a truck. BNSF's history dates all the way back to 1849, so it's a business that has really stood the test of time, which is another feature of many of Buffett's investments.

Plant usually refers to buildings built on pieces of land. It could be a factory, warehouse, office building, retail store, and a host of other things. Berkshire-owned Dairy Queen stores may be a Berkshire "plant" long-term asset you have visited in the past. Berkshire also owns the paint retailer Benjamin Moore. If you've ordered things such as balloons or napkins from your favorite sports team for a party, it may have come from Berkshire's toy and novelties unit, Oriental Trading Company. If you live on the West Coast perhaps you've been to a See's Candy store, another Berkshire company. You get the point; plant refers to places where work gets done. If the firm owns the real estate, it winds up on the PP&E portion of the balance sheet.

Let's tackle the "E" part, or equipment. Equipment is also easy to visualize. It refers to machines that produce the things a firm sells, such as a milkshake machine for Dairy Queen or a candy-making machine for See's Candy. It could be a truck that transports Berkshire's products to retail stores. Or a forklift in the factory. Even computers used by Berkshire employees. Machines usually last a long time, but they eventually break down. Think about a car. Tires lose their tread, brakes grind down, engines wear out, and so forth. Companies account for this wear and tear of a long-term asset with an accounting term known as **depreciation**. The life of an asset differs for various items, depending on how long it typically lasts. It might be 3 years for a computer, 5–7 years for a car, and 30 years for a building. We won't bore you with the details.

Next, we get to **long-term investments**. These represent Berkshire's investments in external, or third-party, firms or securities, such as the stock Berkshire holds in Apple, Coca-Cola, Wells Fargo, and Kraft Heinz. Although Berkshire owns billions of dollars of these firms' securities, it doesn't own a **controlling interest**. Controlling interest means Berkshire has the power to run the firm. That's why these investments are listed under the long-term investments field and not fully combined or **consolidated** into Berkshire's regular financial statements. In other words, if Berkshire owned a controlling interest in Coca-Cola, the beverage maker's revenues would be partially or fully included in Berkshire's revenues on its income statement. Since it doesn't own controlling interest, Berkshire's holdings are filed under the long-term investments section of its balance sheet.

The Other item in Berkshire's Assets includes a host of things, but we'll discuss one category called **intangibles**. Intangibles related to **patents**, **trademarks**, **copyrights**, and other items usually fall under the name, or umbrella, of **intellectual property**. Rules governing intellectual property prevent someone from stealing a firm's ideas or inventions. For example, if you were able to open up a store and call it McDonald's, you would instantly have a bunch of customers who know and love the food. Same goes for Disney, Nike, Apple, and many other companies. But you can't do this, of course, since someone else owns these firms and their related intellectual property.

The sum of the left-hand side of Berkshire's balance sheet totals to an amazing $817.729 billion. That's a lot of bread! Hang in there. We're half done with the balance sheet. Now let's shuffle over to the right-hand side of the balance sheet. It focuses on who has claims or dibs to the assets. These claimholders basically fall into two areas. First is the group that lent the firm money, or that provided it with products or services. In aggregate, this group is generally known as **creditors**. The second area is the owners, which we know are the stockholders. They get what's left over after paying all the bills. The gravy, so to speak. And with Berkshire's we'll see there is a whole lot left.

Liabilities

In everyday usage, a liability refers to a weakness. Maybe you've heard the expression "Achilles' heel." Tom Brady is a great football player, but his liability is running for a gain, or scrambling in football lingo. NBA Hall of Famer, Shaquille O'Neal, was so bad at making free throws, that teams invented a strategy to try to beat him. It involved fouling him on purpose so he would have to shoot free throws, a strategy dubbed Hack-A-Shaq.

By now it should be clear that virtually everyone and everything has liabilities. As we noted above, a liability on the firm's balance sheet means it owes something to someone—an outside vendor, an employee, a bank, or a host of other creditors. As with the left-hand side of the balance sheet, we are going to break things into two categories, short term and long term. And short-term, or **current, liabilities** plus **long-term liabilities** equals **total liabilities**.

Current Liabilities

Current liabilities are amounts owed by the firm where payment is due within one year. **Accounts payable** is the flip side of accounts receivable. In this instance, Berkshire received a product or service and hasn't paid yet. A more generalized interpretation of accounts payable would also include paying the company's employees. Even Warren Buffett doesn't work for free! With most companies, employees work for 2 weeks or a month before receiving a paycheck. Berkshire had $36.437 billion in accounts payable at the end of 2019.

Long-Term Liabilities

Long-term liabilities represent money owed to creditors, but the money is due more than one year from today. In Berkshire's case, much of the money owed is to investors who bought Berkshire's bonds, to the tune of $99.425 billion! We also have an entry called "other." It's a humongous number in Berkshire's case, $257.076 billion, so let's give an example of what might fall in this category. Berkshire has a big **insurance** unit as one of its businesses. Insurance protects you, by giving you money, if something bad happens to your car, property, or person. We mentioned GEICO before, one of the largest auto insurance firms in the world. Berkshire sells many other kinds of insurance, including **life insurance**.

Life insurance makes a payment to the surviving heirs (e.g., spouse or kids) of a person after they die. Many companies provide life insurance as one benefit, or **perk,** to their employees. Most of these workers are on the younger side and healthy. We mentioned in a prior chapter that a big chunk of the people who are on the earth today are going to live to be at least 100 years old, so it may be several decades before Berkshire has to pay death benefits on life insurance policies (i.e., long-term liabilities) even though it receives a policy payment (known as an **insurance premium**) on a regular basis. The money earned on the spread between the amount paid on an insurance policy and the premiums received by the insurance company is often called **float**. It's not quite as scrumptious as a root beer float, but you can do a lot of things with it. One option is to put it in a safe bank account and earn some interest. Buffett and Berkshire tend to be more aggressive with their float and invest much of it in stocks and other investments. Total liabilities for Berkshire added up to a whopping $392.938 billion at the end of 2019.

Stockholders' Equity

Now we get to the gravy, the icing, or what is left over after paying your bills. Accountants call it **shareholders' equity**, **stockholders' equity**, or **owners' equity**. Yet some other terms for the same thing are **net worth** or **book value**. Like the $80 billion or so Buffett is personally worth. Its calculation is a cinch, for either a company or a person. It's simply total assets minus total liabilities. In Berkshire's case it's a hefty $424.791 billion. And, of course, our balance sheet has to balance, so the sum of total liabilities and stockholders' equity equals the same $817.729 billion on the left-hand side, or total assets side, of the balance sheet.

Book value is listed on the balance sheet of a firm and it's something that can be measured by following accounting rules. We mentioned the term "intrinsic value" in the last chapter. It's an *estimate* of what the firm is worth today, or what we called a price target. Buffett distinguished between the two values in his 1993 Letter to Berkshire Shareholders, writing, "Of course, it's per-share intrinsic value, not book value, that counts. Book value is an accounting term that measures the capital, including retained earnings, that has been put into a business. Intrinsic value is a present-value estimate of the cash that can be taken out of a business during its remaining life."

He goes on in that same letter with an analogy that describes book value as the cost of a college education, while intrinsic value is a measure of how much money a person will make over the course of their career. For example, a college student who becomes a engineer will likely make more money over their lifetime than a person that studied to be a social worker, even if their college education cost the same amount of money. Tip 30 focused on Buffett's preference for intrinsic value for evaluating the worth of a firm, so we won't create a duplicate tip here.

We don't want to confuse you, but the stockholders' equity value or book value is not necessarily equal to a firm's market capitalization, which we know is the price of firm's stock times its shares outstanding. For example, as we are writing this book, Berkshire's market value is a little bit over $500 billion while the stockholders' equity is roughly $425 billion. This happens to be the case for many firms, such as Facebook, Starbucks, Tesla, and indeed for the vast majority of firms. One reason for this difference is that the rules for creating financial statements tend to err on the conservative side. They record assets at cost. For example, if your grandparents bought an apartment in New York City or San Francisco 40 or 50 years ago, its price today would probably be much, much higher than what they paid for it. So when the market value is higher than the purchase price or book value, you can better understand this discrepancy.

Buffett likes to use the ratio of operating income to shareholders' equity as one measure of company performance. It's a measure of "bang for the buck," or what the shareholders make from their regular course of business (the operating income), given the equity capital they have in the firm. He thinks the number should be greater than the average for the entire market over a five-year period and that a company shouldn't use too much debt or accounting gimmicks to get there.

Buffett criticized the approach of just looking for a company that has increasing earnings per share. A company can show rising earnings per share simply due to compound interest and not skill of management. For example, the cash balance of a company's bank account will increase, due to interest, pushing up earnings per share, other things equal. He expressed these thoughts in his 1979 Letter to Berkshire Shareholders, writing, "We continue to feel that the ratio of operating earnings (before securities gains or losses) to shareholders' equity with all securities valued at cost is the most appropriate way to measure any single year's operating performance. . . . The primary test of managerial economic performance is the achievement of a high earnings rate on equity capital employed (without undue leverage, accounting gimmickry, etc.) and not the achievement of consistent gains in earnings per share."

There's a lot of accounting terminology in Buffett's quote, but let's summarize these thoughts with a Tip.

Buffett Tip 45:

The ratio of operating earnings to shareholders' equity is a good metric of performance for most firms.

In his 2009 Letter to Berkshire Shareholders, he drilled down further on the type of firms he likes. He wrote, "Indeed, the best businesses by far for owners continue to be those that have high returns on capital and that require little incremental investment to grow." Thus, a firm like See's Candy that generates high profits relative to the money invested in the business *and* that doesn't require a lot of new investment is the kind of firm that he's referring to here. In contrast, a car company such as GM or Ford has fairly low **profit margins** (i.e., profits as a percentage of sales) *and* requires investments in new car models, engines, transmissions, electric vehicles, and even "years down the road" investments in things such as driverless cars. Let's summarize Buffett's point with a Tip.

Buffett Tip 46:

The best businesses by far are those that have high returns on capital and that require little incremental investment to grow.

A Quick Note on the Statement of Cash Flows

There is a third major financial statement called the **statement of cash flows** that measures cash coming in and out of the business. It has three sections. The first section is **cash flow from operating activities (CFO)**, which, as the name indicates, is cash generated from the firm's regular activities. For Berkshire, some element of CFO may be from selling insurance, candy, or ice cream. The second section is **cash flow from investing activities (CFI)**, which refers to funds spent on long-term investments, such as PP&E and acquisitions of or investments in other firms. For Berkshire, it may include a new power plant, Dairy Queen store, or investment in Apple stock. The third section is **cash flow from financing activities (CFF)**. This section includes things such as issuing or buying back equity or debt or the payment of dividends. The statement of cash flows can be derived from the income statement and balance sheet, but we'll leave the details aside for now. We sense you've probably had enough of accounting for the moment . . . or year.

Summary

You can trust that roughly 99-plus percent of the financial statements published by firms are accurate. By accurate we mean they are prepared under the rules of GAAP. Two of the main people running the firm, the chief executive officer and the chief financial officer, have to personally certify that the statements are true and accurate, or they risk going to jail. And, by the way, many people have gone to jail for falsifying financial statements. You can look up the names of Bernie Ebbers and Jeff Skilling if you want to learn about the high-profile financial fraud cases involving WorldCom and Enron. That being said, companies will try to put the best "spin" possible on their financial results while staying within the boundaries of GAAP. They often try to bury things in the footnotes that may not have yet affected the company's financial statements but may result in some bad news down the road.

Buffett is aware of these games that executives sometimes play with their financial numbers and wrote in his 1988 Letter to Berkshire Shareholders, "Further complicating the problem is the fact that many managements view GAAP not as a standard to be met, but as an obstacle to overcome. Too often their accountants willingly assist them. ('How much,' says the client, 'is two plus two?' Replies the cooperative accountant, 'What number did you have in mind?') Even honest and well-intentioned managements sometimes stretch GAAP a bit in order to present figures they think will more appropriately describe their performance." Let's include a Tip about being a bit wary with the reported numbers.

Buffett Tip 47:

Companies will try to put the best "spin" on their financial reports. You need to look beneath the surface to truly understand what is happening with the company.

Accountants may seem nerdy. But Buffett embraces his inner nerdiness, and so should you. He spends much of his day reading financial reports. It can be pretty cool to have your financial house in order. It's one of our main goals in writing this book. And some basic knowledge of accounting and financial statements can help you do that. Berkshire's or Buffett's A+ balance sheet and income statement is a "stretch goal" worth aspiring to.

Buffett's Tips from Chapter 7

Buffett Tip 43: Take all the accounting courses you can. Accounting is the language of business.
Buffett Tip 44: Don't take one year of accounting figures very seriously. Focus on periods of five or more years in your analysis.
Buffett Tip 45: The ratio of operating earnings to shareholders' equity is a good metric of performance for most firms.
Buffett Tip 46: The best businesses by far are those that have high returns on capital and that require little incremental investment to grow.
Buffett Tip 47: Companies will try to put the best "spin" on their financial reports. You need to look beneath the surface to truly understand what is happening with the company.

References

"Apple Inc. (AAPL) Income Statement." Yahoo! Finance. Accessed June 27, 2020. https://finance.yahoo.com/quote/AAPL/financials?p=AAPL.

"Berkshire Hathaway Inc. New (BRK-B) Balance Sheet." Yahoo! Finance. Accessed June 27, 2020. https://finance.yahoo.com/quote/BRK-B/balance-sheet?p=BRK-B.

"BNSF Railway—News, Reports & Features for Rail Industry Professionals." *Progressive Railroading*. Accessed June 27, 2020. https://www.progressiverailroading.com/bnsf_railway/.

Buffett, Mary, and David Clark. *Warren Buffett and the Interpretation of Financial Statements The Search for the Company with a Durable Competitive Advantage*. London: Simon & Schuster, 2011.

Buffett, Warren. "Letter to Shareholders of Berkshire Hathaway Inc." Berkshire Hathaway, Inc., 1979. https://www.berkshirehathaway.com/letters/1979.html.

Buffett, Warren. "Letter to Shareholders of Berkshire Hathaway Inc." Berkshire Hathaway, Inc., 1983. https://www.berkshirehathaway.com/letters/1983.html.

Buffett, Warren. "Letter to Shareholders of Berkshire Hathaway Inc." Berkshire Hathaway, Inc., 1986. https://www.berkshirehathaway.com/letters/1986.html.

Buffett, Warren. "Letter to Shareholders of Berkshire Hathaway Inc." Berkshire Hathaway, Inc., 1988. https://www.berkshirehathaway.com/letters/1988.html.

Buffett, Warren. "Letter to Shareholders of Berkshire Hathaway Inc." Berkshire Hathaway, Inc., 1993. https://www.berkshirehathaway.com/letters/1993.html.

Buffett, Warren. "Letter to Shareholders of Berkshire Hathaway Inc." Berkshire Hathaway, Inc., 1998. https://www.berkshirehathaway.com/letters/1998.html.

Buffett, Warren. "Letter to Shareholders of Berkshire Hathaway Inc." Berkshire Hathaway, Inc., 2009. https://www.berkshirehathaway.com/letters/2009.html.

CNBC. "Warren Buffett's Advice to Teen Investor," July 31, 2014. https://www.cnbc.com/video/2014/07/31/warren-buffetts-advice-to-teen-investor.html.

Penman, Stephen H. *Financial Statement Analysis and Security Valuation*. New York: McGraw-Hill Higher Education, 2013.

8

Buffett's Approach to Portfolio and Risk Management

"Rule No. 1: Never lose money. Rule No. 2: Never forget rule No. 1."
—Warren Buffett, *Rules That Warren Buffett Lives By*

Introduction

Putting all of your eggs (or investments) in one basket is too risky for nearly everyone. The basket could fall, breaking all of the eggs. Similarly, a specific stock could go bankrupt, potentially wiping out all, or a good portion, of the value of your investments. That's really taking the L. Even brand-name stocks such as Kodak, General Motors, Enron, WorldCom, and Lehman Brothers went bankrupt, taking their stock prices to $0. In **Chapter 2**, we mentioned that most people diversify their investments, or spread them across different assets. It's one of the fundamentals of investing for most people.

A portfolio is a basket of investments, but we'll mostly use the term **diversified portfolio** in this chapter and for the remainder of the book to describe what your overall, or aggregate, portfolio might look like. But how do you best diversify your investments, known in the investment world as selecting an **optimal portfolio**? There are several approaches, and—not surprisingly—Buffett has weighed in on the subject. Selecting a portfolio goes hand in hand with risk, since risk and return are two sides of the same coin. We emphasized this point back in **Chapter** 2, illustrated with the famous coin flipping example, the Saint Petersburg Paradox. And yes, Buffett has weighed in on risk too. In fact, one of his most humorous quotes is on risk. He said, "Rule No. 1: Never lose money. Rule No. 2: Never forget rule No. 1."

Of course, you can't invest in something, other than an FDIC-insured bank product or a highly rated short-term government bond, and *never* lose money. But Buffett's quote makes it clear that investors should have a keen focus on risk before investing any money. That mind-set merits a Tip.

Buffett Tip 48:

Rule No.1: Never lose money. Rule No. 2: Never forget rule No.1. ***(Focus on the risks of an investment before investing any money.)***

To further show why it's important not to lose money, consider the following example on the difficulty of recovering from losses. If you start with $100 and lose 10%, you have $90 left. It requires a subsequent return of about 11% to breakeven, getting you back to your original $100 stake. But if you lose 50%, going from $100 to $50, you need a subsequent return of 100% to breakeven. In plain English, the bigger the hole you get into, the harder it is to get out of. Buffett knows this well and hence the reasons for his Rule No. 1 and Rule No. 2.

The Key to Selecting a Well-Diversified Portfolio: Correlation

There are a lot of approaches to selecting a portfolio. You can take a "shotgun" approach and randomly pick a bunch of different investments. That doesn't sound too smart. A lot of people choose to equal weight their portfolios at inception. For example, this may mean if you have $10,000 to invest, you might put $1,000 each into 10 different investments. Behavioral economists actually have a name for this approach, called the **1 over N (1/N) heuristic**. A heuristic is a rule of thumb that people use to solve a problem. So if you have 10 choices, you'd put 10%

in each option under the 1/N heuristic. If you had 20 choices, you'd put 5% in each choice. The 1/N heuristic isn't bad, but it doesn't look beneath the surface at what drives risk, at least according to one metric that we'll discuss next.

Correlation is a term that measures how two assets move—or don't move—together. Mathematically, it's a number that ranges between positive one and negative one. If two investments have a correlation of −1, when one investment goes up, the other investment *always* goes down. Similarly, if one investment goes down, the other investment *always* goes up. In a minute, we'll give you an example with two investments that shows if they have a correlation of −1, it is possible to construct a portfolio with *zero* risk.

If the correlation between two investments is +1, then one investment is essentially a carbon copy of the other. When one goes up, the other *always* goes up, and when one goes down, the other *always* goes down. As you might guess, this type of investment pair provides no meaningful amount of risk reduction. If the correlation between two investments is 0, it means there is no relationship between them. When one goes up, the other may go up, down, or remain unchanged. Two investments that have a correlation of 0 provide good risk reduction properties, but not as good as if it were −1. Let's illustrate this concept with an example.

A (Theoretical) Portfolio with No Risk

To illustrate the power of two investments with negative correlation, suppose there are only two companies in the entire stock market. We like the beach, so let's assume one company sells suntan lotion and the other company sells umbrellas. We know some people purchase umbrellas to shield themselves from the sun, but let's assume most buy them to keep themselves from getting wet on a rainy day.

Suppose on sunny days the suntan lotion company is making a killing. Let's say it's up 30% due to its huge swell of profits. But on rainy days, not too many people are coming to the beach, and the firm loses 10% due to the fixed costs of running the business (e.g., rent and salaries). But on rainy days, it's the umbrella company that's making a killing. Let's say it's making 30% to keep the numbers symmetric. On sunny days, let's also assume it loses 10% due to the costs of running the business and not too many people buying umbrellas, except for the people trying to shield themselves from the sun.

Okay, we're almost ready for the punchline. Let's assume the chance of rain or shine is the same, 50%. If you put all of your money in one company, either the suntan lotion company or the umbrella company, your wealth is entirely dependent on something you have *no* control over—the weather. You either make 30% or lose 10%. But if you put half your money in the suntan lotion company and half your money in the umbrella company, you are guaranteed a profit on the overall portfolio, rain or shine. Instead of rolling the dice on the weather, you make money when it is sunny with the suntan lotion company, which more than offsets the loss from the umbrella company. When it rains, the profits you make on the umbrella company more than offset the losses from the suntan lotion. So there we have it. A guaranteed profit rain or shine! In this fictional example, the correlation between the suntan lotion and umbrella company is negative one.

The art of selecting an optimal portfolio is to find investments that don't move in synch with each other (low correlation in mathematical terms). In practice, many investments have a positive correlation since they are all part of the same economic boat—the world economy. But intelligent diversification can still meaningfully reduce risk. Not all companies move in lockstep fashion, especially if they are from different industries and located in different countries. Berkshire itself is the combination of many companies that are unrelated, or what economists call a **conglomerate**. After all, car insurance has little to do with an electric utility, railroad, furniture store, or candy shop. As we know, these are just a handful of Berkshire's many businesses.

Selecting an Optimal Diversified Portfolio: The "Business School" Approach

We'll first cover what business schools teach as the optimal way to select a portfolio, since the purpose of this book is to improve your financial literacy. We'll cover later in the chapter two approaches that Buffett favors. The "business school" approach to selecting an optimal portfolio was developed by a young graduate student named Harry Markowitz, back in the 1950s. Since recent changes to his approach have been merely incremental in nature, it still falls under the umbrella of "Modern Portfolio Theory"—more than 60 years later.

Markowitz's approach relies heavily on the concept of correlation, which we just covered, since selecting investments that have low correlation among each other results in the creation of portfolios with relatively lower amounts of risk. He also realized that people made trade-offs between things when making decisions. For example, you might look cool in an expensive Ferrari, but you probably can't afford it. When purchasing a car, you balance what you want versus what you can afford. When selecting a portfolio, you have to balance its risk with the expected return. We use the term "expected return" since your actual return can only be determined at some point in the future, after you've selected the investments.

Although the past is a very rough guide to the future, in some instances, you can't rely on it. Otherwise, investors would simply pick the stocks that went up the most in the past (e.g., Apple, Amazon.com, Microsoft, and Berkshire). Future competition, new inventions, and the missteps of companies may result in their future returns looking a lot different from their past returns. Buffett has a humorous quote on the topic, citing the **Forbes 400**, an annual list of the richest people in America. He said, "If history books were the key to riches, the Forbes 400 would consist of librarians." It's a spin on the standard investments disclaimer, "Past performance is no guarantee of future results." Let's put Buffett's quote in as a Tip to cement the idea that the future performance of an investment might look a lot different than its past performance.

Buffett Tip 49:

If history books were the key to riches, the Forbes 400 would consist of librarians. ***(Past performance is no guarantee of future results.)***

Markowitz coined the term "**efficient portfolio**," which maximizes the expected return of your portfolio, given the risk you are willing to take. Since risk and return are two sides of the same coin, an efficient portfolio is also one that minimizes risk, given an expected return that you want to receive. If you map out all of the possible efficient portfolios for a given set of investments, it results in a curve (technically a parabola) called an **efficient frontier**. A picture of an efficient frontier is shown in Figure 8.1.

You can view the efficient frontier as the menu of good diversified portfolios. Investments that fall below the efficient frontier are inefficient and are dominated by the good ones. The inefficient ones have less return for the same amount of risk or more risk for the same amount of return. There are a lot of analogies that we can use to explain this

Figure 8.1 Selecting an Optimal Portfolio from the Efficient Frontier

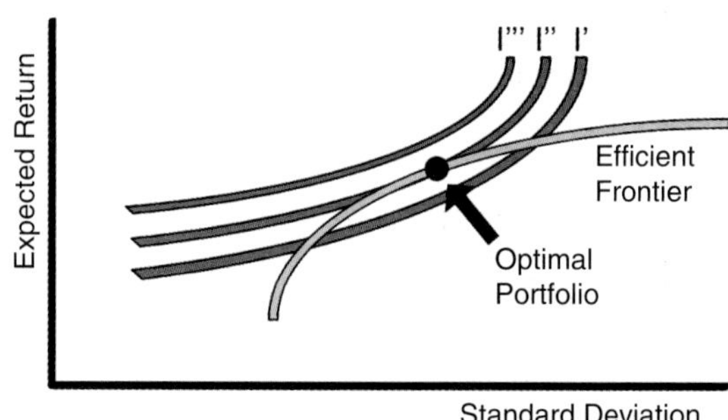

concept. Most people can relate to food. The efficient portfolios are similar to a menu of good food items at a Chinese buffet. (We could use any cuisine, but buffet sounds similar to Buffett, and we don't want you to spell Buffett's name incorrectly, so we expect this note to stick in your mind). The bad (or inefficient) food at the Chinese buffet either tastes poorly, isn't fresh, or isn't worthy of making it on the menu. So now we can get to the question next addressed by Markowitz. That is, "What is the optimal diversified portfolio for *me*?"

Sticking with our Chinese buffet analogy, even though you might like Chinese food, you probably won't eat everything on the menu. Similarly, Markowitz used a way to measure your willingness to trade off things, specifically, risk and return. The formal term for measuring this trade-off is with something economists call an **indifference curve**. In a portfolio selection context, it measures your willingness to trade off between two things, risk and return. You might be willing to take on a little more risk if you expected to get a little bit more return. Similarly, you might be willing to take a little bit lesser return if your portfolio had less risk. The optimal diversified portfolio matches the efficient frontier (the menu of good investment combinations) with your indifference curve (the items at the Chinese buffet that you like), which measures your willingness to trade off risk and return. The **optimal portfolio** is shown in **Figure 8.1** as the point of tangency between the two curves, the efficient frontier and your unique indifference curve.

If you find this approach compelling, there is some free software online that can help you select an optimal portfolio. One good website that helps with the portfolio selection problem using the Markowitz approach is:

https://www.portfoliovisualizer.com/optimize-portfolio.

Most investment firms also have software that can perform something similar for their clients.

Buffett's First Approach to Portfolio Selection: Index Funds

Buffett has two approaches to picking a portfolio. For most people, he suggests an index fund, such as the S&P 500, which consists of 500 large American stocks spread across a range of industries. We've mentioned index funds before and listed their benefits as a prior Tip. It's basically a "set it and forget it" buy-and-hold strategy of a basket of investments that charges minimal fees. We'll focus on stock indexes here since it may be the main holding for a young person, but there are index funds on bonds, real estate, and other assets. If a stock index portfolio has too much risk for you, mixing it with other index funds should lower the overall risk of the portfolio over time.

Besides the low expenses and minimal effort involved, stock index funds have the advantage of owning some of the largest and most successful firms in America, such as Apple, Alphabet (Google), Exxon Mobil, Starbucks, Microsoft, Berkshire Hathaway, Johnson & Johnson, and many others. These large firms are less likely to go bankrupt and many also pay a dividend. The S&P 500 is a value- or market capitalization–weighted index, which means the larger, more valuable stocks, such as Microsoft, have a greater effect on the index's returns than the smaller ones.

Since no one can time when to get in and out of the market with any high degree of certainty, Buffett further advises investors to buy index funds periodically over time. This approach is known as **dollar cost averaging**. It guarantees that you won't buy near the market high, or the market low. It also relates to how most people typically invest, taking money out of their paychecks and putting it into their retirement plans every couple of weeks or month.

Buffett's Second Approach to Portfolio Selection: Expert Mode

Buffett's second recommended approach is for someone who is a "know something" (as opposed to know nothing) investor. Knowing *something* is a minimal hurdle, so we'll refer to someone picking their own investments as a person operating in "expert mode," at least within their circle of competence. By that expression, we mean someone willing to put the time and effort into understanding what a firm does and what it is worth, before investing. This approach also requires following the firm closely to make sure the reasons why you purchased the stock are still valid. For example, in **Chapter 6** we talked about companies having a moat that helps them fend off competition. If the moat of a firm is eroding, it might be time to sell. Buffett typically puts a large percentage of his assets in a relatively small group of stocks. Folks on Wall Street often call this a **high-conviction** or **best-ideas** approach, which involves putting the bulk of your assets in a relatively small number of investments. It results in highly concentrated portfolios as opposed to a broadly diversified index fund.

For example, Buffett once put roughly 40% of his investors' assets in a single stock, American Express, when the firm ran into problems back in the 1960s. Forty percent is a huge amount to put in any investment, so hopefully you can see how we view Buffett's high-conviction approach to creating a portfolio as falling under the "expert mode." A few bad decisions in a highly concentrated portfolio could put yourself in a big hole that is hard to recover from.

Buffett has always operated this way and not just during his young, gunslinger days. Large investment managers (i.e., those managing more than $100 million) have to file quarterly reports with the SEC, called **Form 13-F**, that detail some of their holdings. There are various websites that track this data. Our favorite site that tracks 13-F data is WhaleWisdom.com. A **whale** in Wall Street jargon refers to a large investor. For example, at the end of 2019 Berkshire Hathaway had more than 67% of its investments in only five stocks: Apple (29.7%), Bank of America (13.5%), Coca-Cola (9.2%), American Express (7.8%), and Wells Fargo (7.2%). These firms are generally regarded as high-quality companies that pay a dividend and have a long operating history. These attributes are some of the ways Buffett aims to control risk, as well as his detailed understanding of each company that he invests in. Notice that in his top holdings there are no recent IPOs, companies that are losing money, that or don't have a long-term history. Buffett thinks six stocks are enough for someone operating a portfolio in "expert" mode.

In a talk Buffett gave to students at the University of Florida, he said, "If you can identify six wonderful businesses, that is all the diversification you need. And you will make a lot of money. And I can guarantee that going into a seventh one instead of putting more money into your first one is gotta be a terrible mistake. Very few people have gotten rich on their seventh best idea. But a lot of people have gotten rich with their best idea. So, I would say for anyone working with normal capital who really knows the businesses they have gone into, six is plenty." Let's turn the essence of that quote into a Tip.

Buffett Tip 50:

Six wonderful businesses is all the diversification that you need. Very few people have gotten rich on their seventh-best idea. But a lot of people have gotten rich with their best idea.

In his 1993 Letter to Berkshire Shareholders, Buffett expanded on his thoughts on diversification. He said, "We believe that a policy of portfolio concentration may well *decrease* risk if it raises, as it should, both the intensity with which an investor thinks about a business and the comfort level he must feel with its economic characteristics before buying into it." Let's also summarize that quote with a Tip.

Buffett Tip 51:

Portfolio concentration may *decrease* risk if it raises both the intensity of your effort and comfort level with the companies you own.

A Compromise Solution to Portfolio Selection

If you don't have the interest, time, or expertise to follow the Buffett "expert" mode approach to selecting a portfolio, a compromise might be to construct your own diversified "mini index." One approach that we like is to select the biggest firm, by market capitalization, in each industry. We call it the "terminator portfolio" in homage to a famous cyborg character Arnold Schwarzenegger played a couple of decades ago. These firms, like the Schwarzenegger character, tend to dominate the competition. For example, the portfolio might consist of the largest oil firm in the US, ExxonMobil, the largest consumer firm, Apple, the largest restaurant, McDonald's, the largest bank, J.P. Morgan, and so forth. This "mini index" portfolio would likely return something similar to the S&P 500 since it would account for roughly 80% of the market capitalization weight of the S&P 500. You might also learn something by watching these leading firms closely (i.e., you automatically get an annual report of each stock owned) and may eventually transition into an "expert mode."

One way to get practice with investing, even if you have no money, is to use a free investment simulator. A simulator allows you to manage a "paper portfolio" of any amount (e.g., $1 million in fictional money) and track the results. There are several investment simulators out there. Our favorite free one can be found at Investopedia.com. Click for the "Simulator" link and proceed from there. You could even set up multiple paper portfolios corresponding to different investment strategies until you find your favorite approach.

How Many Stocks Make a Diversified Portfolio?

Buffett thinks diversification "makes little sense if you know what you are doing." However, most people aren't comfortable with the notion of a highly concentrated portfolio. This raises the question of "What is adequate diversification?" The answer depends on what is in your portfolio.

For example, a single S&P 500 index fund may be adequate diversification for someone's stock holdings since this single investment holds the equivalent of 500 stocks. So let's tackle the question of what might be adequate diversification for someone picking their own individual stocks and are not quite ready to go into the Buffett expert mode of a highly concentrated portfolio. Fortunately, there have been many studies on the topic. In **Chapter 2** we mentioned that one way of measuring risk is by looking at the standard deviation of an asset's returns.

If you have a portfolio with only one stock, decades of academic research find it has a ton of risk, or a standard deviation of roughly 30% in statistical terms. But the good news is that risk is reduced rapidly as you keep adding securities to your portfolio. By the time you have 10 stocks in the portfolio, studies find the risk is cut by about 40%. Once you get to about 30 securities your risk is cut by almost half. Once you get past 100 stocks, there is not much more risk reduction to be had. Plus 100 stocks is a lot to follow. So to answer the question we posed at the top of this section, to have a well-diversified portfolio, 30 is a good round number of how many stocks you need. If you're more adventurous, even 15 to 20 might be enough.

However, we emphasize that the 30 stocks should be spread across a number of different industries (at least 15). Owning 30 tech stocks (or others in the same industry) is not likely to provide much additional risk reduction since the correlation among the securities will probably be high.

The "Business School" Approach to Risk

Buffett takes issue with how business schools usually teach the subject of risk. To better understand Buffett's critique and to enhance your financial literacy, we'll cover the essence of the major theory on risk and return taught in most business schools. It's called the **Capital Asset Pricing Model (CAPM)**, and it's an extension of Markowitz's work. To get there, let's start with a picture that we've labeled as **Figure 8.2.**

The more stocks you add to the portfolio, the more risk is reduced. Here we are still using standard deviation of the stock's returns (i.e., its volatility) as the measure of risk. As you keep adding more and more stocks to the portfolio, the diversifiable—or company-specific—risk is reduced. Notice that even if you own all the stocks in the market (e.g., an index fund with thousands of stocks), you still can't get rid of the market risk. One easy way to see this is that the market goes up or down on a daily basis. If market risk could be completely diversified away, the market would never go down. But we know that it does, and sometimes by huge amounts.

Academics call market risk by the Greek alphabet letter **beta**. It's also known as systematic risk, since it's tied to the economic system. Here's the insight that academics believe is important. The only risk worth paying for (i.e., that should give you a meaningful return) is the risk

Figure 8.2 Graph of the "Business School" Approach to Risk

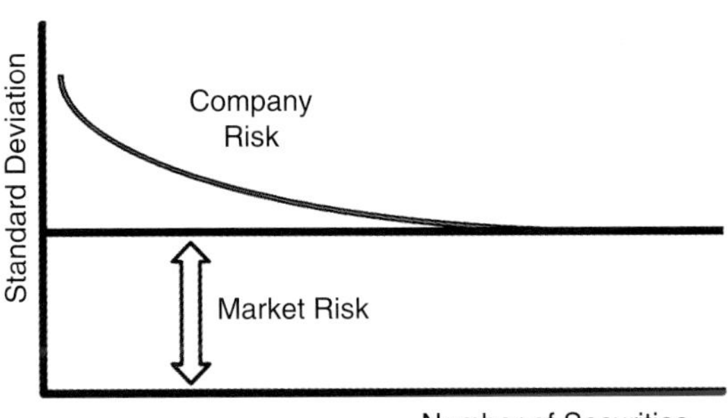

that can't be diversified away, beta. According to the theory, company-specific risk should then be irrelevant when buying a stock, since if you diversify enough, it will disappear.

The CAPM says that the expected return on any stock is equal to the risk-free rate of interest plus the product of stock's beta and another item we'll cover in a second. In practice, the risk-free rate of interest is a government bond with a maturity equal to your time horizon (e.g., one year). Any investment worth its salt should beat the risk-free rate of interest, on average; otherwise, no one would invest in it. We've just covered beta, a measure of market risk. Not all stocks have the same beta. The beta for the market as a whole is 1. Some stocks have a beta less than 1. These tend to be large, well-established firms, or companies that operate in less volatile industries, including food, beverages, utilities, and large pharmaceutical firms. But some firms have a beta greater than 1. These often include small firms and firms in more volatile industries, such as technology, biotechnology, banks, autos, and some retail stocks.

Getting back to the CAPM, we have the risk-free rate of interest, beta, and one more factor. This last factor is tied to market psychology. It relates to how much risk investors are willing to take in the market as a whole. It's called the **market risk premium** and is the difference between the expected return on the stock market and the risk-free rate of interest. To make this concept less abstract, the US stock market historically returns about 10% per year, and the risk-free rate of interest, as represented by a Treasury bill, historically returns about 3% a year, even though today it's close to 0%. This analysis would give a historical market risk premium of about 7% a year. But market psychology is fickle, as we discussed with our Mr. Market and pendulum analogies in our chapter on stocks. Sometimes people are fearful, and the market risk premium might spike to around 10% or more. Other times people are greedy or complacent and the number shrinks to 2% or 3%. In this case, people don't require much more extra return to invest in stocks. The market risk premium number is the same for all stocks in the market and is not tied to its beta.

Putting it all together, the CAPM says the expected return for any stock is equal to the risk-free rate of interest plus the stock's beta, times the market risk premium. It results in a straight-line relationship between expected risk and return as shown in **Figure 8.3**. In case you're mathematically inclined, we put the full CAPM equation in an endnote.

Summing this section up, in business school they teach that beta (market risk) is the main way of measuring risk. Sometimes they combine

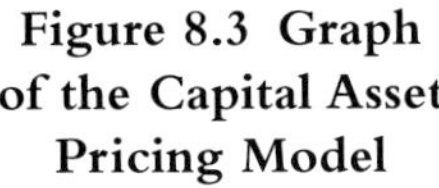

Figure 8.3 Graph of the Capital Asset Pricing Model

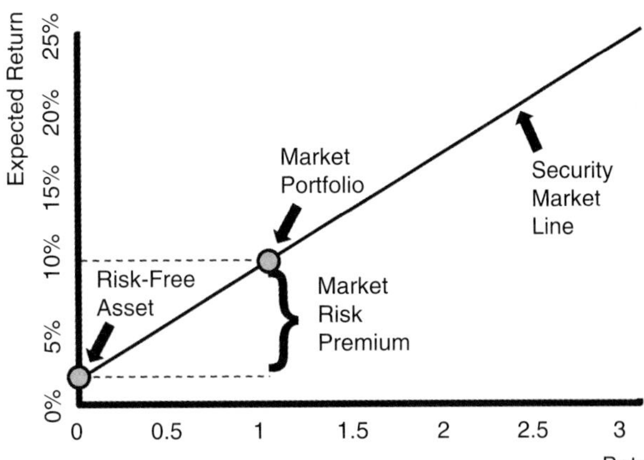

it with things that we discussed in **Chapter** 5, such as size (i.e., large cap vs. small cap), style (i.e., growth vs. value), as well as the recent trend in price, known as **momentum**.

Buffett's Critique of the Business School Approach to Risk

There's a good reason why we discussed beta and the CAPM model, even though you may have found it about as dull as dirt. Buffett has an issue with how they define and teach risk in business schools. We touched upon some of these issues but will now add more detail to his critique. And because he's Buffett, we think he's right. First, back in **Chapter** 2 we noted Buffett's definition of risk—the possibility of loss or injury. We also noted that he said, over the long run, bonds and cash are riskier than stocks since they often fail to keep up with inflation, especially on an after-tax basis.

But he has more to say on the topic of risk, and we needed to cover specific measures of risk such as standard deviation and beta in more depth in order to address his critique further. Having a concentrated portfolio, and its usual corresponding high levels of standard deviation, doesn't bother Buffett since he thinks standard deviation is a flawed measure of risk. He doesn't give it a second thought.

He thinks beta is flawed too. He couldn't care less about it either. In his 1993 Letter to Berkshire Shareholders, he wrote, "Employing data bases and statistical skills, these academics compute with precision the 'beta' of a stock—its relative volatility in the past—and then build arcane investment and capital-allocation theories around this calculation. In their hunger for a single statistic to measure risk, however, they forget a fundamental principle: It is better to be approximately right than precisely wrong."

This last sentence is a similar comment to our prior tip on "beware of geeks bearing formulas," but since it's a direct attack on what is taught in business schools, we'll put the essence of his critique as a separate Tip.

Buffett Tip 52:

Beta is not risk. It is better to be approximately right than precisely wrong.

Buffett's Approach to Risk

Buffett's approach to risk is to focus on what the company does and how it may be affected by its competition, or what we called the strength of its moat. He thinks it's crazy to say a firm with the same beta as Coca-Cola or Gillette (now owned by Procter and Gamble, P&G) has the same risk as some "fly by night firm" that is new or has shaky financials. This firm, let's called it Beta Inc., likely doesn't have the history and moat of Coke or P&G and therefore shouldn't have the same risk. In his 1993 Letter to Berkshire Shareholders he wrote:

> The competitive strengths of a Coke or Gillette are obvious to even the casual observer of business. Yet the beta of their stocks is similar to that of a great many run-of-the-mill companies who possess little or no competitive advantage. Should we conclude from this similarity that the competitive strength of Coke and Gillette gains them nothing when business risk is being measured? Or should we conclude that the risk in owning a piece of a company—its stock—is somehow divorced from the long-term risk inherent in its business operations? We believe neither conclusion makes sense and that equating beta with investment risk also makes no sense.

He goes on to say, "In assessing risk, a beta purist will disdain examining what a company produces, what its competitors are doing, or how much borrowed money the business employs. He may even prefer not to know the company's name. What he treasures is the price history of its stock. In contrast, we'll happily forgo knowing the price history and instead will seek whatever information will further our understanding of the company's business."

Let's summarize these views on risk with another Tip.

Buffett Tip 53:

The risk of a firm is related to what a company produces, what its competitors are doing, and how much money a company has borrowed.

When you want to buy something and it drops in price, you probably think you're getting a good deal. The risk that you overpaid for the product or service you purchased is reduced. Buffett says the same concept should apply to investing. In his 1993 Letter to Berkshire Shareholders, Buffett said, "For example, under beta-based theory, a stock that has dropped very sharply compared to the market—as had *The Washington Post* when we bought it in 1973—becomes 'riskier' at the lower price than it was at the higher price. Would that description have then made any sense to someone who was offered the entire company at a vastly reduced price? In fact, the true investor *welcomes* volatility."

That's great advice from the Oracle of Omaha, even though it's hard for many people to follow. Why? When a stock you own falls in price, it decreases your net worth, leaving you poorer. This causes many investors huge anxiety and has them reaching for some antacids. Let's put the last line in Buffett's quote in as a Tip.

Buffett Tip 54:

The true investor *welcomes* volatility.

Buffett on Gold

Gold is often considered a safe-haven asset. That is, it typically goes up when stocks fall sharply. It often has a negative correlation to stocks, so academics usually like it for its diversification properties. So what does Buffett have to say about gold? Like with Bitcoin, Buffett is not a fan. Buffett doesn't believe gold is a productive asset. By that, we mean the following: A farm produces food. Real estate produces rent or serves as a home. Bonds pay interest, in addition to the principal. Stocks represent ownership in a business and often pay dividends. But gold? It looks nice and can be used for jewelry, but Buffett doesn't think it has much value. In his 2011 Letter to shareholders he wrote:

> Today the world's gold stock is about 170,000 metric tons. If all of this gold were melded together, it would form a cube of about 68 feet per side. (Picture it fitting comfortably within a baseball infield.) At $1,750 per ounce—gold's price as I write this—its value would be $9.6 trillion. Call this cube pile A.
>
> Let's now create a pile B costing an equal amount. For that, we could buy all US cropland (400 million acres with output of about $200 billion annually), plus 16 Exxon Mobils (the world's most profitable company, one earning more than $40 billion annually). After these purchases, we would have about $1 trillion left over for walking-around money (no sense feeling strapped after this buying binge). Can you imagine an investor with $9.6 trillion selecting pile A over pile B?
>
> A century from now the 400 million acres of farmland will have produced staggering amounts of corn, wheat, cotton, and other crops—and will continue to produce that valuable bounty, whatever the currency may be. Exxon Mobil will probably have delivered trillions of dollars in dividends to its owners and will also hold assets worth many more trillions (and, remember, you get 16 Exxons). The 170,000 tons of gold will be unchanged in size and still incapable of producing anything. You can fondle the cube, but it will not respond.

It's a long quote, but one worth remembering the next time some doomsayer tells you to put a big chunk of your money in gold. Let's summarize his views on gold with a Tip.

Buffett Tip 55:

Gold is a nonproductive asset. So, despite its diversification properties, gold shouldn't represent a meaningful part of your portfolio.

Summarizing Buffett's Views on Risk

Risk isn't an easy topic to grasp on first sitting, but it's one of the most important subjects for your financial and personal well-being. To summarize some of Buffett's views, risk is having an investment that can't outperform inflation on an after-tax basis. It's investing in businesses that you don't understand, that have poor management, have too much debt, have no competitive advantage, or are overvalued.

He laid it out more formally in his 1993 Letter to Berkshire Shareholders. It's sort of a lengthy quote, but hang on a bit longer since you've finally reached the end of this chapter. Plus, it's not an equation like you might find in a textbook on investments. According to Buffett, risk is determined by:

1. The certainty with which the long-term economic characteristics of the business can be evaluated;
2. The certainty with which management can be evaluated, both as to its ability to realize the full potential of the business and to wisely employ its cash flows;
3. The certainty with which management can be counted on to channel the rewards from the business to the shareholders rather than to itself;
4. The purchase price of the business;
5. The levels of taxation and inflation that will be experienced and that will determine the degree by which an investor's purchasing-power return is reduced from his gross return.

Endnote on CAPM

The main CAPM equation (often called the **Security Market Line**) is listed below, using IBM as an example.

$$E\left(R_{IBM}\right) = R_f + \beta_{IBM} \times \left[E\left(R_{mkt}\right) - R_f\right]$$

It says the expected return on IBM is equal to the risk-free rate of interest plus the product of the beta for IBM and the market risk premium. The risk-free rate of interest and the market risk premium, theoretically, are the same for all firms, so differences in expected return for different assets essentially boil down to differences in beta, according to CAPM.

Buffett's Tips from Chapter 8

Buffett Tip 48: Rule No.1: Never lose money. Rule No. 2: Never forget rule No.1. *(Focus on the risks of any investment before investing any money.)*
Buffett Tip 49: If history books were the key to riches, the Forbes 400 would consist of librarians. *(Past performance is no guarantee of future results.)*
Buffett Tip 50: Six wonderful businesses is all the diversification that you need. Very few people have gotten rich on their seventh-best idea. But a lot of people have gotten rich with their best idea.
Buffett Tip 51: Portfolio concentration may *decrease* risk if it raises both the intensity of your effort and comfort level with the companies you own.
Buffett Tip 52: Beta is not risk. It is better to be approximately right than precisely wrong.
Buffett Tip 53: The risk of a firm is related to what a company produces, what its competitors are doing, and how much money a company has borrowed.
Buffett Tip 54: The true investor *welcomes* volatility.
Buffett Tip 55: Gold is a nonproductive asset. So, despite its diversification properties, gold shouldn't represent a meaningful part of your portfolio.

References

Bodie, Zvi, Alex Kane, and Alan J. Marcus. *Investments,* 10th edition. New York: McGraw-Hill *Education*, 2013.

Buffett, Warren. "Letter to Shareholders of Berkshire Hathaway Inc." Berkshire Hathaway, Inc., 1993. https://www.berkshirehathaway.com/letters/1993.html.

Buffett, Warren. "Letter to Shareholders of Berkshire Hathaway Inc." Berkshire Hathaway, Inc., 2011. https://www.berkshirehathaway.com/letters/2011.html.

Buffett, Warren. "Warren Buffett: Why Stocks Beat Gold and Bonds." *Fortune*, February 9, 2012. https://fortune.com/2012/02/09/warren-buffett-why-stocks-beat-gold-and-bonds/.

Investment Master Class. "Diversification or Concentration? Quotes from Some of the Best Investors." *ValueWalk*, January 15, 2017. https://www.valuewalk.com/2017/01/diversification-concentration-quotes-best-investors/.

Kroll, Luisa, and Kerry A Dolan, eds. "The Forbes 400 2019." *Forbes*, October 2, 2019. https://www.forbes.com/forbes-400/.

LeylandPAM. "Warren Buffett speaks with Florida University." YouTube Video, 1:27:35, July 2, 2013, https://www.youtube.com/watch?v=2MHIcabnjrA.

Loiacono, Stephanie. "Rules That Warren Buffett Lives By." *Yahoo! Finance*, February 23, 2010. https://web.archive.org/web/20111229015815/http://finance.yahoo.com/news/pf_article_108903.html.

Markowitz, Harry. "Portfolio Selection." *Journal of Finance* 7, no. 1 (1952): 77–91. https://doi.org/10.2307/2975974.

Markowitz, Harry. *Portfolio Selection: Efficient Diversification of Investments*. New York: Wiley, 1970.

Saft, James. "Buffett Champions Conglomerates, Don't Believe Him," March 4, 2015. http://blogs.reuters.com/james-saft/2015/03/04/buffett-champions-conglomerates-dont-believe-him/.

Udland, Myles. "Warren Buffett Defends Berkshire's Conglomerate Structure—and Fires a Huge Shot at Private Equity." *Business Insider*, February 28, 2015. http://www.businessinsider.com/warren-buffett-on-conglomerates-and-private-equity-2015-2.

Whitby, Jason. "The Illusion of Diversification: The Myth of the 30 Stock Portfolio." *Investopedia*, June 25, 2019. http://www.investopedia.com/articles/stocks/11/illusion-of-diversification.asp.

9

Business 101: Companies You Should Know

"My response time to the next glaringly attractive idea will be slashed to well under 50 years."

- Warren Buffett, 1989 Letter to Berkshire Hathaway Shareholders

Introduction

Imagine if you met someone who didn't know who LeBron James was. Or Taylor Swift, Jay Z, Tom Brady, Beyoncé, Katy Perry, Michael Jordan, Wayne Gretzky, Lady Gaga, Tiger Woods, Drake, or your superstar of choice. You'd probably say or think, "Are you from Mars? Have you been living under a rock?" Well, to be financially literate, you should know many of the key firms and businesspeople in the world economy today. They're the people and firms that help shape the world we live in. That's what this chapter and the next one are all about. In this chapter, we'll focus on the stocks of many of the leading firms in the world. In the next chapter, we'll focus on some of the leading businesspeople. So let's get started!

The Dow Jones Industrial Average: The Oldest Diversified US Stock Market Index

When thinking about some of the most important companies in the world, we think a good place to start is by checking out blue-chip firms. And when thinking about blue-chip firms, the first group that comes to mind for most financial professionals in the Dow Jones Industrial Average, or the Dow. The Dow is the oldest diversified stock market index in the US, if not the world.

We previously defined a stock market index as a basket or portfolio of stocks. There is often some sort of theme to the index. Dow Jones & Company, now owned by News Corp, is the publisher of *The Wall Street Journal*, the most widely read business periodical in the US, if not the world. Anyway, there was a person, Charles Dow, who co-founded this now internationally famous newspaper back in 1889.

People following or investing in the stock market typically have a couple of important questions. First, they may ask, "How did the stock market do today?" The time period—today, this week, month, year—can be any horizon, but to answer this question, you need a stock market index. Answering this question is one of the main reasons why Charles Dow created the Dow for his newspaper back in 1896.

A second question—not fully answered by the Dow or any market index—is, "How is *my* investment portfolio doing?" To answer this question rigorously, you should compute the performance of your portfolio and compare it to the performance of the market, assuming the two had similar risk. Here, we're talking about relative performance, like with a grading curve on an exam. If your teacher gave you a really tough exam and the average was 70, you might be pleased if you scored an 80. In contrast, if the average was 90 and you scored an 80, you might be disappointed. If you don't care about your performance relative to others, then good for you! Buffett would say you are following your Inner Scorecard (Tip 8), following your own belief system without paying attention to the thoughts of others.

Let's drill down on the concept of performance a bit, in the context of stocks. If your portfolio is up 15% and the market is up 10%, that'd be fantastic. The difference between your portfolio's returns and those of the market is called **alpha**, assuming the portfolios had similar risk.

If they didn't have similar risk, it's not an "apples to apples" comparison, and we'd have to make some adjustments, which we aren't going to get into here. If your portfolio is up 15% and the market is up 20% then perhaps you didn't do so well, your alpha is –5% in this case.

How the Dow Is Calculated

The calculation is pretty simple on the surface. You can think about adding up the prices of the 30 stocks in the Dow and then just dividing by 30. Piece of cake! It's almost that simple. Originally, there were only 12 stocks in the index, but the number increased to the familiar 30 in 1928. So the increase from 12 to 30 stocks is one adjustment that needed to be made. There are two other adjustments that get us to the present-day Dow levels.

Occasionally, stocks get removed from the index. Why? Rarely, another firm will buy them. Less rarely, but still uncommon, the folks at Dow Jones who run the index kick some firms out and replace them with new firms. They usually have shrunk in size or are no longer considered blue chip. There have been less than 60 changes in the Dow since it began back in 1896. That's not a ton of changes (less than one every two years), but it still required an adjustment. For example, there were once stocks in the Dow that went by the name of American Sugar Company, U.S. Leather Company, and Laclede Gas Company. The most recent changes occurred on August 31, 2020, when Amgen replaced Pfizer, Honeywell replaced Raytheon Technologies, and salesforce.com replaced Exxon Mobil.

Buffett has written about once-great companies that have faltered. In his 2014 Letter to Berkshire Shareholders, he wrote,

> My successor will need one other particular strength: the ability to fight off the ABCs of business decay, which are arrogance, bureaucracy and complacency. When these corporate cancers metastasize, even the strongest of companies can falter. The examples available to prove the point are legion, but to maintain friendships I will exhume only cases from the distant past. In their glory days, General Motors, IBM, Sears Roebuck and U.S. Steel sat atop huge industries. Their strengths seemed unassailable. But the destructive behavior I deplored above eventually led each of them to fall to depths that their CEOs and directors had not long before thought impossible. Their one-time financial strength and their historical earning power proved no defense.

Let's summarize the quote about companies gradually losing their power with a Tip.

Buffett Tip 56:

Avoid companies that are susceptible to the ABCs of business decay: arrogance, bureaucracy, and complacency.

The third reason for an adjustment to how the Dow is computed is something called a **stock split.** We'll define it in more detail in the next section, but for now you can think of it as changing a $10 bill for two $5 bills. It's more or less an accounting trick that has no real economic value. We know you're dying of suspense, wondering why firms might do this. The answer will be revealed in the next section. The key thing for now is the price of stock gets lowered *and* the number of shares outstanding increase, even though there has been no real effect on the company.

It's pretty easy to see why an adjustment is needed by looking at some basic numbers. Today, the Dow is trading at levels greater than 27,000. And, other than Berkshire Hathaway—which is not currently a member of the Dow—there is no company in the US with a stock price greater than $27,000. So how can adding up the prices of the 30 stocks in the Dow and dividing by 30 result in a number like 27,000? Because of the 3 reasons we mentioned, but mostly because of stock splits.

The Dow is a **price-weighted index**. This means stocks with a high price, such as Visa in recent years, count for a greater weight in the index than a firm with a lower price, such as Coca-Cola. To give a school analogy, a test usually counts for more than a quiz when determining your overall grade for a class. In this case, the high-priced stock (Visa) is like your test grade, while the low-priced stock (Coca-Cola) is like your quiz grade.

A more common type of index is a **value-weighted** or **market cap–weighted index**. The S&P 500 is probably the most common value-weighted index. Here the weight of the stock in the index calculation isn't determined by its price per share but rather the price per share times the number of shares outstanding, the definition of market cap. For example, Microsoft was recently valued at more than $1.6 trillion. It's weight in a value-weighted index, such as the S&P 500, would count more than 1000 times than a firm with a market cap of only $1.6 billion. Sticking to our grade analogy, Microsoft would be the equivalent of a huge final exam, and the $1.6 billion stock would be the equivalent of a trivial homework assignment.

One last term for this section. A **point** means a dollar change, or a change in whatever unit of currency you are using. If a stock went up 2 points, in the US it means 2 dollars. In Germany, it would mean 2 euros. In Great Britain, 2 pounds. Of course, it could go down points as well. The term also applies to a market index such as the Dow or S&P 500 as well.

A move of, let's say, 5 points may or may not be meaningful. If Berkshire (Class A) stock goes down 5 points, it's barely a rounding error. However, if it's a stock such as Coca-Cola, currently trading in the $50 a share range, it would be a big move. So one point to remember is that it's the *percentage change* in the price of a stock, portfolio, or index that counts since it most closely relates to how your wealth is changing.

An Explanation of Stock Splits

As we mentioned a minute ago, a stock split is an accounting trick or gimmick that essentially changes a $10 bill into two $5 bills. Obviously, the amount of money you have, $10 in this case, is unchanged. That's why it's simply accounting sleight of hand. Let's do a similar calculation with a stock. Suppose you own 100 shares of stock that is worth $50 a share. Multiplying 100 shares times $50 equals a value of $5,000.

With a stock split, the company specifies the ratio of the split, with the most common being 2 for 1. So, in our example, after a 2-for-1 split, you would have 200 shares of stock (2 times 100), but the stock price would be cut in half, ($50 divided by 2), from $50 a share to $25 a share. The dollar value of your position, $25 a share times 200 shares, is still $5,000.

Why go through all of this trouble if the value of your shares is still the same? Well, it's mainly due to investor psychology. If you walk up to the typical investor on the street and ask them, "Would you rather have 100 shares of stock or 200 shares?" nearly everyone will say 200 shares and not bother to ask about the effect on the share price. On the surface, you sound richer owning more shares, but we know if the price of the stock is cut in half after a 2-for-1 split, you really aren't richer. Some naïve people also think that since the price of the stock is now $25 and yesterday it was $50, it's cheaper and a better deal. That line of thinking is flawed since is the intrinsic value of the firm (i.e., the present value of its future cash flows) or a multiple of current earnings that counts, not the actual price.

In fact, we can make a case that Berkshire Hathaway (class A shares) are cheap at more than $300,000 a share, while many firms trading at $10 a share or less are expensive. How? Berkshire may be trading at a low price compared to the present value of its future cash flows or a multiple of its current earnings, while the $10 stock may be selling at a high valuation, or have little to no prospects for earnings.

Besides preying on investor psychology, why do many firms split their stock? A phrase you see used in press releases by firms splitting their stock is "increased market liquidity." We've discussed this concept several times. As a refresher, a liquid asset is one that may be sold quickly and at fair market value. So the company may believe that by splitting its stock, the lower share price will make it accessible to more investors and that may result in more trading and lower transaction costs. This may have been true many years ago when it was required that investors had to buy a **round lot** of shares. A round lot means 100 shares or more. Transactions less than 100 shares were often sent to the **odd lot desk**, where trading of orders less than 100 shares took place. Today, it is not necessary to purchase a round lot in order to have lower transaction costs. Most brokerage firms will charge you a flat fee, say $10, for any buy or sell transaction up to 1,000 shares. In fact, many brokerage firms, such as Schwab, Fidelity, and Robinhood, have gone to a $0 commission structure, making the distinction even of less relevance today. Furthermore, some brokerage firms have the capability of allowing their clients to own a fraction of one share.

We don't want to go off on too much of a tangent, but there is also something called a **reverse split**, where the number of shares you own are reduced but the price per share goes up. For example, if you owned 1000 shares of a stock trading at $1 a share, after a 1-for-10 reverse split, you would own 100 shares of a stock now trading at $10 a share. The total value, price times number of shares, is still $1,000. Why would firms do this? Most exchanges require the stock to be at least $1 a share to remain listed on the exchange. Although this is still an accounting gimmick, stocks usually go down after a reverse split since it provides a signal that the company is in somewhat dire straits. Companies that no longer trade on the exchange are the equivalent of bad kids being kicked out of school, not a good idea under almost all circumstances.

Different Share Classes and Buffett on Stock Splits

Buffett has weighed in on stock splits, and as you might guess given Berkshire's stock price, he is not a fan of them. In Berkshire's 1983 Shareholder Letter, he wrote, "Were we to split the stock or take other actions focusing on stock price rather than business value, we would attract an entering class of buyers inferior to the exiting class of sellers...People who buy for non-value reasons are likely to sell for non-value reasons. Their presence in the picture will accentuate erratic price swings unrelated to underlying business developments." Since a stock split is basically an accounting trick, there is no fundamental value to it. Let's summarize his quote with a Tip.

Buffett Tip 57:

People who buy for non-value reasons are likely to sell for non-value reasons. They tend to increase the volatility of prices.

As Berkshire's shares rose dramatically in price without splitting, some people couldn't afford even a single share. Several stock promoters sprang up that would sell investors a fraction of a Berkshire share, while earning the promoter a fat sales fee or commission. Buffett wasn't a fan of this structure so he decided to create Class B shares of Berkshire Hathaway to make them more accessible to smaller investors. You may be thinking, "What are Class B shares and why would a firm have them?" We're glad you asked.

Most companies have only one share class. One share of a stock for these firm entitles its holder to have one vote on company matters sent for voting to their shareholders. Shareholders of a firm often vote on matters related to who should be appointed to the board of directors that runs a firm, and they select the accounting firm that audits a firm's financial statements, as well as many other items. A small percentage of firms have two share classes, with the main difference between the two share classes being the right to vote on company matters. Firms such as Alphabet/Google and Under Armour have two share classes. Having two share classes provides the founders, or their heirs, a way to maintain control of a firm even if their ownership share falls below a 50 percent majority.

In Buffett's case, he didn't create Class B shares of Berkshire to maintain control of the firm. He and his close friends own the majority of Berkshire shares. Rather, he did it to foil the plans of the promoters who were earning large fees at the expense of the small investor. Thus, in 1996, he created Class B shares of Berkshire Hathaway, which currently sell for 1/1,500 the price of Class A shares. Other than the price and voting rights, everything else is the same for Class B shareholders. They are still entitled to share in the same businesses that Class A owns and the related profits. If Berkshire paid dividends, Class A and Class B would get the same share of dividends on a percentage basis.

One advantage of owning at least a single Class B share of Berkshire is that you will get invited to the annual Berkshire Hathaway shareholder meeting, known in the financial press as "Woodstock for capitalists." Tens of thousands of people attend in person each year, and millions more view the proceedings online, streamed by Yahoo! The meeting was moved to an all-virtual meeting for 2020 in the wake of the COVID-19 pandemic. Woodstock may have occurred well before your time, but it was an epic music and art festival back in the summer of 1969 that featured a bunch of future "hall of fame"-type bands including Jimi Hendrix, The Who, Santana, Jefferson Airplane (later Starship), Crosby, Stills, Nash & Young, Sly and the Family Stone, and the Grateful Dead. The other advantage to owning shares in Berkshire Hathaway, of course, is owning a piece of a fantastic business, managed by Buffett and his colleagues.

Current Stocks in the Dow Jones Industrial Average

And now on to the main event, a brief discussion of the current 30 stocks in the Dow, followed by another brief discussion of some other global blue-chip stocks. The past and current selectors of stocks in the Dow want to get a mix of companies, just like there's a diverse range of companies in the economy. We'll organize the companies by **sector**. The stock market is made up of individual stocks, which roll up or combine into an **industry**. The industries roll up into sectors. The sectors then roll up to the aggregate or overall market. For example, technology is a market sector that is comprised of industries including computer software, computer hardware, and computer services. In this section, we'll cover the sectors of the Dow, but you should be aware that the S&P 500 has some slightly different categorizations that we won't cover here.

Materials Stocks in the Dow

The sector materials refers to stocks that are involved in commodities, such as oil, natural gas, crops, and chemicals.

Chevron (NYSE: CVX)

Chevron, formerly Chevron Texaco, is one the largest energy firms in the world. There are three main parts to the oil business. The upstream segment finds and drills for oil and gas. The midstream segment refines or cleans and transports the (dirty) crude oil pulled from the ground or sea. The midstream segment mainly consists of oil refineries and pipelines. The downstream segment includes selling oil and gas products at the retail or consumer level. For example, Costco sells gasoline at some of its stores and is part of the downstream segment but doesn't have any businesses in the upstream or midstream segments. A firm that is active in all three segments, such as Chevron, is called fully integrated. It might surprise you to learn that that many of the products that we use are (at least partially) made from oil, including plastics, candles, and ChapStick lip balm.

Dow Chemical (NYSE: DOW)

Dow Chemical is, as its name suggests, a chemical company and it has no relation to Dow Jones. Dow Chemical merged with DuPont, another large chemical firm, back in 2015. DuPont was the firm that was first part of the Dow index, not Dow Chemical. But guess what? Dow and DuPont split into three companies in 2019, with the third component now known as Corteva. We know, kind of crazy, but it's a story we'll leave for another day. Chemicals go into tons of products, including cleaning agents and pesticides, and are often derived from oil.

Consumer and Business Services Stocks in the Dow

As the name indicates, firms in the consumer and businesses services sector sell goods or services to consumers and businesses. You probably have the most interaction with consumer firms in this sector since they include restaurants, clothing retailers, and department stores.

Home Depot (NYSE: HD)

Home Depot is the largest home improvement retailer in the world. Pretty much anything you need for your home you can find at Home Depot. They have more than 2,200 stores worldwide, mostly in the US, Mexico, and Canada. They also do a ton of business with home building–related firms and contractors, who install or repair items in a home. Their primary competitor is Lowe's, although they also compete to a certain extent with Wal-Mart and Amazon.com. One of the few products where Amazon.com may not be able to compete effectively is cement. The shipping costs are often more than the price of the product itself!

McDonald's (NYSE: MCD)

McDonald's is one of the pioneers of the fast food industry and one of the largest restaurant chains in the world. McDonald's was one of the first restaurants to apply assembly line techniques to selling food. Fast food is known for being inexpensive and served quickly but often is not considered the most nutritious. There is a relatively new segment of the fast food industry known as fast casual. Fast casual firms serve food quickly, its customers are often not expected to leave a tip, and the food tends to be more nutritious than what's served at McDonalds, Burger King, Hardee's, and Wendy's. Chipotle and Panera Bread are perhaps the two best known fast casual firms that you've probably come across.

Walmart (NYSE: WMT)

Walmart is the largest retailer in the world, measured by annual sales. It might surprise you to learn that they are the biggest seller of groceries and long-lasting consumer products, known in industry terms as dry goods. They are even one of the biggest sellers of diamonds in the US. Diamonds? Say what? For some people, especially in rural areas, Walmart is pretty much the only game in town. Walmart's main competitors are Target, Costco, and Amazon.com.

One of Buffett's biggest regrets is not buying stock in Walmart when it was a much younger growth firm. It was a business he understood and operated on a bigger scale than some of Berkshire's successful retail subsidiaries, Nebraska Furniture Mart (NFM) and Borsheims, a jewelry store. In his 1989 Letter to Shareholders, he wrote, "NFM and Borsheims follow precisely the same formula for success: (1) unparalleled depth and breadth of merchandise at one location; (2) the lowest operating costs in the business; (3) the shrewdest of buying, made possible in part by the huge volumes purchased; (4) gross margins, and therefore prices, far below competitors'; and (5) friendly personalized service with family members on hand at all times." There are some important lessons in this quote for stockholders and business owners alike, so we'll include it as one of our most verbose Tips.

Buffett Tip 58:

The formula for success for a retail business includes: (1) unparalleled depth and breadth of merchandise at one location; (2) the lowest operating costs in the business; (3) the shrewdest of buying, made possible in part by the huge volumes purchased; (4) gross margins, and therefore prices, far below competitors'; and (5) friendly personalized service with family members on hand at all times.

Consumer Goods Stocks in the Dow

There is some overlap with the consumer goods sector and the consumer and business services sector we discussed above. The main difference hinges on the words "services" and "goods." A consumer services firm, such as Walmart, sells the products of many other firms. In contrast, a consumer goods firm, such as Nike, may operate some of its own stores, but it sells the bulk of its products through other companies, such as Foot Locker, Dick's Sporting Goods, and DSW.

Apple (NASDAQ: AAPL)

Apple is one of the most profitable, valuable firms in the world and perhaps best known for its iPhone product. Apple started out as one of the pioneers of the personal computer business. They also created a number of other wildly popular products such as the iPod, iPad, and Apple Watch. Yeah, we know most people view Apple as mostly a technology firm, but research firms put it in the consumer goods sector since it sells most of its products, especially iPhones, to consumers. Apple usually ranks among the most valuable stocks in the world, currently worth more than $2 trillion!

Apple is currently Berkshire's biggest stock position even though Buffett historically has shied away from tech stocks since he claims he doesn't understand the industry. But he likes Apple's customer loyalty and the firm's ability to raise prices and have customers buy new versions of its products due to this intense loyalty. In an interview on CNBC discussing Apple and the iPhone, he said, "You can't move people by price in the smartphone market remotely like you can move them in appliances or all kinds of things. People want the product. They don't want the cheapest product. . .It's a very, very, very valuable product to people that build their lives around it. And that's true of 8-year-olds and 80-year-olds." We think there is Tip in there.

Buffett Tip 59:

Buy stock in companies whose customers build their life around the company's products.

Coca-Cola (NYSE: KO)

Virtually everyone knows Coke. It's one of the most recognized brands in the whole world. Coca-Cola is the largest non-alcoholic beverage company in the world, with operations in more than 200 countries. Their brands include Coke, Diet Coke, Sprite, Tab, Fresca, Dasani, Powerade, and Minute Made juices. Their main competitor is PepsiCo, which somewhat surprisingly makes most of its profits from selling snack foods such as Lays Potato Chips, Tostitos Tortilla Chip, and Doritos. One last note on Pepsi: they are the maker of Gatorade. Smaller competitors to both Coke and Pepsi include Cadbury Schweppes and Dr Pepper Snapple.

Coke has been one of Buffett's best investments. He's made more than ten billion dollars from it since his first purchase back in 1988. But he tells a fascinating story in his 1989 Letter to Shareholders that he should have bought the stock much sooner. He writes:

> I believe I had my first Coca-Cola in either 1935 or 1936. Of a certainty, it was in 1936 that I started buying Cokes at the rate of six for 25 cents from Buffett & Son, the family grocery store, to sell around the neighborhood for 5 cents each. In this excursion into high-margin retailing, I duly observed the extraordinary consumer attractiveness and commercial possibilities of the product.
>
> I continued to note these qualities for the next 52 years as Coke blanketed the world. During this period, however, I carefully avoided buying even a single share, instead allocating major portions of my net worth to street railway companies, windmill manufacturers, anthracite producers, textile businesses, trading-stamp issuers, and the like. (If you think I'm making this up, I can supply the names.) Only in the summer of 1988 did my brain finally establish contact with my eyes.
>
> In fact, if I had been thinking straight I would have persuaded my grandfather to sell the grocery store back in 1936 and put all of the proceeds into Coca-Cola stock. I've learned my lesson: My response time to the next glaringly attractive idea will be slashed to well under 50 years.

There's an important lesson in this humorous story that we'll include as our next Tip.

Buffett Tip 60:

Act quickly if you see a glaringly attractive idea.

Nike (NYSE: NKE)

Nike is the largest athletic shoe (i.e., sneaker) company in the world. Their Air Jordan and Nike LeBron brands are their most popular sneakers. Converse is also owned by Nike, after they purchased the firm in 2003. Nike also sells all sorts of athletic apparel and equipment including T-shirts, shorts, cleats, and jerseys. They are known for their catchy marketing slogans, such as "Just Do It," and their celebrity endorsers including Michael Jordan, LeBron James, Tiger Woods, Zion Williamson, Maria Sharapova, and Christian Ronaldo. Their main competitors include Adidas, Puma, and Under Armour.

Procter & Gamble (NYSE: PG)

Procter and Gamble (P&G) is one largest consumer product firms in the world. They sell a bunch of the stuff you'll find in the supermarket. Some of their main brands include Ivory Soap, Covergirl, Head and Shoulders, Cheer, Tide, Oxy, and Tropicana. Their main competitor is Unilever, a Netherlands-headquartered firm with global operations.

Walgreens Boots Alliance (NASDAQ: WBA)

Walgreens Boots Alliance is mainly known for its US drug store chains, Walgreens and Duane Reade. If you haven't been in one of their stores, they may be viewed as retail stores that sell healthcare products, cosmetics, and convenience items. The Boots Alliance part of the name relates to international pharmacies Walgreens acquired in a 2014 merger. The combined company is huge—they operate about 15,000 stores worldwide.

Walt Disney (NYSE: DIS)

Disney is a large media and entertainment firm. You probably know about their theme parks, movies, and Disney+ video on demand service. Did you also know they own ESPN and ABC TV? In recent years, they bought some other movie companies: Pixar (maker of computer animated films), Marvel (maker of comic books and related movies), Lucasfilm (creator of the Star Wars and Indiana Jones franchises), and the film and TV business of Fox. They also own a majority stake in Hulu, another subscription-based video service.

Financial Stocks in the Dow

Financial stocks are somewhat self-explanatory. They include banks, credit card companies, insurance firms, investment management firms, and investment banking firms.

American Express (NYSE: AXP)

We previously mentioned American Express in our discussion on credit cards and charge cards, as well as with our recounting the tale of Buffett's purchase of the stock when it was suffering from the effects of the salad oil scandal. Amex was originally in the business of express mail delivery, money orders, and traveler's checks. American Express is one of the pioneers of the rewards programs in credit cards, where the card issuer provides you with nice perks such as free airline tickets and cash back on purchases. They also provide credit cards for many businesses and their employees who pay for business-related expenses on the company's dime.

Goldman Sachs (NYSE: GS)

We previously mentioned Goldman Sachs as an example of Buffett putting his maxim to work—"Be fearful when others are greedy. Be greedy when others are fearful"—during the Great Recession. Goldman Sachs is one of the largest and most prestigious financial firms in the world. For many who work or want to work on Wall Street, it's their dream to work at Goldman Sachs. It is sort of like the New England Patriots, New York Yankees, or Golden State Warriors of the financial world. That is, they consistently win. Goldman has large investment banking, investment management, and securities trading units, as well as a growing online retail bank.

JPMorgan Chase & Co. (NYSE: JPM)

JPMorgan Chase is one of the largest financial firms in the world. It was founded in 1871 by J.P. Morgan, a person we'll discuss in the next chapter. They provide a mix of traditional banking and investment banking services to both individuals and companies around the world. Chase is their retail unit, which accepts deposits, provides loans, and issues credit cards, among other activities. They also have a large investment banking division and a wealth management unit, primarily geared towards individuals with $10 million or more in assets. We hope you'll get there someday by following the lessons in this book!

Travelers (NYSE: TRV)

Travelers is one of the largest insurance firms in the US. Perhaps you've seen their famous red umbrella logo. There are all sorts of insurance products. Car insurance is likely the first insurance product that most people purchase. Other types of insurance products you'll probably use in your lifetime include homeowner's insurance (in case something happens to your home) and life insurance (providing money for your heirs after passing away, hopefully a long, long time from now).

Visa (NYSE: V)

We discussed credit cards in **Chapter 3**. Visa is the largest credit card company in the world. You may not know how they primarily make money. Let's say you buy a shirt at Macy's for $20 and pay for it with your Visa credit card. Macy's doesn't net $20 from the sale. It makes about 97 or 98 percent of it ($19.40–$19.40). You might say, Visa gets 2 to 3 percent of billions and billions of dollars of sales for doing practically nothing? Well, they do a lot behind the scenes including reimbursing customers whose cards have been lost or stolen and operating some of the "plumbing" of the financial payments system.

Health Care Stocks in the Dow

Health care stocks include firms that provide health insurance, develop prescription drugs, and sell and distribute prescription drugs, as well as firms that sell all sorts of medical devices ranging from insulin pumps to artificial hearts.

Amgen (NASDAQ: AMGN)

Amgen is one of the largest biotechnology firms in the world. As the name indicates, biotechnology firms use technology to discover new drugs, in contrast to the traditional test tube and trial-and-error process of drug discovery. Since there are several pharmaceutical stocks in the Dow, we'll give you a really quick primer on the FDA approval process, for which there are three phases. Phase 1 aims to make sure the drug is relatively safe. Of course, virtually all drugs have side effects, but the main goal of phase 1 is to make sure the side effects of the drug for most people aren't worse than the disease. The goal of phase 2 is to make sure the drug works for most people, formally known as testing the efficacy of the drug. Phase 3 tests the drug on a larger sample of people and also against a sugar pill, known as a placebo. If the trial is double-blind, neither the patient nor the doctor knows who is getting the real drug. The patients taking the real drug should have better results than those taking the sugar pill. It might surprise you, but less than 0.1 percent of drugs make it from the test tube to the market!

Johnson & Johnson (NYSE: JNJ)

Johnson and Johnson (J&J) is one of the largest health care firms in the world. It has three main segments: A consumer segment, which sells products such as Band Aids and Tylenol; a pharmaceutical segment, which sells prescription drugs; and a medical device segment, which sells things such as artificial hips, knees, and heart stents, which are designed to keep blood vessels open.

Merck & Co. (NYSE: MRK)

Merck is another large health care firm that sells pharmaceutical products, mostly of the prescription drug variety. One factoid that you may not know: It often takes more than a decade to bring a drug from the lab testing phase to the market as a final US Food and Drug Administration (FDA)–approved product. This is one reason why patents often last up to 20 years. Otherwise, there would be little incentive to do all the costly research and development work.

UnitedHealth Group (NYSE: UNH)

UnitedHealth Group is the largest provider of health insurance in the US. Health insurance pays the doctors, hospitals, and pharmacists that may treat you. Many people get health care insurance as a **benefit**, a form of non-cash compensation, from their job. Seniors often get health care services through **Medicare**, a government health program for the elderly.

There are also a number of other important government-sponsored health care plans. Health care generally isn't free. Even if you get health insurance from your employer as part of your benefit plan, it's usually not free. You often have to pay part of the bill, known as a **co-pay**. For many people, especially the elderly, health care is one their largest expenses.

Industrial Goods Stocks in the Dow

Industrial goods stocks typically make some sort of equipment or provide products that are used as input into other products. For example, one of GE's biggest products is selling aircraft engines. To throw you for a loop, Rolls-Royce is also in the aircraft engine business. Rolls-Royce doesn't even make its namesake cars anymore. It sold the rights to BMW more than a decade ago. That's right, Rolls-Royces are produced by BMW!

Boeing (NYSE: BA)

Boeing is one of the largest makers of commercial aircraft, a fancy term for the jets most people fly on. Perhaps you've flown on a 737, 747, or their new Dreamliner jet. Their main competitor is the European firm Airbus. Boeing also has a large national defense business and was one of the main companies involved in producing the space shuttle.

Caterpillar (NYSE: CAT)

Caterpillar is the world's largest maker of earthmoving equipment. That's the kind of things you see at many construction sites, such as cranes, diggers, bulldozers, and steamrollers. They are well known for the yellow and black colors that adorn their equipment. These days, much of the construction around the world is taking place outside of the US, especially in China and India. Most of their sales are outside the US making them a truly global firm.

Honeywell (NYSE: HON)

Honeywell makes a variety of products, too numerous to mention in detail, but most consumers know them from the thermostats that regulate the temperature in their homes. The firm also is heavily involved in the aerospace, defense, surveillance, fire protection, and software industries. For example, the firm competes with Google Nest's range of wireless enabled devices, a segment known as "the Internet of things." Honeywell returned to the Dow in 2020 after a roughly ten-year absence. Like Berkshire, Honeywell is considered a conglomerate, or a firm with businesses that span a range of unrelated industries.

3M Company (NYSE: MMM)

3M was originally known as Minnesota Mining and Manufacturing company. They aren't in the mining business anymore and are known primarily as an industrial firm. You almost certainly know a couple of their products, Scotch Tape and Post-It Notes. Yep, that's MMM. During the COVID-19 pandemic, there was a shortage of their N95 masks. They have a bunch of other business lines besides tape or adhesives, including automotive, health care, security, electronics, and energy.

Technology Stocks in the Dow

The technology sector covers several industries including computer hardware, software, and services. One thing to remember about the Dow is the companies included in the index all have a multi-decade history. So, despite the recent success of Facebook, it is not yet included in the index. Since the Dow is a price-weighted index, it's unlikely that super-high-priced stocks such as Berkshire (Class A), Alphabet, and Amazon.com will make it into the Dow, unless they split their stock. The founders of the latter two firms have expressed their admiration for Buffett and Berkshire, so we don't think their inclusion is likely anytime soon. And we know Buffett won't split Berkshire's stock, although we do think there is a chance that its Class B shares may make it a candidate for the Dow someday.

Intel (NASDAQ: INTC)

Intel is one of the largest computer chip makers in the world. Wall Street calls computer chip makers semiconductor firms. Intel is best known for their central processor unit (CPU) chips, which power most laptops and computers around the world. Intel also owns the antivirus software maker McAfee. Intel recently purchased another chip company called Mobileye, which makes the computer chips that may help power many driverless cars.

International Business Machines (NYSE: IBM)

International Business Machines (IBM) is one of the largest makers of computers in the world. They focus on large computers, the kind that used to fill up whole rooms. Perhaps you saw the hit movie *Hidden Figures*. If so, you got a glimpse of what IBM's computers looked like several decades ago. IBM has been around more than 100 years, and computers were created in the 1940s and 1950s. What did they sell before then? The answer lies in IBMs full name. It sold business machines, including things such as cash registers. They also have a large information services (IT) business, running all or part of the computer departments for many firms around the world. When a company farms out something it historically does itself, such as IT services, it's called **outsourcing**. IBM also has a renewed focus on artificial intelligence (AI) software through their Watson product, which is similar to Siri, Alexa, and other voice-activated assistants. In an effort to increase their sluggish growth, IBM purchased Red Hat in 2019, a firm that focused on cloud-based open-source software, such as Linux.

Microsoft (NASDAQ: MSFT)

Microsoft is the largest computer software company in the world. They are best known for their computer operating system, Windows, and MS Office, recently renamed Microsoft 365, a package of software productivity programs. It includes Microsoft Word, Excel, and PowerPoint. Microsoft also produces the X-box gaming unit, a competitor to Sony's PlayStation and Nintendo's Switch. A few years ago, Microsoft purchased Nokia's phone unit, but they haven't yet made much headway against Apple's iPhone and Samsung's Galaxy line of phones. They also own Skype, a software program that lets you make calls around the world for virtually nothing, and LinkedIn, a job-oriented website that we'll touch upon in **Chapter 15** on careers. The resurgence of Microsoft's stock over the past several years has been due in large part to the success of their cloud computing unit, Intelligent Cloud.

salesforce.com (NASDAQ: CRM)

The stock symbol of salesforce.com, CRM, provides a clue to the types of services that the firm provides. Specifically,CRM is the acronym for customer relationship management software. For example, if you call your cellphone provider, they probably have notes in your account about the last time you called, the type of phone you have, the features of your service plan, and so forth. salesforce.com is pioneer of keeping their software in the cloud, making it easily accessible via smartphone or laptop to users on the go. Their products are sold as part of a subscription model known as software as a service (SaaS). They also purchased the Tableau, a firm that is best known for its data visualization products, in 2019. And yes, the company refers to itself in all lowercase, but thanks for keeping us honest with your grammar vigilance. :-)

Telecommunications Services Stocks in the Dow

Telecommunications services refers to companies that help enable phone calls, the Internet, or the equipment used to power these industries.

Cisco Systems (NASDAQ: CSCO)

Cisco is a shortened form of the city San Francisco, a city located near the company's headquarters in Silicon Valley, California. Cisco is best known for selling networking equipment, which provides the backbone of the Internet. We don't want to bore you too much with technical details, but one of the earliest types of products that Cisco sold is called an Internet router. When you visit a webpage, the router is the piece of equipment that helps send the webpage from the computer server of the host company (such as Yahoo.com) to your computer, tablet, cell phone, or other Internet-viewing device. In recent years, the company has become much more diversified, selling a range of hardware, software, and security-related products.

Verizon (NYSE: VZ)

Verizon was once part of AT&T (a long story) and is the largest cell phone provider in the US. They also own a large cable TV network under the brand name FIOS. In recent years Verizon has expanded into the Internet business. They purchased America Online (AOL) several years ago and more recently purchased Yahoo!, one of the most widely visited websites in the world.

So those are the 30 blue-chip firms in the Dow and a brief mention of some of their competitors. But there are a lot more important companies out there. Let's briefly discuss some of the key firms in the US and also from the rest of the world.

Some Blue-Chip US Stocks That Aren't in the Dow

Since the Dow is an old index that consists of blue-chip stocks, its selection committee tends to be conservative regarding any additions. They don't want to pick some shooting star or flash in the pan and then have the stock flame out. We also mentioned the performance distortion issues with including high-priced new stocks in the Dow, such as Berkshire (Class A).

The FANG Stocks—They Don't Bite

Let's start with the so-called FANG stocks. FANG is the acronym for Facebook, Amazon.com, Netflix, and Google (now formally known as Alphabet).

Facebook is a leading social media firm with well over a billion active users each day. Social media is an electronic platform that enables people to share ideas, comments, pictures, videos, career interests, and much more. Facebook is a convenient way for keeping in touch with your friends and a whole lot more. Facebook also owns Instagram, a photo-sharing and social media company They also own WhatsApp, an app that allows you to text and make phone calls at virtually no cost. WhatsApp also has over a billion active users.

We've mentioned Amazon.com several times in this book. It is hard to describe how many ways this firm touches your life beyond shopping. One of their popular consumer products is Echo. On the surface it's a speaker, but it's really a virtual assistant. As AI expands its capabilities, you'll be able to use Echo for a lot more than playing music, checking the weather, or purchasing items. We can't wait to see how it unfolds. As with Microsoft, Amazon.com also generates much of its profitability from its cloud computing unit, Amazon Web Services. They also expanded into the grocery space in a meaningful way with their acquisition of Whole Foods in 2017.

Netflix is a great way to watch movies, TV shows, educational videos, and other items. They started out renting DVDs through the mail. Today, most of their business involves the online streaming of video content. They are likely the biggest user of Internet bandwidth (i.e., traffic) in the world. Netflix users often engage in a behavior known as binge watching. In the past, when a TV show aired, you had to watch one episode a week. With binge watching you can watch a whole season in one weekend. Increasingly, consumers are "cutting the cord" from their traditional cable provider and moving to a video streaming service, such as Netflix, to meet their entertainment needs. In case you are looking for a TV show to add to your binge-watching list, consider Breaking Bad, a Buffett favorite.

Everyone knows Google as the most popular search engine in the world. But they also own YouTube and are working on some other cool projects such as driverless cars. Google Maps is the most popular navigation app in the world. If you prefer Waze as your navigation app, they own that too. Since they are doing a lot more than search, the firm decided to rename itself Alphabet. Google is still the core, but like Amazon.com they continue to amaze us with what they have up their sleeve.

Tesla is another company that gets many of the financial headlines today, although it is technically not a member of the FANG stocks. It pioneered the development of the electric car. The cars are so impressive that Consumer Reports gave their Model S sedan its highest rating ever. You have to tip your hat to a company that has a car that is as fast as a Ferrari and handles like a Porsche, despite some of their challenges with consistently generating profitability. Wall Street clearly believes in their potential, since their market cap is larger than Ford, GM, Volkswagen, and Daimler (Mercedes) combined! They also merged with SolarCity, a leading provider of solar roofs. Its CEO, Elon Musk, has a vision of colonizing Mars with one of his other companies, SpaceX. Now that's thinking big! We'll get back to Elon Musk in the next chapter on "Who's Who in Business."

China's Emerging Titans

China currently has the second-biggest economy in the world in terms of GDP, and they are poised to pass both the US and the European Union (EU) in our lifetimes. We'll briefly mention the "Big 3" of China's tech firms, Alibaba, Baidu, and Tencent. A fourth large tech firm, ByteDance, which owns TikTok, is privately held. It is currently caught in the crossfire of a skirmish between the US and China and may be sold, in part, to Oracle. Alibaba is like the eBay plus Amazon.com plus PayPal of China. They not only have a platform to sell products to consumers, but they also have a robust **business-to-business** (**B2B**) platform. What does B2B mean? Let's say you have a business that sells T-Shirts. Your business might need a firm to manufacture the T-Shirts in bulk. That's where Alibaba comes in. By searching their website, you may be able to find a firm that manufactures your T-Shirts cheaply. You could then focus on other aspects of your business, such as marketing and finding places that will stock your T-Shirts, a process known as **distribution**. Alibaba also has an electronic payments system, similar to what we discussed with PayPal in **Chapter 3**. It's called Alipay and is part of Alibaba's financial arm, called Ant Financial.

Baidu is similar to the Google or Alphabet of China. They are the leading search engine in China (Google is currently banned there, outside of Hong Kong). Not coincidentally, they also have a driverless car and other AI projects that may spur their next legs of growth. We also want to mention Tencent. No relation to 50 Cent, the musician. Facebook is currently banned in most of China, and Tencent has emerged to be the leading social media firm in the country. They are also the leading mobile gaming firm in the world (i.e., playing games on your phone, computer, or tablet) and dominate the Chinese instant messaging market. Perhaps the most valuable part of Tencent is their app WeChat, which also doubles as a payment system, like Alipay. We have no doubt that you'll be hearing a lot more about these three firms in the decades to come.

Some International Energy Titans

Energy is one of the most important industries in the economy. Most of us use energy for transportation (cars, trucks, airplanes, trains, etc.) and for heating our homes (natural gas, heating oil, and coal). Saudi Aramco, largely owned by the royal family that rules Saudi Arabia, owns virtually all of the oil fields in Saudi Arabia. It also has a large market share in the midstream and downstream segments that we discussed. The government sold a small piece of Saudi Aramco to investors in 2019 and plans to use the money to help develop new industries that may thrive when the oil eventually runs out. Shortly after its IPO the stock peaked at roughly $2 trillion, making it the most valuable stock in the world at the time. Today the market cap of the firm is closer to $1.75 trillion, a number that would even make Buffett envious.

Other major international energy firms include Gazprom (largely owned by the Russian Government), British Petroleum (BP), Royal Dutch Shell (a British-Dutch Firm), PetroChina (China), Petrobras (Brazil), Total S.A. (France), and Eni (Italy). We should also mention the American energy titan Exxon Mobil. We noted earlier in the chapter that it was kicked out of the Dow in 2020 and replaced with salesforce.com, primarily to increase the technology weight in the index after Apple completed its 4:1 stock split.

Some Global Consumer Titans

We mentioned earlier in this chapter that Unilever is a Netherlands-based consumer products firm that is most similar to America's Procter & Gamble. Some of Unilever's best-known brands include Breyer's, Ben & Jerry's, Dove (soap), Hellmann's (mayonnaise), Lipton (tea), Vaseline, and Q-Tips. You probably have some awareness of the major global auto firms. Ford, General Motors, and Tesla in America. Toyota, Honda, and Nissan are from Japan. Daimler (Mercedes Benz), BMW, Porsche, and Volkswagen are from Germany. Stellantis is the new name of the auto firm that combines Fiat, Chrysler, and Peugeot. Some of Stellantis' sub-brands include Jeep, Dodge, Ram, Alfa Romeo, and Maserati. Tata Motors in a leading Indian-based auto manufacturer, which also owns Jaguar and Land Rover. China's leading auto companies, SAIC Motor, Dongfeng, FAW, Chang'an, BYD, Chery, and Geely, may someday become known on a global scale. Geely is already known outside of China, mainly due to their acquisitions of Volvo and Lotus. Speaking of cars, you may not need one anymore with Uber and Lyft, ride-sharing services, now available around much of the word and also two publicly traded stocks. Uber and Airbnb, a home rental firm, are leaders of what is known as the "sharing economy."

Some Global Financial Service Firms

We mentioned some large American financial firms, such as J.P. Morgan and Goldman Sachs, that are in the Dow. Their main American competitors include Bank of America, Citigroup, Wells Fargo, and Morgan Stanley. Some overseas competitors include Bank of China and the Industrial and Commercial Bank (ICBC) of China, Deutsche Bank of Germany, Union Bank of Switzerland (UBS) and Credit Suisse (both Swiss Banks), and Barclays, a British bank. BlackRock and Vanguard are the two largest asset managers in the world, primarily running mutual funds and exchange-traded funds for their customers. Both manage in excess of $6 trillion in assets.

Congratulations, you now have literacy in many of the leading publicly traded firms of the day! Of course, there are a bunch of firms that are currently private such as Fidelity Investments (financial services) and Cargill (agricultural services) that are important too. By following the business press or financial websites such as WSJ.com, Yahoo! Finance, Google Finance, Bloomberg, CNBC.com, and MSN Investor, you can keep up to date on these firms and the new ones that will inevitably emerge.

Buffett's Tips from Chapter 9

Buffett Tip 56: Avoid companies that are susceptible to the ABCs of business decay: arrogance, bureaucracy, and complacency.

Buffett Tip 57: People who buy for non-value reasons are likely to sell for non-value reasons. They tend to increase the volatility of prices.

Buffett Tip 58: The formula for success for a retail business includes: (1) unparalleled depth and breadth of merchandise at one location; (2) the lowest operating costs in the business; (3) the shrewdest of buying, made possible in part by the huge volumes purchased; (4) gross margins, and therefore prices, far below competitors'; and (5) friendly personalized service with family members on hand at all times.

Buffett Tip 59: Buy stock in companies whose customers build their life around the company's products.

Buffett Tip 60: Act quickly if you see a glaringly attractive idea.

References

Belvedere, Matthew J. "Warren Buffett: I Used Berkshire's Insights into the Furniture Business to Figure out Apple's Worth," May 8, 2017. https://www.cnbc.com/2017/05/08/billionaire-investor-warren-buffett-says-its-very-easy-tosee-where-apple-is-with-consumers-at-any-time.html.

Buffett, Warren. "Letter to Shareholders of Berkshire Hathaway Inc." Berkshire Hathaway, Inc., 1983. https://www.berkshirehathaway.com/letters/1983.html.

Buffett, Warren. "*Letter to Shareholders of Berkshire Hathaway Inc.*" Berkshire Hathaway, Inc., 1989. https://www.berkshirehathaway.com/letters/1989.html.

Chang, Sue. "The Dow's Tumultuous History, in One Chart." *MarketWatch,* February 3, 2018. https://www.marketwatch.com/story/the-dows-tumultuous-120-yearhistory-in-one-chart-2017-03-23.

"Dow Jones Industrial Average (DJIA)–Overview, History, & Components." Corporate Finance Institute. Accessed June 28, 2020. https://corporatefinance institute.com/resources/knowledge/trading-investing/dow-jones-industrial average-djia/.

"Drug Approvals–from Invention to Market. . .A 12 Year Trip," July 14, 1999. https://www.medicinenet.com/script/main/art.asp?articlekey=9877.

ETMarkets.com. "Warren Buffett Biggest Regret: Not Investing in This Technology Giant!," May 6, 2017. https://economictimes.indiatimes.com/markets/stocks/news/warren-buffett-biggest-regret-not-investing-in-this-technology-giant/articleshow/58551975.cms?from=mdr.

Lawler, Alex, Marwa Rashad, and Saeed Azhar. "Exclusive: Saudi Aramco Valuation Gap Persists as IPO Talks Resume - Sources," August 7, 2019. https://www.reuters.com/article/us-aramco-ipo-exclusive/exclusive-saudi-aramco-valuation-gap-persists-as-ipo-talks-resume-sources-idUSKCN1UX1PD.

Victor, Daniel. "Consumer Reports Gives New Tesla Its Highest Score Ever," August 27, 2015. https://www.nytimes.com/2015/08/28/automobiles/tesla model-s-p85d-consumer-reports-perfect-score.html.

10

Business 101—Past and Present Business Leaders, or Who's Who in Business

"All families in my upper middle–class neighborhood regularly enjoy a living standard better than that achieved by John D. Rockefeller Sr. at the time of my birth."
—Warren Buffett, 2015 Letter to Berkshire Hathaway Stockholders

Introduction

In the last chapter, we covered the Dow Jones Industrial Average and other companies you should know a little something about in order to be considered financially literate. Otherwise, businesspeople might view you like someone who recently arrived from Mars—that is, a person pretty clueless about business and the financial markets. This chapter focuses on some important business leaders (past and present) that you should know. Knowing who these men and women are will provide you with a greater understanding of how our present-day economy came to be and where it might be going. George Santayana, a famous philosopher of the 19th and 20th centuries, said, "Those who cannot remember the past are condemned to repeat it," so that's another reason not to zone out on this chapter.

We'll organize the chapter into two big segments, past business leaders and present business leaders, similar to a business "Hall of Fame." How does this all tie in with Buffett? Well, Buffett knows or has commented on many of the business leaders we'll discuss. Many of the living businesspeople that we'll discuss have also signed the Giving Pledge. There are a handful of nuggets in this chapter that we'll turn into Buffett Tips. Let's get started.

Past Business Leaders

Alexander Graham Bell

Alexander Graham Bell is generally credited as the inventor of the first telephone, although there is some controversy surrounding this claim. Bell founded the Bell Telephone Company, which eventually morphed into AT&T. AT&T dominated the telecommunications industry in the US until the government ordered its breakup in 1982. Martin Cooper of Motorola is credited with inventing the cell phone, in case you were wondering.

Rose Blumkin (Mrs. B)

We've mentioned Rose Blumkin (Mrs. B) a few times in this book. She built Nebraska Furniture Mart (NFM) into the largest furniture store in the country and ultimately sold her business to Berkshire. She worked until she was 103 years old and was one of NFM's best salespeople, in addition to running the business. Buffett regards her as one of the most talented business executives of all time. Buffett met with hundreds of college students each year for decades—John went several times—and included a visit to the NFM as a key part of the itinerary. In his 2013 Letter to Shareholders, Buffett wrote, "Aspiring business managers should look hard at the plain, but rare, attributes that produced Mrs. B's incredible success. . . . If they absorb Mrs. B's lessons, they need none from me." That's a pretty powerful endorsement. Let's use one of Mrs. B's most famous quotes: "Sell cheap and tell the truth" as our next Tip. We know Buffett would approve.

Buffett Tip 61:

Sell cheap and tell the truth. ***(Courtesy of Mrs. B.)***

Andrew Carnegie

Andrew Carnegie was known as a steel baron and philanthropist. His steel holdings, with the help of financier J.P. Morgan (discussed below), were eventually consolidated into US Steel, the first billion-dollar corporation in the US. His charitable efforts resulted in the creation of thousands of libraries around the world, as well as the highly ranked Carnegie Mellon University (then called Carnegie Tech) in Pittsburgh, Pennsylvania.

Walt Disney

Walt Disney began his entertainment career as a cartoonist, with Mickey Mouse being his most famous creation. He not only developed a very successful movie business but also expanded into the theme park business in a big way. Disneyland opened in California in 1955 and since then, several more enormous Disney theme parks and resorts have opened around the world. Disney is probably the person most associated with family entertainment, that is, forms of entertainment rated G or PG that delight kids and adults alike. As we mentioned in the last chapter, Disney is a member of the Dow.

Thomas Edison and Jack Welch

Thomas Edison is known as perhaps the greatest inventor who ever lived, obtaining patents on the light bulb, phonograph (record player), motion picture camera, and more than a thousand other items. He founded the company, with the help of financier J.P. Morgan, that evolved into General Electric (GE), which was one of the 30 stocks in the Dow Jones Industrial Average for more than 100 years, until its removal in 2018. Another GE executive, Jack Welch, who died in 2020, was regarded as one of the most successful corporate executives of all time, helping turn

GE into one of the most valuable stocks in the world at the time of his retirement in 2000.

Henry Ford

Henry Ford didn't invent the automobile (that distinction generally goes to Karl Benz of Daimler/Mercedes Benz), but he helped mass produce the car using **assembly-line techniques**. That is, each worker was responsible for adding a single or small number of parts to the car, such as a tire. Ford, with his Model-T car, made the automobile affordable to the masses, forever changing the world of transportation. Ford is probably most responsible for putting the "buggy whip" (i.e., a horse-drawn carriage) largely out of business, to the benefit of horses everywhere.

Katharine Graham

Katharine Graham was the first female CEO of a Fortune 500 company, *The Washington Post*. During her tenure leading *The Washington Post* from 1971 to 1991, its stock returned 3,315% vs. a gain of only 227% for the Dow. Graham played an important role in helping Buffett improve his social skills and provided him with an introduction to a "Who's Who" of business and government leaders around the world. Buffett strongly recommends reading Graham's book *Personal History*. It details her personal story of being thrust into running *The Washington Post* after her husband's suicide, her doubts as an executive, and her ultimate triumph. Sounds like a great Lifetime movie, except it's all true.

William Randolph Hearst

William Randolph Hearst, for a time, ran the largest newspaper and magazine business in the world. He was active in business from the late 1800s to early 1950s. At one point during the 1920s, one in four Americans read a paper owned by Hearst. His organization also published magazines that are still popular today, including *Cosmopolitan*, *Harper's Bazaar*, and *Good Housekeeping*. The articles in his papers weren't always of the highest standards and were often called "yellow journalism" by critics, a reporting technique based on speculation and half-truths. One of his famous and most criticized quotes was "You furnish the pictures and I'll furnish the war." Many of the articles in his papers were like a combination of the *National Enquirer* or *TMZ* plus *The Washington Post*. But his newspapers also conducted some serious journalism, such as uncovering corruption in many instances. The classic movie, *Citizen Kane*, is loosely based on the rise and fall of Hearst.

Steve Jobs

Steve Jobs was co-founder (with Steve Wozniak) of Apple, which played a major role in ushering in the personal computer age. Before Apple, most computers were used for business purposes and were large enough to fill up a room. Apple also played an important role in popularizing the graphical user interface (GUI) used in most computers today. The GUI relies on icons or pictures, rather than memorizing and typing commands. We'll make a long story short. Jobs was fired from Apple (by its board of directors) in 1985, but he returned to lead the company in 1997. There's a pretty good Ashton Kutcher movie (*Jobs*, 2013) on the subject if you're dying to know the full story. Another movie (*Steve Jobs*, 2015) isn't quite as good, at least according to the Jobs family. Jobs led the development of a slew of revolutionary products including the Mac, iPod, iPad, and iPhone and helped turn Apple into, at one point, the most valuable company in the world. If that's not enough of an accomplishment, he also founded and led Pixar, an animated film studio, that he sold to Disney for $7.4 billion in 2006.

Ingvar Kamprad

Ingvar Kamprad was the Swedish founder of IKEA, a large, high-quality discount furniture store. Like Buffett, Kamprad favored frugality, simplicity, and enthusiasm. As an example, much of IKEA's furniture is shipped unassembled. This not only results in lower prices but also allows the boxes that contain the furniture to be relatively flat. Shipping costs are lower, and IKEA's stores are able to hold a large amount of inventory. Customers can leave with their furniture loaded in their car, SUV, or pickup truck and not wait weeks for delivery. IKEA aims to make the assembly of their furniture relatively easy, having less customers dread the phrase "Some assembly required." Like Buffett, Kamprad was often ranked among the richest people in the world and lived a fairly plain existence. For example, despite his multi-billionaire status, Kamprad drove a 1993 Volvo for two decades, shopped at flea markets, and flew coach when traveling. Even Buffett will skip on that last item!

Ray Kroc

Ray Kroc didn't found McDonald's. That distinction belongs to the McDonald brothers, Maurice and Richard. Kroc eventually bought them out, with some controversy, as depicted in the movie *The Founder*. However, Kroc helped popularize the fast food industry and turned McDonald's into the biggest restaurant chain in the world. Most McDonald's restaurants are **franchised**, rather than company owned. Franchised means an independent owner follows the business approach set up by the company (McDonald's in this case) and pays the company (McDonald's again in this case) a percentage of its sales. McDonald's also makes a good chunk of its money from real estate, since the franchisee usually pays rent to McDonald's for its store. This aspect of McDonald's goes to a main point on financial literacy: understanding the business model of a firm, which is how it makes money. Like Disney, McDonald's is a Dow 30 stock.

Estee Lauder

If you've ever walked by a cosmetics or fragrance counter in a department store, you've must have seen some of Estee Lauder's products. Estee Lauder co-founded the cosmetics and fragrance firm that bears her name. She was the only woman on *Time* magazine's 1998 list of the 20 most influential business geniuses of the 20th century. For a time, she was the richest self-made woman in the world. She was especially known for her marketing skills and popularized the now common practice of giving a free gift with the purchase of a cosmetic or fragrance product.

J.P. Morgan

We mentioned J.P. Morgan earlier in the book as the founder of what today is known as JPMorgan Chase & Co. He also beared a strong resemblance to the banker in the game Monopoly. The central bank in the US, the Federal Reserve, was created in 1913. Before that time, if there was a recession, then often known as a panic, the government relied on powerful bankers, such as Morgan, to bail the country out. For example, Morgan was widely credited with ending the Panic of 1907. He also played a key role in creating some of the largest companies in the world at the time through mergers and raising capital. Morgan had a big hand in the creation of three firms we previously mentioned, AT&T, General Electric, and U.S. Steel. The Rothschild banking dynasty in Europe is probably the only other family that rivals the power that J.P. Morgan had at his peak.

John D. Rockefeller

We came across John D. Rockefeller, perhaps the richest person in modern history, in **Chapter 5** in the context of his quote on his love of receiving dividends. Rockefeller created the largest corporation in the world at the time, then known as Standard Oil. The firm controlled much of the oil industry in the US, especially on the refining side, until it was forced to break up into 34 separate companies. The main Standard Oil component that remains today is known as Exxon. Other Standard Oil "siblings" include Mobil (which has since merged back with Exxon), Chevron, and Amoco.

Buffett had a profound thought on John D. Rockefeller and the standard of living that most Americans enjoy today. He said due to the advances in technology, health care, farming, and so forth, even middle-class Americans live better in many respects than the perhaps the richest person ever. We have better health care, cars, phones, food, airplanes, computers, televisions, and thousands of other items that either didn't exist in Rockefeller's time or were of poorer quality.

In his 2015 Letter to Shareholders, Buffett wrote:

> All families in my upper middle-class neighborhood regularly enjoy a living standard better than that achieved by John D. Rockefeller Sr. at the time of my birth. His unparalleled fortune couldn't buy what we now take for granted, whether the field is—to name just a few—transportation, entertainment, communication, or medical services. Rockefeller certainly had power and fame; he could not, however, live as well as my neighbors now do.

According to Buffett, it's the American system of commerce and innovation that provides real gains to its citizens over time, and it explains why most of us are fortunate to live better than the world's first billionaire. He also wrote in the same 2015 Letter, "For 240 years it's been a terrible mistake to bet against America, and now is no time to start. America's golden goose of commerce and innovation will continue to lay more and larger eggs." Let's summarize Buffett's powerful thoughts on Rockefeller and the American economic system with a Tip.

Buffett Tip 62:

The American system of commerce and innovation provides real gains to most of its citizens over time and enables many of us to live better than John D. Rockefeller, perhaps the richest person in modern times.

Cornelius Vanderbilt

Cornelius Vanderbilt, who had the nickname Commodore, made a fortune in the shipping and railroad industries during the 1800s. By some estimates, he'd have a net worth of more than $200 billion today—more than Buffett, Gates, and Bezos, after adjustments to present-day dollars. Before there were automobiles and paved highways, railroads were the dominant form of transportation that helped power the economy, and Vanderbilt was the biggest railroad baron of his time.

Sam Walton

Sam Walton was the founder of Walmart, the largest retailer in the world. *Fortune* magazine ranks the top 500 firms in the US by revenues in an annual list known as the **Fortune 500**. Walmart has topped the list for the past several years, even though Microsoft, Amazon.com, Apple, and other firms have a bigger market cap. Not too long ago, Walmart was a small-fry company run out of Bentonville, Arkansas. The name of the firm comes from part of Walton's last name as well as Walmart's larger competitor at the time the firm was founded, Kmart. Sears was also a much larger firm and a Dow 30 stock when Walmart was founded back in 1962. Walmart helped pioneer the "superstore" concept and provided its customers with low prices on a wide range of goods. It too, of course, is a Dow 30 stock today.

Thomas Watson Jr.

Thomas Watson Jr. helped turn IBM into the most powerful computer company in the world from the 1950s through the 1970s. It had great success selling computers to businesses and governments, as well as to individuals, after the personal computer revolution was ignited by Apple. IBM still has a large business presence today but has since been eclipsed by Microsoft, Facebook, and Alphabet (Google) in the technology world. It still remains a Dow 30 stock. Watson had some struggles as a student but was admitted to Brown University as a favor to his father, Thomas Watson Sr. Buffett is fond of quoting Watson, who said, "I'm no genius, but I'm smart in spots, and I stay around those spots." It's a slight twist on Buffett's circle of competence belief and one that we think is worthy of a Tip for all of us non-geniuses.

Buffett Tip 63:

You don't have to be a genius to be successful. Everyone is smart in certain spots. Stay around those spots. *(Courtesy of Thomas Watson Jr.)*

Present Business Leaders

Companies that completely dominate their industries aren't easy to come by. They arrive perhaps a few times in a generation. Companies that would fall, or fell, into this category include IBM in the 1950s–1970s, Microsoft in the 1980s–present, Intel from the 1980s through the early 2000s (until the smartphone began its rise), Google 2006–present, and Facebook 2012–present. Alibaba and Tencent also have very powerful positions within their industries in China today.

Bernard Arnault

Bernard Arnault is the chairman and CEO of LVMH Moët Hennessy—Louis Vuitton SE (LVHM). If you want to flex your wealth, sporting some Louis Vuitton is one way to do it, since they are perhaps the most premier luxury goods firm in the world. Their popular brands, besides Louis Vuitton, include Christian Dior, Fendi, and Dom Pérignon. LVMH is in a battle over acquiring Tiffany, one of the preeminent jewelry firms in the world. Arnault is currently worth over $80 billion, making him one of the richest people in the world.

Mary Barra

Mary Barra is CEO of General Motors (GM), one of the oldest and largest car companies in the world. GM's brands include Cadillac, Chevy, Buick, and GMC Trucks. Mary Barra is revered for her approach to dealing with a crisis. She was dealt a bad hand when she took over as CEO of GM. The company admitted to sweeping under the rug a problem with faulty ignition switches on hundreds of thousands of its cars. The faulty ignition switches could result in the car engine shutting off while driving, preventing the airbags from inflating in the event of an accident. At least 100 people died from this severe mechanical problem with GM cars. Barra publicly acknowledged the problem, apologized, and recalled a massive 30 million cars. GM was able to move on from the scandal and provided an example, albeit belated, on how to deal with product recalls.

In his 2005 Letter to Shareholders, Buffett dispensed some advice on how to deal with a problem. He wrote, "When a problem exists, whether in personnel or in business operations, the time to act is now." Barra followed Buffett's advice as soon as she took over as GM's CEO, and this advice is certainly Tip worthy.

Buffett Tip 64:

When a problem exists, whether in personnel or in business operations, the time to act is now.

Better yet, try to prevent mistakes from happening. Hurricane Katrina devastated the New Orleans region of Louisiana in 2005. It was one of the worst hurricanes ever to hit the US, resulting in the loss of 1,800+ lives and an estimated $125 billion worth of storm damage. Places near or below sea level are often protected by a type of floodwall designed to withstand water surges called a levee. It obviously failed for New Orleans when Hurricane Katrina barreled into the city. In Buffett's 2005 Letter to Berkshire Shareholders, he wrote, "The time to have considered—and improved—the reliability of New Orleans's levees was before Katrina."

Buffett suggests that you should be aware of your likelihood to make certain mistakes or to be exposed to certain risks and then you should think of a plan in advance to reduce the negative effect. For example, maybe you are prone to impulse buying on something you don't need, are tempted to put all your money in a single risky investment, or are in a situation that can lead to trouble. Follow your Inner Scorecard to try to resist mistakes that may arise from peer pressure. If you are prone to impulse buying, do your best to make sure it's on something that you can return quickly without penalty. In advance of any purchase, try to have a written plan for the type of investments that make sense and a risk management plan for reducing the losses.

Jeff Bezos

We've discussed Amazon.com several times in this book. The founder of this incredible company is Jeff Bezos. Amazon started out a seller of books on the Internet and billed themselves as "The World's Largest Store." Eventually they expanded the business to sell almost everything on their website. And with their purchase of the organic grocery store Whole Foods, Amazon has moved into the physical retail store business—known as a brick-and-mortar store in Wall Street speak—as well. They've also started to roll out their own branded Amazon stores. They are piloting cool technologies such as cashierless stores that allow you to avoid waiting in line, everyone's least favorite part of shopping. Amazon also powers many of the most widely visited websites in the world, such as Netflix, through their Amazon Web Services unit. And their home speaker Echo/Alexa is likely to morph within your lifetime into a true virtual assistant that can answer many of your questions.

Buffett regards Jeff Bezos as the best business executive of the current generation. He praised Bezos for building a business that delights the customer. In speaking to a group of small business owners, he said,

"Bezos set out every day to delight his customer by fast delivery, by lower prices, whatever it took. . . . And today, he is thinking about how to delight his customer." Let's turn this thought into a Tip.

Buffett Tip 65:

Delight the customer if you are a business owner. Buy companies that delight their customers if you are an investor.

Richard Branson

Richard Branson is a billionaire businessman best known for two things—his Virgin brand of businesses and feats of adventure. Let's start with the adventure part first, since it's more exciting. In 1991, he set a record crossing the Pacific Ocean in a hot air balloon. He also crossed the Atlantic Ocean on a separate trip and set a record crossing the English Channel, the body of water that separates England from France, in an amphibious vehicle. That is, something that can both drive and float. He also currently owns Virgin Galactic, a firm with the goal of flying passengers in outer space. His firms include(d) Virgin Records, Virgin Mobile (a cell phone company), and Virgin Atlantic Airways (an airline). Branson battled dyslexia and poor grades as a young person before achieving his incredible business success. At last count, he had a net worth exceeding $4 billion.

Michael Bloomberg

Michael Bloomberg may be best known as the former mayor of New York City, which he led from 2002 to 2013. He also vied for the Democratic presidential nomination in 2020 but didn't make the cut. He made most of his $50+ billion fortune as the founder of Bloomberg L.P., a business information and media firm. A "**Bloomberg machine**" can be found on most Wall Street trading desks, and Bloomberg TV/radio are popular business channels/stations. A Bloomberg machine provides an efficient way to get data, analytics, news, and messaging on one platform. It also acts as a tool to do trading for many of its customers, especially in the bond market. If you work on Wall Street one day, we think it's a good bet that you'll have a Bloomberg machine on your desk or at least one shared machine in your department. Mike Bloomberg's story also provides a lesson in perseverance. He was laid off (i.e., asked to leave) due to a slowdown in business from his prior job at the Wall Street investment bank Salomon Brothers before starting his eponymous company.

Sergey Brin, Larry Page, and Sundar Pichai

Sergey Brin and Larry Page are the co-founders of Google, now known as Alphabet. There were lots of search engines before Google came on the scene. There was Yahoo! and MSN Search / Bing (Microsoft) as well as names that now are somewhat obscure, such as AltaVista, Excite, Infoseek, and Ask Jeeves. Google won out because it had the best product. Brin and Page started the company while graduate students at Stanford University. The Internet revolution provides a great example of the fact that young people can literally change the world. Sundar Pichai is currently the CEO of Alphabet and also a person to watch in the decades ahead.

Another one of Buffett's biggest investment regrets is not buying Google's (now Alphabet's) stock, even though he was an avid user of the company's search engine. Although Buffett usually stays away from technology stocks, he understood that Google had elements of a **natural monopoly**. A natural monopoly means there is one seller of a product and the advantage happened naturally (i.e., through the quality of a company's product(s) and its business acumen), as opposed to government regulation. Of course, Google isn't the only search engine, but it has roughly 80% market share in the US, so it's close enough.

Buffett said during his 2017 shareholders meeting, "Just imagine having something every time to just hit a click, you know, a cash register rung somewhere out in California. So it was and is an extraordinary business and it has some aspects of a natural monopoly. I mean, it's very easy for me when I go to a computer." Let's turn Buffett's investing mistake on Google into a Tip.

Buffett Tip 66:

Buy companies that have a natural monopoly.

Shawn Carter, Beyoncé Knowles, Sean Combs, and Andre Young

Shawn Carter, Beyoncé Knowles-Carter, Sean Combs, and Andre Young started out as musicians. You likely know them better by their "stage names" of Jay-Z, Beyoncé, P Diddy (or Diddy or Puff Daddy), and Dr. Dre, respectively. Beyoncé Knowles-Carter, who is married to Jay-Z, is so famous that she only needs to go by her first name, like Cher or Madonna. It may surprise you that these artists made most of their money in the business world and not by selling records. All are on the path to becoming billionaires and some, such as Jay-Z, already are.

Jay-Z's business empire include(d) a record company (Roc-A-Fella Records), clothing line (Rocawear), sports agency (Roc Nation Sports), alcoholic beverage firms (D'Ussé cognac and Ace of Spades Champagne), and a subscription-based music streaming service (Tidal). Jay-Z did meet with Buffett on at least one occasion to listen to the oracle's advice on building a successful business. Beyoncé is another hugely successful musician (Destiny's Child, Beyoncé), actress (with *Austin Powers in Goldmember*), and businessperson in her own right. She has an ownership stake in two clothing lines, House of Deréon and Ivy Park, as well as in Tidal. She also has a very successful fragrance line, Heat, and endorsements for Pepsi, American Express, Nintendo, L'Oréal, and many other firms.

Sean Combs earned his business stripes not only from a successful music career but more significantly through his business interests. Combs Enterprises is, or has been, owner of a clothing and fragrance line (Sean John), record company (Bad Boy Records), and spirits company (Cîroc Vodka). Dr. Dre scored his biggest business win when he sold Beats, a headphones company he co-founded, to Apple for $3 billion in 2014. His record company, currently known as Aftermath Entertainment, has played a large role in the success of other superstar musicians, such as Snoop Dogg, Eminem, and 50 Cent.

Tim Cook

Tim Cook is the Chairman and CEO of Apple, which is among the most powerful companies on the planet. Under Tim Cook's watch, Apple at one point became the most valuable company in the world, valued at more than $2 trillion. Tim Cook used to run the operations part (i.e., day-to-day and nuts and bolts) of the business and was put in charge by Steve Jobs after he became terminally ill.

Jamie Dimon

Jamie Dimon, chairman and CEO of JPMorgan Chase & Co, is probably the best-known financial services executive today, other than Buffett. Dimon steered his company through the Great Recession of 2008–2009, perhaps better than any other banking executive in the world. However, it hasn't always been smooth sailing for Dimon. In Chapter 15, we're going to talk about careers, networking, and mentoring. A mentor is someone who provides advice and is helpful to your career. Dimon had a great mentor in Sandy Weill for many years but ultimately got in a conflict with Weill and was fired by his mentor. However, Dimon eventually rebounded and led JPMorgan to new heights. Like Buffett, he writes a widely read, detailed letter for his shareholders each year.

Jack Dorsey

Jack Dorsey may be the closest thing we have today to Steve Jobs, an executive running two very high-profile companies that he co-founded, Twitter and Square. Twitter, of course, is the wildly successful social media platform that has, in some respects, replaced the newspaper. President Trump is a big fan of the service and his tweets often roil the financial markets. Square produces a hardware/software product that allows small vendors to accept credit card payments. Dorsey also made headlines for donating $1 billion in 2020 to fight COVID-19 and to support a number of other worthwhile ventures.

Bill Gates, Paul Allen, and Steve Ballmer

Bill Gates is usually ranked among the richest people in the world—$110+ billion at last count, along with Buffett and another person on our list, Jeff Bezos of Amazon.com. Gates is the co-founder of Microsoft. The other co-founder was a lower profile billionaire by the name of Paul Allen, who left working at Microsoft on a day-to-day basis in 1982. If you're a sports fan, you may have known Paul Allen as the owner of the

Seattle Seahawks in the NFL and Portland Trailblazers in the NBA. He passed away in 2018. Steve Ballmer was one of the early employees of Microsoft and was CEO for many years after Bill Gates stepped down from day-to-day management of the firm. He is currently owner of the Los Angeles Clippers NBA team.

Bill Gates is good friends with Warren Buffett, and Buffett has volunteered to donate most of his money to Bill Gates's charitable foundation. We'll discuss this enormous and generous gift further in our last chapter, on philanthropy and charity. They both co-founded the philanthropic organization that we mentioned in **Chapter 1**, the Giving Pledge.

Reed Hastings

Reed Hastings is co-founder of Netflix, the huge online video service. Many families have quit their cable providers ("cord cutters") making Netflix a growing force in the entertainment industry. For many, Netflix, Google's YouTube, and Amazon's Prime Video are their TV. Netflix's original business model was renting DVDs through the mail, but now most of their customers stream content over the Internet. Legend has it that Hastings started Netflix since he was upset paying late fees for a movie rental (*Apollo 13*) that he didn't return promptly. The rest is history. Creating a better or more customer-friendly product is the recipe for many successful businesses. Netflix has branched out to creating original movies and TV shows making it a competitor of Disney, AT&T/Time Warner, and other media companies.

Kylie Jenner and Robyn Fenty

Kylie Jenner built a cosmetics empire using her and her family's social media presence as a key marketing engine. She became the youngest working billionaire in history after Coty, a large cosmetics firm, purchased a majority stake in Jenner's cosmetics business. You may know Robyn Fenty better by her middle and stage name, Rihanna. Like Jay-Z, Beyoncé, P. Diddy, and Dr. Dre, she used fame garnered from her musical talents to expand into the business world. Like Jenner, Rihanna has a thriving cosmetics and fashion business. She is reported to have a net worth of at least $600 million while still in her early 30s. That figure would be way ahead of where Buffett was at that age, even when adjusted for inflation.

Phil Knight

Phil Knight is co-founder and former chairman and CEO of Nike, the largest athletic shoe (i.e., sneaker) and apparel company in the world. In case you are wondering where the name Nike came from, Nike was the ancient Greek goddess of victory. A cool name for an athletic company, in our view.

After you finish reading this book, we strongly recommend that you check out Phil Knight's fascinating autobiography, *Shoe Dog: A Memoir by the Creator of Nike*. It may surprise and inspire you to learn that the firm was far from an overnight success. Phil Knight started his business as an importer of Japanese sneakers that he sold out of the trunk of his car at track meets. Eventually, he turned this reseller of sneakers, then known as Blue Ribbon Sports, into Nike. Of course, we know how the story ended—a humongous success!

Jack Ma, Pony Ma, and Robin Li

Jack Ma, Pony Ma (no relation), and Robin Li are co-founders of three of China's largest tech companies—Alibaba, Tencent, and Baidu—respectively. We briefly mentioned them in the last chapter on important companies in today's global economy. China is currently the second-largest economy in the world, as measured by GDP, behind only the US. Since China has a population of roughly 1.4 billion people and it is using the technology found in most developed markets, as well as educating its citizens, it is poised to surpass the US in total GDP terms within our lifetimes. And these three gentlemen, through their firms, are shaping the way China will look in the years ahead.

Rupert Murdoch

Rupert Murdoch is the Australian-born founder and co-chairman of News Corporation. He is one of the most successful news and media professionals with a net worth in excess of $15 billion. You may know News Corporation best for their Fox TV channels and 20th / 21st Century Fox film units. As we noted in the last chapter, the bulk of the entertainment part of the business was sold to Disney. In Europe and Asia, they were also well known for their cable TV company, Sky, which is now owned by Comcast. News Corp is also one of the largest newspaper publishers in the world. Their best-known paper is *The Wall Street Journal,* but they also publish a number of other popular papers including the *New York Post* and *The Sun*. Real estate fans may also know News Corporation as the owner of the popular website realtor.com.

Elon Musk

Elon Musk first became widely known to the business world as one of the founders of PayPal, a firm we came across in our discussion of electronic payments in **Chapter 3**. Today Musk is better known as co-founder and CEO of Tesla, a pioneering electric car company. Musk is also the founder of SpaceX, a firm that blasts rockets and satellites into space for corporate and government customers. SpaceX has a much more ambitious goal—to colonize Mars! Don't laugh, it may happen in your lifetime. Musk and Bezos are probably the two most visionary business leaders in the world today, taking over the mantle from the late Steve Jobs, whom we discussed earlier in this chapter.

Amancio Ortega

Amancio Ortega is the Spanish founder of Inditex, a multinational clothing company, and he's also one of the richest people in the world. He recently had a net worth of $65 billion, putting him in Buffett's, Gates's, and Bezos's territory. Zara is perhaps the best-known retail clothing chain in Ortega's empire. Ortega's contribution to the business world falls under the heading of "fast fashion." No, it's not the clothing wear of former Olympic sprinter Usain Bol:-). It refers to getting clothing from the headlines (e.g., a star wearing a certain outfit) into the store very quickly. By quickly, we mean Zara can develop a new product and get it into a store in as little as one week, in contrast to the several months it takes most companies.

Howard Schultz

Howard Schultz is the founder and former chairman/CEO of Starbucks, the world's most popular coffeehouse chain. Schultz helped develop the

"Starbucks experience"—a cool place to hang out, socialize, and do work. He came up with the concept after being inspired by Italian coffee shops during a trip to Milan. In contrast, at many restaurants most people just eat and leave. Most Starbucks location have Wi-Fi and swanky furniture, providing an inviting atmosphere. This cool vibe allows Starbucks to charge high prices for its coffee, while still getting repeat business.

Oprah Winfrey

Oprah Winfrey was once the most widely watched talk show host on the planet. Her show, *The Oprah Winfrey Show*, dominated its time slot—the main way people watched TV before the days of binge watching—for more than 20 years. However, she turned herself into a billionaire by becoming a media and sales mogul. She started out as an employee of the talk show company but became so successful and powerful that she eventually set up her own company, Harpo Productions (Harpo is Oprah spelled backward), that owned the talk show.

When she retired from the daily talk show business in 2011, she hosted a series of TV specials and focused on developing her media empire, including a magazine (*O, The Oprah Magazine),* website (Oprah.com), satellite radio station (Oprah radio), and cable network (Oxygen) and co-produced two other enormously popular talk shows that she helped launch (*Dr. Phil* and *The Dr. Oz Show*). If that's not enough, she was also a contributor to the highly regarded weekly news program *60 Minutes* and is (a roughly 10%) owner of Weight Watchers International, a weight management services firm.

Mark Zuckerberg and Sheryl Sandberg

Mark Zuckerberg is co-founder, chairman, and CEO of Facebook, the largest social media firm in the world, with over 1.2 billion active daily users. He started the business out of his dorm room at Harvard and later dropped out of college as his business took off. Bill Gates did the same thing a generation or two before Zuckerberg. Normally, we wouldn't encourage you to drop out of school, but if you're on the path to becoming a billionaire, we'll give it a thumbs up:-). In the prior chapter, we also mentioned that Facebook also owns Instagram, Facebook Messenger, and WhatsApp.

Sheryl Sandberg is the chief operating officer of Facebook, running the firm on a day-to-day basis. Before she joined Facebook in 2008, she was an executive at Google. When Sandberg joined the firm, Facebook was losing tens of millions of dollars a year. Today it is making more than $15 *billion* a year. She is also author of the bestselling book *Lean In: Women, Work, and the Will to Lead*. It's a highly acclaimed book that gives advice, especially to women, about succeeding in business.

Of course, there are tons of other important business executives, past and present, but this list provides you with a good start. A fun exercise might be to peruse the lists of the Bloomberg's Billionaire's Index, the Forbes 400, and Nobel Prize winners. The stories of these men and women may inspire you. There are other people worth mentioning such as Satoshi Nakamoto, the pseudonym of the inventor(s) of Bitcoin, but his/her/their identity is currently unknown.

Buffett's Tips from Chapter 10

Buffett Tip 61: Sell cheap and tell the truth. *(Courtesy of Mrs. B.)*
Buffett Tip 62: The American system of commerce and innovation provides real gains to most of its citizens over time and enables many of us to live better than John D. Rockefeller, perhaps the richest person in modern times.
Buffett Tip 63: You don't have to be a genius to be successful. Everyone is smart in certain spots. Stay around those spots. *(Courtesy of Thomas Watson Jr.)*
Buffett Tip 64: When a problem exists, whether in personnel or in business operations, the time to act is now.
Buffett Tip 65: Delight the customer if you are a business owner. Buy companies that delight their customers if you are an investor.
Buffett Tip 66: Buy companies that have a natural monopoly.

References

"About Us: Nebraska Furniture Mart: Nebraska Furniture Mart." Nebraska Furniture Mart. Accessed June 15, 2020. https://www.nfm.com/about-us.

"All Nobel Prizes." NobelPrize.org. Accessed June 28, 2020. https://www.nobelprize.org/prizes/lists/all-nobel-prizes.

"Bloomberg Billionaires Index." Bloomberg.com. *Bloomberg News.* Accessed June 10, 2020. http://www.bloomberg.com/billionaires/.

Buffett, Warren. "Letter to Shareholders of Berkshire Hathaway Inc." Berkshire Hathaway, Inc., 2005. https://www.berkshirehathaway.com/letters/2005.html.

Buffett, Warren. "Letter to Shareholders of Berkshire Hathaway Inc." Berkshire Hathaway, Inc., 2013. https://www.berkshirehathaway.com/letters/2013.html.

Buffett, Warren. "Letter to Shareholders of Berkshire Hathaway Inc." Berkshire Hathaway, Inc., 2015. https://www.berkshirehathaway.com/letters/2015.html.

Buffett, Warren, et al. "2017 Berkshire Hathaway Shareholders Meeting (Full Transcription)." *Vintage Value Investing, May* 9, 2017. https://www.vintagevalueinvesting.com/2017-berkshire-hathaway-shareholders-meeting-full-transcription/.

"Estée Lauder Biography." Biography.com. A&E Networks Television, August 22, 2019. https://www.biography.com/people/est%C3%A9e-lauder-9374625.

Farnam Street. "The 'Circle of Competence' Theory Will Help You Make Vastly Smarter Decisions." *Business Insider,* December 5, 2013. https://www.businessinsider.com/the-circle-of-competence-theory-2013-12.

Graham, Katherine. *Personal History*. New York: Random House, 1997.

Knight, Phil. *Shoe Dog*. New York: Simon & Schuster, 2018.

Kroll, Luisa, and Kerry A. Dolan, eds. "The Forbes 400 2019." *Forbes,* October 2, 2019. https://www.forbes.com/forbes-400/.

La Roche, Julia. "Warren Buffett: Your Business Will Succeed If You Execute This 3-Word Mission." Yahoo! Finance, June 7, 2016. https://finance.yahoo.com/news/warren-buffett-best-advice-for-small-business-owners-203913790.html.

Oyedele, Akin. "Buffett on Google: Imagine Having a Business Where 'a Cash Register Rung Somewhere out in California' Every Time Someone Clicks." *Business Insider,* May 8, 2017. http://www.businessinsider.com/warren-buffett-says-google-has-some-aspects-of-a-natural-monopoly-2017-5.

Peterson-Withorn, Chase, and Madeline Berg. "Inside Kylie Jenner's Web of Lies—and Why She's No Longer a Billionaire." *Forbes*, June 1, 2020. https://www.forbes.com/sites/chasewithorn/2020/05/29/inside-kylie-jennerss-web-of-lies-and-why-shes-no-longer-a-billionaire/.

Sandberg, Sheryl. *Lean In*. New York: Alfred A. Knopf, 2013.

11

Being Thrifty like Buffett: Ways to Save Money

"Too often, a vast collection of possessions ends up possessing its owner."
—Warren Buffett, *Giving Pledge Letter*

Introduction

The Merriam-Webster dictionary defines the word "thrifty" as frugal. It has a related definition which is "economical management." Say what? It means being careful, smart, and not wasteful with your money. It doesn't mean cheap or stingy, which are almost always viewed in a negative light. Buffett had a personalized license plate for his car not too long ago. He didn't drive a Rolls Royce or some other super-exclusive car. Rather, he drove a nice, but somewhat modest, Lincoln Town Car. A Town Car was often used by firms providing car service to business travelers. Do you know what it said on his license plate? You guessed it! Thrifty. This chapter discusses things you can do to save money, with a healthy dose of Buffett throughout. Remember, if you can't save money, you can never have it grow and ultimately work for you.

Living within your means is one of the major themes of this book. But that doesn't mean you have to live the life of a pauper or monk. We want you to be smarter with your money. You might recall one of Walmart's famous slogans, "Save money. Live better." We think that's the proper mindset when it comes to spending money. And we know Buffett's giving virtually all of his money away to charity, so we're confident he's not cheap or miserly.

In this chapter, we're going to discuss a lot of things you can do to save money. In at least one respect, a mindset of saving money is more important to your net worth than making money. If you make money, you have to pay taxes on much of it, often 25% or more. In contrast, saving money goes right to the "bottom line," resulting in a dollar for dollar increase in your net worth. We'll discuss the names of real companies and products or services to make the discussion actionable. We have no affiliation with any of the firms mentioned but often use some of their products or services. To make it easier to digest we'll break it down into a number of smaller categories and leave you with a bunch of websites and apps that you might want to refer to well after you're done with this book. Of course, you're welcome to read this book more than once. ;)

We'll start out with some things you can do for free and then gradually work up to some bigger-ticket items. The topics of cars, homes, and college are big-ticket items that are so important that we're going to devote other chapters to them. So, they'll receive minimal discussion here, but we haven't forgotten about them by any stretch of the imagination.

Your Library: Free Books, Magazines, Newspapers, Music, Movies, and More

If you're reading or listening to this book, we hope you like books. The medium (reading on a screen, reading a physical book, or listening to a book) through which you consume information shouldn't matter much. We're big fans of audiobooks. You can listen to them while driving (or being driven), on the train, at home, or virtually anywhere. Audible, an Amazon.com company, is the leading provider of audiobooks. There's also audiobooks.com, iTunes, and other providers. OverDrive is an app used by many libraries that allows for the free download of books in various digital formats.

We mentioned in **Chapter 1** that Buffett read more than 100 books, outside of what was required for school, by the time he finished high school. He said, "By the age of 10, I'd read every book in the Omaha public library about investing, some twice. You need to fill your mind with various competing thoughts and decide which make sense." That's good advice and merits a Tip.

Buffett Tip 67:

Read a lot. You need to fill your mind with various competing thoughts and decide which make sense.

We know that Buffett is a super rich guy, but we mentioned another **tycoon** (i.e., an extraordinarily rich businessperson) in our last chapter, steel baron Andrew Carnegie. If you adjust for inflation and the size of the economy when Carnegie was around versus today, he'd be even richer than Buffett. By some estimates, he'd be worth more than $300 billion!

When Carnegie decided to become a philanthropist, one of his main causes was the construction of a network of libraries around the world. And man, did he deliver! He donated the funds to build more than 2,500 libraries around the world between 1883 and 1929, with the bulk of them in the US. The towns that received the libraries had to help too. For example, they usually donated the land where the library was built and used their own funds to run the library after it was constructed.

Carnegie was an active reader as a young man and realized that the knowledge obtained from books could help people achieve their dreams. Carnegie was an immigrant to the US who arrived from Scotland in the United Kingdom and worked his way up to becoming one of the richest people the world has ever seen. He was mostly known as a steel **baron** (a synonym of tycoon), and his main firm, U.S. Steel, still exists today. Carnegie believed in a merit-based economic system by which someone who worked hard and became educated had an increased chance of being successful. Some refer to this belief as the **democratization of knowledge**. You can count Google in that camp as well.

Google has also created a virtual library online, containing many freely available books in electronic or digitized form. Their plan is to scan and put online every book that has been ever written, with the permission of their publishers, of course. The author of a book receives a copyright, providing them with royalties, which are payments for their work. The rules for copyright vary a bit, but in general they last for 70 years after the author dies. Thus, if an author writes a book at age 20 and lives to be 100 years old, the copyright will last 80 plus 70 years, or 150 years in total! Google currently has more than 25 million books scanned online and estimates there are currently a total of 130 million books in the world. They hope to get them all online in the not too distant future.

Today, libraries have all sorts of free things you can borrow besides books. They have movies, music CDs, newspapers, magazines, and even Internet access. In our household, we often borrow movies from the New York Public Library. They have a huge selection of most of the popular movies, but sometimes it takes awhile to get your top choices.

Free Educational Courses: Khan Academy, Coursera

We've all heard the comment "Seeing is believing." There are all sorts of ways to learn. Many people are visual learners, learning best by seeing. Two popular and free websites for learning in a video format are Khan Academy and Coursera. We'll briefly discuss each website, which may be viewed on your phone, laptop, PC, Mac, iPad, and numerous other devices.

Khan Academy was created in 2006 by Salman Khan. A couple of years earlier, he tutored one of his cousins remotely over the Internet. He eventually decided to turn his tutoring activities into a nonprofit business. Khan originally worked in the financial services industry, but his true passion and calling is teaching. So he quit his high-paying financial job and took his educational business to the next level. The motto of Khan Academy is "A free, world-class education for anyone, anywhere." It currently offers thousands of free courses on most of the topics taught from grade school through high school. It also offers PSAT, SAT, ACT, and AP preparation courses.

How can Khan Academy do all of this for free? The firm has received substantial financial support from the Bill Gates Foundation, Google, AT&T, the Carlos Slim Foundation, and others. Carlos Slim is also one of the richest men in the world and made his fortune in a variety of Mexican-based businesses.

Khan Academy's courses may be found on YouTube, or through Khan Academy's own website (KhanAcademy.org). In case you're not an Internet guru, .org (organizational) generally means the firm running the website is a nonprofit. The suffix .gov relates to government websites, .edu to traditional educational websites, and the familiar .com stands for commercial or profit-seeking websites.

Curious about what a college course is like? Well, then you should check out Coursera at Coursera.org. Coursera offers free access to more than 3,000 college courses taught at top universities around the world including Yale, The University of Pennsylvania, Stanford, Duke, Johns Hopkins, Rutgers, Fudan University in China, and many, many more. We think it's a cool way to remotely sit in on a real college class and learn without the stress of taking the exams. Of course, you don't get a degree by simply watching Coursera videos, but you can learn a ton. They do offer programs that offer degrees, but it generally costs something. Coursera has several competitors worth checking out as well including Udacity, and edX. For free, short, educational, and inspiration talks that are not college courses we recommend the 2,500+ TED (Technology, Entertainment, Design) talks available at TED.com. Many TED talks can also be found on YouTube.

Websites for Free Stuff

Who would give away something for free? Lots of people! Sometimes they are moving and want to get rid of possessions they don't need. Other times they purchased a new item, such as a TV, and want to get rid of the old one. And it's not just people giving things away. Sometimes its organizations. Libraries occasionally give away old books to make way for new ones. Churches often give away items to their parishioners, beyond the soup kitchens they often run to feed the poor. For-profit firms also give away products (e.g., "free samples") since they want you to try their product and become a repeat customer. Firms may also try to lure you into getting something for free in the hopes that you will buy another item at its regular price.

In **Chapter 3** we discussed banks offering free savings and checking accounts. The strategy of giving away something for free falls under the banner of **loss leader** strategies. That is, the product that the firm leads with (e.g., the free sample of food) gives the firm a loss, but if the customer purchases another item at full cost (e.g., a regular meal), then the business may ultimately turn a profit. This strategy also falls under the umbrella of **cross-selling**. This means the firm tries selling the customer another product once they have obtained their current product. Most credit cards charge no annual fee, but the banks offering them make money by charging interest to their customers who don't pay their bill in full each month. Hopefully, after reading this book, that's not you! Banks may also try to sell their credit card customers checking accounts, mortgage loans, and wealth management products to illustrate some other possible cross-selling opportunities.

Perhaps the most popular website for getting free stuff is Craigslist.org. Yes, the business was started by a guy with the first name Craig. Craigslist is the most widely used online **classified** website. A classified is an advertisement where someone is trying to sell something. Sometimes they are looking for things, such a person to fill a job in a "help wanted" ad. Classified ads originally appeared in newspapers, but they are increasingly found online. Other popular websites that may help you get free items include the appropriately named Facebook Marketplace, FreeStuff.com, FreeSamples.org, BzzAgent, and WomanFreebies.com. There are dozens of websites that we came across that offer free stuff, including some sponsored by large firms, such as Target.

Free Activities

It almost goes without saying, but one way to save money is to do things that you find to be enjoyable that are virtually free. For example, you can hang out with friends, watch TV, listen to music, play sports, go to the park or beach, walk, exercise, work out, shoot pool at a friend's house, play cards, play board games, and many, many other things.

We realize in some cases you may need equipment or have to buy a board game, but over time the cost spread across many months or years is really small. For example, searching Amazon.com, we found a new deck of Bicycle playing cards for $4. You can find a used deck for less than half that or even lower at a garage sale. A deck of cards should last you 5 to 10 years. A small price today for something that might provide you with a decade or more of fun.

By the way, Buffett is a huge fan of the card game Bridge. He thinks it's a game with some parallels to investing, namely, making decisions based on incomplete information and the actions of others. It also involves teamwork since most variations of the game involve two teams of two people. He sometime plays bridge online under the handle T-Bone. Here's one of his quotes on the value of playing bridge:

> You have to look at all the facts. You have to draw inferences from what you've seen, what you've heard. You have to discard improper theories about what the hand had as more evidence comes in sometimes. You have to be open to a possible change of course if you get new information. You have to work with a partner, particularly on defense.

Amazon.com: The World's Biggest Store

Moving on to the frugal, but not so free category, we feel compelled to start with Amazon.com, a firm that needs no introduction. Virtually everyone not living under a rock has heard of Amazon.com. The name is related to the Amazon River, generally regarded as the biggest on earth. Amazon does have a huge selection of products and many are selling at very attractive prices. Plus, there are millions of customer reviews on the website, often giving you a somewhat independent view of the product's usefulness.

Jeff Bezos, founder of Amazon.com, started out selling books online, but ultimately wanted to create the biggest store in the world. Mission accomplished, at least in terms of the value of his firm. The value of Amazon.com's stock is greater than that of Walmart's ($1.5 trillion vs. $385 billion), even though Walmart still leads it in annual revenue ($542 billion vs. $332 billion). The difference may be explained by stock market investors speculating that Amazon.com's incredible growth will continue into the future, well outpacing that of Walmart.

Pretty much anyone with an Internet or cell phone connection can use Amazon's website, but virtually half of US households are members, including ours. Membership in Amazon Prime costs $119 a year. One advantage to being a student is Amazon.com will give you a break, six months of free membership and then $59 per year afterward. Membership in Amazon Prime has a ton of benefits that you get for "free"—outside of the membership costs.

Perhaps the main benefit is free and expedited shipping on products sold directly by Amazon. They also have a relationship with Kohl's, where you can return Amazon.com purchases at some Kohl's stores. Amazon also sells products from outside vendors that want access to Amazon's platform of a website viewed by millions of people, but there usually isn't free shipping for these external, or third-party, vendors. You might be wondering why Amazon would allow its website to be used by third-party vendors. Good question! It gets a piece of the sale made by the third-party vendor without having to purchase any inventory. The shipping costs are also handled by the third-party vendor. In essence, Amazon.com is renting the equivalent of shelf space in its market to these vendors for a fee. It also tends to be a win for the vendor since they would never have access to the millions and millions of Amazon's customers without this arrangement.

Amazon Prime's other benefits include free videos, music, and books. You can download one audiobook per month, although the selection is not quite as large as their (pay site) subsidiary, Audible. Amazon Prime has a huge selection of movies and original content programs, although we don't think it's quite as good as Netflix's—yet. Amazon Prime members can also upload an unlimited number of photos and 5 GB of videos to the cloud, a way to store information in the Internet. Yet another benefit of Prime membership is early access to sales, which may come in especially handy during the holiday shopping season.

There are more benefits to Amazon Prime, which you may find at the link below or by typing "Amazon Prime benefits" in any major search engine.

https://www.amazon.com/gp/help/customer/display.html?nodeId=201910360.

Amazon even tested out shipping items purchased from the website with a drone. It's not yet quite ready for prime time—yes, pun intended. We're also excited about their Amazon Go stores, which allow you to purchase things without waiting in line for a cashier or a self-scanner.

Comparison Shopper Tools: Your New Best Friend

There's a ton of stuff out there on the web. How do you find the best price for something you want to buy? That's where comparison shopper websites come into play. Think of it as a search engine, with a laser focus on finding what you want at the best possible price. Not surprisingly, Google/Alphabet is one of the leading firms in the space. Their comparison shopper tool is called Google Shopping and may be found at www.google.com/shopping.

Let's look at an example of how it might work. Let's say you're looking for a fitness tracker, Fitbit Charge 3. By typing that phrase in Google Shopping's search box, we get the following analysis, as show in **Figure 11.1**. There's a range of prices for the product from $86.00 to $149.99. That's a difference of about 75% for the same exact product!

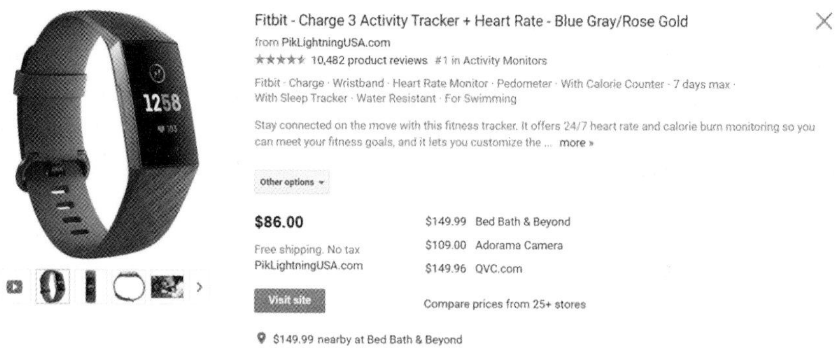

Figure 11.1 Google Shopping Fitbit Charge 3 Results
Source: Google Shopping.

Most of these comparison shopper tools also provide reviews from people who have purchased the product and tell you which physical stores near your home have the item in stock. Other leading comparison websites include PriceGrabber (PriceGrabber.com), eBay's Shopping.com, shopzilla (Shopzilla.com), and wikibuy (wikibuy.com)

Buffett is an avid user of Google and likes saving money on his purchases. In his 2007 Letter to Berkshire Shareholders, he wrote, "Long ago, Ben Graham taught me that 'Price is what you pay; value is what you get.' Whether we're talking about socks or stocks, I like buying quality merchandise when it is marked down." That's good advice, worth of a tip.

Buffett Tip 68:

Price is what you pay; value is what you get. Buy quality merchandise when it is marked down. ***(with an assist from Ben Graham)***

Barter: Turning a Cell Phone into a Porsche Convertible

Barter means to trade products or services, usually without cash changing hands. Maybe you traded lunches with a friend when you were a kid or holiday presents during a grab bag at school or with a sibling. That's barter in action.

Barter has been going on since the beginning of recorded history. Eventually money (in coin, paper, and electronic forms) replaced barter as the primary means of acquiring things, but barter still occurs. One problem with barter is that it requires what economists call a **double coincidence of wants.** That is, both people must want something that the other has. For example, it might be hard to imagine us bartering with Kim Kardashian, Jennifer Lawrence, or even Warren Buffett. What do we have that they could possibly want?

But before you think barter is a waste of time, consider this incredible example. (Then) seventeen-year-old Steven Ortiz bartered a cell phone and eventually turned it into a Porsche convertible! That's a savage trade! Young Mr. Ortiz started with a cell phone that was actually a gift from a friend. Thus, in some respects he started with nothing and turned it into a Porsche! But let's continue the story. He bartered the cell phone into an iPod touch. He bartered the iPod touch for a dirt bike. He bartered the dirt bike into a MacBook Pro laptop. The MacBook Pro laptop eventually bartered into a 1987 Toyota 4Runner. The Toyota then bartered into another Sport Utility Vehicle (SUV), a classic 1975 Ford Bronco. The 1975 Bronco was bartered into a 2000 Porsche Boxster. We've left out a few steps to the story, but all told Steven engaged in 14 barter transactions over a two-year period to ultimately turn his (free) cell phone into a sweet ride that must have made his high school classmates envious.

There's one example that we are familiar with that is even more extreme. A man bartered a single red paperclip for what *eventually* turned into a house! It's true! Kyle MacDonald is a young man who accomplished this incredible feat, with the help of some friends and external publicity. He operates the aptly named website http://oneredpaperclip.blogspot.com/ where you can read all about it. Not surprisingly, he wrote a book, *One Red Paperclip*, about his odyssey.

Our point about barter is that it might be an option to save you money, although it takes time and a double coincidence of wants. There are numerous barter websites out there. Steven Ortiz used the barter section on Craigslist.org to turn his cell phone into a Porsche Boxster. A few of the more popular ones include swap.com, U-Exchange (http://www.u-exchange.com/barterusa), TradeAway (http://www.tradeaway.com/), and SwapRight.com.

Eat a Low-Cost Meal, Periodically

Let's talk about saving money on food. We're not going to advise you to fast (i.e., skip meals). We'll leave that type of advice to your doctor or dietician. But we can suggest one way of saving money. Perhaps one day or more a week (1 day out of 7 = 14.3% of the time) consider eating meals that don't cost much. It doesn't mean starving. It means watching what you are spending for the food that you put in your body. A stereotypical example is young entrepreneurs running a start-up business while living on a diet heavily laden with Ramen noodles and Macaroni & Cheese. A 12 pack (3 ounces each) of Ramen noodles goes for $1.94 on Walmart.com. A 3 pack of Kraft Macaroni and Cheese (14 ounces each) goes for $6.48.

In fact, Buffett usually heads to the McDonald's drive-thru on most days for breakfast. If he's feeling prosperous, he'll splurge on a bacon, egg, and cheese biscuit for $3.17. On days when the stock market's down and he's not feeling quite as prosperous, he'll pay $2.61 for two sausage patties. True story, discussed in an HBO documentary on the life of Buffett.

For something healthier consider eggs, oatmeal, cereal, or rice. Once again, sticking with Walmart prices, since it's the largest seller of groceries in the US, we found a dozen grade A eggs selling for $0.90. A 42-ounce container of oatmeal (30 servings per container) goes for $3.88. A box of Cinnamon Toast Crunch cereal (11 servings per container) goes for $2.98. For something less sugary, a box of Kellogg's Corn Flakes (12 servings per container) costs $3.64. You may want to add milk to your cereal at a cost of $3.00 a gallon (16 servings per container). Winding up our example of cheap staple foods, we find a 5-pound bag of enriched white rice costs only $2.67. With all these food prices, we think you're ready to be contestant on the game show *The Price is Right*!:-)

If you have time and property, you can even plant seeds at minimal cost and create your own mini-garden. One of America's founding fathers, Thomas Jefferson, viewed agriculture as "the most precious of arts." One of his more famous quotes, outside of writing The Declaration of Independence, of course, was "I am entirely a farmer, soul and body, never scarcely admitting a sentiment on any other subject." Thomas Jefferson was down with farming!

The cheapest thing to drink is tap water. It's also one of the healthiest. Tap water should be fine in most locations. In fact, much of the bottled water that is sold to consumers is from the same source as tap water in many communities. Usually a lake or mountain spring. If you are less than thrilled with the quality of your tap water, you can buy a filter for around 20 bucks that will last you at least a year.

Shop Private Label and Generic Items

We've mentioned Amazon.com and Walmart. Let's add another couple of discount stores to the mix, focusing mostly on food. We bring you Aldi and Costco. Aldi is a discount supermarket that originated in Germany and operates over 10,000 stores worldwide. They have more than 1,900 stores in the US. It's probably one of the few retail stores that are often less expensive than Walmart on select items. Aldi has a sister store chain, Trader Joe's, which sells many organic food items at prices that are generally less than what you may find at Whole Foods, at least before it was acquired by Amazon.

Aldi sells some name brand products, such as Gatorade, but they are also known for selling "no name" items. Using Gatorade as an example, a "no name" brand would be a sports drink with similar ingredients, but with a name you probably wouldn't recognize, such as SportsAde. Apologies to any real firm using that name.:-)

When a company slaps its own label on a product manufactured by an outside firm it's called **private label**. Sometimes the word **generic** is interchanged with private label, especially in the case of selling pharmaceutical products. Walmart uses the private labels Sam's and Equate on some of the items it sells. Aldi uses private label brands such as Clancy's and Friendly Farms. Costco uses the private label name Kirkland for many of the items in its stores. A rough rule of thumb is that private label products cost at least 20% less than their branded counterparts. For example, a 12 pack of Sam's Cola cans recently sold for $2.17. A 12 pack of Coca-Cola cans recently cost $4.28 at Walmart. That's almost double the price for a product with virtually the same ingredients! Yes, we know Buffett is a huge fan and owner of Coke and drinks five cans a day!

Costco is known for selling items in bulk. Instead of a pack of gum, they might sell a box of 24. Instead of selling a single razor, they might sell a pack of 26. On a per unit basis, the price is cheaper, but if you don't use the bulk items within a certain period of time (a year for the chewing gum example) it may not make sense. Costco also sells some non-bulk items at great prices. They are famous for selling a hot dog and soda for only $1.50 since the mid-1980s and a full rotisserie chicken for only $4.99.

Costco requires a membership fee to join—$60 annually for individuals. But you can often get one membership plan for the entire family, making the expense more palatable. Other firms in the same business, sometimes called a warehouse club, include Walmart's Sam's Club and

BJ's Wholesale Club, which charge annual membership fees of $45 and $50, respectively. All of these "wholesale clubs" sell things besides food, including electronics, clothes, health care products, and items used to furnish and maintain a home.

What might surprise you is the branded firm is often selling the private label product to Walmart, Costco, Aldi, and so forth. Why would they do this? One reason is to avoid the expense of marketing or selling the item. Examples of marketing expenses include commercials and (print or online) advertisements.

Clothes: Outlet Stores, Vintage Items, and Buying Off-Season

Teens and young adults are big purchasers of clothes since they are growing rapidly physically and tend to be fashion conscious. Of course, clothes are for everyone, regardless of age. Who doesn't like some cool threads? We have nothing against paying full or retail prices for something that you *love*, but most of the major apparel brands have **outlet stores**, which sell items at a big discount, usually anywhere from 25% to 70% off. In fact, there are some malls that are predominately populated by just outlet stores. One of the more popular ones on the East Coast is Woodbury Common Premium Outlets in Orange County, New York. The place is huge and has over 200 stores. Shopping heaven for some! People literally fly in from China and other countries to shop there. We won't list all 200 stores, but here are some you'll probably recognize: Adidas, American Eagle, Calvin Klein, Gap, J. Crew, Levi's, Nike, Oakley, Puma, Reebok, The North Face, Timberland, Under Armour, and many, many others.

The goal of this chapter is to help you save money, but for those able to afford higher-end or luxury brands, Woodbury Commons also has outlet stores for Armani Exchange, Hugo Boss, Brooks Brothers, Burberry, Coach, Fendi, Gucci, Jimmy Choo, Kate Spade, Neiman Marcus Last Call, Polo Ralph Lauren, Versace, and many, many others. In case you get hungry, there are a bunch of places to grab a bite to eat, including Applebee's, Chipotle, Cinnabon, Shake Shack, Starbucks, and yes, McDonald's.

T.J. Maxx is a national store chain with over 1,000 locations whose business emphasizes selling name brand goods at deep discount prices. They have a large selection of clothing and accessories from major brands including Adidas, Calvin Klein, Kate Spade, Michael Kors, Ralph

Lauren, Puma, Tommy Hilfiger, Under Armour, and many others. Ross Stores is another national chain selling similar goods at a deep discount.

Vintage clothing is a fancy name for used clothing. Most people have a positive impression of the words vintage or antique, while the term "used" is undesirable, just like Chilean seabass sounds more appetizing than its original name, Patagonian toothfish. While buying someone else's clothes may sound skeevy to some, it's a large industry. Many of the clothes have been barely worn, and the prices are typically 50% to 90% off the retail price of a new item. For example, a new pair of ripped jeans generally costs from $50 to $200. We found a bunch of vintage ripped jeans on eBay (ebay.com) for between $10 and $20. Similar bargains exist for most other clothes. There are vintage clothing shops in most cities that you can check out in addition to websites such as eBay, Etsy (Etsy.com), and Rusty Zipper (RustyZipper.com).

A central concept of investing is that if you have a long horizon, you may be able to profit from distressed sellers. Distressed sellers need the money, for one reason or another, and often sell at low prices. An expression in the investing world for buying stocks on sale is "buying a straw hat in the winter." Yeah, we know that straw hats may be perceived as nerdy or uncool in many parts of the country today, but when they were popular, most were purchased in the summer or warm weather months. Applying this concept to clothes, if you buy something outside the season, like a bathing suit during the fall in cold regions of the country, you might find a great deal on brand-new merchandise. At the end of each season the retailer is usually trying to clear out inventory to make way for the next season's expected big sellers. For example, removing the bathing suits from the shelves in the Northeast in September and replacing them with long-sleeve shirts or jackets.

Buying Gasoline

Gas, like food, tends to be another part of your budget that is hard to avoid. At least for those who drive or don't live in a city with excellent mass transit systems. Gas prices differ dramatically by company, but the quality tends not to differ too much for the same octane levels. Octane is a measure of the quality and performance of fuel—the higher the number, the better. Most of your "no name" gas stations actually purchase their gasoline from major oil companies, such as Exxon Mobil, Chevron, BP, and Royal Dutch Shell.

When you need to fill up your tank, don't just go to the nearest place, unless you are running on E, of course! Consider using an app or website such as GasBuddy (GasBuddy.com). Simply type in the zip code where your car is, or an address, and hit "Find Gas." The site will then show a list of gas stations in the area sorted by price—lowest to highest. In our experiences, warehouse clubs such as Costco, Sam's Club, and BJ's Wholesale usually offer the lowest prices on gas. They typically save you 10% or more from the prices of most gas stations. The downside is that the lines are sometimes long, unless you fill up at off-peak hours. Over the course of a lifetime, saving money on gasoline could be huge. Using our compound interest and future value formulas, introduced in **Chapter 2**, saving $100 a year for 50 years and putting the savings in the stock market at a rate of 10% per year adds up to more than $100,000!

One last note on gasoline purchases. It might be possible to own an automobile without paying for *any* gas. The prices of electric vehicles (EV) are coming down every day. The US government has provided tax incentives to own these cars, giving discounts known as **electric vehicle federal tax credits** from $2,500 to $7,500. A new Nissan Leaf costs about $30,000, before any tax credits. The Chevy Volt starts at about $33,000. The Tesla Model 3 EV starts at $39,990, giving you up to 322 miles of range on a full charge. Most auto manufacturers have, or are developing, their own electric cars too. And the price of used cars, of course, is almost always a lot less. Our next chapter will provide you with more details on buying or leasing a car.

Coupons, Double-Couponing, Triple-Couponing, and Groupon

When we discussed the bond market in **Chapter 4**, we mentioned that the interest the issuer of a bond pays is known as the coupon. Most people are familiar with coupons that give you a discount on a purchase, and that's what we're focusing on here. Here's a funny story on Buffett and coupons. He took Bill Gates to McDonald's and used coupons to help pay the bill! Oh, to be a fly on the wall, watching two of the richest people ever, eating cheap food, at an inexpensive restaurant, using coupons!

Earlier in this chapter we mentioned the concept of a loss leader. That is, selling one product at a loss, in the hopes of selling other items at a profit that will more than make up for the loss. This strategy is especially popular during the holiday season when some firms, such as

Best Buy, offer "door buster" specials with a limited number of a highly desired item, like an X-Box, sold at a huge discount. Many stores sell a small portion of their goods at a steep discount on a regular basis. Sometimes they send a flyer in the mail in the form of a coupon.

Let's say your local Stop & Shop supermarket is having a sale on Friendly's Cookies 'n Cream Ice Cream at a price of $2.00 a gallon when the normal price is $4.00. That's a sweet 50% discount. Manufacturers (Friendly's in this case) also issue coupons that can be combined with those offered by the store selling the ice cream. When you combine two coupons it's called **double-couponing**. Let's say you have a Friendly's coupon that provides another 50 cents off a gallon of ice cream. Applying this "double discount" results in a price of $1.50 a gallon, a cool 62.5% discount. Occasionally, it'll even be possible to get a **triple-coupon**, where the store (supermarket in our case) offers another discount, such as 10% off any order over $25.

There are a bunch of firms that specialize in coupons. Valpak is one of the larger firms known for sending coupons in the mail. Supermarkets such as Kroger, Acme, A&P, Stop & Shop, and Shop Rite often put their own coupons, sometimes called a circular, in the mail too. Some websites that specialize in coupons include Retail Me Not (RetailMeNot.com), Honey (JoinHoney.com), and Coupons.com.

Groupon (Groupon.com) is a popular website that teams up with companies to offer deep discounts on products and services. They began in the US but are now in 48 countries around the world. Groupon started out selling a "deal of the day" that would often be active for 24 to 36 hours and then disappear. Today they offer all sorts of deals, at prices typically ranging from 25% to 75% off. Groupon often partners with small local companies who face the challenge of finding a steady stream of customers. One way for these small companies to be "discovered" is to have Groupon advertise their business to its millions of members with a special "deal of the day." The small business might break even or lose money on this first sale, but hopefully the customer will be satisfied and come back for more at their regular, higher price.

Rewards Programs

Many companies offer reward programs for their customers. They know that repeat customers are a good way to build a long-term business. They often create rewards programs to offer discounts, or "members only" sales, providing an incentive to join. For example, Dunkin' Donuts' rewards program is called DD Perks. Members get points for each purchase they make. They get free beverages when they sign up, on their birthday, and after accumulating 200 points. Starbucks, Panera, Chili's, and tons of other companies offer similar programs.

Airlines also offer their customers popular rewards programs, sometimes called **frequent flyer programs**. Each time you fly on an airline you accumulate miles or points. These miles, if large enough, can be cashed in to get free flights. Other times, you might get upgraded from coach to cushy business class or first class. Awesome! On the topic of airlines, there are websites such as Kayak, Booking.com (Priceline), Expedia, and Travelocity that can search for your flights and find the best prices. In Priceline's case you can actually bid on the price you are willing to pay. In **Chapter 3** we discussed credit cards providing a range of benefits from cash back to discounts on food, gasoline, and clothes. The bottom line is this. Is there a store or business that you use on a regular basis? If so, ask if they have a rewards program and see if you can save money on something you are already doing.

Negotiate with Cell Phone, Cable, and other Service Providers

Many prices aren't etched in stone. They're subject to negotiation. The art of haggling over prices is practiced in many countries around the world. It's an uncomfortable process for many, such as in haggling over the price of a used car, but improving your negotiating skills will pay off for you over the long term. That's one of the reasons why we're going to cover the teachings of a guy by the name of Dale Carnegie (no relation to Andrew Carnegie) in **Chapter 13**, covered in his best-selling book, *How to Win Friends and Influence People.*

There are many items that you purchase that may be reduced in price if you ask nicely—especially if the company thinks you're going to leave and take your business to another competitor. Now, we are not suggesting that you should lie, but if you are genuinely thinking about switching, it may be worth mentioning this to your service provider. Among the bills that that may be negotiated are your cell phone bill and your cable/satellite TV (e.g., DirecTV, DISH network) bill. You might start by asking the customer service representative if there are any discounts. There often are if you are willing to commit for at least a year. If that doesn't work, you can show them an advertisement developed by one of their competitors showing good prices and see if there is anything your original company can do to match.

On the topic of cell phones, we know that they're crucial to the lives of most people today. The pricing plans can be more confusing than a Rubik's cube! Fortunately, there are some websites out there that will help you make sense of things and find the best plan for you. Some of these cell phone comparison websites include WhistleOut, WireFly, NerdWallet, and Consumer Reports.

Based on our experience and informal surveys, having access to a smartphone is more important than the phone itself, since it's the apps that matter. Although we are huge fans of the iPhone, there are also great and cheaper phones out there made by Samsung (not the one that blows up!), Google, LG, Sony, Huawei, Xiaomi, and others. The following analogy will explain our logic.

During the 1990s, when the Internet was fairly new, you connected to the Internet through an Internet Service Provider (ISP) such as America Online, MSN Online, CompuServe, and others. Although you might find this hard to believe, many people spent much of their time online within that service provider's ecosystem (i.e., its own websites). For example, there was a page for AOL news, AOL sports, AOL shopping, and so forth. Eventually, people spent much of their time outside their ISP's ecosystem and on great external websites, such as ESPN.com, Instagram, Facebook, and so forth. After all, there are now millions of websites out there. Our point is you should shop around for the phone and cable/Internet carrier that meets your needs.

Now, we're not going to tell you to ditch your smartphone, but you might be surprised to learn that Buffett still uses a Nokia flip phone! He joked, "This is the one Alexander Graham Bell gave me." He also has sent only one email in his life, and it was subpoenaed in a court hearing. Buying an older smartphone may save you some money and using an ancient cellphone, like Buffett's flip phone, may save you a lot of money, if you are so inclined.

Yard Sales, Flea Markets, and More: Turning Trash into Treasure

A **yard sale**, called a **garage sale** in some communities, is where people sell items to the public they don't need anymore. It's a way to earn some extra money if you're selling. On the flip side, if you're buying, it's a way to find some great deals. Pretty much anything can be sold in a yard sale, but common items are clothes, toys, games, sporting equipment, and home furnishings. It brings to mind the well-known expression "Turning someone's trash into your treasure."

There have been rare occasions where someone sells an item at nominal cost, without knowing its value, and then the item is later revealed to be worth millions of dollars. Now that's a real treasure! Not that we think you can bank on that happening to you, but here are a couple of examples. Rick Norsigian paid $45 for two boxes of what appeared to be regular glass plates back in 2000. Turns out the plates were actually photographic negatives of the American photography pioneer Ansel Adams. The value of the photographic negatives may be worth up to $200 million! In 2009, Teisha McNeal paid $2 at a yard sale for a reportedly fake Picasso. Well, she bought the real thing, and it may be worth up to $2 million!

Many yard sales are done on a community basis. That is, many of the people on the block have a yard sale on the same day. It increases the traffic, since potential customers can peruse the yard sales of many families and not just one. Something related to a garage sale is called a **flea market**, where dozens, if not hundreds, of vendors all meet at the same place to sell their goods. Each vendor typically sets up a table and places their items on the table for potential customers to examine. Like with a garage sale, you might earn some extra cash by selling, or score some great deals by buying.

A similar place worth considering is called a **thrift shop**. Most of the items for sale are donated to the thrift shop. They are often run by charitable or religious institutions. Goodwill Industries is one of the largest firms in this space. Thrift shops typically sell many items, including clothes, shoes, books, toys, sporting goods, electronics, and home furnishings. Before you scoff at such an idea, you might be surprised to learn who has purchased things at thrift shops. Buffett's wife, Astrid Menks, is said to be a fan of thrift shops even though she is married to one of the richest people in the world. You are never too rich to save money!

Lastly, for this section, a **pawn shop** may also be a place to find some great deals. We hope you are never in this situation, but sometimes people need money for a variety of reasons. If they have something of value, say a fancy watch, they may be able to loan it to a pawn shop. Let's say the watch is worth $200. The pawn shop owner may give the person $100 and keep the watch as collateral, a term we encountered in

Chapter 3 in our discussion of bank loans. The person who sold their watch to the pawn shop has a finite period of time, typically 30 to 90 days, to pay back the $100 plus interest. If not, the pawn shop owner will keep the watch and then sell it. In our running example of the watch, the selling price may be between $100 and $200.

Pawn shops used to have a somewhat seedy reputation since some were used to turn stolen goods into cash for thieves, but popular TV shows, such as *Pawn Stars*, have increased the legitimacy and status of these stores. There are even some pawn shops trading on the American stock exchanges, such as FirstCash (symbol FCFS), which is valued at roughly $2 billion!

Do-It-Yourself

There are a lot of things you can "do-it-yourself" to save money. The standard example is bringing your own lunch to school or work ("brown bagging") instead of buying one. Washing your car (if and when you get one) instead of going to a car wash is another one. Some of your family members and close friends might appreciate a personalized, homemade gift more than one that's store bought. Doing things around the house can save you money, such as painting, cleaning, cutting the grass, and so forth. Using a "smart thermostat" such as Nest may also save you money over time since it can adjust the temperature of your home when you aren't around. You get the idea. There are probably hundreds of things you can do to save money if you really think about it and put it into action. Remember the numbers we cited earlier in this chapter. Saving $100 a year can add up to more than $100,000 over the course of a lifetime. To put it even more dramatically, saving $1,000 a year ($83.33 a month) can save $1,000,000 over the course of a lifetime for a young person on the early road to building wealth.

Donate Things to Charity

If you have things that can't be sold on eBay, Craigslist, at a yard sale, or in some other way, then why not donate them? Many thrift shops or community centers may be interested in things you no longer have use for, or interest in. Your donation may help someone in need or a person searching for a good bargain. Plus, when you make enough money to pay income taxes, the donation will likely qualify as a tax deduction, reducing your overall tax bill. Seems like a win-win to us!

Avoid Shooting Yourself in the Foot with Bad Habits

There are a lot of little things to do that may save you money if you put your mind to it. In **Chapter 3**, we discussed the importance of paying off your credit card bills, if you have one, in full each month. You'll save on interest expense. Hopefully, you haven't picked up (or will pick up) any bad habits, such as smoking, drinking, unhealthy food, and so forth. Eliminating this type of behavior will likely be as good for your health as it will be for your wallet or pocketbook.

Being happy with what you have is a good mindset to develop. It's a challenge to think that way given the peer pressure that all people face and the pressure to "keep up with the Joneses"—or Kardashians. When in doubt, it might help to turn to Buffett's wisdom for advice. In a 2006 article in *Fortune* magazine discussing his pledge to donate most of his money to charity, he said, "Some material things make my life more enjoyable; many, however, would not. I like having an expensive private plane, but owning a half-dozen homes would be a burden. Too often, a vast collection of possessions ends up possessing its owner. The asset I most value, aside from health, is interesting, diverse, and long-standing friends." Let's summarize that sage advice with a Tip.

Buffett Tip 69:

Too often, a vast collection of possessions ends up possessing its owner. The more stuff you have, the more stuff you have to worry about.

Tying It All Together in a Budget

We'll finish this chapter with setting up a **budget**, which is a plan that describes your spending and savings over a period of time. Budgets for teens are a lot different than budgets for retired people, as well as at every age in between. We'll focus on a budget for someone just starting in the workforce, such as a recent college graduate, earning $50,000 a year before taxes. We're pretty sure Buffett could live on $50k if he needed to. He'd have to ditch his private jet though!

At this point in the book, you should know that you can't accumulate wealth without spending less than what you take in. It sounds trivial, but many people wind up in a vicious cycle where they spend more than they take in, often accruing high rates of interest on debt. This behavior often results in living a paycheck-to-paycheck existence. We don't want this to be you! The concept of having net savings was hardwired into Buffett's brain probably at birth. It was never a problem for him, since even as a young person he envisioned himself as the richest person in the world.

Budgets take into account your income, which is typically earned from a full-time job, but it may come from other sources, such as investment income, gifts, and a side gig. Earning **multiple streams of income** is a great way to accelerate the growth in your wealth. Budgets also take into account your expenses, including food, shelter, entertainment, health, education, and so forth. Everyone's income and expenses are different, but for financially literate people, the key point is that inflows should exceed the outflows most of the time. An obvious exception might be paying for college, since it's an expensive investment that often overwhelms your income at the time.

While you may dread making a budget, an easy place to start is by making a list of all of your expenses as well as sources of income. Credit card statements will often break down expenses by category, potentially making a convenient list for you. It's good discipline to create a budget with the help of a spreadsheet. There are also a bunch of free, or freemium, apps that easily let you create and track a budget, such as those created by Mint, PocketGuard, You Need A Budget (YNAB), and Goodbudget. One way to get motivated to create a budget is to write down your goals. For example, you may want to save for a house, car, retirement, education, and so forth.

Once you have decided on your financial goal(s), you should enter your sources of income. Let's assume you earn $50,000 from your main job. Let's further assume you receive $1,000 in gifts, $1,000 in investment income, and $4,000 from your side gig as an Uber driver. This all adds up to $56,000, but we think it's good technique to reinvest your investment income and not spend it so "the miracle of compound interest" can work for you. That gives us $55,000 in pre-tax income.

A sizeable part of being financially literate is about having the proper mindset. "Paying yourself," or saving, is the first "expense" we'll start with. Of course, it's not an expense, but it's a good technique and often a tax-free deduction when done through a retirement plan such as an IRA or 401(k), which we'll discuss in **Chapter 15**. "Supersavers" aim to save 50% or more of their income, but it may take awhile to get there. Saving 10% is more realistic for most people and Fidelity Investments recommends 20%. Let's start at 10%, or $5,500, with the goal of getting this number up to 20%+ in a few years by pocketing future raises in your income.

We'll also assume you are living on your own. Housing is the largest expense for most people, and a good rule of thumb is that it should cost no more than 30% of your total income, even though its weight is closer to 40% in the CPI. Many people got in over their heads in the period just prior to the Great Recession by purchasing homes they couldn't afford. Let's say you don't have to have the swankiest pad and can get by on spending 25% of your income on housing, or $13,750 per year, which comes out to $1,146/month. We realize this amount won't go too far in places such as New York City, unless you have some roommates. Some apartments include utilities, such as electric, gas/oil, (basic) Internet/cable/Netflix, and water, in the price of the housing, but we'll add another 5%, or $2,750, to our budget.

As another rule of thumb, transportation should cost about 15% of your income or less. That's $8,250 per year or $688 per month. Although that sounds like a sweet budget, don't get ready to purchase that new BMW you've had your eye on! By transportation expenses, we refer to those related to automobiles, trains, buses, subways, insurance, parking, and repairs. If you live in a city with great mass transit, you can reduce this number drastically, although the cost of your home will likely be much higher. **Carpooling** (i.e., sharing a work commute) may be another way to reduce these expenses, especially if you live in the same area as one of your work colleagues. Working from home is an option for many people, especially in the way that the world has changed in the wake of the COVID-19 pandemic.

Health care is typically a work benefit, but with most firms you still have to pay something in excess of what your employer provides. Most young people are very healthy and can use a high deductible plan, which has the effect of lowering your health care cost, unless you wind up with a lot of doctor / hospital visits. Let's put it at 5% in our budget, some of which is usually tax deductible. We'll make your gift giving $600, instead of $1,000, due to your newfound ability to shop at great prices and growing penchant for homemade gifts. ;-)

Based on our earlier discussion, we showed that food costs vary widely and can be reduced significantly if you try hard enough by shopping wisely, bringing your own lunch to work, and eating in a lot during nights and weekends. Let's put it at 10% ($5,500), unless you have a weakness for eating out a lot. Otherwise you'll have to cut somewhere else, as long as it is not your savings rate!

We'll put clothes at 3% of your annual budget, or $1,650. This may seem like a low number, but it's not that bad, considering that these are annual additions to your already existing wardrobe. Sorry—you may not be able to afford anything you see on the runway in Fashion Week on this tight budget. We'll call another category entertainment and other. It's a catch-all category for things entertainment related, including your cell phone, dating, vacations, and personal items. We'll put it at 5%, or $2,750. Once again, if this number seems too low, you will have to rob from Peter to pay Paul, so to speak.

An **emergency fund** should help with any major unforeseen expenses, such as job loss, a medical problem, or car trouble. A savings account is often a good location for emergency funds, due to its safety and high liquidity. An emergency fund of 5% every year is a good rule of thumb. Over time, the fund should grow to cover at least 3 months of living expenses and preferably six months.

We can't escape the tax man or woman, but we're able to reduce taxes with some of our health and retirement plan deductions, and the standard single deduction of $12,400 for individuals. We estimate the income taxes for this person at around $8,750, assuming you don't live in a high-tax region. If you do, you'll probably need a roommate to cut your housing costs in our example. We're also assuming you don't have a large student loan to pay. See **Chapter 14** for a discussion on college and its related expenses.

We've included our fictional budget, in spreadsheet form, in the **Appendix**. So that's a wrap for this chapter. We know it was long, but it may be the chapter most directly tied to your wealth down the road.

Buffett's Tips from Chapter 11

Buffett Tip 67: Read a lot. You need to fill your mind with various competing thoughts and decide which make sense.

Buffett Tip 68: Price is what you pay; value is what you get. Buy quality merchandise when it is marked down. *(with an assist from Ben Graham)*

Buffett Tip 69: Too often, a vast collection of possessions ends up possessing its owner. The more stuff you have, the more stuff you have to worry about.

Appendix: Sample Budget

Goals: Save money for retirement and for purchasing a home

Income Sources	Amount
Full-time job	$50,000
Investments*	$1,000
Gifts	$1,000
Side job	$4,000
Total	$56,000
Adjusted total**	**$55,000**

*Plan to reinvest

**Assumes reinvestment of investment income

Expenses	Amount
Retirement savings ***	$5,500
Housing	$13,750
Utilities	$2,750
Transportation	$8,250
Food	$5,500
Health care	$2,750
Clothing	$1,650
Entertainment & other	$2,750
Gifts	$600
Emergency fund	$2,750
Taxes	$8,750
Adjusted total	**$55,000**

***Start at 10% with a goal of moving to 20%+

References

Becoming Warren Buffett. Directed by Peter W. Kunhardt. HBO, 2017

Belvedere, Matthew. "Amazon's Jeff Bezos Is 'the Most Remarkable Business Person of Our Age,' Says Warren Buffett." CNBC, May 5, 2017. http://www.cnbc.com/2017/05/05/amazons-jeff-bezos-is-the-most-remarkable-business-person-of-our-age-says-warren-buffett.html.

Blank, Adam. "Teen Barters Phone for a Porsche Convertible." CNN. Cable News Network, July 22, 2010. http://www.cnn.com/2010/LIVING/07/22/teen.barter.cell.porsche/.

Buffett, Warren. "Letter to Shareholders of Berkshire Hathaway Inc." Berkshire Hathaway, Inc., 2007. https://www.berkshirehathaway.com/letters/2007.html.

Buffett, Warren. "My Philanthropic Pledge." *Fortune,* June 16, 2010. http://archive.fortune.com/2010/06/15/news/newsmakers/Warren_Buffett_Pledge_Letter.fortune/index.htm.

Carnegie, Dale. *How to Win Friends and Influence People.* New York: Simon & Schuster, 1936.

Crippen, Alex. "Warren Buffett: Playing Bridge Theoretically More Interesting Than Naked Woman." CNBC, April 2, 2014. http://www.cnbc.com/id/23234847.

Davis, Matt. "7 Garage Sale Finds That Were Worth Millions." *TheRichest, May* 10, 2014. http://www.therichest.com/luxury/most-expensive/7-garage-sale-finds-that-were-worth-millions/.

"The Definitive Collection | Buffett in His Own Words." Warren Buffett Archive. CNBC, May 4, 2020. http://www.warrenbuffett.com/12-interesting-facts-you-didnt-know-about-warren-buffett/.

Elkins, Kathleen. "Warren Buffett Eats the Same Thing for Breakfast Every Day—and It Never Costs More than $3.17." CNBC, January 30, 2017. https://www.cnbc.com/2017/01/30/warren-buffetts-breakfast-never-costs-more-than-317.html.

Elkins, Kathleen. "Warren Buffett Once Bought Bill Gates Lunch at McDonald's with Coupons." CNBC, February 19, 2017. https://www.cnbc.com/2017/02/17/warren-buffett-once-paid-for-bill-gates-mcdonalds-meal-with-coupons.html.

Elkins, Kathleen. "11 Of Warren Buffett's Funniest and Most Frugal Quirks." CNBC, May 9, 2017c. https://www.cnbc.com/2017/05/09/11-of-warren-buffetts-funniest-and-most-frugal-quirks.html.

Elkins, Kathleen. "Here's How Much of Your Income You Should Be Spending on Housing." CNBC, June 6, 2018. https://www.cnbc.com/2018/06/06/how-much-of-your-income-you-should-be-spending-on-housing.html.

Fidelity Viewpoints. "How Much You Should Save and Spend." Fidelity, March 3, 2020. https://www.fidelity.com/viewpoints/personal-finance/spending-and-saving.

Greutman, Lauren. "Aldi vs. Walmart—Which One Is Really Less Expensive than the Other One?" Lauren Greutman, April 22, 2016. http://www.laurengreutman.com/aldi-walmart/.

Leadem, Rose. "25 Surprising Facts About Warren Buffett." *Entrepreneur.* Accessed June 15, 2020. https://www.entrepreneur.com/article/290381.

Loomis, Carol J. "Warren Buffett Gives Away His Fortune." *Fortune,* June 25, 2006. https://archive.fortune.com/2006/06/25/magazines/fortune/charity1.fortune/index.htm.

Loomis, Carol J. *Tap Dancing to Work: Warren Buffett on Practically Everything, 1966–2012.* London: Portfolio Penguin, 2014.

Mathews, Brendan. "Warren Buffett Finally Explains Why Being Cheap Leads to Happiness." The Motley Fool, June 8, 2014. https://www.fool.com/investing/general/2014/06/08/warren-buffett-finally-explains-why-being-cheap-le.aspx.

MacDonald, Kyle. *One Red Paperclip: Or How an Ordinary Man Achieved His Dream with the Help of a Simple Office Supply.* New York: Three Rivers Press, 2007.

Skillings, Jon. "'Red Paperclip' House up for Bids." CNET, June 18, 2008. https://www.cnet.com/news/red-paperclip-house-up-for-bids/.

"Top 10 Richest of All Time: Celebrity Net Worth Ranks Wealthiest in the World." nydailynews.com. *New York Daily News.* Accessed June 15, 2020. http://www.nydailynews.com/news/top-10-richest-people-time-gallery-1.1186737?pmSlide=1.1186732.

Zheng, Ruonan. "Woodbury Commons as 'Essential as the Empire State,' Say Chinese Tour Operators." *Jing Daily,* January 10, 2018. https://jingdaily.com/woodbury-outlet-chinese-shopping/.

12

Buffett's Views on Cars and Homes

"All things considered, the third best investment I ever made was the purchase of my home."
—Warren Buffett, 2011 Letter to Berkshire Hathaway Shareholders

Introduction

It's considered part of the American Dream to own your own home. You know, the proverbial house with the white picket fence. Although Buffett is a huge fan of stocks, he considers his home in Omaha to be the third-best investment of his life. In case you're wondering what the two best investments Buffett thinks he made, they are marrying his two wives, Susie and, after her death, Astrid.

Despite being a billionaire many times over, Buffett has lived in the same house since 1958, which he bought for $31,500. It's a nice home, but it's not a mansion. Odds are some of the nicer homes in your neighborhood are probably more luxurious than Buffett's home. Nonetheless, he said in one interview, "For me, that's the happiest house in the world. And it's because it's got memories, and people come back, and all that sort of thing." He also said, "All things considered, the third-best investment I ever made was the purchase of my home, though I would have made far more money had I instead rented and used the purchase money to buy stocks." Despite Buffett's preference for stocks, let's turn his views on owning your own home into a Tip.

Buffett Tip 70:

A home will likely be one of the best investments you'll ever make.

You want to be smart about all of your purchases, but especially related to the big-ticket items, such as cars and homes. These aren't only purchases but may also be considered investments in many respects. Let's tackle these big-ticket items in the order that you'll likely encounter them. First, owning your own car and then owning your own home. As usual, Buffett has had a lot to say on these topics, so we'll weave his comments in when appropriate. We'll discuss one more big-ticket item—paying for college—in **Chapter 14**.

Do You Need a Car?

Although the driverless car is on its way, it's not yet here in full force. Some people live their entire lives without owning a car, especially those living in large cities with well-developed mass transit systems. Others choose to use Uber or Lyft to get around, the equivalent of taxis run by regular people. In Denmark, 9 out of 10 people own a bicycle and many people ride it to work, even in the winter! It saves money, and the exercise keeps the Danish fitter than people from most other countries. However, most young people in America today still want a car since it often provides them with extra freedom. Freedom to get to school, work, shopping, and social activities. Of course, having a car also results in extra expenses—the cost of the car, repairs, insurance, and gasoline. It's a rite of passage into adulthood for many teens.

Buffett was, and is, a fan of cars. He once said, "When I was 16, I had just two things on my mind—girls and cars. I wasn't very good with girls. So I thought about cars." In contrast to his frugal behavior today, Buffett and a friend each owned half of an old Rolls Royce when he was in high school. They bought it to impress girls and tried to rent it out to earn extra money. They paid $350 for the car and rented it out for $35 a day. He also co-owned another car when he was in high school, a hearse, which is the car used to carry a coffin in funeral processions. Buffett once picked up a date in a hearse. As you might guess, the date didn't go too well, and he later said his approach "wasn't the smoothest thing." Today, he drives a Cadillac XTS, a nice car, but nothing too extravagant. He puts about 3,500 miles a year on the car, mostly driving from his home to the office and McDonald's with it.

In the next few sections, we'll address the main issues related to car ownership, such as new versus used, buy versus lease, and the best time to buy a car. Of course, the answer is "It depends," but we'll provide you with a general framework for thinking about these issues and give you some rules of thumb. So let's roll.

New Cars vs. Used Cars

No doubt, from a financial standpoint, a used car is a lot cheaper, at least with the sticker price. You've probably heard the expression that as soon as you drive a new car off the dealer lot, it falls 20% in value. We encountered the term "depreciation" in our accounting chapter. It refers to the drop in the value of an asset, such as a building, car, or machine, due to its age and wear and tear. Depreciation differs dramatically by car make and model, but it often tends to be the least for Toyotas, Hondas, Nissans, and Jeeps. These cars tend to be reliable and aren't too expensive to fix when things go wrong. Expensive cars, such as Mercedes, BMWs, Cadillacs, and Lincolns, tend to depreciate the most, since they often cost a huge chunk of change to repair. Someone buying a used car tends to be cost conscious, so hefty repair bills aren't a good fit for these folks.

Older cars tend to break down more than newer cars. Their **warranties**, which fix problems at no or low cost, also expire over time. **Certified pre-owned** (CPO) cars are newer used cars that are in good condition with relatively low mileage, and they often come with extended manufacturer warranties. They tend to be less than five years old and have fewer than 50,000 miles, but CPO requirements vary by make and model. CPO cars typically cost about 20% more than a similar used car without the warranty and stamp of approval, since it reduces the risk that you've bought a "**lemon**," or a car with a bunch of problems.

Newer cars also usually look nicer and have fancier features, making them desirable for a lot of consumers. For example, many new cars have Wi-Fi and perfectly synch with your smartphone. Even high-end cars from a decade ago, costing $100,000 or more when new, wouldn't have these features since they didn't exist. New things will surely be invented in the future that we'll want to have in our cars, say, artificial intelligence software that *effectively* eliminates the urge to read and respond to texts or emails while driving. Think about a Siri or Alexa app that can perfectly read and respond to texts or an app that can effortlessly find you a parking spot during at a busy location. We know some cars aim to offer these features, but they aren't ready for prime time. And, as we said at the chapter opening, the widespread arrival of driverless cars is just a matter of time.

New cars also usually have better fuel efficiency and faster 0-to-60 times, a great combination for most drivers. Today, you can find new cars that go from 0 to 60 in in less than 5 seconds *and* also get 30+ miles per gallon. That was virtually impossible a decade or two ago. And electric cars, such as Tesla's Model 3, are changing the automotive landscape requiring no gas and fewer items to repair and often have tremendous acceleration to boot. When you flip on a modern light switch, the light appears instantly. Similarly, electric cars have full power, or torque, as soon as they are turned on, providing neck-snapping acceleration in some cases. For more on that topic, do a search on Tesla's Model S in Ludicrous Mode, hitting 0 to 60 in less than 2.3 seconds! To top that, they have a reboot of their Tesla Roadster car in 2020 with a 0-to-60 time of 1.9 seconds!

So what's better to buy, a new or used car? Financially it's usually more beneficial to buy a used car, but it really depends on what role a car plays in your life. If you want something to get from point A to point B, a used car is undoubtedly cheaper. If you view a car as an important extension of your personal brand (i.e., the coolness factor) and really hate having to wait around while your car is in the repair shop, then a new car may be best for you. Plus, some people hate the idea of buying something that is used, which by definition means you got someone's leftovers. A recent study aimed to determine what type of used car may be optimal for most people. Picture a U-shaped curve where the cost depreciates each year, but it is offset by higher repair costs over time.

A detailed analysis posted anonymously on Reddit, a social media and bulletin board website, estimated the cheapest strategy for buying a car over the long term taking into account things such as the cost of the car, depreciation, repairs, insurance, and the cost of gasoline. The result? Buy a 10-year-old car, hold it for 5 years, sell it, and then repeat the process. The most expensive approach was to buy a new car every 5 years, selling it at the end of each 5-year period. With this latter method you are absorbing the biggest depreciation years of the car, essentially locking into a loss of 50% or more each time you buy a car, as well as paying more expensive insurance.

Buying vs. Leasing a Car

Let's say you've made a decision to get a new car, even though used cars tend to be a better way of saving money. Obviously, the cost of the car can vary greatly. You can buy a brand-new Nissan Versa or Chevy Spark for $13,000 or less. If you're the next Justin Bieber, Miley Cryus, or Kylie Jenner, you could afford a multimillion-dollar Bugatti or Koenigsegg. You still have to go through a buy-or-lease decision regardless of the price of your car, if you care about money. A lease is the rental of a new car, usually for a period ranging anywhere from one year to four years. A two- to three-year lease is most common for cars. With a lease you don't own the car but have the right to use it for a fixed period of time, so the monthly payment is cheaper. With most leases, you have the option to purchase the car after the lease term ends, but it usually is more cost effective to buy the car from day one if that is your plan.

There are several buy-vs.-lease calculators on the web, such as those at Cars.com, Lease.Guide.com, or BankRate.com. We'll give you the intuition of what's going on with them, while not getting bogged down too much in the details. The best-selling vehicle in America is usually not a car but rather a truck. Specifically, the Ford F-150, which is typically purchased more than 900,000 times a year. Trucks are widely used in business, such as in the construction industry, but many people simply like driving trucks. The Ford F-150 is usually followed in the rankings by two other trucks, the Chevy Silverado and RAM trucks. RAM was formerly a model under the Dodge brand but now has evolved into its own separate brand. The Toyota Rav4 is typically the best-selling non-truck in America, with about 400,000 purchases a year. It's a sport utility vehicle (SUV) and in recent years has outsold its sister car, the Toyota Camry.

A new Toyota Rav4 or Camry starts at about $25,000. It can cost $10,000 more than this with a high-end option package. Let's use the base model as the basis for our buy-vs.-lease calculation. Further, let's assume you have put no down payment, known as a **capitalized cost reduction** in the auto world, to reduce the purchase price and that you don't have an older car or truck to trade in to reduce the price of the new one. Most states charge a **sales tax** on car or truck purchases, which is exactly what it sounds like: a tax that goes to the state government for sales of goods or services. Sales tax on cars varies widely by state, ranging from 0% to more than 11%, so let's assume 5% is the sales tax rate.

We've talked a lot about interest rates and the time value of money in this book, so you probably have the intuition that the level of interest rates also affects the price of a car. The lower the interest rate, the cheaper your car payment. Sometimes lease calculators use a variation on interest rates called the **money factor**, which can be estimated by taking the interest rate and dividing it by 2400. Let's also assume a 5% interest rate, even though interest rates are currently abnormally low, and that the car depreciates 40% over a three-year period.

Buying the Rav4 or Camry with a three-year loan results in a payment of $786 per month. Leasing the same car over a three-year period, the most common lease period, results in a monthly payment of $379 per month. Obviously, the purchase payment is a lot higher than the lease payment, but you actually own the car after three years. Many car loans are over a five-year period since paying the $786 a month in our example is a pretty steep number for most people. Using the same numbers, it would result in a monthly payment of $495 a month over five years. Still significantly more than the lease payment. Plus, the bumper-to-bumper warranty for a Toyota, and most other cars, expires after three years, so you would be on the hook for most repairs after the three-year period since the bulk of the warranty expires. Toyota does provide a powertrain warranty, which covers the engine, transmission, and a few other items, for five years or 60,000 miles.

If the buy-vs.-lease calculation seems a bit confusing to you, don't worry, we'll give you a simple rule of thumb in a minute. But first, a couple of more details on leasing. When you lease a car or truck, you can only use it for a certain number of miles, or else you have to pay a penalty for any miles over that amount. The typical penalty is an extra 15 to 25 cents per mile for anything over the limit. Car leases generally permit you to average 7,500 to 15,000 miles per year over the lease term. The most common mileage limits are 10,000 or 12,000 miles per year. Also, if you trash the car and don't have the repairs covered by insurance, then you have to pay extra fees to repair the damage.

So here's the bottom line. Under most scenarios, if you don't drive a lot of miles (i.e., 12,000 per year or less) *and* you want a new car every few years or less, it's generally more efficient to lease the car. Plus, if you have a business, there are some advantages to leasing that may reduce your tax bill. This rule of thumb brings to mind an expression credited to the late oil tycoon J. Paul Getty, once the richest person in the world and the founder of Getty Oil: "If It appreciates, buy it. If it depreciates, lease it." Even though Buffett didn't give that quote, it merits a tip that Buffett would likely approve of, since we mentioned his views that reinvesting the money he allocated toward his home would have earned much higher returns if he put it in stocks.

Buffett Tip 71:

If it appreciates, buy it. If it depreciates, lease it. ***(Courtesy of J. Paul Getty)***

Stocks, bonds, and homes usually appreciate. Cars and most other things that you buy depreciate. One last point before moving on to the next section. **Classic cars** often *increase* in value. Classic cars are generally *at least* 25 years old and are also in demand by collectors. Thus, an older Ferrari or Corvette may be considered a classic, but a 25-year-old Camry probably wouldn't be. Classic cars could be a hobby or an investment but are usually not the primary means of transportation for someone. Therefore, we'll stick to Getty's rule of thumb. Buy what appreciates and lease or sell what depreciates, unless you drive a lot of miles, or would like to own the car for many years. That latter point is what Buffett has followed in recent times, typically owning his car for at least eight years and not being concerned about looking cool or having the latest high-tech features.

The Best Time to Buy or Lease a Car

Like with many items, you can get a good deal if you buy at certain times. For example, if you buy holiday items such as a Christmas tree after January 1, you can probably get it for 50% or more off. If you buy a bathing suit or shorts in the fall, you can probably get a good deal too. If you rent a car on a weekend, it's usually cheaper than a weekday since fewer businesspeople use cars on weekends. If you buy a plane ticket about two months before your flight, it's usually cheaper than buying it way in advance or at the last minute. There is also some advice you can use to get a better deal on buying or leasing a car.

Buying or leasing a new car during the last few months of the year (October–December) often provides you with an opportunity to get a good deal since dealers want to make room for the new model/year cars that are coming on the lot. Many car salespeople have minimum sales hurdles, known as **quotas**, to meet, so you can often get a good deal at the end of the month since their quotas are usually based on the number of vehicles they sell each month. Using simple supply-and-demand analysis, if fewer prospective customers are in the dealership, you can probably get a better deal. Most people shop for cars after work hours, on weekends, or on holidays. So going to a car dealership during a weekday in the morning or afternoon might be a good time to snag a great deal.

If you hate haggling with car dealers over prices, you can try using Costco's car buying service or websites such as TrueCar.com to put you in a better buying position. You can also get a good deal on a car if it will no longer be made or if the model is undergoing a significant style change. For example, you probably see a bunch of cars on the road that are no longer made, such as those made by Pontiac, Saturn, Oldsmobile, Plymouth, or Mercury. If you bought one of these cars during the last year that they were produced, you probably could have negotiated a very good deal. The manufacturer will still honor the warranty over the full period or else they would have had extreme difficulty selling the car. The 2019 Toyota Rav4 was a significant revamp from the 2018 model, so dealers were probably extra motivated to get rid of the 2018 models since they look out of date compared to the new model.

One last word on cars before we move onto the next section, homes. You might think, "Why don't I rent a car when I need it, rather than paying the full cost of buying or leasing a car?" This statement might be especially true for someone who doesn't need a car to get to work or school. It might make sense if you are 25 years of age or older. In one of the last few areas of legal discrimination, most car rental companies won't rent a car to someone under the age of 21. The same goes for being an Uber or Lyft driver to earn some extra cash with the help of your car. Firms think young people, without a lot of driving experience, are more likely to be unsafe drivers. Even if you are 21, you will probably have to pay an extra underage driving fee until you reach the age of 25 to rent a car. If you are able to rent a car, you can use car rental search engines, such as Kayak or Travelocity, to find a good deal. Costco and AAA also can help you score some good deals. Some companies, such as Zipcar, also let you rent a car for a portion of a day. Instead of going through a rental car company, such as Avis, Hertz, Budget, or Thrifty, an additional option is to rent an individual's car through websites such as Turo. It's the car rental version of Airbnb, a firm that allows you to stay in someone's home for a fee, instead of a hotel.

Home Basics

It's been said that buying a home (e.g., apartment, condominium, townhouse, or house) is the most important purchase of your life. It's probably true since it will be one of your largest purchases, and it also has a big effect on your credit rating. It will most likely be the biggest expense that you have that will be tracked by credit agencies, and therefore it will be an important part of your credit score. The main reason is that unless you're rich and can afford to pay for the home entirely in cash, you'll probably have to borrow money to help buy your home. We mentioned earlier in this book that money borrowed to help pay for the purchase of a home is called a mortgage. Most mortgages last between 15 and 30 years, so a mortgage might weigh as an anchor on your credit report, since it will be there for a really long time. But paying your mortgage every month on time also gives you a chance to demonstrate the responsible use of credit and may ultimately increase your credit score. Let's start with a discussion of the basics.

The first thing you should consider is if you plan on staying for at least a few years in the area where you want to buy a home. If that's the case, then buying a home usually makes financial sense instead of renting. If you are renting a home, you're basically throwing money away, helping the **landlord**, or homeowner, build wealth at your expense. A landlord is someone who purchases a home with the purpose of renting it out to someone. In many cases they own multiple homes. A **slumlord** is a landlord who spends little money on maintenance and repairs of a rental home and often rents it to low-income people. Most homes also go up in value over time, building wealth for the homeowner. Plus, there are some great tax benefits to owning a home that we'll get into, not to mention the great memories that Buffett alluded to in our opening section.

So why then would someone rent a home? Well, owning a home is a big financial commitment. First you need to come up with a **down payment** on the house, which you can view as a deposit to protect the bank or other lender that provides you with a mortgage. It's typically a serious chunk of change in the tens of thousands of dollars or more. Many people can't get over that hurdle. Plus, if you don't pay your mortgage consistently, you might wind up bankrupt, which would result in a terrible hit to your credit rating, as well as the eventual loss of your home. In addition, when you sell a home you typically have to pay a real estate agent a **commission**, which is the sales fee they (and their agency) get from selling the home. Commissions vary, but 5% or 6% is typical. So, a 5%

commission on a house sold for $200,000 would result in a $10,000 sales fee to the real estate agent, sometimes known as a real estate broker, and their firm. That might be enough to wipe out the financial benefit from owning a home. Some online real estate firms, such as Zillow and Redfin, charge lower commission rates, but it's still a sizeable amount.

In order to move on to the next section, home ownership, let's summarize the boxes you need to check off for it to be worthwhile. First, you need enough money for the down payment. Second, you should plan to stay in the area at least a few years. Third, you should have a steady income. The last point is important because it will be hard to get a mortgage from a lender without one, unless you have someone, such as a parent, **co-sign** the mortgage loan for you. If someone co-signs a loan, they agree to pay the mortgage if the original borrower (i.e., you) does not. Being a co-signer is a legal obligation, which affects their credit rating. So think carefully about co-signing for another person, or, if someone is co-signing for you, thank them for their generosity.

Finding A Home

You should know the general area where you want to live. It's likely near your job, family, or a place that makes you happy. Some people, such as writers, the self-employed, and those able to work remotely, can live almost anywhere. They might choose to live near the beach, a mountain, a park, or any other place that speaks to them. You can drive around the area and look at homes with "For Sale" signs, but a more efficient way to find a home is through the use of a search engine or a real estate agent. A real estate agent probably knows the neighborhood well and can do a search that is custom-tailored to your needs (e.g., 2+ bedrooms, 2+ bathrooms, or property size). The most common database real estate agents and buyers search is called the **Multiple Listing Service** (**MLS**).

You can also do your own search for real estate and then take that "short list" of homes to the real estate agent for a more efficient buying process. Most of the homes on MLS can be found on Realtor.com, Zillow.com, or Redfin.com. Craigslist often lists homes **For Sale by Owner** (**FSBO**). Someone with a FSBO listing is trying to sell their home but wants to avoid the commission paid to the real estate agent. Both the buyer and seller usually each use the services of a real estate attorney to make sure everything is legit. The real estate attorney fees vary, but they usually range from a few hundred to a few thousand dollars, often with higher fees for more complex cases and sometimes for more expensive homes.

Bidding for a Home

Okay, let's say you found your dream home—or at least a home that you think you'll be happy with. The next step is making an offer. Unless you are making an offer for an FSBO property, the offer is usually made through the real estate agent. Both the buyer and seller typically have their own agent, who communicate with their respective clients. In most cases the seller is the only one who pays a commission, and it's split in some manner between the buyer's and seller's agents and their respective firms. A fairly common split is 50/50. However, in some markets both the buyer and seller may pay commissions.

Although you know the list price of a home when you see it, the actual sale price is subject to negotiation. Home prices, like most things, are subject to supply and demand. The price at which the seller is willing to finally sell the home is subject to a bunch of factors. Some of these factors include how motivated the seller is (i.e., Do they need the money? Are they relocating to a new job?), how long the home has been on the market, the condition of the home, the price the seller paid for the home, the number of offers (if any) the seller has, the number of similar homes for sale in the same market, and so forth. In general, most sellers are willing to lower the price anywhere from 1% to 5%, with a 1% or 2% discount from the list price being the most common. On the other hand, during "hot" markets, you might have to pay more than the list price if the property has multiple buy offers.

If you're looking for a deep discount (i.e., 25–50%) on the price of the home relative to its market value, you might want to look into buying a **foreclosed home** or a home through a **short sale**, which we'll define in a minute. A foreclosed home is one that is taken back by the lender after the homeowner stops paying the mortgage, in part or full. A mortgage is a legal contract and obligation to pay. If you don't pay, the bank or other lender will take the house back from you. A well-known legal expression is "The wheels of justice grind slowly but surely." In other words, think carefully about missing any mortgage payments because there will be consequences. The foreclosure process must go through the legal system and takes a while to occur, usually about 1 to 2 years after the person began missing payments. Properties foreclosed by banks are often called bank **real estate owned (REO)**.

A home that is in **pre-foreclosure** means the current owner has missed payments and that the lender is in the process of taking the home back or negotiating new payment terms with the owner. A foreclosure sounds like a great deal for the new buyer, and it can be sometimes. But there are some things you should keep in mind. First, a lot of homes sold after foreclosure require a full cash payment, with no mortgage. Foreclosure homes are also usually sold "as is," and you often can't inspect the inside of the house before you buy it. So if the prior tenant trashed the place, the new owner would be responsible for the repairs. In some cases, the former owner remains in the home, and the new buyer has to evict them. Not fun!

We used the term "short sale" in one of our stock market chapters, **Chapter 5**. A short sale when talking about stocks is a bet that the stock is going to drop in price. Short sale investors benefit from drops in a stock price. A short sale in the context of a real estate transaction is when the owner sells the home at a price less than the current mortgage value. Why would the owner do that? At least two reasons. First, maybe the owner overpaid for the house when they first bought it. Let's say they paid $250,000 for a house and, due to a recession or some other reason, similar houses in the neighborhood are now selling for less than $200,000. A second reason is similar to the case of a foreclosure. Perhaps the current owner can't afford the home anymore, or is in a rush to sell, and wants to get out of the mortgage contract before they spiral into bankruptcy and trash their credit rating. The mortgage company usually has to approve a short sale but often prefers it to the long, drawn out foreclosure process.

Paying for a Home: The Down Payment

Earlier in the chapter, we said you need to come up with a down payment. How much? It varies. Before the Great Recession of 2007–2009 it was possible, under certain circumstances, to purchase a house with virtually no down payment. The financial press referred to these loans as "liar loans" or "NINJA" loans. Liar means that that the applicants lied on the mortgage application about their ability to pay, fabricating their income and/or assets. NINJA is short for "No Income, No Job, No Assets." Why would lenders approve these people for mortgages? Well, home prices usually rise in price. So if the buyer stopped paying at some point, the lender could simply take the home back and try to resell it at the higher price. Also, some lenders sell the mortgage to other lenders, essentially "passing the buck." They'd then view it as someone else's problem. A lot of new financial laws were passed after the Great Recession, such as the Dodd-Frank Act, that now require banks have rigorous paperwork and that purchasers must make a down payment. There is one valid exception. If you're a member of the US Military, you can often qualify for a **US Department of Veterans Affairs (VA) Loan**, which may be obtained with as little as nothing down.

Okay, getting back to the down payment, the typical down payment is 10–20% of the purchase price of the home, but in some circumstances you only have to put down 3.5%. We'll explain all of these numbers in a minute. If you're lucky, your parents or grandparents might help with the down payment of your home, but we'll assume for most people that isn't the case. Buffett didn't do it for his kids, preferring they develop a strong work ethic before providing them with any meaningful amount of money. Bank lenders also consider the **loan-to-value ratio (LTV)** of an investment. For instance, a $200,000 mortgage loan on a $250,000 home has an LTV ratio of ($200,000/$250,000 =) 80%.

Buffett suggests putting at least 10% down. In his 2008 shareholder letter, which he wrote in the midst of a housing crisis during the Great Recession, he said:

> Home ownership is a wonderful thing. My family and I have enjoyed my present home for 50 years, with more to come. But enjoyment and utility should be the primary motives for purchase, not profit or refi possibilities. And the home purchased ought to fit the income of the purchaser. The present housing debacle should teach home buyers, lenders, brokers, and government some simple lessons that will ensure stability in the future. Home purchases should involve an honest-to-God down payment of at least 10% and monthly payments that can be comfortably handled by the borrower's income. That income should be carefully verified.

Let's summarize that sage advice with a Tip.

Buffett Tip 72:

Home ownership is a wonderful thing. The home you buy should fit your income.

The government knows the down payment is a major obstacle to home ownership for many people, so they offer some special programs, especially for those in the low- to middle-income range, in order to help them purchase a home. The **US Department of Housing and Urban Development (HUD)** is the branch of the federal government that plays a key role in the housing market. **The Federal Housing Authority (FHA)** is a unit of HUD that insures loans made by private lenders, such as banks. That is, if the borrower fails to pay the loan, the FHA (backed by the credit of the US government) will ensure the loan is paid. Due to the government support, you can often purchase a home even if you don't have a great credit score, one as low as 580. Banks will not only consider your credit score when applying for a mortgage but also your income and assets relative to the size of your planned mortgage loan. A rough rule of thumb is a bank will give you a mortgage loan 3–4x your **gross income**. That is, before any taxes are taken out. So, if your income is $50,000 and you have a good credit score, you can typically get a mortgage for $150,000 to $200,000.

The FHA offers programs that allow first time homeowners to put down as little as a 3.5% down payment and also provides the homebuyer with up to 6% of the value of the home for **closing costs**. Closing costs include things such as paying for the first month's mortgage and property taxes in advance, **homeowners insurance**, **title insurance**, and attorney fees. Homeowners insurance covers problems with the home due to fire, vandalism, lightning, wind, hail, and several other reasons. Title insurance is designed to protect the buyer in the event that the seller didn't own the home "free and clear" before it was sold. Since purchasing a home is a huge financial commitment, most people enlist the services of a real estate attorney to help them with the legal paperwork.

Paying for a Home: The Mortgage

Few people, especially younger individuals, can afford to pay for the full price of a home in cash. The median price of a home in the US is roughly $250,000. In some neighborhoods in Manhattan and San Francisco, the median price exceeds a million dollars! You'd need a Buffett-like wallet to afford them. Most people purchasing their first home borrow anywhere from 80% to 96.5% of the purchase price. A 20%

down payment is a good number to shoot for. That would be $50,000 on the median home price of $250,000. That's a big number for most people. By definition, there are 50% of homes that sell for less than the median price in all areas. These are often referred to as **starter homes**, especially for those at the lower end of the income spectrum. Over time many people trade up to a nicer home, hence the "starter" name. Most mortgages are referred to as conventional, but a large mortgage is called a **jumbo mortgage**. The definition of jumbo varies by location, but it usually refers to a mortgage of at least $510,400, although it could be as high as $765,600 in higher-priced areas, such as New York City, Los Angeles, Miami, and San Francisco.

If you purchase a home by putting less than 20% down, you usually have to purchase **private mortgage insurance** (**PMI**). Some real estate professionals use the term "**lenders mortgage insurance**" (**LMI**), but we'll stick with PMI in this book. PMI protects the lender in the event the borrower doesn't pay the mortgage. The insurance pays the lender in case the borrower is unable or unwilling to make a payment. PMI typically results in an extra expense of 0.5% to 1.0% a year on the amount of the mortgage.

Once the equity (i.e., the value of the house minus what you still owe on the mortgage) in your home is at least 20% of the value of the home, you typically can cancel the PMI, since the lender would now have a sufficient cushion in case you didn't pay on time. You can get to the 20% threshold by paying your mortgage on a regular basis and also by having the house go up in value. If your cash flow is great, you can even pay more than your required payment to get rid of your PMI as soon as possible. Most houses do appreciate over time, roughly 2–3% per year, but the numbers may vary dramatically by location, bringing to mind the real estate slogan, "Location, location, location."

It pays to shop around for the lowest mortgage rates. A small difference in mortgage rates can really add up over the life of the mortgage, typically 15 to 30 years. A $200,000 mortgage at an interest rate of 4% for 30 years results in a monthly payment of $955 and total payments of $343,739. Increasing the interest rate just 1%, to 5% on the same property, results in a monthly payment of $1,074 and total payments of $386,512. We're sure you could find good use for that extra $40,000+ difference. Popular search engines that help you sort out mortgage rates offered by banks include LendingTree.com and BankRate.com.

A "House Hack": Getting Someone to Pay (Most of) Your Mortgage

What's better than getting a home at a good price? Having someone pay the bulk of your mortgage, legally. Real estate investor and author Brandon Turner uses the term "house hack" to describe the case when someone purchases a multi-family home and rents out part of it. It's easy to envision this scenario in the case of a **duplex**, which is a house divided into two apartments or condominiums, with a separate entrance for each. If you have more money, you could purchase a triplex or fourplex—residences for three and four persons/families, respectively. The basic idea is the rent-paying person pays enough money to cover all, or part, of the mortgage of the full property. Full payment of the mortgage may be hard in a duplex, but it's possible in a triplex or fourplex. A 3.5% down payment is also possible with some of these multi-family homes.

The downside of a multi-family home, other than the higher price, is that it puts you in the landlord business. You are then responsible for fixing problems with the other units when something goes wrong—a leaky faucet, broken heater, clogged toilet. Of course, you can hire outside plumbers and contractors to fix these problems, but that costs money. What happens if your tenants don't pay the rent or damage the place? Well, you might have to take them to court to have them pay or kick them out. That doesn't sound like a lot of fun to us. Thus, a house hack will work for some enterprising people but not all.

Looking Under the Hood of a Mortgage

Looking under the hood of a mortgage is not as exciting as what you might see under a Corvette's hood. But it's important, since knowing some of the details may save you big money over time. A mortgage, like most bonds, has two parts, principal and interest. Principal in this context is the amount of money you borrowed, at least when the mortgage starts. The amount owed on the mortgage, the principal, goes down a little bit each time you make a payment. As we know, virtually all loans, including mortgages, charge interest. The **mortgage servicer** is the financial firm that collects your monthly mortgage payment. Besides the principal and interest, the mortgage payment usually includes some other payments—**property taxes**, homeowners insurance, and PMI (if needed).

Property taxes are used to pay for the services offered by your local city or town. The bulk of property taxes usually go to pay for the public school system, but they also pay for police, firefighters, local government administrators, snow removal, road repair, and many other services. Property taxes are usually paid quarterly, and your mortgage payment usually occurs monthly. The mortgage servicer keeps some of the money from the monthly payments in **escrow**, in order to pay the property taxes when they are due on a quarterly basis. Escrow is a legal term that means money is held by a third party (the mortgage servicer in this case) and given to the appropriate firm or person (the city or town) by the due date (i.e., quarterly for property taxes).

Getting back to the main part of the mortgage payment, the principal and interest, the way most mortgages work is that in the early years (i.e., during the first half of the mortgage life) the bulk of your mortgage payments goes toward paying interest. In later years (i.e., during the last half of the mortgage life) the bulk of the payment goes to pay down the principal. The relationship of paying off debt and interest is called an **amortization schedule** and can be seen in **Figure 12.1**. Although tax laws are always changing, as of today,

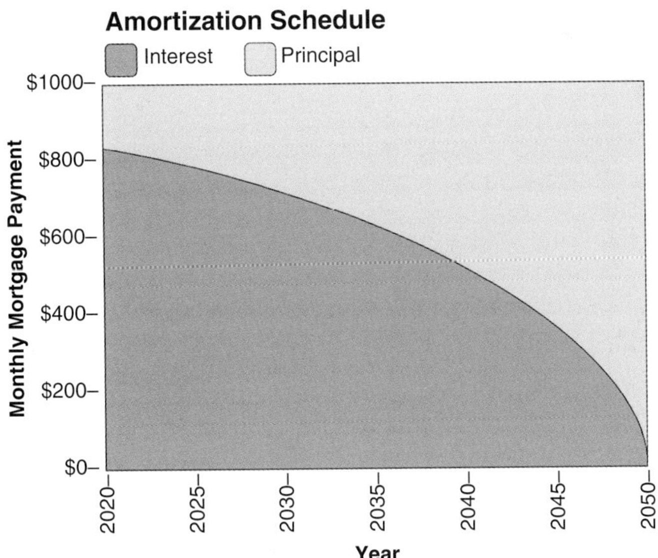

Figure 12.1 Amortization Schedule for a Typical Mortgage
Source: Based on http://www.engineeryourfinances.com/2010/06/how-to-compare-rates-for-mortgage-refinancing/

interest payments on mortgages (up to $1,000,000) are tax deductible. This means if you **itemize** your taxes (i.e., list all your expenses), you might save money on your income taxes. All of your itemized deductions would have to be greater than the **standard deduction**, which is the amount anyone can claim without listing expenses. The current standard deduction is $12,400 for single filers and $24,400 for married couples filing jointly. Property taxes also used to be tax deductible at the federal tax level. They are still tax deductible for paying state taxes (if any). In short, there may be some good tax breaks to owning a home, besides the pride and wealth-building opportunities that usually come with home ownership.

Most mortgages last for 30 years, but one way to reduce the total amount of interest you pay is to take out a 15-year mortgage. Let's use the same numbers as we did earlier with the 30-year mortgage ($200,000 mortgage, interest rate of 4%), which resulted in a monthly payment of $955 and total payments of $343,739. The difference between $343,739 and $200,000 is $143,739 in interest payments. A 15-year mortgage with an interest rate of 4% results in a monthly payment of $1,479, total payments of $266,288, and $66,288 in interest costs. The lesson is, if you can afford the (54.9%) higher monthly payment, you can save a huge amount in interest costs. In this case $77,451. Sometimes when people pay off their mortgage, they throw a party, often called a "mortgage burning party." When the biggest expense in your life vanishes, it's probably a good reason to party!

If you own a home through a (15–30 year) mortgage, you aren't locked into it for life. If you sell the house, the price is usually high enough to pay off the old mortgage. The profit on your old home can be tax free if you roll it into a new home utilizing a part of the tax code called a **1031 Exchange**. Many individuals can get an exemption up to $250,000 in profit, once every two years, if the home is their primary residence. Check with an accountant or real estate attorney for the nitty gritty details on how to do this exchange while legally avoiding IRS scrutiny.

If interest rates fall, it often makes sense to **refinance** your mortgage. Essentially, you rip up your old mortgage and take out a new one. Using the example we cited earlier, if the interest rate on your mortgage was 5% and you could get a new one for 4%, it would save you $119 per month. One word of caution. When you refinance a mortgage, you incur closing costs again, such as title insurance, appraisal fees, application fees, and so forth, so you want to make sure the drop in your mortgage payments is enough to offset these costs. It depends on the value of your mortgage, but one rule of thumb is that your new interest rate must be at least 1% less than the rate on your old mortgage for a refinance to make financial sense.

Buffett generally eschews debt but is a fan of mortgages, calling them a "one-way bet." Since the interest rates on mortgages are fixed, if rates rise, you are fortunate to be locked into the relatively low rate on the mortgage. If rates fall, as we mentioned above, you can refinance and lock into the lower rate. Buffett once had a second home in California and took out a mortgage on that property, even though he could have easily afforded to purchase the home in cash. He used the extra money to buy Berkshire stock, which, of course, turned out to be a huge home run.

Here's his full quote, "If you get a 30-year mortgage it's the best instrument in the world, because if you're wrong and rates go to 2%, which I don't think they will, you pay it off. It's a one-way renegotiation. I mean it is an incredibly attractive instrument for the homeowner and you've got a one-way bet." Let's try to summarize Buffett's ideas on mortgages with a somewhat wordy Tip.

Buffett Tip 73:

Most debt is bad. Mortgage debt, as long as it is affordable, can be a positive since it amounts to a one-way bet.

We don't recommend it, but sometimes your home can become the equivalent of an ATM, if you've built up some equity in it. You can often get a **home equity loan** against some of the equity that you've built up in your home, usually any equity over the 20% mark we mentioned earlier. We generally don't recommend it since you will then have two payments due on your house, your regular mortgage payment and another payment due to the home equity loan. The exception, of course, is if you already had your mortgage burning party and paid off your mortgage. One advantage of a home equity loan is that the interest rates are usually less than what you can get from borrowing money against your credit card. Plus, the interest paid on a home equity loan is usually tax deductible. Thus, under some circumstances, getting a home equity loan to pay off credit cards or other high-interest debts may make financial sense.

What Determines Home Prices?

The interaction of supply and demand determines the price of virtually everything, including homes. But, to be more specific, several things affect real estate prices. Lower, or falling, interest rates make homes more affordable. Therefore, home prices usually increase more in a low or falling interest rate environment. Homes that are part of a good school district are highly valued by some buyers, especially those with children or who are planning to have some.

Homes close to major forms of transportation, such as a train station, are often in great demand from buyers since it makes it easier for many people to get to work. Using that same line of thinking, homes close to where the jobs are plentiful (e.g., New York City, Chicago, Seattle, Silicon Valley, Boston, Austin, or Washington, DC) tend to sell at higher prices. Most people prefer new or newer homes to older ones, so the age is often a determining factor in price. Old homes, though often unique in character and beautiful, tend to break down more and require more to maintain it. Larger properties—both in square footage of the home and land area—are usually more expensive than smaller homes. Homes with a beautiful view, near a body of water or mountain range, usually sell at higher prices than a "plain vanilla" one or one located on a busy road. Homes tend to sell at lower prices if the features mentioned above aren't in place as well as during recessions. In sum, owning a home is something we and Buffett strongly recommend, but there is a lot of variability in home values, and the home buying process requires a fair amount of homework. The sooner you can get on the path to home ownership and "livin' the dream," the better, in most cases.

Buffett's Tips from Chapter 12

Buffett Tip 70: A home will likely be one of the best investments you'll ever make.

Buffett Tip 71: If it appreciates, buy it. If it depreciates, lease it. *(Courtesy of J. Paul Getty)*

Buffett Tip 72: Home ownership is a wonderful thing. The home you buy should fit your income.

Buffett Tip 73: Most debt is bad. Mortgage debt, as long as it is affordable, can be a positive since it amounts to a one-way bet.

References

"2020 Chevrolet Spark Review, Pricing, and Specs." *Car and Driver.* Accessed June 17, 2020. http://www.caranddriver.com/chevrolet/spark.

"Buying a Home in 10 Steps." *Money Essentials.* CNN, February 15, 2018. https://money.cnn.com/pf/money-essentials-home-buying/index.html.

Capparella, Joey. "25 Best-Selling Cars, Trucks, and SUVs of 2019." *Car and Driver,* January 6, 2020. https://www.caranddriver.com/news/g27041933/best-selling-cars-2019/.

Cordes, Henry. "Warren Buffett: New Lease for Corporate Headquarters Is Good News for Omaha and Berkshire." *Omaha World-Herald,* May 12, 2019. https://www.omaha.com/money/buffett/warren-buffett-new-lease-for-corporate-headquarters-is-good-news-for-omaha-and-berkshire/article_a2b19bf6-3cfd-511f-a850-98f747a03c21.html.

Demuro, Doug. "How Much More Does a CPO Car Cost?" *Autotrader,* October 31, 2014. https://www.autotrader.com/car-tips/how-much-more-does-a-cpo-car-cost-231072.

Elkins, Kathleen. "Here's Why Warren Buffett Thinks You Should Buy a Home." CNBC, January 2, 2019. https://www.cnbc.com/2017/03/06/heres-why-warren-buffett-thinks-you-should-buy-a-home.html.

Flannery, Joseph. "Warren Buffett's Golden Advice on Refinancing Your Mortgage." *SELFi,* August 20, 2019. https://selfi.com/warren-buffett-advice-refinancing-mortgage/.

Green, William. "I've Followed Warren Buffett for Decades and Keep Coming Back to These 10 Quotes." *Observer,* May 4, 2015. http://observer.com/2015/05/ive-followed-warren-buffett-for-decades-and-keep-coming-back-to-these-10-quotes/.

GuruFocus.com. "Warren Buffett: Why Berkshire Hathaway Doesn't Invest in Real Estate." *Yahoo!,* June 24, 2020. https://www.yahoo.com/news/warren-buffett-why-berkshire-hathaway-210202230.html.

Jenkins, Aric. "This Is the Best Time to Buy a Plane Ticket." *Fortune,* April 6, 2017. http://fortune.com/2017/04/06/best-time-to-buy-plane-tickets-domestic/.

"Just How Frugal Is Billionaire Warren Buffett? You'd Be Surprised." *South China Morning Post,* February 8, 2019. https://www.scmp.com/magazines/style/people-events/article/2184930/just-how-frugal-billionaire-warren-buffett-youd-be.

Kagan, Julia. "NINJA Loan Definition." *Investopedia,* February 21, 2020. https://www.investopedia.com/terms/n/ninja-loan.asp.

Little, Kendall. "How to Buy a Car—10 Best Car-Buying Tips." Bankrate, November 29, 2018. http://www.bankrate.com/loans/auto-loans/10-best-car-buying-tips-for-2017/.

Lowenstein, Roger. *Buffett: The Making of an American Capitalist.* New York: Random House Trade, 2008.

Martin, Ray. "Why You Should Lease a Car Now." CBS News, February 28, 2012. https://www.cbsnews.com/news/why-you-should-lease-a-car-now/.

Pearl, Michael. "When Is the Best Time to Buy a Car?" Bankrate, March 11, 2019. http://www.bankrate.com/loans/auto-loans/when-is-the-best-time-to-buy-a-car/?ic_id=home_smart+spending_homepage-financial-goals_car-buying_when-is-the-best-time-to-buy-a-car.

Reklaitis, Victor. "Why Buying a 10-Year-Old Car Is a Savvy Move." *MarketWatch, December* 29, 2017. http://www.marketwatch.com/story/the-cheapest-and-priciest-approaches-to-car-ownership-in-one-handy-chart-2017-06-26?siteid=yhoof2.

Schroeder, Alice. *The Snowball: Warren Buffett and the Business of Life*. New York: Bantam Books, 2009.

Szczypinski, Sarah. "Should You Rent or Buy a Home?" CNNMoney, October 9, 2017. http://money.cnn.com/2017/10/09/real_estate/rent-or-buy/index.html?iid=hp-stack-dom.

Taibi, Catherine. "The 16 Best Things Warren Buffett Has Ever Said." *The Huffington Post*, December 6, 2017. http://www.huffingtonpost.com/2013/08/30/warren-buffett-quotes_n_3842509.html.

"The Danish Cycling Culture: Read Why Danes Bike Everywhere." Denmark.dk. Accessed June 17, 2020. https://denmark.dk/people-and-culture/biking.

"US Existing Home Median Sales Price:" YCharts. Accessed June 17, 2020. https://ycharts.com/indicators/sales_price_of_existing_homes.

"Warren Buffett Quotes (Author of The Essays of Warren Buffett)." Goodreads. Accessed June 17, 2020. https://www.goodreads.com/author/quotes/756.Warren_Buffett.

"Warren Buffett's Advice to Teen Investor." CNBC, July 31, 2014. http://video.cnbc.com/gallery/?video=3000297529.

13

Buffett on Dale Carnegie, Communication Skills, and Emotional Intelligence

"The chains of habit are too light to be felt until they are too heavy to be broken."
—Warren Buffett, *Tap Dancing to Work: Warren Buffett on Practically Everything, 1966-2012*

Buffett Learns Life-Changing Skills in a Dale Carnegie Course

Back in **Chapter 1**, we mentioned the only diploma that Buffett hangs on his office wall is from Dale Carnegie Training. That's an amazing statement considering Buffett has attended some great universities, such as the University of Pennsylvania, University of Nebraska, and Columbia University. He went so far to say that the skills he learned in a Dale

Carnegie course "changed his life." Pretty powerful stuff! Who was Dale Carnegie and what did Buffett learn from the workshops he attended? We'll address that topic in this chapter, along with the related topics of communication skills, emotional intelligence, and getting along with people—skills Buffett claimed he didn't have as a young person, but ones he developed into a strength over time. As we also mentioned in **Chapter 1**, there is a financial dimension to these skills. Buffett claims improving them will increase your earnings power by 50% over the course of your life. That's an awesome payoff!

Buffett describes his younger self as a basket case with respect to public speaking and social skills. Carol Loomis, his longtime friend, editor of his annual shareholder letter, and *Fortune* columnist, wrote about Buffett:

> When he was young, he was terrified of public speaking. So he forced himself to take a Dale Carnegie course, filled, he says, "with other people equally pitiful." Today he gives speeches with ease, drawing them entirely from an outline in his head—no written speech, no notes—and lacing them with an inexhaustible supply of quips, examples, and analogies (for which a professional writer would kill).

That's some turnaround! And it's not just Buffett who has dealt with some social anxiety, shyness, and communication issues. Some of the most famous people in the world deal with similar issues. A-list movie stars Ryan Reynolds and Blake Lively, who happen to be married to each other, claim they are very shy. Lively said, "We're really shy people who express ourselves best when we're acting, when we're hiding as someone else."

Another A-lister, Johnny Depp, perhaps best known for his role as Captain Jack Sparrow in the *Pirates of the Caribbean* movies, said more bluntly, "I'm f*ckin' shy, man. I'm living, in a sense, like a fugitive. I don't like to be in social situations." Retired football star and former Heisman Trophy winner Ricky Williams occasionally conducted post-game interviews with his helmet on so he could avoid looking at reporters. The late rock star David Bowie's social anxiety and shyness led him to develop his onstage characters, such as Ziggy Stardust.

Actress Daryl Hannah, famous for her roles in hit movies such as *Splash, Wall Street*, and *Kill Bill*, has succeeded at the highest levels of Hollywood despite an autism diagnosis since childhood. Music superstar and business mogul Dr. Dre also suffers from social anxiety. In an interview with *Rolling Stone*, he said, "I have social anxiety. I don't like being in the spotlight, so I made a fu★★ing weird career choice. That's the reason for my mystique and why I'm so secluded and why everybody knows nothing about me." Author Susan Caine's highly regarded book *Quiet: The Power of Introverts in a World That Can't Stop Talking* documents widespread evidence of the success of introverted people across virtually all fields.

The bottom line is social anxiety and communication deficiencies, in all of their forms, don't result in a permanent barrier to success, especially if one desires to improve these skills, as the young Warren Buffett did. So let's make the first Tip in this chapter related to the young Buffett taking that important step to improve his communication skills.

Buffett Tip 74:

If you know you are weak in an important skill, try to improve it.

If you are weak in a skill that is less important, say being a top-ranked mixed martial arts (MMA) fighter, you are certainly welcome to improve on it, but let's characterize it as a less sensible use of your time. We don't want to say it will be a waste of your time in case you become a champion MMA fighter and punch us out.:-) Be like Buffett and compute the (financial or psychic) return on improving your skills. There is always an opportunity cost of doing something more valuable with your limited time and energy. Now let's move on to cover some of the things Buffett learned from the Dale Carnegie program he graduated from.

CliffsNotes Version on Dale Carnegie and *How to Win Friends and Influence People*

Let's expand a bit on the brief introduction to Dale Carnegie that we gave back in **Chapter 1**. Dale Carnegie was born in 1888 with the original name Dale Carnagey. He changed it in 1922 to have the same surname as the steel magnate we mentioned back in **Chapter 10**, Andrew Carnegie, who we noted was one of the richest men to ever live.

You are certainly welcome to read the Carnegie book. It's about 300 pages. You can also sign up for a course at DaleCarnegie.com. If you don't have the time or money for those options, we'll summarize some of the highlights of the book. You can send us a thank-you note after you come out of your shell or send us one beforehand as practice.:-) Our summary is based on the book itself, as well as an article on the book by a blog called *Farnam Street*. The Wikipedia entry on Dale Carnegie also has a pretty good summary, even though we know it's not a primary source. By the way, Farnam Street is the name of the street where Buffett lives and works. Not surprisingly, he lives less than two miles down the road from where he works. How's that for a commute! He is perfectly happy with where he lives and works and knows his time is extremely valuable, so Buffett's work-life setup is perfectly logical and consistent with his character.

You might object to the ideas in Carnegie's book, our book, or any other book you come across. Many people object to the "fake it till you make it" mentality that sometimes comes with a self-help or self-improvement book. If things are going great for you, then there is probably no need to change anything. Continue living your charmed life. However, if you aren't getting the results you want, then you probably have to take a hard, honest look at yourself and change something. Carnegie's techniques are suggestions that have some track record of success over many years, but they aren't etched in stone.

Now let's hit some of the highlights of Carnegie's book, especially those most relevant to Buffett. We'll have a slightly more detailed section related to each of the key parts of his book. These topics include a list of things the book will do for you, fundamental techniques in handling people, six ways to make people like you, how to win people to your way of thinking, and being a leader. Let's get started.

Things *How to Win Friends and Influence People* Will Do for You

Carnegie's description of what his book will do for you sounds like a dream. He was a salesman and probably overstated his case, but his agenda for the book was quite ambitious. Among other things, he claimed following the principles outlined in his book will increase your earnings power, popularity, influence, prestige, and ability to get things done. And that's just for starters. He also claimed his book will enable you to make friends quickly and easily and become a better speaker and conversationalist. For those of you already engaged in business, Carnegie claimed his book will make you a better salesman, help you win new customers and inspire your colleagues, better enable you to handle complaints, and help you avoid arguments. If the book accomplished a fraction of that for most people, it would be worth its weight in gold! The book has sold more than 30 million copies and resulted in countless workshops, so it must be doing something right.

Now, we doubt Carnegie's techniques are solely, or even primarily, responsible for Buffett's success, but they certainly had a great influence on him, since we heard it from the horse's mouth (i.e., in Buffett's own words). Buffett has become one of the most popular and inspirational people in the world. He has experienced massive business success. He is a witty speaker and engaging conversationalist and has friends ranging from Bill Gates to LeBron James, as well as a few adversaries. In short, he is probably a best-case outcome of what Carnegie's techniques can do for you. Let's keep going on the Carnegie-Buffett connection.

Techniques in Handling People According to *How to Win Friends and Influence People*

Carnegie discussed three techniques for handling people in his landmark book.

1. Don't criticize, condemn, or complain;
2. Give honest and sincere appreciation; and
3. Arouse in the other person an eager want.

Buffett has a lot to say about the first two techniques, so we'll turn a variation of them into a Tip. The word "never" is a strong word. It's probably unrealistic to say that you should never criticize someone or complain, especially if an injustice or some form of discrimination occurs. However, most people are reasonable, and when you meet someone, it is probably wrong to jump to conclusions about how bad that person may be. The old expression "Never judge a book by its cover" comes to mind when meeting someone new. Buffett's shareholder letters give numerous examples of him praising star performers. He rarely criticizes anyone, and even then, it's usually not specifically by name. If you do want to criticize someone, some good advice is to wait or sleep on it for a day to avoid making "heat of the moment" decisions. Here's our Tip based on Buffett's actions.

Buffett Tip 75:

Praise people by their name. Criticize people by their category, not personally.

Carnegie's third point, about arousing in the other person an eager want, is not really part of low-key Buffett's personality. He is far from the pushy salesperson type. But we'll close the loop on this section with some insight from (retired) marketing Professor Robert Cialdini. His book *Influence: The Psychology of Persuasion* has sold more than three million copies and analyzes the topic in broad terms. He finds six factors that are able to influence people, often eagerly. They are:

- *Reciprocity*: People feel obligated to help someone who helps them;
- *Commitment and Consistency*: People don't like to go back on their word. Often, if they agree to a small step, they will take a larger step down the road;
- *Social Proof*: People often follow what others are doing;
- *Authority*: People often listen to authority figures, such as a politician, doctor, or professor;
- *Liking*: People are more apt to buy something from somebody they like, such as a celebrity spokesperson; and
- *Scarcity*: People are more likely to purchase something if it is in limited quantity, or available for a limited time.

Getting back to **Tip 75**, let's discuss some specific examples. In Berkshire's annual shareholder letters, Buffett routinely lavishes praise on people who have had a positive effect on his life, some of the top managers of Berkshire's subsidiary firms, and administrative staff as well. It seems natural to start with his financial mentor, Ben Graham. In Berkshire's 2000 Shareholder Letter, Buffett wrote:

> A bit of nostalgia: It was exactly 50 years ago that I entered Ben Graham's class at Columbia. During the decade before, I had enjoyed—make that loved—analyzing, buying, and selling stocks. But my results were no better than average. Beginning in 1951 my performance improved. No, I hadn't changed my diet or taken up exercise. The only new ingredient was Ben's ideas. Quite simply, a few hours spent at the feet of the master proved far more valuable to me than had 10 years of supposedly original thinking. In addition to being a great teacher, Ben was a wonderful friend. My debt to him is incalculable.

Buffett calls Tom Murphy ("Murph"), who used to run Capital Cities/ABC and still serves on Berkshire's board of directors, "The best overall business manager I've ever met." In Berkshire's 2005 Annual Letter to Shareholders, Buffett wrote, "It's appropriate that I say a few words here about Murph. To put it simply, he is as fine an executive as I have ever seen in my long exposure to business. Equally important, he possesses human qualities every bit the equal of his managerial qualities. He's an extraordinary friend, parent, husband and citizen. In those rare instances in which Murph's personal interests diverged from those of shareholders, he unfailingly favored the owners. When I say that I like to be associated with managers whom I would love to have as a sibling, in-law, or trustee of my will, Murph is the exemplar of what I mean."

Buffett often praised Tony Nicely, who ran Berkshire's GEICO Insurance unit for many years. In the 2005 Shareholder Letter, Buffett also wrote, "Credit GEICO—and its brilliant CEO, Tony Nicely—for our stellar insurance results in a disaster-ridden year. One statistic stands out: In just two years, GEICO improved its productivity by 32%. Remarkably, employment fell by 4% even as policy count grew by 26%—and more gains are in store. When we drive unit costs down in such a dramatic manner, we can offer ever-greater value to our customers. The payoff: Last year, GEICO gained market share, earned commendable profits, and strengthened its brand. If you have a new son or grandson in 2006, name him Tony."

Ajit Jain is vice-chairman of Berkshire and one of two people, with another Berkshire vice-chair, Greg Abel, in line to replace Buffett as Berskhire CEO someday. Here's a quick snippet from Buffett in the 2009 Chairman's Letter to illustrate the point. Buffett wrote, "If Charlie, I, and Ajit are ever in a sinking boat—and you can only save one of us—swim to Ajit." His reference to Charlie, of course, is Berkshire's longtime vice-chair and Buffett's BFF, Charlie Munger. Yeah, we know having three vice-chairs is a lot, but it speaks to what Buffett thinks of these colleagues.

Buffett routinely praises his staff too, not just bigshots. Carrie Sova helped run Berkshire's annual meeting for several years. This is a big deal since tens of thousands of rabid fans attend the meeting, as well as a number of internal and external companies. At the 2017 Meeting, Buffett said:

> Before we start, I'd like to make a couple of introductions, the first being Carrie Sova, who's been with us about seven years. And can we have a light on Carrie? . . . And she has dozens and dozens and dozens of

> exhibitors that she works with and, as you can imagine, with all of what we put on and all of the numbers of you that come, the hotels and the airlines and the rental cars and everything, she does it as if, you know, she could do that and be juggling three balls at the same time. She's amazing, and I want to thank her for putting on this program for us.

Buffett doesn't criticize people that often. When he does, he usually doesn't single one person out but rather a group of people that he disagrees with. One frequent target is the investment bankers that sometimes push Berkshire, and many other firms, to make questionable acquisitions. The bankers earn high fees when a deal gets done and usually leave empty-handed when no deal occurs. In Berkshire's 2014 Chairman's Letter, Buffett wrote, "The Street's denizens are always ready to suspend disbelief when dubious maneuvers are used to manufacture rising per-share earnings, particularly if these acrobatics produce mergers that generate huge fees for investment bankers."

Buffett also routinely criticizes high-fee investments, such as hedge funds and private equity. These are investment products usually sold to rich people and large institutions. They often charge high fees, 2% of the assets managed, and take 20% of the profits they generate. Compare these fees to those of a simple index fund that usually charges a tiny fraction of 1% of assets and often close to nothing. Buffett calls these high-fee investment firms, and the financial advisors who sell them, "Helpers." And he doesn't mean that term in a good way, like the late Mother Teresa, declared a saint by the Vatican in 2016, helping out at an orphanage. In Berkshire's 2005 Chairman's Letter, he gave a "bottom line" assessment of these "Helpers," writing, "The burden of paying Helpers may cause American equity investors, overall, to earn only 80% or so of what they would earn if they just sat still and listened to no one." Ouch! That is, if you are a Helper. Fact check alert. Buffett was a "Helper" when he managed a hedge fund early in his career, but he made his clients a ton of money after any fees he charged, in contrast to most hedge funds today, so we'll sort of give him a pass on his critique of helpers.

Six Ways to Make People Like You According to *How to Win Friends and Influence People*

Below we list the six points related to making people like you, according to Carnegie. Again, we won't go over every point on this topic, just a few that are the most relevant to Buffett and financial literacy.

1. Become genuinely interested in other people;
2. Smile;
3. Remember that a person's name is to that person the sweetest and most important sound in any language;
4. Be a good listener. Encourage others to talk about themselves;
5. Talk in terms of the other person's interests; and
6. Make the other person feel important—and do it sincerely.

Smiling, on paper, is the easiest thing to do. It's free, friendly, and takes a small amount of time. But it can be hard to do naturally, especially if you are in a new or stressful situation. It might seem fake, but here is one relatively harmless instance where a "fake it till you make it" approach might be warranted. If you meet someone for the first time, such as a teacher or employer, you want and hope that they will be friendly. A brief smile is one way to convey this characteristic. If you made a scowl or looked stressed, would this create a good impression? Probably not, unless you are at a Halloween party or goth metal concert.

Carnegie thought it was extremely important to remember someone's name. However, it's really easy to forget someone's name, especially if you meet a bunch of people at once. It also becomes harder to remember things as you age, especially items related to your short-term memory, such as someone's name that you meet for the first time. One trick to remembering someone's name is to think about something unique related to their name or look. The more outlandish, the easier to remember. Let's say you met Mike Tyson, the former heavyweight boxing champion, before he was famous. Alliteration, words that begin with the same first letter, is often one technique that makes things easy to remember. You might think of him as Mike, the mauler or marauder. Or if you shook hands with him, you might picture him wearing boxing gloves while shaking hands. If you need a more dramatic image, you could think of him punching someone—hopefully not you! If none of these ideas work for you, then consider something else, such as picturing him eating some Tyson chicken nuggets while shaking your hand.

Buffett usually addresses people by their first names and has people call him Warren in order to keep everyone on the same level. A good clue to someone's character is to notice how they treat people who perform a lower-level job, such as a janitor, food service worker, cashier, or secretary. A high character person will treat everyone with respect, absent a strong reason to do otherwise. A quote illustrating this point, attributed to civil rights activist Jesse Jackson, is "The only time you should look down at someone is when you are helping them up." In the prior section we gave examples of Buffett praising people—Graham, Murphy, Nicely, Jain, Sova—in a sincere manner and making them feel important, another Carnegie touchstone.

Carnegie felt it was important to be a good listener and that people are more inclined to like you if you listen and let them talk about themselves. Listening is easy to do for most people, especially for introverts such as Buffett. Listening is also part of developing good communication skills, a point that Buffett has often stressed.

Buffett routinely listens to the managers who report to him, since they largely run that particular business. Buffett then can provide more meaningful input once he understands in greater detail what is going on with the business. This skill helps him wisely allocate money across Berkshire's different subsidiaries. For example, Berkshire still owns the company that sells *World Book Encyclopedia*, a product that easily runs into several hundreds of dollars for the full hardcopy set. Although Wikipedia may not have great editorial controls, it's free, fast to find on the Internet, and does a good job with millions of topics. Accordingly, Buffett is probably not allocating a bunch of money to *World Book* today but rather, to other divisions at Berkshire that have a higher return on capital.

How to Win People to Your Way of Thinking, According to *How to Win Friends and Influence People*

In this section of the book Carnegie lists a dozen or so ways to win people to your way of thinking. You know the routine by now. We'll do something akin to a Venn diagram on Carnegie's and Buffett's thoughts, rather than a detailed overview. Carnegie suggests beginning your discussion with someone in a friendly way, since it disarms people and reduces stress. It's similar to the point we just mentioned on smiling. Friendly is part of Buffett's DNA, perhaps in part to his Midwestern roots. Buffett's sense of humor and friendly, plain-spoken nature are undoubtedly an important part of his nearly universal charm.

Carnegie suggested trying to see things from the other person's point of view. Buffett also learned this perspective from Charlie Munger, who told him to always invert, a math term you might recall, which means to turn an equation inside out. In Berkshire's 2009 Chairman's Letter to Shareholders, Buffett had a couple of quips about inversion. He wrote, "Long ago, Charlie laid out his strongest ambition: 'All I want to know is where I'm going to die, so I'll never go there.' That bit of wisdom was inspired by Jacobi, the great Prussian mathematician, who counseled, 'Invert, always invert' as an aid to solving difficult problems. (I can report as well that this inversion approach works on a less lofty level: Sing a country song in reverse, and you will quickly recover your car, house, and wife.)"

He then got more serious in the 2009 Letter and discussed how he and Charlie apply the concept of inversion to running Berkshire. He wrote:

> Here are a few examples of how we apply Charlie's thinking at Berkshire: Charlie and I avoid businesses whose futures we can't evaluate, no matter how exciting their products may be. In the past, it required no brilliance for people to foresee the fabulous growth that awaited such industries as autos (in 1910), aircraft (in 1930), and television sets (in 1950). But the future then also included competitive dynamics that would decimate almost all of the companies entering those industries. Even the survivors tended to come away bleeding. Just because Charlie and I can clearly see dramatic growth ahead for an industry does not mean we can judge what its profit margins and returns on capital will be as a host of competitors battle for supremacy. At Berkshire we will stick with businesses whose profit picture for decades to come seems reasonably predictable. Even then, we will make plenty of mistakes.

We'll turn those thoughts into a Tip, with assists from Carnegie, Munger, and Jacobi.

Buffett Tip 76:

Always invert, or consider the other person's point of view.

Carnegie believed that if you are wrong, you should admit it quickly and emphatically. Buffett readily admits his mistakes, often couched with a bit of self-deprecating humor. Let's look at some examples. For Berkshire, 1999 was a rough year since investors at that time were enamored with Internet stocks and not humdrum stock, such as Berkshire's. In his 1999 Chairman's Letter to Shareholders, Buffett wrote:

> The numbers on the facing page show just how poor our 1999 record was. We had the worst absolute performance of my tenure and, compared to the S&P, the worst relative performance as well. Relative

> results are what concern us: Over time, bad relative numbers will produce unsatisfactory absolute results. Even Inspector Clouseau could find last year's guilty party: Your Chairman. My performance reminds me of the quarterback whose report card showed four Fs and a D but who nonetheless had an understanding coach. "Son," he drawled, "I think you're spending too much time on that one subject."

If you aren't a fan of classic movies, Inspector Clouseau is the bumbling detective from the *Pink Panther* movies. One of Buffett's biggest financial mistakes was buying a shoe company, Dexter Shoe, for $434 million that turned out to be almost worthless. The mistake was compounded by paying for it with Berkshire shares instead of in cash. Today, the shares would be worth about $10 billion! In his 2001 Chairman's Letter to Shareholders he fully took the blame, writing:

> I've made three decisions relating to Dexter that have hurt you in a major way: (1) buying it in the first place; (2) paying for it with stock; and (3) procrastinating when the need for changes in its operations was obvious. I would like to lay these mistakes on Charlie (or anyone else, for that matter) but they were mine. Dexter, prior to our purchase and indeed for a few years after prospered despite low-cost foreign competition that was brutal. I concluded that Dexter could continue to cope with that problem, and I was wrong.

Let's combine some of the thoughts on mistakes from Carnegie and Buffett into a Tip.

Buffett Tip 77:

Admit your mistakes quickly, and try to learn from them.

Although Carnegie was averse to criticizing people, he wasn't against throwing down a challenge once in awhile to prove a point. Buffett occasionally does the same thing. Back in **Chapter 5** we spoke of Buffett's enthusiasm for low cost, tax-efficient index funds, even though he is generally regarded as the greatest stock picker ever. Earlier in this chapter we spoke of Buffett's criticism of the high fees charged by private equity and hedge fund managers. You can probably see where we are going with this topic. In 2007, Buffett challenged a professional investor to pick a portfolio of hedge funds and said this hand-picked portfolio of funds would not outperform the S&P 500 Index fund over the next decade. He put his money where his mouth was, with each participant betting $1 million, with the winnings going to the charity of choice of the victor. Well, the results are in, and not surprisingly, Buffett won the bet. The S&P 500 beat the pants off the picks of the hedge fund manager, returning 7.7% per year over the 10-year period, relative to the 2.2% for the portfolio of hedge funds.

There is another section in Carnegie's book, called "Be A Leader: How to Change People Without Giving Offense or Arousing Resentment." Some of the points in this last part of Carnegie's book, such as giving honest appreciation and talking about your own mistakes, have substantial overlap with points that we've already covered, so we'll move on to some other topics tied to communication, emotional intelligence, and getting along with others.

What Is Emotional Intelligence (EQ)?

Carnegie's book, although still highly relevant, was published over 80 years ago. You might be wondering, what else has come on the scene tied to communication and social skills that has gained a strong following? One topic that comes to mind for us is the concept of **emotional intelligence**, or **EQ**. Sometimes it's also referred to as **EI**, but we'll stick with EQ. EQ measures ability to recognize, understand, manage, and influence emotions.

The concept of EQ was proposed by Daniel Goleman, a science journalist who wrote for *The New York Times* for many years. Goleman's 1995 book, *Emotional Intelligence*, has sold more than 5 million copies since its publication and has been translated into more than 40 languages.

There are different ways of being smart. Smart kids, and some adults, are often characterized as being either book-smart or street-smart. The first group probably aced most of their school classes and scored well on their exams. The second group learns well from personal experience and has keen awareness of the situations they are in and of the persons they interact with. Buffett started out as book smart but eventually increased his street smarts. Buffett did well in school and was always a wiz with numbers—the book-smart part. As he has aged, his raw brainpower has declined, but he describes himself as a better judge of people relative to his younger years. That's the street-smart part, which increased in part from his life experiences but also from his desire to improve on his weaknesses and the influence from important people in his life, most notably from his two wives, as well as Katharine Graham, who ran *The Washington Post*, and Charlie Munger.

Nearly everyone is familiar with the term "**intelligence quotient**" (**IQ**). A person's IQ measures their cognitive ability, or how a person reasons, calculates, comprehends, and solves problems. It's usually measured with standardized tests. Although the SAT and ACT are not formally considered IQ tests, there is a strong correlation between high scores on these college entrance exams and high IQ scores. The average IQ of the general population is about 100 and its distribution can be approximated with a bell curve. Typically, someone in the upper right-hand tail of the curve is considered to be a "genius." The "genius" IQ number typically starts somewhere in the 130–140 range, and in extremely rare cases it can exceed 200.

Buffett has often said that an IQ higher than 130 is probably at the upper end of what someone needs to be a successful investor. He said super-high IQ people tend to think they won't make mistakes and often take too much risk. They may also believe they have risks under control. The textbook example he cites is the former investment management firm Long-Term Capital Management (LTCM). The *CliffsNotes* version on LTCM is that the once multi-billion dollar investment firm run by a bunch of geniuses used a crazy amount of borrowed money (a.k.a. leverage) and their fund blew up and almost took down the entire global financial system. Fortunately, they didn't, after a bailout was orchestrated by the Federal Reserve and financed by a bunch of big Wall Street banks. If your curiosity is piqued and you would like to learn more about the LTCM story, check out Roger Lowenstein's excellent book, *When Genius Failed: The Rise and Fall of Long-Term Capital Management.*

Increasingly, different ways of measuring intelligence have been developed beyond IQ, EQ being one of the most prominent. Bill Gates said, "Intelligence takes many different forms. It is not one-dimensional. And not as important as I used to think." Goleman's EQ framework is also sometimes described as including emotional *and* social intelligence. It has four main parts: self-awareness, self-management, social awareness, and relationship management.

Emotional Intelligence (EQ): Some Details

Let's look at each of the four parts of EQ in a little bit of detail, doing the Venn diagram thing again with Buffett and EQ.

Self-awareness: Goleman defines this part of EQ as "the ability to understand your own emotions and their effects on your performance." Buffett's famous quote **(Tip 27)** "Be fearful when others are greedy and greedy when others are fearful" might be the best example of this element of EQ. How do you develop better self-awareness? Goleman suggests knowing one's strengths and limits or weaknesses is one way. Keeping a journal related to your important decisions and their outcomes and learning from them applies to all elements of EQ.

Another important point that Buffett learned over time is that sometimes when things go wrong, it might eventually result in something better down the road. A blessing in disguise, so to speak. Perhaps the most famous example tied to the early Buffett is the rejection of his admission application from the graduate school at Harvard but eventual acceptance at Columbia. Regarding this incident, *Fortune* columnist Carol Loomis writes:

"In the summer of 1950, having applied to Harvard Business School, Buffett took the train to Chicago and was interviewed by a local alum. What this representative of higher learning surveyed, Buffett says, was 'a scrawny 19-year-old who looked 16 and had the social poise of a 12-year-old.' After 10 minutes the interview was over, and so were Buffett's prospects of going to Harvard. The rejection stung. But Buffett now considers it the luckiest thing ever to have happened to him, because upon returning to Omaha he chanced to learn that Ben Graham was teaching at Columbia's business school, and immediately—and this time successfully—applied."

Angela Duckworth in her best-selling book, *Grit,* describes the ability to bounce back from setbacks as having a growth mindset. That is, you should strive to develop the ability to not only learn but also grow from setbacks. Let's summarize these thoughts with a Tip, which is a bit different from our prior one, with an assist from Angela Duckworth.

Buffett Tip 78:

Sometimes, when things go wrong, better times lie ahead. Develop a growth mindset. ***(Assist from Angela Duckworth)***

Self-management: Goleman says this part of EQ "refers to managing ones' internal states, impulses, and resources." While self-awareness mostly focuses on understanding your emotions and the effect they have on your life, the self-management component more directly relates to doing something about it. Goleman suggests that keeping your emotions in check, being adaptable, and taking the initiative with opportunities directly relates to the self-management aspect of EQ. Let's circle back to the young Buffett. He was a nervous wreck speaking in public as a youngster, so he took the Dale Carnegie course. He even won a prize one week from the class instructor for making the most progress. His accomplishment? Asking his first wife, Susie, to marry him. Fortunately, she said yes!

Buffett knew he needed to keep practicing public speaking to make it a lasting skill, so he forced himself to teach an investments course at the Municipal University of Omaha, which would later become the University of Nebraska Omaha. In fact, he taught the course for a full decade (1952–1962). Buffett's confidence was certainly bolstered by his mastery of the investment subject, although he still felt awkward around people back then.

Now, Buffett's diet of hamburgers and Cherry Coke won't win any awards from the US Department of Agriculture (USDA) for healthy eating, but he keeps his mind sharp and does enough exercise to be in decent shape at roughly 90 years of age. He commented on the importance of supporting your mind and body. He said, "You have only one mind and one body for the rest of your life. If you aren't taking care of them when you're young, it's like leaving (that) car out in hailstorms and letting rust eat away at it. If you don't take care of your mind and body now, by the time you're 40 or 50, you'll be like a car that can't go anywhere."

That advice merits a Tip.

Buffett Tip 79:

You have one mind and one body for the rest of your life. Take care of them now.

Social awareness: Goleman says this part of EQ "refers to how people handle relationships and awareness of others' feelings, needs, and concerns." Goleman suggests developing empathy and having a service orientation as ways to improve your social awareness skills. Former President Bill Clinton was a master of at least appearing to be empathetic. His ability to "feel someone's pain" helped him to establish a personal connection with people and got him elected as president twice. Buffett's service orientation is most evident in his establishment of the Giving Pledge as well as the decades he spent meeting with hundreds of college students each year. As noted in **Chapter 1**, John personally benefited from this generosity, taking several trips with Rutgers students to meet with Buffett in Omaha.

However, Buffett is far from perfect in the social awareness and empathy realms. His biggest regret in life is letting his first wife, Susie, move to California in 1977 to pursue a singing career without him, which affected their relationship forever. They remained married until her death in 2004, but their relationship clearly changed when she left. In fact, it was Susie who introduced Buffett to Astrid Menks, who moved in with Buffett and became his second wife roughly two years after Susie's passing. We'll skip the love triangle details and leave that for TMZ and related gossip sites.

In our discussion of Dale Carnegie, we mentioned Buffett lavishing praise on many of his employees. Recognizing talent falls under the social awareness realm. He also understands that not only Berkshire, but also America itself, can't be at its best unless it utilizes the talents of its entire population. In his 2001 Chairman's Letter to Shareholders, Buffett wrote on the importance of better utilizing the talents of women, racial minorities, and all people regardless of religious views or sexual orientation. He said:

> The closer that America comes to fully employing the talents of all its citizens, the greater its output of goods and services will be. We've seen what can be accomplished when we use 50% of our human capacity. If you visualize what 100% can do, you'll join me as an unbridled optimist about America's future.
>
> In neither the purchase of goods nor the hiring of personnel, do we ever consider the religious views, the gender, the race or the sexual orientation of the persons we are dealing with. It would not only be wrong to do so, it would be idiotic. We need all of the talent we can find, and we have learned that able and trustworthy managers, employees and suppliers come from a very wide spectrum of humanity.

These ideas, although obvious to most of us today, still merit a Tip.

Buffett Tip 80:

It's wrong and idiotic to discriminate. Talent comes from a wide spectrum of humanity.

Relationship management: Goldman says this part of EQ "concerns the skill or adeptness at inducing desirable responses in others." It could involve working as part of an effective team, providing inspirational leadership, resolving disagreements, and acting as a catalyst for change, among other factors. Buffett has clearly provided inspirational leadership to his hundreds of thousands of employees and millions of worldwide fans. He works especially well as part of a team with his BFF, Charlie Munger, as well as with Berkshire's senior managers. He helped save his investment in the Wall Street firm Salomon Brothers, by resolving a dispute between the firm and the US government. More on this story in our final chapter.

Although Buffett doesn't get involved in the day-to-day operations of his subsidiary companies, he does focus on big-picture issues, such as compensation. Buffett discussed his approach to doling out the Benjamins in his 2010 Chairman's Letter to shareholders, writing, "We want a compensation system that pays off big for individual success but that also fosters cooperation, not competition." For example, he and the two younger investment management professionals (Todd Combs and Ted Weschler) at Berkshire regularly share investment ideas. Todd and Ted are paid on the long-term performance of their investments, relative to the S&P 500, and if subsequent returns go bad, Berkshire can "claw back" some of the compensation.

If this EQ business all seems a little too abstract or theoretical for you, then you might want to cut to the chase and consider a mindfulness app, basically, an app that gets you to chill and be your best self. You probably need a little more guidance than Netflix and chill. Clearly, sometimes you want to be amped up, like in advance of a big sports game. (See Forest Whitaker's character in the classic high school movie *Fast Times at Ridgemont High* for a hilarious example.) But if your emotions are making it hard to think clearly or are stressing you out, then a mindfulness routine might be right for you. Headspace is perhaps the most popular mindfulness app out there. They run on a freemium model. If you want something completely free (we know Buffett would approve), there are tons of mindfulness videos on YouTube where they take you through a bunch of mental exercises. Consider watching a few and pick something that works for you.

Have A Great Posse

Buffett has a lot to say on the type of people you should associate yourself with, both in business and in your personal life. We'll devote this last section to some of his thoughts on this topic, even though they probably fall under Goleman's heading of relationship management.

The people you spend the most time with—your posse, crew, gang, friends, co-workers, family, or any other term to your liking—may have a bigger effect on you than you realize, especially during your formative years. Not only do they take up a lot of your time, but they play an important role in shaping your personality and moral framework. Jim Rohn, a motivational speaker who had great influence on self-help guru Tony Robbins, succinctly described the role of your circle of friends on you with his quote "You are the average of the five people you spend the most time with." If your friends are a bunch of slackers, or worse, it will be hard to get ahead and accomplish great things. They might even drag you down or get you into trouble.

Buffett largely agrees with Rohn's sentiment of associating with good people. You want to spend your time with people who motivate, lift, and inspire you to achieve great things or be a better person. Buffett said it slightly differently from Rohn, noting, "It's better to hang out with people better than you. Pick out associates whose behavior is better than yours, and you'll drift in that direction." That quote is worthy of a Tip.

Buffett Tip 81:

It's better to hang out with people better than you. Pick out associates whose behavior is better than yours, and you'll drift in that direction.

We have noted throughout this book Buffett's life-altering relationships with people such as Benjamin Graham, Charlie Munger, Bill Gates, Katharine Graham, and his wives, Susie and Astrid. They and his family helped shape him into the person he is today: a widely respected man with millions of fans around the world—including the two of us.

In Buffett's 1989 Chairman's Letter to shareholders, Buffett expanded on this thought applied to the business world when he wrote the following:

> After some other mistakes, I learned to go into business only with people whom I like, trust, and admire. As I noted before, this policy of itself will not ensure success: A second-class textile or department-store company won't prosper simply because its managers are men

> that you would be pleased to see your daughter marry. However, an owner—or investor—can accomplish wonders if he manages to associate himself with such people in businesses that possess decent economic characteristics. Conversely, we do not wish to join with managers who lack admirable qualities, no matter how attractive the prospects of their business. We've never succeeded in making a good deal with a bad person.

Buffett provides further insight for young people on shaping their future personalities. In Loomis' book, based on a series of *Fortune* magazine articles, he said:

> Pick out the person you admire the most, and then write down why you admire them . . . And then put down the person that, frankly, you stand the least, and write down the qualities that turn you off in the person. The qualities of the one you admire are traits that you, with a little practice, can make your own, and that, if practiced, become habit forming.

This last point relates to another famous quote: "The chains of habit are too light to be felt until they are too heavy to be broken." Although Buffett frequently cites this quote, it has been attributed to Samuel Johnson, Bertrand Russell, and others. By this quote he means, when you're young you want to develop good habits. When you're older, it may be too hard to change bad habits. Let's end this chapter with a flurry of Tips based on Buffett's insights on business and personal relationships.

Buffett Tip 82:

Only go into business with people whom you like, trust, and admire.

Buffett Tip 83:

It's very hard to make a good deal with a bad person.

Buffett Tip 84:

The chains of habit are too light to be felt until they are too heavy to be broken. ***(Courtesy of Samuel Johnson)***

Buffett's Tips from Chapter 13

Buffett Tip 74: If you know you are weak in an important skill, try to improve it.
Buffett Tip 75: Praise people by their name. Criticize people by their category, not personally.
Buffett Tip 76: Always invert, or consider the other person's point of view.
Buffett Tip 77: Admit your mistakes quickly, and try to learn from them.
Buffett Tip 78: Sometimes, when things go wrong, better times lie ahead. Develop a growth mindset. *(Assist from Angela Duckworth)*
Buffett Tip 79: You have one mind and one body for the rest of your life. Take care of them now.
Buffett Tip 80: It's wrong and idiotic to discriminate. Talent comes from a wide spectrum of humanity.
Buffett Tip 81: It's better to hang out with people better than you. Pick out associates whose behavior is better than yours, and you'll drift in that direction.
Buffett Tip 82: Only go into business with people whom you like, trust, and admire.
Buffett Tip 83: It's very hard to make a good deal with a bad person.
Buffett Tip 84: The chains of habit are too light to be felt until they are too heavy to be broken. *(Courtesy of Samuel Johnson)*

References

"American Business Magnate, Investor, and Philanthropist." Wikiquote. Accessed June 18, 2020. https://en.wikiquote.org/wiki/Warren_Buffett.

Arpaia, Alex. "The Best Meditation Apps 2020." *New York Times*, March 24, 2020. https://www.nytimes.com/wirecutter/reviews/best-meditation-apps/.

Buffett Family & UNO. Genius of Warren Buffett. University of Nebraska Omaha (course). Accessed June 18, 2020. https://www.unomaha.edu/college-of-business-administration/genius-of-warren-buffett/buffett-and-uno/index.php.

Buffett, Warren. "Letter to Shareholders of Berkshire Hathaway Inc." Berkshire Hathaway, Inc., 1989. https://www.berkshirehathaway.com/letters/1989.html.

Buffett, Warren. "Letter to Shareholders of Berkshire Hathaway Inc." Berkshire Hathaway, Inc., 1999. https://www.berkshirehathaway.com/letters/1999.html.

Buffett, Warren. "Letter to Shareholders of Berkshire Hathaway Inc." Berkshire Hathaway, Inc., 2000. https://www.berkshirehathaway.com/letters/2000.html.

Buffett, Warren. "Letter to Shareholders of Berkshire Hathaway Inc." Berkshire Hathaway, Inc., 2001. https://www.berkshirehathaway.com/letters/2001.html.

Buffett, Warren. "Letter to Shareholders of Berkshire Hathaway Inc." Berkshire Hathaway, Inc., 2005. https://www.berkshirehathaway.com/letters/2005.html.

Buffett, Warren. "Letter to Shareholders of Berkshire Hathaway Inc." Berkshire Hathaway, Inc., 2009. https://www.berkshirehathaway.com/letters/2009.html.

Buffett, Warren. "Letter to Shareholders of Berkshire Hathaway Inc." Berkshire Hathaway, Inc., 2010. https://www.berkshirehathaway.com/letters/2010.html.

Buffett, Warren. "Letter to Shareholders of Berkshire Hathaway Inc." Berkshire Hathaway, Inc., 2014. https://www.berkshirehathaway.com/letters/2014.html.

Cain, Susan. *Quiet: The Power of Introverts in a World That Can't Stop Talking.* New York: Broadway Books, 2013.

Carnegie, Dale. *How to Win Friends and Influence People Featuring Dale Carnegie.* New York: NBC, 1938.

Carrig, David. "Warren Buffett Wins $1M Bet against Hedge Funds and Gives It to Girls' Charity." *USA Today,* January 3, 2018. https://www.usatoday.com/story/money/markets/2018/01/02/warren-buffett-bet-against-hedge-funds-girls-charity/996993001/.

Chiglinsky, Katherine, and Tom Metcalf. "Walmart Heir, Buffett to Give Away $4.8b." NNY360, July 2, 2019. https://www.nny360.com/news/walmart-heir-buffett-to-give-away-b/article_2850c23d-79ca-5a14-911f-5a0e7f7ff2b9.html.

Cialdini, Robert. *Influence: The Psychology of Persuasion.* New York: Harper Business, 2006.

Clifford, Catherine. "Bill Gates Shares His 2 Best Pieces of Advice for Young People Headed Back to School." CNBC, September 5, 2018. https://www.cnbc.com/2018/09/05/bill-gates-shares-his-best-advice-for-students.html.

CNBC. "Morning Session—2017 Meeting," May 6, 2017. https://buffett.cnbc.com/video/2017/05/06/morning-session—2017-berkshire-hathaway-annual-meeting.html.

Daniel, Goleman. "How Emotionally Intelligent Are You?," April 21, 2015. http://www.danielgoleman.info/daniel-goleman-how-emotionally-intelligent-are-you/.

Duckworth, Angela. *Grit: The Power of Passion and Perseverance.* New York: Scribner, 2018.

Farnam Street Team. "How to Win Friends and Influence People: The Best Summary." Farnam Street. Accessed June 18, 2020. https://fs.blog/2012/07/how-to-win-friends-and-influence-people/.

Fast Times at Ridgemont High. Directed by Amy Heckerling. Universal Pictures, 1982.

Goleman, Daniel. *Emotional Intelligence: Why It Can Matter More Than IQ.* 10th ed. New York: Bantam Books, 2005.

Goleman, Daniel. "Harvard Researcher Says the Most Emotionally Intelligent People Have These 12 Traits. Which Do You Have?," June 9, 2020. https://www.cnbc.com/2020/06/09/harvard-psychology-researcher-biggest-traits-of-emotional-intelligence-do-you-have-them.html.

Loomis, Carol J. "The Inside Story of Warren Buffett." *Fortune,* April 11, 1988. http://fortune.com/1988/04/11/warren-buffett-inside-story/.

Loomis, Carol. *Tap Dancing to Work: Warren Buffett on Practically Everything, 1966–2012*. London: Portfolio Penguin, 2014.

Lowenstein, Roger. *When Genius Failed: The Rise and Fall of Long-Term Capital Management*. New York: Random House, 2001.

Phelan, David. "Here's How Headspace Turns Your Stressful Phone into a Source of Calm." *Independent,* April 26, 2019. https://www.independent.co.uk/life-style/gadgets-and-tech/features/headspace-meditation-app-ios-android-download-review-interview-a8888186.html.

Van Der Meer, Erin. "Blake Lively Says She and Ryan Reynolds Are 'Really Shy People.'" *Grazia*. Accessed June 18, 2020. https://grazia.com.au/articles/blake-lively-ryan-reynolds-shy/.

Ward, Marguerite. "There Are 9 Types of Intelligence. Bill Gates Says Finding Yours Is Key." CNBC, May 17, 2017. https://www.cnbc.com/2017/05/16/why-bill-gates-says-finding-you-unique-type-of-intelligence-is-key.html.

Willingham, Emily. "'Wall Street' Actress Daryl Hannah Is an Autistic Woman," September 29, 2013. https://www.forbes.com/sites/emilywillingham/2013/09/29/wall-street-actress-daryl-hannah-also-autistic-woman/.

Zoe Segal, Gillian. "Billionaire Warren Buffett: 'This $100 College Course Gave Me the Most Important Degree I Have'—and It's Why I'm Successful Today," March 22, 2019a. https://www.cnbc.com/2019/03/21/billionaire-warren-buffett-says-a-100-dollar-course-had-the-biggest-impact-on-his-success.html.

Zoe Segal, Gillian. "Warren Buffett Wants Young People to Know: Ignoring This Is like 'Leaving a Car out in Hailstorms.'" CNBC, April 15, 2019b. https://www.cnbc.com/2019/04/12/billionaire-warren-buffett-greatest-advice-to-millennials-the-1-thing-in-life-you-need-to-prioritize.html.

14

Buffett's Tips for College

"The best education you can get is investing in yourself."
—Warren Buffett, Speech at Ivey Business School, 2012

Introduction

According to Buffett, selecting a career and a spouse are the two most important decisions you'll make in your life. We'll focus on the career advice, although Buffett has weighed in on the marriage topic too. His advice? Marry someone who is a better person than you and who agrees with you on important points. In this chapter, we'll focus on college-related issues. For most people, starting a career begins after college, so we'll cover this important life decision in the next chapter. Roughly 70% of high school graduates attend college. Buffett has a lot to say on college and careers, and his comments will act as the backbone of this and the next chapter. For example, Buffett has said, "The best education you can get is investing in yourself." That merits a Tip in our book, literally.

Buffett Tip 86:

The best education you can get is investing in yourself.

College: The Basics

Buffett readily admits that college isn't for everyone, but the odds are it will help greatly if you want a high-paying and/or intellectually challenging job. We briefly touched on this topic in **Chapter 1** when we noted that income typically increases with your education level. Or, as Buffett liked to say in the Secret Millionaire cartoon series, "The more you learn, the more you earn." (**Tip 3**)

College is a huge financial commitment, with many private colleges "all in" (i.e., tuition, housing, food, books) costing well over $75,000 a year. Multiply that by the typical four or five years that most people take to complete an undergraduate degree, and you get an astronomical $300,000 to $375,000 expenditure, assuming no financial aid from the school. Fortunately, two-thirds of students get some sort of financial assistance, and public colleges are often a high quality, cheaper option. We'll cover some of the sources of financial aid in this chapter, as well as discuss the different types of colleges. But when you're talking about six-figure expenses, it makes you pause and think if taking the money earmarked for college and putting it in the stock market, or some other investment, would result in a better long-term result.

We're writing this section under the assumption that college is in your future, regardless of your age. Graduate students often range in age from early 20s to 50-plus. But we know that college isn't for everyone. Some join the military right out of school, choosing to serve their country while gaining valuable skills and leadership experiences. Others become **entrepreneurs** and create and run their own businesses right out of high school. This was Buffett's preference, but he attended college on the advice of his father. In **Chapter 1** we noted Buffett's early businesses ventures related to pinball machines, newspaper routes, farmland, and a gas station, all of which may be viewed as entrepreneurial activities. Yet others might be best served learning a trade (e.g., electrician, plumber, mechanic, chef) either through an **apprenticeship** or a **trade** or **vocational school**. It's a popular career path in Germany and has shown great results for that country, which often ranks among those with the lowest unemployment rates in the world.

An apprentice is someone who learns a craft by working side by side with an expert for a number of years. A trade or vocational school is focused on practical courses and the hands-on experience learning a specific trade. For example, if you want to learn how to be a mechanic, you might take some courses related to different systems of a car and work on cars as part of a practical lab experience. At these schools, you're less likely to take courses on English literature or advanced mathematics. Those attending a trade or vocational school typically spend one or two years there, in contrast to the four or more years at most colleges. We're not going to make much of a distinction between a college and university. A university typically offers several advanced degrees (i.e., master's and doctoral) programs and often places greater emphasis on original research. Most undergraduate degrees are called bachelor's degrees. The term has nothing to do with being single! The two most common bachelor's degrees are a bachelor of arts (BA) and a bachelor of science (BS).

A **community college** offers a two-year degree program, usually called an **associate's degree**, at a fairly low cost. This program takes two years for students attending full-time; of course, you may attend on a part-time basis as well. Community colleges are sometimes called **junior colleges, JC**, or **JUCO** for short. Most community colleges are state owned and cost a fraction of the amount of even low-cost public colleges. The figures can differ widely by state and college, but a ballpark estimate is that many community colleges cost about $3,000–$4,000 a year in tuition and fees. The acceptance rate is typically close to 100% for most JUCOs.

Most community colleges are geared toward students who live at home and who commute to school. Many students who complete their associate's degree move on to a four-year college. Most or all of the credits typically transfer to the new college, although this policy varies widely by school. If all credits transfer, then you could receive your bachelor's degree in the same 4–5-year time period, saving you a bunch of money. But transferring from a community college to a four-year college is not for everyone, despite the likely cost savings. You might have to start over, making new friends and joining student clubs. Many of your peers would have had a 2-year head start in these areas if they joined the college right out of high school. In addition, the admissions standards at most universities are much higher than community colleges, so there may be a transition period getting used to the increased academic rigor.

Getting into a College

Acceptance rates (i.e., the number of admitted students divided by the number of students who applied) range from the low single digits to the nearly 100% acceptance rate at most community colleges. In general, the most competitive colleges look at a range of factors including SAT/ACT scores, high school grades, SAT subject exams, extracurricular activities, volunteer work, and personal essays. If you are applying to graduate school, work experience may also be important.

Before taking the SAT/ACT, many high school students in the US take a precursor test called the Preliminary SAT (PSAT). It's good practice for the "real thing" and, as noted below, high-performing students are eligible for scholarships. Perhaps the most important advice for preparing for standardized tests is the same way you get to Carnegie Hall, arguably the most prestigious place for classical musicians to perform: practice, practice, practice. Practice may literally include taking the practice tests (some prior tests are released), utilizing websites such as Khan Academy, and reading books geared toward standardized tests (e.g., Kaplan, Barron's, or Princeton Review). If money isn't a big issue, you might want to consider taking a formal review course or using the services of a tutor.

There are literally thousands of colleges in the US, and most do a good job for their students. However, you really need to stand out to be accepted at the most competitive schools, including those in the Ivy League, Stanford, MIT, Caltech, the University of Chicago, Duke, and the military academies. This list of highly competitive schools is far from exhaustive. There are a multitude of great schools out there, and some may surprise you. For example, the College of the Ozarks in Missouri has an acceptance rate that rivals many Ivy League schools. Their motto is "Hard Work U" since most students graduate with little to no debt, due to financial aid, including scholarship and work study programs (discussed further below).

The top schools have boatloads of applicants with strong grades and standardized test scores. Extracurricular activities at these schools can make a huge difference. Extracurricular can be anything outside of your regular classroom work including sports, music, theater, community service activities, science competitions, entrepreneurial activities, publications, and a multitude of other activities. Although some schools prefer well-rounded students, others seek students who are what is sometimes termed as a "super spike"; that is, being world-class in some academic or extracurricular activity. There are a couple of other things that could improve your admission chances at competitive schools; one is within your control, and the other may be outside it.

Early decision refers to applying to a *single* school early (i.e., usually in mid to late October of your senior year of high school). It should be one of your top choices, if not the top choice. You typically receive your acceptance, deferment, or rejection letter by mid-December. The acceptance rates for early admission may be two to three times higher than those of regular admission at the most competitive schools. However, if you are given an acceptance offer, it is a legally binding contract. You should withdraw any pending applications at other colleges. It is unethical and may even result in civil penalties if you enroll at another school after receiving acceptance through the early decision process. In some cases, the early decision applicant is deferred and evaluated with the regular applicant pool and will receive a final decision during the spring. One downside of being accepted via the early decision process is that you can't compare financial aid packages if you are accepted at multiple schools.

Another factor that may improve your admission chances is through what is termed **legacy admissions**. This involves having a familial relationship at the university. The most common example is having a parent who graduated from the college that you are applying to. The rules vary for different schools, but it could also relate to grandparents, siblings, or other ancestors having attended, or even having a parent serve on the faculty of the college. Legacy admissions tend to be more relevant at private schools, but some schools don't take legacy relationships into the admission process at all.

Graduate School: Optional for Some Jobs, Mandatory for Others

Since we are on the topic of college, it is appropriate to mention a few words on graduate school. After all, Buffett got a master's degree in economics from Columbia Business School in New York City while he was in his early twenties.

Some professions, such as being a doctor, lawyer, or professor, virtually require a graduate degree. For example, practicing physicians in the US are required to have an MD (doctor of medicine) or DO (doctor of osteopathic medicine) degree. Medical school typically requires four years of training after receiving an undergraduate degree. Furthermore, many doctors choose to specialize in a specific area, such as dermatology, cardiology, or neurology. This specialization path usually requires two or more years of additional training. Lawyers in America in the vast majority of cases have received an JD (juris doctor) degree, which usually requires three years of study beyond an undergraduate degree. Professors at top colleges almost always have a PhD (doctor of philosophy) degree, which usually requires three to five years of graduate education to complete.

Graduate degrees in education and business are among the most popular. Obviously, education graduate degrees are popular for teachers and school administrators. Many people in the business world hold a master's of business administration (MBA) degree. Most MBA programs require two years of full-time study, although recent trends have shortened this period to one or one-and-a-half years at some schools. Our advice on graduate school is as follows. Back in **Chapter 1** we gave you some stats that showed, on average, the more education you have, the more money you'll make. So you should be biased toward getting further education if money is important to you. Obviously, if you want to pursue a profession that requires a graduate degree, such as being a doctor or a lawyer, you basically have no choice. For other jobs, if your career is going well, you may not need to purse a graduate degree, or perhaps you may pursue it on a part-time basis (i.e., nights, weekends, or online). If you feel stalled in your career or are not getting the job opportunities that you desire or deserve, pursuing a graduate degree may be a good path to jumpstarting your career or taking it to the next level.

If you go down the road of graduate school someday, you should take it seriously, studying extremely hard for the entrance examinations and, of course, after you enroll in your graduate school classes. For example, the MCAT is the standardized test for students pursuing medical school, the LSAT for law school, the GMAT for business school, and the GRE for a range of other graduate programs. You could certainly prepare for these exams on your own, but taking a review course and/or employing the services of a tutor may give you a further edge, as with the SAT/ACT. Not only is there usually a significant cost to attending graduate school (tuition is almost always higher for graduate programs versus undergraduate ones), but you will also likely stop or curtail your job while pursuing your full-time graduate degree, resulting in a double whammy of less income and higher expenses. Attending the best schools will give you a better chance at the most desirable jobs, since companies often limit their recruiting to a small number of target schools.

One more point on education: professional credentials. We strongly encourage you to pursue these if they are related to your desired career. Many professions, besides the obvious ones in medicine and law, offer professional certifications. Lawyers have to pass the bar exam to practice law in a particular state. Patients often look for doctors who are board certified, which requires the passing of certain exams by doctors. Many accountants pursue the certified public accountant (CPA) designation. We noted in **Chapter 7** that CPAs are often considered the equivalent of black belts in accounting, and the designation is required to perform certain functions, such as audits (verifying a company's financial statements). Many financial analysts and professional investors pursue the **chartered financial analyst (CFA)** designation. Obtaining the CFA charter is not an easy task since it involves passing three comprehensive examinations, as well as having four years of work experience in the securities analysis profession.

Paying for College: Scholarships and Grants

The best way to pay for college is by not paying at all. How can you do that? By getting a **scholarship** or **grant**. Both are examples of free money, so we won't make much of a distinction between the two. A grant usually comes from some sort of government organization, while a scholarship usually comes from the college, its alumni, corporations, nonprofit organizations, and others. It's not easy to get one, and they can cover anything from a small part of your college expenses to the whole thing (i.e., a free ride). You are probably most familiar with athletes that are given scholarships to play sports, such as football and basketball. Not everyone on a sports team has a scholarship. Those without one are called walk-ons, since they literally just walk on the team after trying out and making the cut. Sports have a way of building school pride and a sense of community. Think Duke University basketball or Alabama or Notre Dame football. There is also some evidence, albeit controversial, that strong athletic programs result in increased alumni donations.

There are many academic scholarships too. Why do schools award academic scholarships? Many schools want to attract the best and brightest students. Many of these students go on to achieve great success. This success attracts other strong students and may also result in alumni donations down the road. Many alumni want to pay it forward, helping others in a similar way that they were supported in the past. We'll expand on these concepts in our last chapter on philanthropy and charity.

A Pell Grant is one of the most common academic grants and is based on financial need. The awards range from several hundred to several thousand dollars. The National Merit Scholarship Program is one of the most prestigious academic scholarships in the US. Its awards are based primarily on PSAT and SAT scores and to a lesser extent on high school grades and extracurricular activities. Awards are typically about $2,500. Students can apply for the prestigious Rhodes, Fulbright, and Gates scholarships, which are primarily for students pursuing international graduate degrees.

How can you find out about scholarships and grants? The college that you attend will often automatically consider you for some once admitted. However, there are many scholarships offered by organizations outside of the college that you will attend. Scholly is one popular app that allows you to search for scholarships and grants that fit your personal profile. This app has indirectly helped students receive over $100 million in scholarship funds. That's a cool app in our book!

Some states, such as New York, offer free tuition for students attending state/city universities as long as you or your parents don't have too high an annual income—currently defined to be about $125,000. There is another catch with the New York program. After graduation you must live and work in New York state for the same number of years that you received the award. If you don't, the award will convert into a 10-year student loan that must be repaid. At least the loan would have to be repaid without interest, a good deal for any type of borrowing activity.

Paying for College: The Three-Year Plan for Super Achievers

Another approach to reducing your college expenses requires a *ton* of work, at least compared to most of your college peers. Although most students take four or five years to graduate from undergraduate college, a small percentage of high achievers graduate in three years by taking a high course load and/or by receiving credit for a bunch of AP classes. This may be a monumental task for most, but it's a technique worth mentioning, which may reduce your college expenses by 25% or more and get you into the workforce or graduate school a year before most of your peers.

Paying for College: 529 Plans

529 plans are tax-advantaged investment vehicles used for qualified educational expenses from kindergarten through college years. The name comes from Section 529 of the IRS tax code. The gains on the investment accumulate tax free as long as they are spent on qualified expenses. Qualified expenses include things such as tuition, room, board, books, supplies, and equipment. Some states also provide tax deductions for 529 contributions.

There are two types of 529 plans, savings plans and prepaid plans. Savings plans are more common. The money for 529 savings plans is placed into market-based investments. The amount varies with the performance of the underlying investments over time. Prepaid plans are offered by some states to purchase tuition credits (i.e., you buy something today that can be used to pay tuition in the future). They increase in value at the same rate of tuition for that particular college.

The investment vehicles are similar to mutual funds and typically contain a mix of stock and bond investments. As you approach the date that you need the funds (i.e., right before you enter college), many plans shift the investment mix to a higher allocation of bonds since they are less likely to crash over short periods of time. Money to 529 plans can be contributed by almost anyone, including yourself, parents, grandparents, relatives, and some other benefactor. The amount contributed to 529 plans can range from nominal amounts to several hundred thousand dollars. Accordingly, it might be a good, tax-advantaged way to sock away money for educational expenses.

Paying for College: Student Loans

We mentioned that many private colleges cost over $75,000 a year all included. Even families that have diligently saved over the years may not be able to afford all of the costs, after grants and scholarships. Typically, when you apply to college you also fill out a form called **Free Application for Federal Student Aid** (**FAFSA**), which helps determine your eligibility for financial aid. Loans are another form of financial aid. The vast majority of loans include interest, so you will pay out in dollar terms more than you have borrowed. A mix of institutions offer loans for both students and their parents/guardians. A recent online article by *Forbes* found that the average recent college graduate had $38,390 in student loans. That's some serious coin that could pay for a new car or be used as the down payment on a home.

The main US **government-sponsored enterprise** (**GSE**) focused on the student loan market is SLM Corporation, formally known as the

Student Loan Marketing Association. Its nickname is Sallie Mae. A joke, probably not funny to those with large student loans, is that Sallie Mae is the only college friend you'll have for the rest of your life.

On Sallie Mae's website they provide an overview of the different types of federal and private student loans, the latter of which are usually provided by banks. We reproduce this list below.

Types of federal student loans:

- **Direct subsidized loans** are based on financial need.
- **Direct unsubsidized loans** are not based on financial need. They're not credit-based, so you don't need a cosigner. Your school will determine how much you can borrow based on the cost of attendance and how much financial aid you're receiving from other sources.
- **Direct PLUS loans** are credit-based, unsubsidized federal loans for parents and graduate/professional students.

Types of private student loans:

- **Private student loans** are taken out by the student; they're often cosigned by a parent or another creditworthy individual.
- **Parent loans** are another way to get money for college. A parent or other creditworthy individual takes out the loan to help their student pay for college.

There are some differences with each of these loans. In general, you should prefer a loan with a lower interest rate, other things equal. In addition to a low interest rate, you should prefer loans where the interest doesn't start compounding until after you have finished your education. That is, with some loans the interest "clock" starts ticking on the day you receive the loan, while with others the clock starts after you graduate or terminate your college studies.

By the way, if you are thinking about getting rid of student debt in a bankruptcy filing, you can pretty much forget it. Students loan debt can't be discharged except under extreme circumstances, where you have to prove it "will impose an undue hardship on you and your dependents." We don't have time to go into the details here, but it's not an easy hurdle to clear. If you die with student loan debt, for government loans, the debt may be discharged, but it usually can't for private loans. Your estate, or what is left of it, may be on the hook for payments.

Paying for College: On- and Off-Campus Jobs

Going to college is a full-time job for most, but some students try to earn money by working during the school year. We'll cover summer internships later in this chapter, since they are often a stepping-stone to full-time, permanent positions. An off-campus job could be anything, from working at your local fast food joint to a job at the hippest or swankiest firm out there—think Alphabet (Google), Goldman Sachs, Apple, Amazon.com, and so forth.

On-campus jobs are often provided by the college itself. Sometimes it goes under the name **work study** and is part of the financial aid package a student receives. These jobs may include a range of positions, such as working in a computer lab, library, or student housing. For example, a **preceptor** is usually an upper-class student (i.e., a junior or senior) who acts as a sort of counselor and administrator on a dormitory floor. The preceptor usually doesn't have to pay for their housing and sometimes receives some additional pay. They generally have their own room, which can be a big bonus if you like to study alone or are prone to conflicts with a roommate.

Speaking of student housing, it's likely that the people who live in your dormitory or apartment building are, or will be, among the best friends of your entire life. Buffett relayed a powerful story about a Holocaust survivor and her litmus test for a true friend.

> Bella Eidenberg was a Polish Jew who was at Auschwitz and some of her family didn't make it. Twenty years ago she said she was slow to make friends, and that the real question in her mind was always, 'WOULD YOU HIDE ME?' If you have a lot of people that would hide you, you've had a very successful life. That can't be bought. I know people that have billions of dollars and their children would say, "He's in the attic."

A story that memorable deserves a Tip.

Buffett Tip 86:

A true friend is one who will help you at the risk of grave danger to themselves. ***(Courtesy of Bella Eidenberg)***

If you pursue a PhD or some other graduate degree, it may be possible to work as a teaching or research assistant. It's less common, but still possible, for undergraduate students to also receive assistantships.

Students with these positions may help or fully teach an undergraduate course or help professors with research projects. These jobs are not easy to come by, but they often provide free tuition, benefits, and a modest, but livable wage. Academic scholarships, distinct from the teaching and research assistantship positions, at the graduate (usually doctorate) level are sometimes referred to as **fellowships**.

College is probably the best stepping-stone to getting a permanent job, so let's move on to that crucial topic. The process of getting a job often starts with creating a resume. Most people create their first resume toward the end of their high school years or near the beginning of their college careers. Let's talk a little bit about resumes, even if you have already created one.

Your Resume: A Snapshot of Your Qualifications for a Job

A **resume** is a snapshot of your qualifications for a job. You usually send it to someone, or an organization, when you are looking for a job. It's also often posted online. It's good to keep your resume up to date even if you aren't looking for a job. You may be approached with a new job someday, even if you are happy with your current job. In fact, you are probably in a better bargaining position in that case, since to paraphrase a famous expression from the classic movie *The Godfather*, they'd have to "make you an offer you can't refuse." That is, too good to pass up.

Your resume should fit on one page (one side), at least for students and recent college graduates. Why? Most people spend only a few minutes looking at a resume, so you need to make it short and sweet. As your career progresses, it is more acceptable to have a resume that is more than one page. In that case, your resume typically starts with a "summary" section, in case someone doesn't want to read the whole thing. In some industries, such as academia, it's common to create an expanded version of your resume, called a **curriculum vitae** (**CV**). For example, most professors create CVs that list all of their publications (which could measure in the hundreds), research grants, service activities, and so forth. CVs often span dozens of pages. Thankfully, we'll stick to the one-page resume here.

We suggest saving your resume in Adobe Acrobat PDF format since the formatting sometimes becomes changed if someone opens it on a different program (e.g., Microsoft Word) than the software (and version) that you used to create the document.

Putting Together Your Resume

We've created a resume for the fictitious Pat Jones and placed it in the **Appendix**. Sorry to all the real Pat Joneses out there, in case it attracts unwanted attention for you. We purposely chose the name Pat since it is gender neutral and can stand for Patrick, Patricia, and perhaps a few other names. We picked Kardashian, uh Jones, for the expression we mentioned earlier in the book, "Keeping up with the Joneses."

We started with a resume template from Microsoft Word, but you can find a lot of free ones on the Internet. The sections of the resume that we'll cover: objective, education, work experience, and so forth, are very common, but you can change them a bit to suit your strong points. For example, some students like to include a relevant courses section, especially if they don't have a lot of work experience.

The top of your resume must include your name and contact information, such as phone number, email address, and physical mailing address. You could include other things as well, such as your own website or **LinkedIn** profile, a topic that we'll get to later the next chapter.

The Objective Section

The first formal section in most resumes, objective, lists your near-term career objective. If you are interested in a couple of different jobs or career paths, it's acceptable to have two different versions of your resume. Why shouldn't you have one resume with multiple objectives? You can certainly do that, but one part to getting a job, beyond your qualifications, is about "fit." That is, a prospective employer will think about your passion to pursue this specific career and with their firm. If you give them mixed messages about your career goals, they may not feel confident in extending you a job offer. Hiring is an expensive and time-consuming process, and employers want to find someone who will stick around for a while, ideally for the duration of their full career.

Pat's objective is to get a summer **internship** as an investment banking analyst. Our general preference is to keep your objective short—one or two sentences—since your resume is a valuable piece of "real estate." That is, if you have only one page to pitch yourself to a prospective employer, they are probably more focused on who you are and what you bring to the table. Your objective is a necessary piece of information but unlikely to differentiate yourself from other candidates for the job.

An internship is a temporary job, typically lasting two or three months and 40+ hours per week. It usually occurs over the summer, although it can occur at any time during the year. You can view it as a tryout for a full-time permanent position once you finish your college career. In fact, a good percentage of interns get a full-time offer. According to a survey by Vault.com, about 75% of interns get a full-time offer. With numbers like that, it shouldn't come as a surprise that getting a good internship is extremely competitive. As we mentioned earlier in the book, investment banks help other companies raise money by selling securities and providing advice on mergers and acquisitions, as well as offering many other services.

One last point on short-term jobs: a **cooperative education**, or **co-op**, job is sort of like an internship. It usually refers to a student working for an organization part time, while taking courses during the school year. It also often results in academic course credit. For example, a co-op student may work 20 hours a week at a firm, such as Johnson & Johnson, while carrying a full load of courses during the school year. The student may also be awarded 6 credits in a college course, let's call it Co-op 101, for their efforts, as well as payment for their work. As with internships, co-op jobs are typically meant for college students and are often a tryout for a permanent, full-time position.

The Education Section

The education section lists where you went to school and relevant academic performance and awards. Specifically, it usually includes where you went to school, your grade point average, honors, scholarships, and other relevant information. It generally starts with your most recent information. For example, if you're in college, start with your college education information. If you are in high school, start with your high school information. In fact, once you start college, most people drop the high school education part of their resume. Perhaps the main exceptions are if you went to a prestigious high school (such as the Philips Exeter Academy), were school valedictorian/salutatorian (i.e., ranked first or second in your class, respectively), or won some prestigious honors or awards (e.g., Regeneron Science Talent Search).

Our Pat Jones is what most people would view as a star student, attending Princeton University and having graduated from Princeton High School, generally ranked among the top public high schools in the State of New Jersey and the US. We generally advise listing your grade point average since prospective employers often filter on it to weed out candidates from the many applications they receive and assume the worst if you don't include it. However, some schools suggest (or even require) omitting it since they don't want to foster a cutthroat environment and would prefer the emphasis to be on the other parts of your resume. If an employer really wants to find out your GPA, they can simply ask you for an official copy of your transcript, which lists all the courses you have taken and their corresponding grades.

We advise listing not only your overall cumulative GPA, but also the GPA in your major field of study, especially if it is higher. Of course, you want to get the best grades you can, but one way to offset a relatively lower cumulative GPA is to have a strong GPA in your major. If your grades are not strong, and especially below a B or 3.0 average, hopefully you have strong work experience or other skills to offset it. Pat has a 3.8 cumulative GPA at Princeton, a 4.0 major GPA, and an (unweighted) 4.0 GPA from Princeton High School to boot. Pat's resume also lists an expected graduation date, honors (e.g., Dean's List or Honor Roll), and scholarships such as the Princeton Class of 1966 Scholarship and the National Merit Finalist Scholarship. Some people also include their SAT/ACT scores in the education section, especially if they are impressive (i.e., 90th percentile and higher).

The Work Experience Section

Include relevant work experience, even volunteer positions, that you think may be related to the job you are seeking. In general, try to quantify your accomplishments with specific dollars, percentages, and other numbers. Highlight any promotions you received, or leadership skills developed. If you worked at a place that is not a household name, make it easy for the reader by briefly describing the firm.

Pat worked at Starbucks as a barista, a person who prepares or serves coffee drinks, during the summer of 2018. Virtually any job is a good job, and Starbucks is a great firm and one of the best restaurant stocks of all time. However, a job at Starbucks is not Pat's ultimate career ambition. Notice how Pat described some valuable skills learned, such as the ability to work in a fast-paced team environment and the development of strong interpersonal and customer service skills. Pat also gained some leadership skills by training five new employees and periodically working as shift supervisor. It was a productive summer job for Pat!

The combination of skills that Pat gained while working at Starbucks is useful for most jobs. Pat also made an impact by streamlining the customer order and pickup process, resulting in a 10% increase in store profits. If you want to work for a for-profit firm, uncovering ways to make the firm more money would be a nice feather in your cap when it comes time for a promotion or asking for more money (i.e., a **raise**).

Pat then interned at BlackRock, the largest asset manager in the world, in Princeton, New Jersey, during the summer of 2019. Pat quantifies working for a large ($30 billion) mutual fund, the BlackRock Strategic Income Opportunity Fund. Pat also helped create some "pitchbooks," which are usually PowerPoint or PDF presentations meant for customers or prospective customers. We'll get to the skills section next, where expertise in Microsoft Office would be a plus for most employers.

A quick word on switching jobs. When you're young, it's okay, and perhaps expected, to try out a number of jobs. However, once your career begins in earnest, we would suggest staying a minimum of two years at each position, unless you really hate it or are treated improperly, to avoid getting the reputation of being a "job hopper," that is, someone who quickly leaves jobs on a regular basis. It takes awhile for a firm to train someone to be very productive, so they find it disappointing when someone leaves right when they get up to speed. The firm will have to then go repeat the time-consuming and costly process of finding someone new and training them. Someone reviewing your resume down the road may think, "This person leaves their job every year or two, so they will probably do the same thing with my firm."

The Skills Section

The word "skills" is broadly defined here. Urban Dictionary uses the term "mad skills" to describe "someone who has just pulled off something intensely difficult or seemingly impossible—by way of their immense skills at the task." Like soccer star Carli Lloyd scoring three goals in the first half of the 2015 World Cup final game or Pat Mahomes throwing 50 touchdown passes in his first full year as an NFL quarterback. You don't need Pat Jones's mad skills to have a solid resume. Just work with what you've got.

We purposely gave Pat a wide range of skills, including being fluent in several foreign languages as well as computer languages. Our all-star student Pat has what you would call both left-brain (analytical) and right-brain (creative) skills. It's also a positive from the perspective of an employer if you have experience with widely used software programs. For example, Pat has experience with Microsoft Office (Word, Excel, and PowerPoint).

Pat also cites knowledge of Bloomberg and Aladdin, two widely used software applications in the financial services industry. Wrapping up Pat's skills section is an item noted as financial modeling and valuation skills. Recall, these skills refer to the formal process of building spreadsheets that project a firm's future balance sheet, income statement, and cash flow statement. Valuation, or estimating the value of the firm, is often one key output of the model. These particular skills are desired, if not expected, of investment bankers, Pat's dream job.

The Activities and Interests Section

A resume often wraps up with a section that we've labeled activities and interests, which is exactly what it sounds like. If you don't have a lot of work experience, hopefully you have some strong things to talk about here. For example, if you were an officer in a student club, it provides evidence of some leadership skills, among other things. The ideal employment candidate has strong grades, good work experience, and some evidence of leadership skills.

Pat was the vice president of the Tiger Investments Club at Princeton. Pat also engaged in a lot of volunteer work, helping out with the Special Olympics and the Trenton Area Soup Kitchen. The interests part of the section is also crucial. The people interviewing you want to know something about your personality, especially if they are going to be working 40–100 hours a week with you. Yes, some jobs, such as investment banking, often do require you to work 80–100 hours a week, usually for a few years—thankfully, not for the rest of your life. Interests tie to your personality and the elusive "fit" element, which employers often seek. Pat has interests in Jazz, hockey, the saxophone, and world travel. Maybe the person interviewing you likes one or more of these things as well. Having something in common with the interviewer or developing some sort of rapport can only help you on an interview and will probably relieve some stress.

Cover Letter

A **cover letter** is often attached to the top of the resume, at least if you are giving someone a hardcopy. Otherwise, it is typically included in an email where your resume is attached. The purpose of the cover letter is to more fully explain your qualifications, fit, and desire for the job, but they aren't as widely used in today's electronically dominated world. Sadly, a lot of employers barely read them since they are often overwhelmed with the number of applications they receive, but we encourage you to create a thoughtful one.

The cover letter usually consists of a few paragraphs in prose, rather than the bullet point and short sentence form that is the structure of most resumes. There are several websites you can refer to for sample cover letters, such as ResumeGenius.com. As the name indicates, they have sample resumes on their website as well.

We'll close this chapter with a cautionary Buffett Tip on the importance of building a solid reputation. He said, "It takes 20 years to build a reputation and five minutes to ruin it. If you think about that, you'll do things differently." People are often willing to give someone a pass for mistakes made as teens and high schoolers. However, your reputation and career begin in earnest during your college years. And one bad decision can really affect it. Not that it's impossible to recover from mistakes made during your college years and beyond, but you want to start off on the right foot. Similar to building a solid credit score once you get your first credit card. So file that Buffett Tip in the back of your mind and think twice about doing something that might hurt you down the road.

Buffett Tip 87:

It takes 20 years to build a reputation and five minutes to ruin it.

Buffett's Tips from Chapter 14

Buffett Tip 85: The best education you can get is investing in yourself.
Buffett Tip 86: A true friend is one who will help you at the risk of grave danger to themselves. *(Courtesy of Bella Eidenberg)*
Buffett Tip 87: It takes 20 years to build a reputation and five minutes to ruin it.

Appendix

PAT JONES

123 Main Street, Anytown, NY 10000
Phone: (123) 456-7890
Patjones@yourSchool.com

OBJECTIVE

To obtain a summer internship as an investment banking analyst.

EDUCATION

[B.A. Economics] I Princeton University, Princeton, NJ
9/2018 – 5/2022 (EXPECTED)

3.80 GPA; MAJOR GPA 4.0

Dean's List (all semesters); Class of 1966 Scholarship Recipient

[High School Diploma] I [Princeton High School, Princeton, NJ]
[9/2014] – [6/2018]

4.0 GPA (unweighted)

National Merit Scholar Finalist; Honor Roll (all quarters); National Honor Society member

WORK EXPERIENCE

Summer Analyst Intern I BlackRock, Princeton, New Jersey, NJ
5/2019 – 8/2019

- Provided research support to the BlackRock Strategic Income Opportunity Fund, a 5 Star rated, $30 billion mutual fund.
- Aided in the creation of "pitchbooks" for the fund tailored to institutional and individual investors.

Barista I Starbucks, Princeton, NJ
6/2016 – 8/2018

- Developed leadership skills by training 5 new employees and periodically serving as Shift Supervisor of the store.
- Worked in a fast-paced team environment while developing strong interpersonal and customer service skills.
- Helped improve store profitability by 10% by streamlining customer order/pickup process.

SKILLS

- Microsoft Office (Excel, Word, PPT)
- Java, R, Python programming languages
- Financial Modeling and Valuation
- Fluent in French, German, Spanish
- Bloomberg Certified
- Aladdin Risk Management System

ACTIVITIES & INTERESTS

Vice President: Tiger Investments club, Coffee Club, Princeton member, Special Olympics Volunteer, Trenton Area Soup Kitchen Volunteer, hockey, jazz, saxophone, and world travel.

References

"American Business Magnate, Investor, and Philanthropist." Wikiquote. Accessed June 18, 2020. https://en.wikiquote.org/wiki/Warren_Buffett.

Bary, Emily. "6 Life Lessons from Warren Buffett." *Barron's,* December 7, 2016. https://www.barrons.com/articles/6-life-lessons-from-warren-buffett-1481130853.

Berman, James. "The Three Essential Warren Buffett Quotes to Live By." *Forbes,* April 20, 2014. https://www.forbes.com/sites/jamesberman/2014/04/20/the-three-essential-warren-buffett-quotes-to-live-by/.

Buffett, Warren. *Secret Millionaires Club: Volume 1.* A Squared, 2013. https://www.smckids.com/.

"College Enrollment and Work Activity of Recent High School and College Graduates Summary." US Bureau of Labor Statistics, April 28, 2020. https://www.bls.gov/news.release/hsgec.nr0.htm.

Friedman, Zack. "Student Loan Debt In 2017: A $1.3 Trillion Crisis." *Forbes,* February 21, 2017. https://www.forbes.com/sites/zackfriedman/2017/02/21/student-loan-debt-statistics-2017/.

MarketBeat. "Buffett's 1991 Salomon Testimony." *Wall Street Journal.* Dow Jones & Company, May 1, 2010. https://blogs.wsj.com/marketbeat/2010/05/01/buffetts-1991-salomon-testimony/.

Montag, Ali. "Warren Buffett: Here's How Much College and Grad School Matter." CNBC, October 24, 2017. https://www.cnbc.com/2017/10/24/warren-buffett-on-how-much-college-and-business-school-matter.html.

"Pay for College: Financial Aid: FAQs." CollegeBoard. Accessed June 18, 2020. https://bigfuture.collegeboard.org/pay-for-college/financial-aid-101/financial-aid-faqs.

"Types of Student Loans—Ways to Borrow Money for College." Sallie Mae. Accessed June 18, 2020. https://www.salliemae.com/college-planning/student-loans-and-borrowing/.

Vault Careers. "What Percent of Interns Receive Full-Time Offers?" *Vault,* November 18, 2015. http://www.vault.com/blog/job-search/what-percent-of-interns-receive-full-time-offers.

Young, Elise. "Report Finds Alumni Giving, Among Other Areas, Correlated with Football Success," July 3, 2012. https://www.insidehighered.com/news/2012/07/03/report-finds-alumni-giving-among-other-areas-correlated-football-success.

15

Buffett's Tips for Careers

"Take the job that you would take if you were independently wealthy."
—Warren Buffett, Speech at the University of Florida, 1998

Introduction

In the back half of the last chapter we discussed putting together your resume, which is sort of like a big business card related to your career. In this chapter we'll focus exclusively on other career-related issues, calling on Buffett when appropriate. Buffett has not only had a stellar career, but he's also hired and mentored scores of people. And, like most people, he's also dealt with his fair share of rejection and hardships. We'll get to those stories as the chapter unfolds. Let's get started.

LinkedIn Profile: Your Online Resume

LinkedIn, now owned by Microsoft, is the largest job-oriented social media website in the world. They have more than a half *billion* users. After joining the website, assuming you are age 13 or older, you typically start out by filling out a profile. As with your resume, there are sections for education, work experience, skills, and other items. You can post comments or provide links to articles, like you can do with Facebook and other social media websites. Some people will even write testimonials on your LinkedIn site, saying what a talented person you are or endorse some of your awesome skills. Most people include a picture of themselves in their LinkedIn profile. In America, it's rare to include a personal photo on your resume, but it's common in Europe and many other regions.

Many people use LinkedIn to "stalk" the employer they are interested in and the people they may be interviewing with. The type of "stalking" we refer to won't put you in jail. It means checking out the firm and some of their people. It's likely a good practice in preparing for the interview, but you may not want to refer to it explicitly *during* the interview to avoid freaking someone out. On the topic of "stalking," some employers will examine your own social media accounts, such as Facebook, Instagram, and so forth, and google you as well. In fact, some companies use artificial intelligence software to scope you out. The stuff you post online or text to someone is there forever (often even after you hit the delete key), so keep it clean!

Buffett has a good piece of advice on personal conduct that he communicates to all of his employees and to the students who have visited him over the years. In 1991 he reluctantly became chairman of Salomon Brothers, a Wall Street firm where he had a sizeable ownership stake, after the firm got into some serious regulatory trouble that we'll expand upon in the next chapter. In a speech to a subcommittee of the House of Representatives that was investigating Salomon Brothers, he said, "After they first obey all rules, I then want employees to ask themselves whether they are willing to have any contemplated act appear the next day on the front page of their local paper, to be read by their spouses, children, and friends, with the reporting done by an informed and critical reporter."

We'll use part of the quote—about your actions appearing on the front page of your local paper—in a Tip. We guess the modern-day equivalent of your local paper would be Facebook, Instagram, Snap, TikTok, and now LinkedIn.

Buffett Tip 88:

Act as if all your actions would be shown on the front page of your local newspaper, or its modern-day equivalent (e.g., Instagram, Facebook, TikTok, Snapchat, LinkedIn).

Getting back to LinkedIn, sometimes there are comments about a firm (e.g., culture, dress code, interview questions) on its LinkedIn page and some related news articles or job openings. If you have more than one page of good stuff to fit on your resume, then including a link to your LinkedIn profile might be a smart move, since there is no formal space constraint.

Finding an Internship or Job

There is no one single best way to get a full-time job, other than the point we mentioned last chapter. That is, getting an internship is the best path to landing a full-time job, especially at the entry level. What's the best way to get an internship? The most common ways for getting entry-level or internship positions include hearing about it through family/friends or by applying through the career services department. Most colleges have a career services department, which acts as the matchmaker between employers and students. They also often provide other services such as helping you prepare your resume and with practice, or mock, interviews.

Websites such as LinkedIn, Monster.com (*not* the energy drink), and Craigslist often list jobs. A company's own website may also be a good source for finding out about its open jobs. Your network consists of not only family and friends, but also the alumni of the school that you attend(ed). One advantage of attending a top-ranked college is their alumni probably populate many of the leading companies in the world. People tend to have greater familiarity and comfort with someone who went to the same school as themselves and are more likely to hire from there, rightly or wrongly. The reasons may be as innocuous as an alumnus asking a former professor for some good students.

Of course, you may make friends naturally through your classes and on- or off-campus living situations, but another effective way to meet people who may ultimately be useful for your job search is through school activities. These activities may relate to a club, community service group, fraternity, sorority, and countless other things as well. When companies recruit on campus, they often send recent alumni to do the recruiting. Going back to Pat's search for a job in investment banking, senior members of the economics/finance clubs at Pat's college (Princeton) might be the ones doing the recruiting in a few years. Therefore, strong relationships with the leaders of student clubs may be extremely useful down the road. The same goes with relationships with your professors since they may also act as job referral sources, write you recommendations for graduate school at some point in the future, or act as a job reference.

Creating your own job by starting your own company, being an entrepreneur, is also a good path for many self-starters. Buffett started his own long-term business, an investment management firm, after working for his father and then his mentor (Benjamin Graham) for a handful of years. Of course, he had a bunch of side businesses growing up, as we have mentioned a few times throughout this book. Certain colleges, such as Stanford University in Silicon Valley and Babson College and Northeastern University in the Boston area, are well known, in part, for their entrepreneurial students. Students starting their own businesses coming from these schools, and those with similar reputations for creating new businesses, are more likely to receive funding than an entrepreneur from the proverbial Podunk University. Many businesses require external funding if they are going to become meaningful in size (think about creating a Home Depot competitor from scratch), so the odds are stacked against the Podunk entrepreneur versus the Stanford one.

Lastly, sending blind emails or dialing someone whom you don't know (i.e., cold calling) are largely ineffective ways of getting a job, but it has been done with some success before, sort of like a "Hail Mary" pass in football. If you throw hundreds of passes, you may benefit from a few lucky catches. In short, you should view the process of getting a job as a job and of greater importance than any other class that you may take. After all, we're talking about your career, which Buffett ranks as one of the two most important decisions of your life.

The Job Interview(s): Preparation

If you get an interview, take it very seriously since it means the employer views you as being qualified for the job. Then it often comes down to fit. So if you are bummed out about your 3.5 GPA when other candidates have a 4.0 GPA, get over it. Would you prefer working all day with a person you like or with a jerk or boring person, even if they had strong skills? Of course, there are many great people who did achieve the magic 4.0 GPA number, but our point is leave your GPA at the door in interview situations. And once you start working, no one will ask you about your GPA or SAT/ACT scores; they just want you to work hard, do a good job, and be a nice, thoughtful colleague.

Buffett has weighed in on the topic of the kind of people he likes to work with and hire. We'll include one Tip on his thoughts now and one later in the chapter. In his 1986 Letter to Berkshire Hathaway shareholders, he wrote:

> We intend to continue our practice of working only with people whom we like and admire. This policy not only maximizes our chances for good results, it also ensures us an extraordinarily good time. On the other hand, working with people who cause your stomach to churn seems much like marrying for money—probably a bad idea under any circumstances, but absolute madness if you are already rich.

Buffett Tip 89:

Work only with people whom you like and admire. It maximizes your chance for good results and ensures you an extraordinarily good time.

Buffett wanted to work for Graham, whom he greatly admired, right after he graduated from Columbia in 1951. Graham at first said no, but Buffett kept in communication with him, often sending his former professor investment ideas. Eventually, Buffett was hired by Graham and worked for him in New York City for a few years until Graham decided to retire from the investment business. Buffett thoroughly enjoyed his time working for Graham and learned a ton. Basically, his experience working for Graham epitomized Tip 89.

If you want to do well on a test, you usually have to study for it. Similarly, detailed preparation is often required if you want to give yourself the best chance of getting a job. So before you have your interview(s), read up on the history of the organization and its main products or services. You can often find this information on the company's website, in its annual report, on its LinkedIn website, or on its Wikipedia page. You should also know the name of the company's chief executive officer (CEO) and some of its other top executives. If the company is publicly traded, we also suggest that you know the firm's stock price, stock symbol, market cap, sales, profits, and key competitors. These bits of information will help you answer the common interview question, "Tell me about the firm and why you want to work with us?"

Speaking of questions, if you receive the questions in advance of an exam, you could get expelled for cheating. But, in an interview session, you can often predict a bunch of the questions you'll be asked. Most interviewers aren't terribly imaginative, and they are probably interested in the response to standard questions, such as "Tell me about yourself" "What are your greatest strengths and weaknesses?" "Why did you choose your college?" "Why did you select your major course(s) of study?"

You really want to nail these sorts of questions that you know you're likely to get. You can nail them by practicing and being truthful in your response. If you tell them what you think they want to hear, rather than speaking the truth, you might not come off as genuine. And then your job prospects with that firm are probably over. For example, if you get the common interview question, "What is your greatest weakness?" and you give them a bogus response such as "I work too hard" or "I'm a perfectionist" (i.e., a strength positioned as a weakness) you'll probably lose credibility with the interviewer. Rather, tell them a truth about your weakness (e.g., I'm not the most organized) *but* say what you are doing to fix it (e.g., working on a new system) or how you have improved.

For a legal cheat sheet of interview questions, search the Internet for a "list of the most common interview questions." You'll find there is a ton of stuff out there. Vault.com has a bunch of career guides by discipline, such as investment banking, consulting, marketing, nonprofits, and so forth. Wall Street Oasis is a popular message board for finance-oriented jobs. Glassdoor.com also sometimes lists interview questions for specific firms. More on Glassdoor in a minute. If you have a friend or alumnus of your school working at the place you are interviewing, that person might be your best bet for candid and specific advice. This might be a good reason to "stalk" someone on LinkedIn, emailing something to the effect of, "Hi, I'm Pat Jones, a student at Princeton, and I have an interview at your firm next week. Can you please spare a few minutes of your time to speak with me about your firm?"

Dress appropriately for the firm when you go on the interview. You will usually be able to infer the appropriate dress code by doing your homework on the culture of the organization or by asking the person setting up the interview. For many firms, it may require a suit, while for others, casual attire might be best. For example, jobs in the financial services industry tend to require more formal attire, while those in art or advertising often allow for substantially more flexibility. The same goes for any jewelry, makeup, and so forth. When in doubt, err toward dressing more formally and conservatively. It brings to mind the expression "You never get a second chance to make a first impression." Too bad Buffett didn't come up with this quote or we'd put it as a Tip. There is no agreement on who first said it, but the quote has been attributed to Will Rogers, Oscar Wilde, and the clothing company Botany Suits.

The Job Interview(s): Acing Your Interview

Showing up late for an interview is a surefire way to make a poor first impression. It pretty much kills your chance of getting a job, even if you got stuck in traffic. However, if you show up for the interview too early, some people may find it annoying since they are probably tied up with something else, including interviewing other job candidates, and they may feel obligated to see you. Here is our compromise solution. Show up in the vicinity of where the interview will take place about an hour or two before it occurs. Arriving early will reduce stress and give you time to review your resume and responses to the questions you expect to get asked on the interviews. It will also give you the chance to be on time in case you run into some car trouble or hit terrible traffic. It happens! Psychologist Amy Cuddy, in a famous TED Talk viewed by millions of people, advises practicing some "power poses" (i.e., think Wonder Woman's famous pose with her hands on her hips) as a way to boost your confidence. She calls it a simple life hack, although the results of her study have come under suspicion in recent years.

Arrive at the exact spot for the interview about five minutes before it is scheduled. This will give you a chance to check in and go through any security clearances. Some firms do have airport-like security, requiring you to show ID, be photographed, and go through a scanner. In a post COVID-19 world, we wouldn't be surprised to see temperature scanning as part of a security clearance process as well. Arriving a few minutes early for an interview is fine, and your punctuality may even be viewed as a positive.

While in the waiting area be sure to be courteous to the receptionist or others near the check-in location and try not to look at your phone. Focus on being in the right mindset for your interview (i.e., relaxed and confident), and it's fine to review your resume and interview preparation materials one more time.

Interviews come in many forms. Sometimes firms will conduct a 15–30-minute phone or Skype/Zoom/WebEx interview to weed out potential candidates quickly. For a hilarious example of this type of interview, check out the movie *The Internship*. You can use a phone interview to your advantage since you can have extra information available to you.

For example, you can have your resume, company information, information on the economy and the industry of the job you are interested in, and so forth, spread out on a kitchen island or on the floor of your room. The interviewer might think you are Einstein with all that knowledge at your fingertips! Why not just google in response to questions on a phone interview? It's rude, time consuming, and the person on the phone can probably hear you typing. So ditch the thought.

Most interviews are conducted face-to-face, at least before COVID-19 hit. They are usually with one person at a time, but sometimes there are several people in the same room that fire questions at you, informally known as a "tag team" interview. It's sometimes more efficient for companies to do this, since perhaps one hour of company time will be used instead of two-plus. It's natural to be nervous, especially when the interview first begins. The more interviews you have, the more comfortable you will feel. When first being introduced to someone, smile, look them in the eye, and (before COVID-19) give a firm handshake, making some basic small talk such as, "Hi, I'm Pat. It's nice to meet you < insert person's name here>. Thanks for taking the time to meet with me today."

The interviewer will usually start with some small talk about the weather, if you were able to find the place okay, and so forth. They will typically scan your resume and start asking some questions, including the dreaded "Tell me about yourself." These open-ended questions are not easy to answer precisely, but they are really asking why your unique background makes you qualified for the job as well as trying to see that you are a good fit for the job. In addition to your qualifications, the interviewers want to know that you really want to work for their particular firm and that you are a good fit.

Besides being prepared, there are other things that you can do to help you ace the interview(s). Start by telling the truth, being yourself, and displaying a genuine interest in the firm, position, and interviewers. Often an interviewer will say near the end of the interview, "Do you have any questions for me?" The last thing you want to say is no since it shows a lack of preparation and interest. You don't have to wait for the interview to end before you start asking questions, but you should have a couple of questions in the back of your mind to ask. Something may have come up during the course of the interview that sparked your interest. If you're still at a loss for questions, you can ask them about their career path or the characteristics of people that have done well at a similar position that you are interviewing for or what they like most about the firm.

After your interview is finished, we suggest sending a brief thank-you email or note to each person that you interviewed with. After all, they took time out of their day to meet with you and they could be a future colleague, so you want to make a good impression. Fortunately, you will typically get a business card from each person you meet, so you don't have to panic about remembering their exact names, spellings, and email addresses. Don't write one thank-you note and send the exact same thing to each person you interviewed with. It's lazy and sometimes colleagues forward notes and emails, which would reveal your lack of creativity. Try to say something unique about each conversation you had with a particular person. It's okay to bring a pad of paper while you are interviewing and occasionally take notes. Try to make eye contact and do not look down the bulk of the time at your notepad, even if you're nervous. But don't go overboard and give them some kind of death stare or Kobe Bryant "mamba mode" type of look.

For a full-time position, it usually takes multiple interviews before being extended a job offer. You may be interviewing for the better part of the day over several days. In most cases, they will take you out to lunch. We can't cover a full course on business etiquette here, but there are a bunch of good books on the topic, such as Barbara Pachter's *The Essentials of Business Etiquette: How to Greet, Eat, and Tweet Your Way to Success.*

Here are a few quick points to note while at a business lunch. Eat something you like but that's not too messy. For example, you may like spaghetti, but spending the time and effort twirling it on a fork and then eating it is probably not the best dining option. Don't order alcohol (assuming you are over 21 and it isn't against your religion or moral code) during an interview meal. When sitting at a table with multiple people, it may be confusing to know what dishes and utensils belong to you versus others. You probably learned the mnemonic ROY G BIV to remember the colors of the rainbow. For business meals, think "BMW" for bread, meal, water. Bread is usually served on your left, the plate in the middle, and water on the right. If there are multiple types of utensils, start from the outside for the first course, and then use the inside ones for later courses.

Some firms like to ask brainteaser questions on interviews, especially if you are pursuing an analytical position. These are questions that require detailed computations or deep thought. Here's a well-known example. How many golf balls can you fit in a Boeing 747 airplane? Very few people know the answer to this question with any degree of precision, even those who work for Boeing! The people asking brainteaser questions are mainly interested in your thought process, so don't panic if you don't know the answer. Make some type of logical effort and don't simply give up saying, "I don't know." It is okay to make some quick calculations on a piece of paper or on your phone.

Regarding the golf ball question, you might start by saying a Boeing 747 airplane is about 250 feet long, 20 feet wide, and 20 feet high, excluding the wings, tail, and wheels. Planes and golf balls aren't rectangular shaped, but you might get in the ballpark of the answer by using a formula that pretty much everyone recalls, volume equals length × width × height. (Bonus point if you recall the formula for the volume of a cylinder from high school: volume = pi × radius squared × height). Using the rectangular volume formula gives 250 × 20 × 20 = 100,000 cubic feet.

A golf ball is about 1.5 to 2 inches in length from top to bottom. So if one ball can fit in a 2-inch line, 6 balls can fit in a one-foot line. Multiplying this number by 6 across and 6 up gives, 6 × 6 × 6, or 216 balls per cubic foot. We are now ready to get our final estimate, 100,000 cubic feet times 216 balls per cubic foot for a grand total of 21,600,000.

In case you are wondering, after doing a quick search on the web, we found an estimate that about 23 million golf balls can fit in a Boeing 747. You can google "brainteaser interview questions" for a list of websites that cover some of the most common ones that may turn up on an interview. Reportedly, Google/Alphabet is one firm that is fond of asking them. As we said earlier in the chapter, you should really try to crush the questions you know that you are likely going to be asked. If you don't do so well on brainteaser or other questions that are not in your wheelhouse, it's no big deal. You can still get the job.

The Job Interview(s): Compensation, or Show Me the Money!

Jerry Maguire is a famous movie, starring Tom Cruise, which was released back in 1996. One of the famous quotes from the movie, said by actor Cuba Gooding Jr., is "Show me the money!" This brings us to some advice on the amount of money you'll be paid to do a job. Never be the first person to bring up money! Let the representative of the hiring firm bring it up. For most large firms, the amount of money paid to interns and for entry-level positions is somewhat fixed. The situation is more fluid for smaller firms.

If they ask you something to the effect of, "What type of compensation are you looking for?" there are at least a few ways you can approach it. One resource is Glassdoor.com, a website we mentioned earlier. They list salary information by company, posted by (anonymous) employees. If you join the site, for free, you can get even more detailed information on **salaries** (a fixed payment), **bonuses** (a variable payment often based on performance), and benefits (e.g., health insurance, life insurance, and retirement plans). Getting back to the salary question, you can say, "I read on Glassdoor.com that the average salary for an analyst position at your firm is $60,000. Is this an accurate number? If so, I would be appreciative of something in that range."

If there is no information on Glassdoor, or other Internet websites, you can ask the firm representative if there is a range of compensation for the position. There usually is (e.g., $55,000 to $65,000), but they may not want to divulge the information. If they give you the range, ask for the midpoint, or something a bit above if you are feeling ambitious or have a competing job offer at a higher salary. If you pick a number that is too high, you may seem too greedy or price yourself out of the position, while a number that is too low may be selling yourself short. If you have a contact at the firm (e.g., an alumnus of your school or a friend of your family), they may also be able to give you some frank advice on salaries. If you are in the fortuitous position of having multiple job offers, go with the job that you will enjoy the most and that has better potential growth rather than focusing simply on the money. In the long run it should pay off better in more ways than one, assuming there is not a huge difference to start.

Succeeding on the Job

Working hard is a prerequisite for success in almost any field ranging from sports to a traditional office job. Few people can simply coast on their natural talent and perform at elite levels. What is the definition of hard work? In his bestselling book *Outliers*, Malcolm Gladwell wrote that it takes at least 10,000 hours to become an expert in a certain field. That's the equivalent of about 40 hours a week for 5 years, or 20 hours a week for 10 years. Buffett often cited the hard work of his colleague Rose "Mrs. B" Blumkin, who worked at the firm she helped build, Nebraska Furniture Mart to the ripe old age of 103. We lauded Mrs. B back in **Chapter 10** and with **Tip 61**.

When you are first starting your career, "face time" (i.e., being at the job site), is important since it helps demonstrate your work ethic. So we suggest new employees arrive at work before their supervisors *and* leave after them. If you are working remotely, then log on to your remote work system before your colleagues and be the last to log off. Of course, if you have an occasional important event going on (e.g., wedding or funeral) this advice won't apply. We've heard expressions (that we don't particularly like) said by some supervisors, such as "If I'm here, you're here" and "Your job is to make me look good" that indicate the preference for face time at some organizations. Try to go above and beyond your stated work responsibilities and help others to boot. Your efforts will be noticed.

It's a lot easier to work hard if you have a job that you like. Buffett expressed it slightly differently, saying, "Take the job that you would take if you were independently wealthy." You may not have this luxury early in your career, since the best jobs are often extremely hard to get, but it should be your long-term goal. Buffett first worked for his father's firm, Buffett-Falk & Co., after graduating from Columbia and then eventually created his own firm. He likes the freedom of painting on his own canvas, so to speak. He said, "I feel like I'm on my back, and there's the Sistine Chapel, and I'm painting away." Let's put Buffett's quote near the opening of this paragraph as our latest Tip.

Buffett Tip 90:

Take the job that you would take if you were independently wealthy.

Networking is perhaps an overused and nebulous term, but it has been shown to be a crucial determinant of success. We mentioned networking in the last chapter in the context of college recruiting, but the concept really applies throughout your entire life. You are likely to get hired or be given a strong recommendation by someone in your network. People would rather hire someone who they know is good than some unknown person who looks great on paper.

Other tips for success include a mindset of continuous learning. We previously mentioned Buffett's voracious reading appetite, with his routine of reading roughly six hours each day. Learning can also take place with company-sponsored (internal or external) training classes, listening to audiobooks, watching and actively engaging in college courses on Coursera, YouTube, and TheGreatCoursesPlus.com, as well as reading

Wikipedia articles (despite it not being a primary source). Perhaps most important for new employees, you can earn a lot from your colleagues at work by speaking with them and observing how the most successful workers go about their business. Buffett has often said, "It's difficult to teach a new dog old tricks." Of course, that quip is a spin on a famous quote from the 1500s, "You can't teach an old dog new tricks." In short, respect and learn from the collective wisdom of your more experienced colleagues.

A (usually more senior) colleague may turn into one of your mentors. Buffett stated that his father, Howard Buffett, and his professor, Benjamin Graham, had huge impacts on his business career. Jamie Dimon, CEO of JPMorgan Chase & Co. and a good friend of Buffett's, had the former banking executive Sandy Weil as his mentor. Mentors can provide you with advice, act as a reference, push for your promotion (if you work for the same firm), and sometimes give you the option of following them to new and better jobs. Hitching your wagon to a rising star at the firm may also open up some interesting career opportunities. What can you do to repay your mentor? Here, we'll take another page out of Buffett's playbook and turn it into a Tip. When hiring, he looks for someone with integrity, intelligence, and energy. People at all ages, even rookies on the job, can almost always bring those characteristics to the table. Any mentor would be pleased to know or have someone working for them with those qualities. There is no quicker way to sour a mentor-mentee relationship than to do something that brings embarrassment or dishonor to your mentor.

Buffett Tip 91:

Integrity, intelligence, and energy are highly desired traits.

Having a positive attitude, learning from mistakes, and asking for help are other attributes that may also help you succeed in your career. Although there is no one single most important factor that determines success, the closest thing we know that has been rigorously studied has been dubbed "grit" by University of Pennsylvania psychologist Angela Duckworth. In her 2016 bestselling book *Grit: The Power of Passion and Perseverance*, Duckworth finds that grit, which she defines as a combination of passion and perseverance, is a bigger determinant of success than IQ, socioeconomic status, and a host of other variables. Gritty people not only bounce back from failures, but they also learn from them. Similar to a golfer or ballplayer tweaking their swing. So when things get tough, get gritty, since it may eventually lead to success.

Financial Paperwork After Getting a Job

Since this is a book mostly about financial literacy, we'd be remiss to not include some information about filling out a bunch of financial forms your employers give you when you start working. Some of the most common and important forms are **W-2**, **W-4**, health care plans, retirement plans, and of course the main US Income Tax form, **1040**. We know these topics may be dry as dirt for many, but they are at the heart of building wealth and so necessitate at least a brief discussion. The tax forms mentioned in this chapter may be found at IRS.gov.

Forms W-2 and W-4

The purpose of the Form W-2, or Wage and Tax Statement, is to specify annual wages and taxes paid by an employee. The data on it reflects earnings over the previous calendar year. It's often needed for mortgage or other loan applications. The **Federal Insurance Contributions Act (FICA) tax** withholdings are also reflected on the Form W-2. These are taxes that help fund Social Security and Medicare. Every employer must send their employees Forms W-2 by January 31, since they provide important information used when filling out Form 1040.

The W-2 is organized in a straightforward manner may be found at IRS.gov. It contains a bunch of sections or boxes, the most important of which we briefly cover below. The left side of the form states information about the employer and employee, such as name and address. Information concerning wages earned and taxes paid is stored on the right side of the form. Box 1 contains your wages over the past year, and boxes 3 and 5 show how much of those wages are subject to Social Security and Medicare taxes, respectively. We'll discuss shortly how health care and retirement deductions are taken pre-tax, meaning they cut your tax bill. Boxes 2, 4, and 6 show the taxes that were actually withheld from your paycheck.

Form W-4, also known as the Employee's Withholding Allowance Certificate, is given to every new employee. Its purpose is to record the amount of income tax that will be withheld from each of your paychecks. The top section of the form simply asks for your name and address information. Box 5 may be the most important and asks for the number of allowances you are claiming. Allowances include people, such as yourself, spouse, and dependent children. The more allowances you claim, the less you have withheld from each paycheck, although this behavior may result in a larger than expected tax payment when taxes are due on April 15. If you claim fewer allowances than you deserve, you may get a refund on tax day.

Form 1040: The Annual Income Tax Form and "The Buffett Rule"

Form 1040 is perhaps the most infamous form in the United States, notorious for the copious amount of work often involved with filing taxes every year by April 15, COVID-19-type extensions aside. In plain English, when most people talk about "filing their taxes," this is the form they are referring to. Buffett filed his own taxes, as well as those of his investment partnerships, for many years. If you have a simple case, you should be able to complete your own tax returns, especially with the aid of software such as TurboTax. If your case becomes more complicated, hiring a paid tax preparer may be worth it. They often know nuances of the ever-changing, voluminous tax code that may reduce your overall tax bill. Tax preparers range from one person mom-and-pop shops to national chains, such as H&R Block or Jackson Hewitt. In any case, you need to sign the form and verify the filing is accurate, under the penalty of perjury. Famous mobster Al Capone got away with a lot of things, including murder, but he eventually went to prison for cheating on his taxes.

The first line item or box on Form 1040 asks for your total wages from the previous year. This amount can be found directly on Form W-2 for most people. You may have earned other forms of income, such as interest or dividends from stocks, and these items go in their corresponding locations in boxes 2 through 5. Line 6 asks you to calculate your total income, which is computed by adding up the amounts in boxes 1 through 6. Thankfully, we won't cover each of the 24 lines on Form 1040, just some of the most pertinent.

On line 9 of Form 1040 you are prompted to state your standard deduction or itemized deduction. The standard deduction is a fixed amount you can subtract from your income before you calculate the amount of taxes you owe. Taking the standard deduction saves you a lot of time since you don't have to find receipts to support your expenses. The amount of the standard deduction generally increases each year with inflation. It was recently $12,400 for individuals and higher if you are married (filing jointly) and have kids. That is, if your income (assuming you are single), after deducting for things such as health insurance and retirement contributions, is less than $12,400 you would owe *no* taxes and might even get a refund. Sweet! For many people, taxes owed and paid are a lot higher so they should itemize deductions, such as mortgage interest and property taxes. This approach often requires that you complete a bunch of additional forms that we (mercifully) won't cover here.

Taxes are progressive, meaning the more money you make, the more taxes you are paying, both in dollar amounts and percentage amounts. For example, if your taxable income (after deductions) is between 0 and $9,875, you would pay 10% of it as federal taxes. Let's use a round number. If your taxable income is $5,000, after all deductions, you would owe 10% of $5,000, or $500, to the federal government. Bummer! State and local governments may require that you pay income taxes on top of that as well. Double bummer! Seven lucky states require no income taxes of their residents. Here they are in case you want to work or retire there: Alaska, Florida, Nevada, South Dakota, Texas, Washington, and Wyoming. Getting back to the progressive federal tax table, the taxes owed start at 10%, then increase to 12% for amounts between $9,875 and $40,125, then jump to 22% for amounts between $40,124 and $85,525, and keep going up. There are currently a total of seven tax brackets with the top one starting at an income exceeding $518,400. You'll get there someday! Specific tax tables can be found on pages 67–79 of the IRS's official Instructions for Form 1040, accessible online.

Taxes can be weird since different types of income are taxed at separate rates. For example, income tax rates are usually higher than capital gains tax rates. This has resulted in some strange cases like Buffett paying less taxes, on a percentage basis, than his secretary. Buffett has clearly stated that this is an injustice, although he didn't volunteer to pay more on his taxes. He was just legally taking advantage of the tax code. In 2011, Buffett proposed that people making more than $1 million a year should pay at least 30% of their income in taxes, regardless of tax loopholes, or quirks in the tax code. This proposal became known as The Buffett Rule. Drum roll . . . it didn't happen after Congress debated its enactment.

Moseying down Form 1040, line 9 tells you to subtract the larger of the standard or itemized deductions from your total income, resulting in your taxable income. Once you have your taxable income number, then you can get the taxes you owe from the tax table or tax software program that you are using. Besides TurboTax, other tax-oriented websites include those run by FreeTaxUSA, TaxSlayer, TaxAct, H&R Block, OLT.com, eSmart, and the appropriately named 1040.com and FileYourTaxes.com. Place the number you get from the tax table on line 12 of Form 1040.

The remaining lines on Form 1040 largely relate to additional possible deductions or taxes, such as a **self-employment tax**. That item is exactly what is sounds like, taxes paid by those who operate their own businesses and are used to fund items such as Social Security and Medicare. There is also a spot on Form 1040 for taxes already paid, such as those that are taken out of your paycheck that can be found on your W-2. If the amount of taxes paid is greater than the taxes you owe, then you get a refund (Line 20). Awesome! If the taxes paid are less than the taxes owed, then you have to pay more taxes (Line 23). Aargh!

Retirement Plans

Retirement plans are one of the best vehicles for building long-term wealth. Contributions to your retirement plan are generally tax free, and companies often provide matching funds. We don't need a Buffett Tip to tell you that you should never refuse free money! So your minimum contribution to your retirement plan should be enough to get matching funds, if your employer provides them. Retirement plans often go by the names **401(k), 403(b), IRA, Roth IRA, SEP-IRA**, and **pension plans**. We'll define each of these terms shortly. With most retirement plans you can't take out the money until you reach the age of 59½ or else you have to pay a 10% penalty on the withdrawn funds. There are some hardship exceptions to this rule, such as taking money out to pay for medical expenses.

At a big-picture level, retirement plans often go under the heading of either defined benefit or defined contribution plans. Defined benefit plans are commonly known as pension plans. With this type of plan you typically receive a fixed payment monthly from your retirement date until your death. For example, upon retirement you may receive 60% of your average salary over the final three years you worked before retirement. In general, the longer you work for the firm, the higher the percentage payout. For example, if you work a firm for two years and then move to another company, you're not going to get 60% of your prior salary for life. Pension plans are common with those working for the government, or as teachers, police officers, and in many other fields.

Today, few people stay with one company for decades like Buffett at Berkshire. For them, defined contribution plans often make sense. In this case, the employer often matches a percentage (e.g., 5%) of your salary each year and puts the contribution in a retirement fund, which is usually some type of mutual fund. If you move from one company to another, you can take the money with you. The most popular defined contribution plan is 401(k), named after a provision in the tax code. The nonprofit analog for the 401(k) is the 403(b). The maximum amount of money you can put in is currently $19,500 if you are under the age of 50 and the amount increases roughly by inflation each year. If you are older than 50 you can contribute an additional $6,500 with what is called a "catch-up" contribution.

The self-employed and those working for small businesses often use Individual Retirement Accounts (IRA) as their primary retirement vehicle. The paperwork is often easier for the sponsor, relative to 401(k), 403(b), or defined benefit plans. It is also a common vehicle for "rolling over" 401(k) or 403(b) investments from a former employer.

Most IRAs allow you to contribute money that reduces your taxable income up front. Roth IRAs were introduced in 1997. With the retirement plans we have covered so far, your contributions are tax deductible and when you withdraw funds upon your retirement, the withdrawals are usually taxable. Roth IRAs flip it around. Your contributions are not tax deductible up front, but your withdrawals are tax free. This is beneficial as long as you can deal with the pain of not having the tax-deductible feature up front. There are some income limits to participate in the Roth IRA, currently in the low six figures. The maximum contribution for a Roth IRA, $6,000 if under the age of 50 or $7,000 over 50, is lower than most other plans.

Simplified Employee Pension (SEP) IRA accounts are popular retirement plans for small businesses. They require less paperwork than a traditional defined benefit plan. In addition, the contribution limits are tied to the profitability of the firm, rather than a fixed number. The amount you can save is typically 25% of your overall salary, up to a maximum annual retirement contribution of $57,000.

Becoming a 401(k) or IRA Millionaire

Millions of people have become millionaires through their 401(k) plans. Like the tortoise versus the hare fable, it does take patience to achieve that magic million-dollar milestone. In general, the earlier you start to save and the higher the return on your investments, the more money you will have upon retirement. The retirement plans that we discussed allow your money to grow tax deferred. That is, you don't pay any taxes on any trades until you withdraw the funds upon retirement, assuming no (non-hardship) withdrawals before the age of 59½. The exception is with the Roth IRA since you pay your taxes up front and not upon withdrawal. Tax deferral is an important feature for those who like to pick individual securities, like Buffett. If you make trades in a regular brokerage account, you have to pay taxes on capital gains.

We hope you can start saving for retirement as soon as possible **(Tip 1)**, but let's assume you start saving in earnest at the age of 25, a common age for many people to complete graduate school. Saving $250 a month, or $3,000 a year, at an 8% annual rate of return would make you a millionaire by age 65. If you are super ambitious and want to have $10 million upon retirement, simply multiply the numbers by 10, or save $2,500 a month over the same time period. We know that number would be a stretch for most young people, but it is not a stretch as you progress in your career, especially if you follow the advice of this book. :-)

We've dispensed quite a bit of Buffett's investment wisdom over the course of this book, but here's one more story to think about as you invest for your retirement plan. Almost by definition, retirement plans involve long-term thinking. During Buffett's early years in business, computer input and output was often obtained with the aid of a punch card, a thick piece of paper about 7 inches by 3 inches in size. Punch cards were eventually replaced by the floppy disk, then the CD, and now a flash key or no device at all. With that intro, we're now ready for Buffett's advice, which we'll turn into a Tip, sometimes referred to as the "20 slot rule."

> I always tell students in business school they'd be better off when they got out of business school to have a punch card with 20 punches on it. And every time they made an investment decision, they used up one of their punches, because they aren't going to get 20 great ideas in their lifetime. They're going to get five or three or seven, and you can get rich off five or three or seven. But what you can't get rich doing is trying to get one every day.

Buffett Tip 92:

Invest as if you could only pick 20 investments in your lifetime.

Buffett's Tips from Chapter 15

Buffett Tip 88: Act as if all your actions would be shown on the front page of your local newspaper, or its modern-day equivalent (e.g., Instagram, Facebook, TikTok, Snapchat, LinkedIn).

Buffett Tip 89: Work only with people whom you like and admire. It maximizes your chance for good results and ensures you an extraordinarily good time.

Buffett Tip 90: Take the job that you would take if you were independently wealthy.

Buffett Tip 91: Integrity, intelligence, and energy are highly desired traits.

Buffett Tip 92: Invest as if you could only pick 20 investments in your lifetime.

Appendix

Health Benefits Information

Health care benefits are some of the most valuable parts of a compensation package and, for entry-level positions, they could amount to about 20% of your total comp. That's serious dough, so hopefully we have your attention. Health care benefits are typically offered to most full-time employees, but some firms, such as Starbucks, also offer them to part-time employees. And you thought Starbucks just made awesome coffee! Some companies pay the entire cost for your entire health care benefits while others pay a small portion. It really depends on the firm, but a rule of thumb is you'll probably pay about a quarter to half of the cost that your employer pays for your particular plan. Fortunately, it is a pre-tax deduction, so the cost is also indirectly subsidized by the government since you'll owe less come tax time.

Your health, of course, is your most valuable asset. Perhaps you've heard the quote, attributed to Barbara Hutton, "I've never seen a Brink's truck follow a hearse to a cemetery." A serious health problem, without insurance coverage, may also prove to be financially devastating. Health care, in aggregate, is roughly 18 percent of GDP, so it's of enormous size and complexity. Most people around the world got a wake-up call on the value of health care as the COVID-19 pandemic swept across the globe in 2020. We discussed Buffett's notoriously poor diet in **Chapter 1**, but he does take other aspects of his health seriously. Buffett said a doctor told him, "Either you eat better or you exercise." Buffett chose the second option, calling it "the lesser of two evils."

At a big-picture level, you have a few broad choices when selecting health care plans. One option, generally known as a **Traditional Health Care Insurance Plan**, provides wide choices among doctors and hospitals. It's usually the most expensive option. Another option, known as a **Health Maintenance Organization (HMO)**, has more limited choices of doctors and hospitals but normally costs less money. Why? Typically, the HMO, such as United Healthcare, does the equivalent of buying in bulk and works out a deal with the health care providers, passing along some of the savings to the employee. A third organization, called a **Preferred Provider Organization (PPO)** is a hybrid between the two and costs somewhere in between.

With most health care plans, you pay a fee for each doctor's appointment, called a **co-pay**. The co-pay is usually less than $20, but it ensures that you have some skin in the game—pun intended—paying for your health care and to also provide a disincentive for visiting the doctor for every minor bump or bruise. Often preventative visits, such as an annual physical or flu shot, have no co-pay. Some procedures, such as a magnetic resonance imaging (MRI), may require significant out-of-pocket expenses.

If you're a very healthy person, then a high **deductible plan** may minimize your total health care costs. Let's use $5,000 as the deductible amount. If you visit the doctor on somewhat rare occasions, let's say for your annual physical, a vaccine, or flu treatment, perhaps you pay less than a few hundred dollars in out-of-pocket expenses. But you also pay another monthly fee in the unlikely event that you encounter a serious or expensive illness. Once again, plans vary, but a rule of thumb is the monthly premium you pay the insurance company is about half the amount you pay for one of the traditional plans discussed above. Any amounts over the deductible amount, $5,000 in our example, would be covered by the health insurance. There is often some fine print on the limits of what they'll pay if the costs get prohibitively expensive, but we'll skip the details here.

You may be worried about shelling out up to $5,000, plus the bi-weekly or monthly fee for your health insurance. Fortunately, there is another type of health insurance product that can help. It's called a **Health Savings Account (HSA)**. The amount you can put in an HSA increases with inflation. It's currently $3,550 for individuals and $7,100 for a family. Any unused dollars in the HSA can be rolled over for use in following years. There is a related account called a **Flexible Spending Account (FSA)** that has similar deduction limits, but it has the increased flexibility of being also used for childcare expenses. The catch with FSA money is that it is "use it or lose it." It can't be rolled into future years, so if you put aside $1,000 in your FSA and spend only $700, you lose $300. If you find yourself running into this position, you can always buy some covered health care devices/treatment at a website such as FSAStore.com. In addition, self-employed individuals usually can't set up an FSA, while they can use an HSA. Both HSA and FSA deductions are taken out of your paycheck using pre-tax dollars, once again providing a reduction in your tax bill come tax time on April 15.

Some firms also offer a **Prescription Drug Benefit Plan** that allow members to buy prescription drugs at very attractive prices. The employer's health care plan is typically buying these drugs in bulk, through a health care firm known as a Pharmacy Benefit Manager (PBM). The largest PBMs include firms such as CVS Health/Caremark, Express Scripts, and OptumRx. Money taken out of your paycheck for Prescription Drug Plans is also a pre-tax deduction and typically costs about $100 a month. Other health care benefits may include **disability insurance,** in case you are unable to perform your work due to injury or illness, and **long-term care insurance** that can pay partially or fully for the cost of care in case you become incapacitated or wind up in an assisted living facility or nursing home. Long-term care insurance tends to be very expensive, and you also need to look at the credit rating of the insurer to have confidence they will be around after the 50-plus-year time period when you may first need the insurance (if you are just getting started in your career).

Of course, there are also **dental insurance plans**. Dental plans typically cost less than $100 a month to the employee but usually offer sparse coverage, such as cleanings twice a year, fillings, and x-rays, without significant out-of-pocket expenses. If you want a perfect smile through braces, plastic aligners, or porcelain veneers, it will probably cost you thousands of dollars in out-of-pocket expenses. Dental insurance options are usually analogous to those of health insurance plans with traditional, **Dental Plan Organizations (DPO)**, and preferred provider varieties.

By now, we're sure you've got the feeling that health care is complicated and expensive. Not surprisingly, Buffett is trying to do something about it. Berkshire has teamed up with J.P. Morgan and Amazon to try to create a new approach to health care benefits that reduces costs but also has at least as good patient outcomes. The name of this nonprofit joint venture is Haven. The three firms have about a million employees among them so they may make a good test pilot. Haven has been tight lipped about the details of their plans, so few results are available in 2020. You can check out their website at www.havenhealthcare.com to see their offerings and accomplishments as they unfold.

References

Anonymous. "McKinsey & Company Interview Question: How Many Golf Balls Fit in an . . ." Glassdoor, June 2, 2009. https://www.glassdoor.com/Interview/how-many-golf-balls-fit-in-an-airplane-QTN_5804.htm.

Buffett, Warren. "Letter to Shareholders of Berkshire Hathaway Inc." Berkshire Hathaway, Inc., 1986. https://www.berkshirehathaway.com/letters/1986.html.

Buffett, Warren. "*Letter to Shareholders of Berkshire Hathaway Inc.*" Berkshire Hathaway, Inc., 1988. https://www.berkshirehathaway.com/letters/1988.html.

Collins, Michael. "Who Said: 'You Never Get a Second Chance to Make a First Impression!'?" Quora, Accessed June 18, 2020. https://www.quora.com/Who-said-You-never-get-a-second-chance-to-make-a-first-impression.

Duckworth, Angela. *Grit: The Power of Passion and Perseverance.* New York: Scribner, 2018.

Elsesser, Kim. "Power Posing Is Back: Amy Cuddy Successfully Refutes Criticism." *Forbes*, April 3, 2018. https://www.forbes.com/sites/kimelsesser/2018/04/03/power-posing-is-back-amy-cuddy-successfully-refutes-criticism/.

Gladwell, Malcolm. *Outliers: The Story of Success.* New York: Back Bay Books/Little, Brown, 2009.

Jerry Maguire. Directed by Cameron Crowe. Sony Pictures, 1996.

LeylandPAM. "Warren Buffett Speaks with Florida University." YouTube Video, 1:27:35, July 2, 2013. https://www.youtube.com/watch?v=2MHIcabnjrA.

"Most Common Background Checks for Employers." Paycor, October 4, 2019. https://newtonsoftware.com/blog/2019/03/07/artificial-intelligence-background-check-software/.

Pachter, Barbara, and Denise Cowie. *The Essentials of Business Etiquette: How to Greet, Eat, and Tweet Your Way to Success*. New York: McGraw-Hill *Education*, 2013.

Popomaronis, Tom. "Warren Buffett Loves Teaching This '20-Slot' Rule at Business Schools-and It's Not Just about Getting Rich." CNBC, May 28, 2020. https://www.cnbc.com/2020/05/28/billionaire-warren-buffett-teaches-this-20-slot-rule-to-getting-rich-at-business-schools.html.

TED. "Your Body Language May Shape Who You Are | Amy Cuddy." YouTube Video, 21:02, October 1, 2012. https://www.youtube.com/watch?v=Ks-_Mh1QhMc&t=138s.

The Internship. Directed by Shawn Levy. 20th Century Fox, 2013.

Varchaver, Nicholas. "Buffett Goes to Wharton." CNNMoney, May 2, 2008. https://money.cnn.com/2008/05/01/news/companies/Buffet_Q_A_at_Wharton.fortune/.

16

Buffett's Tips for Philanthropy

"If people whom you want to have love you love you, you're a success."
—Warren Buffett, Fortune, 2013

Buffett's Huge Gift and the Giving Pledge

How can you tell if someone really means what they say? One clue is if they do something for free, or virtually free, and expect nothing in return. We'd put Buffett in that category due to his pledge to donate more than 99% of his net worth to **philanthropy**. The terms "philanthropy" and "charity" are often used interchangeably, but there are some subtle differences. We'll use both terms in this chapter as well without worrying too much about the difference. **Charity** is often associated with short-term causes and gifts, often of an urgent nature (e.g., hurricane relief). Philanthropy, in contrast, often focuses on long-term solutions and active engagement. Both are admirable qualities regardless of the nuances.

Engaging in philanthropic activities isn't just a noble action. It will likely play a positive role in *your own* happiness—a true win-win situation. An ancient Chinese proverb says, "If you want happiness for an hour, take a nap. If you want happiness for a day, go fishing. If you want happiness for a year, inherit a fortune. If you want happiness for a lifetime, help somebody." Boxing legend Muhammad Ali had a slightly different take on philanthropy when he said, "Service to others is the rent you pay for your room here on earth." Helping others adds an interesting, thoughtful dimension to your personality and is almost mandatory as part of the college application process to top schools worldwide. These colleges have their choice from many thousands of student applicants and often choose to create a community of students who think beyond their own interests. Remember the athletic slogan "There is no I in team."

Buffett's plan to donate most of his wealth is unique in several aspects, besides its enormity of roughly $80 billion. He is giving the lion's share of this money to the foundation run by Bill Gates and his wife Melinda. He believes they have been doing a great job with the Gates Foundation and have developed a solid infrastructure to get things done around the world. He's given roughly $35 billon to the Gates Foundation to date. We previously noted that Buffett also teamed up with Gates on forming the Giving Pledge (www.GivingPledge.org), persuading roughly 200 billionaires from more than 20 countries to give away at least half of their fortune within their lifetimes, or shortly thereafter. You might be wondering why all billionaires haven't signed the pledge. They may have different priorities and/or may not want the publicity and incessant requests by people seeking money. Some billionaires, amazingly, told Buffett they couldn't afford it! Buffett quipped that "someone should write a book on how to live on a half billion dollars."

I think we can confidently infer that Buffett is a very philanthropic person driven by a love of what he does—investing money—and not by greed. This chapter will focus on Buffett's comments concerning philanthropy, ethics, and "**paying it forward**," that is, helping others if you have benefited from someone else's generosity. These concepts intertwine with ethics.

There are many ethical codes documented by philosophers and religious scholars across recorded history, and there is no objective measure concerning which one is best. For example, most doctors pledge to follow the Hippocratic Oath, a code of ethics tied to the practice of medicine dating back to between the fifth and fourth centuries BC. "First do no harm" is one of the most popular phrases affiliated with the Oath. Let's just simplify this topic by saying that ethics is "doing the right thing." We'll let you substitute what you think is your best and fairest definition or code of what is right.

Ethical people are often involved in philanthropic and charitable activities, in part because they want to "pay it forward." Few successful people have gotten to where they are without the help of others (e.g., family, friends, co-workers, mentors, teachers). Benjamin Graham once said that every day he "hoped to do something foolish, something creative, and something generous." The "something generous" part of the quote is paying it forward.

Sir Isaac Newton, one of the greatest scientists and mathematicians who ever lived, said, "If I have seen further than others, it is by standing upon the shoulders of giants." Newton's great ideas didn't come out of a vacuum or simply due to the apple that purportedly fell on his head, inspiring his theory of gravity. He built his theories on the fundamentals of what he learned elsewhere.

Noblesse oblige is a French expression that means nobles, or more loosely defined as the rich and powerful, have an obligation to help those less fortunate. If that expression sounds too stuffy, consider the widely cited quote from Spiderman's Uncle Ben character, "With great power comes great responsibility."

Let's get this chapter rolling with Buffett's spin on one of the oldest expressions on kind, charitable, and ethical behavior. It's called the Golden Rule and underpins the philosophy of many world religions. It's usually expressed as, "Treat others as you wish to be treated." In Berkshire's 1983 Letter to Berkshire Shareholders, Buffett put a financial spin on the Golden Rule by saying, "We will only do with your money what we would do with our own, weighing fully the values you can obtain by diversifying your own portfolios through direct purchases in the stock market." Let's shorten that quote a bit into our first Tip for **Chapter** 16.

Buffett Tip 93:

Only do with someone else's money what you would do with your own.

One way of following this Tip is to have some skin in the game. If you are recommending an investment or product to someone else, you should be willing to spend your own money on it since you would suffer if things turned out badly. If you tell someone to be involved in some kind of charitable or philanthropic activity, then you should be willing to engage in it as well.

It's not only with money that Buffett follows his version of the Golden Rule. NetJets is a Berkshire subsidiary that focuses on **fractional jet ownership**. What's that? Of course, private jets are incredibly expensive. They typically go for from $10 million to more than $100 million. Some super wealthy people even customize their own Boeing 747 jets, which costs in the hundreds of millions of dollars. Fractional jet ownership basically allows you to fly on a fleet of jets that are group owned, sort of like a mutual fund for jets. The cost is usually thousands of dollars per hour. Buffett travels a lot, so flying by private jet is one of his few extravagances. But he gets the same treatment as everyone else when he flies on NetJets. In his 2009 Letter to Berkshire Shareholders, he wrote, "We receive exactly the same treatment as any other owner, meaning we pay the same prices as everyone else does when we are using our personal contracts. In short, we eat our own cooking. In the aviation business, no other testimonial means more."

Getting Involved in Philanthropic and Charitable Activities

There are a bunch of ways to get involved in philanthropic and charitable activities. The most obvious route is to support a cause that is important to you. Perhaps you, a family member, or a friend has been impacted by a disease, such as diabetes, cancer, heart disease, or Alzheimer's. Many people volunteered to help in a variety of ways, ranging from health care workers to benefit concerts, during the COVID-19 pandemic. Of course, there are tons of other philanthropic activities, such as helping out at soup kitchens, homeless shelters, hospitals, nursing homes, and even in your own school's community activities. Many religious institutions are actively involved in philanthropic and charitable causes, so that could be another way to get involved, if you are so inclined. If you like sports, volunteering to help with the Special Olympics, an international sports organization for children and adults with intellectual and/or physical disabilities, may be a great fit.

Many young people have had a charitable experience with United Nations Children's Fund (UNICEF). UNICEF provides food and health care services to needy people in more than 150 countries around the world. Perhaps you have collected spare change for UNICEF in one of their famous orange boxes, especially around Halloween time (October 31) in the US.

You've probably heard the expression "There is safety in numbers." If you are still unsure where to get involved, we think another decent place to look may be to examine the activities of the largest charities. A recent article in *Forbes* found that the largest charitable organizations in America were:

1. **United Way Worldwide** *(income, education, and health-related causes)*
2. **Feeding America** *(feeding the hungry)*
3. **Americares Foundation** *(disaster relief and global health)*
4. **The Taskforce for Global Health** *(global health)*
5. **The Salvation Army** *(helping the poor and hungry by meeting their physical and spiritual needs)*
6. **St. Jude's Children's Research Hospital** *(children's catastrophic diseases)*
7. **Direct Relief** *(health care, poverty reduction, and disaster relief)*
8. **Habitat for Humanity International** *(builds homes for people in need)*
9. **Boys and Girls Clubs of America** *(after-school programs for young people)*
10. **The YMCA** *(after-school programs for young people, healthy living, social responsibility)*

Donating your time and energy to a philanthropic or charitable organization may be the most powerful thing you can do at this stage, but even small financial donations can go a long way, especially if practiced by millions of people. We have mentioned Buffett's deep involvement in the Giving Pledge and with the Gates Foundation. He also gave billions of dollars to philanthropic foundations run by each of his three children, Howard, Susan, and Peter.

Buffett has actively supported the Glide Foundation, a San Francisco–based charity that helps the homeless, for more than a decade. Each year the Glide Foundation auctions off a steakhouse lunch with Buffett that goes to the highest bidder. How much do you think this lunch goes for today? A few thousand dollars? Try several million dollars! The record was set in 2019 by cryptocurrency pioneer Justin Sun who had a winning bid of $4.57 million! Since Buffett has come down hard on cryptocurrency, referring to bitcoin as "probably rat poison squared," the conversation at that lunch must have been interesting indeed!

The prior records were set in 2012 and in 2016 with both winner(s) bidding $3,456,789. We're guessing the winners for these years had an affinity for Buffett *and* numbers (notice the sequence 3, 4, 5, . . . , 9). The table in the **Appendix** shows the winning bid each year, which started at "only" $25,000 in 2000 but quickly went into six and seven figures within a few years.

On the great work done by the leaders and volunteers at the Glide Foundation, Buffett said, "Glide really takes people who have hit rock bottom and helps bring them back. They've been doing it for decades. If I can help out by raising some money for them, then I enjoy doing it."

Measuring Performance

How do you know if the charity is doing a good job? We'll share some background info on this topic, supported by some of Buffett's historical comments, as usual. Pretty much all charities are nonprofit, but it doesn't mean that the people there work for free. It might surprise you to learn that some heads of charities earn over a million dollars a year!

Most charities are organized according to a part of the IRS tax code that goes by the number/letter combo of 501(c)(3). There are a few things you should know about **501(c)(3) organizations**. First, donations to them are tax deductible. This point is a biggie, since it makes it a lot easier for them to receive donations. Second, there are a bunch of record-keeping and reporting requirements for the organization. If they don't do this paperwork, there is a chance the charity can get busted and put out of operation. From these reports it's possible to get a rough estimate of how efficient the charity is with the donations it receives. Would you rather donate to a charity that gives virtually all of its money to its primary cause or to its employees? We won't insult your intelligence with an answer to that question.

Let's provide an example of a foundation with an excellent record of both impact and efficiency, the Foundation Fighting Blindness. The Foundation Fighting Blindness "drives research to find preventions, treatments and cures for people affected by retinal degenerative diseases." Since its formation in 1971, the Foundation has raised more than $750 million and has allocated most of the funds toward research and information for those affected by sight loss. They helped fund a prescription drug by Spark Therapeutics, called LUXTURNA™, which uses gene therapy to help restore the sight of some visually impaired patients.

A recent financial report shows that they received about $72.3 million in revenue, primarily from donations. They spent only $2.7 million on administrative expenses, an "overhead" percentage of only 3.7%. Historically, most of their donations went to fund research or to sponsor events supporting their cause and not in the pocket of some "fat cat" administrators. You can track down the tax filings of most 501(c)(3) firms on the Internet since they are public. There are also websites such as Give.org and Guidestar.org that summarize the financial results of thousands of charities. You might want to check them out before you donate your time and money to a specific cause.

Now let's get back to the wisdom of Buffett. He has a nice quote on the importance of checking results. In Berkshire's Annual Report, Buffett consistently lays out some operating principles of his firm. One principle, taken from his 1983 Letter to Shareholders is, "We feel noble intentions should be checked periodically against results." He was actually talking about profit-making enterprises in this case, specifically how well companies reinvest their earnings. He believes firms should deliver to shareholders at least $1 of market value for each $1 retained. However, his point about checking results certainly applies to nonprofits as well, and we think this quote merits a Tip.

Buffett Tip 94:

Noble intentions should be checked periodically against results.

Buffett also provided some guidance on how to measure performance. The performance metric should be specified in advance. It should also be objective and measurable—such as his comment about firms earning more than $1 for each $1 of retained earnings invested. In Berkshire's 1988 Letter to Shareholders, Buffett wrote, "At too many companies, the boss shoots the arrow of managerial performance and then hastily paints the bullseye around the spot where it lands." A variation on this comment is worthy of a Tip.

Buffett Tip 95:

Set objective, measurable performance metrics in advance.

There are probably a ton of examples in your own life where you can set goals in advance and measure them accurately at a later date. For example, you might shoot for a certain GPA if you are still in school, target a percentage of your income to save each year, strive for a certain return for your investments over a period of time, or seek a net worth goal for various age ranges.

Market-Based Economies Are Good . . . Unless You Wind Up as Roadkill

The market-based economic system that operates in most countries around the world has generated enormous amounts of wealth, developed amazing technology, and lifted billions of people out of poverty, but it's not perfect. Go to any major city in the US, and throughout much of the world, and you will see homeless people who have been left behind. Hundreds of millions, if not billions, of people around the world continue to live without access to acceptable levels of food, shelter, health care, and education.

Market-based systems are analogous to Charles Darwin's "survival of the fittest" theory covered in most biology textbooks. Darwin's theory says living organisms need to adapt to their environments or else they risk becoming extinct. The fittest—those that are smart, strong, adaptable—are usually able to make this transition. The economy isn't an organism, but it is dynamic, changing significantly over time. A little over 100 years ago, there were no cars or airplanes. Several decades ago, computers, the Internet, and cell phones didn't exist. Perhaps within your lifetime, Google, Amazon, Facebook, and Uber, didn't exist. Each of these inventions or companies has radically changed the way most people live and work.

We previously mentioned Joseph Schumpeter, an Austrian and Harvard economist, who coined the term "creative destruction" to describe how some companies and industries are "born" and wind up "destroying" other companies and industries. Society as a whole generally benefits from this economic progress—imagine life without your cell phone and all of its apps—but certain segments and people are adversely affected—sometimes severely.

Let's analyze an example that we all can relate to—listening to music. Thomas Edison is credited with inventing the phonograph, which is essentially a record player. Records are pretty bulky, about the size of a super thin pizza, and not easy to carry around, especially in a car. In the mid-1960s, 8-track tapes became a popular way of storing music. They were about the size of a small sandwich and were more portable than records. Perfect for cruising! In the 1970s and 1980s cassette tapes supplanted 8-tracks for most consumers. Cassettes are even smaller than 8-tracks, about the size of a small cellphone. In the late 1980s and early 1990s compact discs (CDs) began to replace cassette tapes for most music listeners. Although they were larger than cassettes, in length and width terms, CDs exhibited superior music quality and durability. By the time the Internet started to pick up steam in the mid-1990s, digital copies of music became the dominant way of maintaining a music collection. Apple co-founder Steve Jobs marketed the iPod music player very effectively by saying it was like "having a thousand songs in your pocket." Who could resist that pitch?

If you worked for a firm that manufactured records, 8-tracks, cassettes, or CDs, you eventually would have lost your job. The same holds true for many other industries, ranging from horse buggy whips to typewriter manufacturers. Technological progress can't be, and shouldn't be, stopped. In the early 1800s in England a group of workers, known as the Luddites, tried to destroy machines in an effort to preserve their jobs. Spoiler alert. The Luddites lost their battle. So what does all of this have to do with Buffett? Make no mistake. Buffett calls himself a "card-carrying **capitalist**." In a capitalist economic system, most of the property and businesses are owned by individuals. The profits go to the owners of the businesses and usually not the workers. The capitalist economy is primarily driven by market forces, not planned by the government, which is the case in some socialist and communist systems. Some individuals in the capitalist system can earn great amounts of wealth, as Buffett did. But he has also weighed in on how the market-based and capitalist system can negatively affect people. He saw firsthand what happened to the textile workers at Berkshire as he unsuccessfully tried to turn around that business for many years.

We've all seen dead animals that have been run over by cars (i.e., roadkill) at some point in our lives. Probably one too many times. When questioned about how economic progress hurts some people, Buffett replied, "We should take care of people who've become roadkill because of something beyond their control . . . I think that's the obligation of a rich country." He then went on to say how in a rich society, like that of the US, the government should find a way to take care of these affected people.

In his 2005 Letter to Shareholders, Buffett recommended at least one specific remedy for those able to find employment—expansion of the **Earned Income Tax Credit**. This tax credit is exactly what it sounds like. It results in less taxes paid for people who work, as opposed to getting a direct cash payment from the government. The tax credits are generally larger for a person with (more) children.

Buffett wrote, "The solution, rather, is a variety of safety nets aimed at providing a decent life for those who are willing to work but find their specific talents judged of small value because of market forces. (I personally favor a reformed and expanded Earned Income Tax Credit that would try to make sure America works for those willing to work.) The price of achieving ever-increasing prosperity for the great majority of Americans should not be penury for the unfortunate." In case you are wondering, penury is one of those SAT/ACT words meaning extreme poverty.

What about helping people who are unable to find new work, especially after unemployment insurance runs out? (Unemployment insurance typically lasts up to six months, but in uncommon circumstances can extend for up to 1.5 years). The question about how to best serve the long-term unemployed is subject to considerable debate and beyond the scope of this book. However, it likely involves some form of education, retraining, (additional) tax credits, and direct cash payments. For example, part of the stimulus package following the COVID-19 pandemic involved direct cash payments to households with a combined income of less than $198,000 per year, or $99,000 for a single filer. One purpose of Buffett's (co-)creation of the Giving Pledge was to help people who became roadkill in the wake of economic progression or health care crises. Let's summarize Buffett's views with a Tip.

Buffett Tip 96:

We should take care of people who've become roadkill because of something beyond their control.

It's Not All About the Benjamins

A **Benjamin** is slang for the US $100 bill, since founding father Benjamin Franklin's face is on its front side. Of course, we know that Buffett has made a ton of money over the years. So it may surprise you that he has left some money on the table, sticking with subpar businesses and the related costs involved, such as employee salaries and taxes paid to state, local, and federal governments. Perhaps Buffett's most prominent example in this regard relates to the many years he tried to turn around Berkshire's original clothing and textile business. A quick glance at the tag on your clothes will reveal that most are manufactured outside the United

States. It's usually a lot cheaper, often 90% less, to make them elsewhere. Eventually, Berkshire shuttered virtually all of its textile manufacturing plants in the US, but he tried to turn the business around for well over a decade. In Berkshire's 1978 Letter to Shareholders, Buffett referred to his community of stakeholders in the following manner:

> (1) Our textile businesses are very important employers in their communities, (2) management has been straightforward in reporting on problems and energetic in attacking them, (3) labor has been cooperative and understanding in facing our common problems, and (4) the business should average modest cash returns relative to investment. As long as these conditions prevail—and we expect that they will—we intend to continue to support our textile business despite more attractive alternative uses for capital.

Buffett and Berkshire's behavior toward underperforming assets largely boils down to a philosophy of being loyal, patient, and having a long-term focus. It also puts Berkshire near the top of the list for owners of businesses looking to sell. After all, if you were selling a business that you grew and nurtured for decades, you'd probably want it to be in good, long-term hands once you're gone. If a business continued to burn cash, like Berkshire's textile business did, it would *eventually* be closed down at Berkshire. In Buffett's 2011 Letter to Shareholders, he expressed it this way:

> Our approach is far from Darwinian, and many of you may disapprove of it. I can understand your position. However, we have made—and continue to make—a commitment to the sellers of businesses we buy that we will retain those businesses through thick and thin. So far, the dollar cost of that commitment has not been substantial and may well be offset by the goodwill it builds among prospective sellers looking for the right permanent home for their treasured business and loyal associates. These owners know that what they get with us can't be delivered by others and that our commitments will be good for many decades to come.

Let's simplify Buffett's comments into a Tip about considering all of the people that interact with a business, known as **stakeholders**. The term stakeholders, with respect to your own life, may be generalized to the people you interact with—family, friends, classmates, co-workers, and so forth.

Buffett Tip 97:

It's not all about the Benjamins—consider all stakeholders when making important decisions.

The Loss of Reputation Hurts More Than the Loss of Money

Way back in September 1987, Buffett invested $700 million in the stock of Salomon Brothers, a well-known Wall Street firm at the time. The investment was in a variation of the type of common stock that we focused on throughout much of this book called convertible preferred stock. Let's not worry about the nuances of this particular type of stock since it's not important to the story. The investment amounted to about 12% of Salomon Brothers and was the biggest dollar investment that Buffett had ever made until that point. The investment didn't get off to a good start because the infamous **Crash of 1987**, where the Dow Jones Industrial Average fell an astonishing 22.6% in one day, happened shortly thereafter! It was the biggest single-day loss ever. Not panicking during times of distress is a Tip we referred to in **Chapter** 5, but our new lesson comes from what happened a few years later.

In 1991, Paul Mozer, a top trader at Salomon Brothers, rigged the auction of US Treasury bonds, one of the largest and most important financial markets in the world. Recall that US Treasury Bonds are the bonds that the US government sells to finance both its short-term operations and huge, long-term debt. In fact, Mozer committed several violations, even after being caught by Salomon's legal department. He eventually went to jail for it. Once the federal government got wind of the illegal actions at Salomon, they threatened to put the firm out of business. This would have likely wiped out the bulk or all of Buffett's massive investment in Salomon, so he promised to step in as chairman of the company and clean up the mess. Buffett isn't a saint. He did this to protect his investment and potentially to minimize the effect on the overall financial system. Salomon did more than just make a promise. They also paid the US government a $290 million fine.

During Buffett's testimony to Congress, detailing what happened at Salomon and the changes that were taking place at the firm to prevent another big problem, Buffett uttered one of his most famous quotes.

"Lose money for the firm, and I will be understanding; lose a shred of reputation for the firm, and I will be ruthless." Buffett's rationale is that damage to the reputation of a firm may have a lasting effect, while the loss of money can often be recovered in the future, especially when the economy or financial markets turn for the better. That thought merits a Tip.

Buffett Tip 98:

The loss of reputation hurts more than the loss of money. ***(Be ruthless in the former behavior and forgiving in the latter.)***

In case you are wondering, Buffett eventually made out just fine on his Salomon investment. The firm was allowed to continue to operate, despite paying the huge fine noted previously, and it was ultimately sold to insurance firm Travelers and subsequently merged into Citigroup. You may be thinking, "Does Buffett practice what he preaches?" We think the answer is yes.

Dairy Queen (DQ) is one of the more high-profile Berkshire companies due to its range of delicious ice cream products and national footprint, although DQ counts for only a tiny percentage of overall firm profits. As we said in **Chapter 1**, in early 2017, James Crichton, a Dairy Queen franchise owner, shouted a racial epithet at a customer and her two children. Almost immediately, Chrichton's Dairy Queen franchise was terminated, and the store was closed. It's unlikely that Buffett got directly involved in the termination due to his hands-off management style, but he set the culture at Berkshire. Dairy Queen's management responded just as Buffett would have, with swift action due to Chrichton's reprehensible comments and also because of the loss of reputation for the firm.

Another more widely cited example concerns the former Berkshire senior executive David Sokol. Some suggested that Sokol was once so well regarded by Buffett, that he was in line to be the CEO of Berkshire, when Buffett eventually left the post.

The short version of the story is Sokol purchased roughly $10 million of an oil-related stock called Lubrizol in early January 2011. What's wrong with that? Well, shortly thereafter he suggested that Berkshire buy the entire company, a transaction that would make Sokol a ton of money quickly. He disclosed his purchase of Lubrizol, so it wasn't illegal insider trading by the letter of the law. At first, Buffett wasn't interested in purchasing Lubrizol, but Sokol kept suggesting the takeover to him. Berkshire eventually did offer to buy the company and Sokol made more than $3 million in a few months. Sokol's actions violate the ethical norms of most companies. In lay terms, they don't pass the "smell test" of ethical behavior.

Once word got out about what happened, a controversy ensued. Sokol offered to resign, and Buffett quickly accepted his resignation. An interesting footnote to the story is that for unrelated reasons Sokol had offered to resign twice in the past and Buffett firmly refused to accept the resignation letters. Buffett later said about the Lubrizol incident, "I obviously made a big mistake by not saying, 'Well, when did you buy it?'" He found Sokol's actions "inexplicable" and "inexcusable." Buffett's actions in the Sokol case weren't as swift or forceful (i.e., allowing a resignation rather than immediate termination) as the Dairy Queen incident, but the message is clear. Lose a shred of reputation for the firm, and he will be ruthless in the end result.

Inheritance Matters

You've probably heard the expression "Charity begins at home." One interpretation of this phrase is that it's great to help others, but don't forget about the people who are part of your family or community. However, leaving family members a wad of money may sap their incentive to work or lead productive lives. Buffett addressed the topic of how much money a wealthy person should leave to their children with a phrase that would make King Solomon, a fabulously wealthy and wise ruler of ancient Israel, proud. He said, leave children "enough money so they would feel they could do anything, but not so much that they could do nothing." When pressed for a hard dollar number, Buffett replied, "A few hundred thousand dollars" for a recent college graduate sounds about right. A few hundred thousand is enough to help someone start a business, put a down payment on a house, pay off student loans, and get a financial head start in life. It's not enough to enable someone to be a couch potato for a decade or more.

A-list actors Ashton Kutcher and Mila Kunis, who as you might know are married to each other, expressed similar views noting that they wouldn't be leaving their kids a trust fund. Kutcher said, "If my kids want to start a business, and they have a good business plan, I'll invest in it." Buffett did something similar decades ago, lending his eldest son, Howard, money to buy a farm while charging him a market rate of interest.

Buffett believes rewards should be earned on merit, not simply because you have a connection to someone who is successful. In an interview with *The New York Times* he expressed a similar thought when he said repealing the **estate tax**, which is a tax on inherited assets, is similar to "choosing the 2020 Olympic team by picking the eldest sons of the gold-medal winners in the 2000 Olympics." Let's close this section by putting Buffett's quote about the amount a wealthy person should leave their kids as a Tip.

Buffett Tip 99:

Leave your children enough money so they would feel they could do anything but not so much that they could do nothing.

Buffett's Definition of Success

Buffett has seen and accomplished a tremendous amount over his amazing life and has certainly developed some worldly wisdom. He views himself as being very lucky to have been born to loving parents and in a country that rewarded his particular set of skills—a knack for making money. He refers to his good fortune as winning the ovarian lottery. In a *Fortune* magazine interview, he said, "My wealth has come from a combination of living in America, some lucky genes, and compound interest. Both my children and I won what I call the ovarian lottery."

Although this book has a primary focus on financial matters, and in particularly financial literacy, we think it's fitting to end it with Buffett's definition of success. It might surprise you, but his definition is decidedly non-financial in nature.

In an interview with *Fortune* magazine in 2013, Buffett said, "If people whom you want to have love you love you, you're a success." It's a powerful quote, but especially coming from one of the richest people who ever lived. A man who knows the value, or lack thereof, of money. We think that's a great last Tip for our book and one that should never be forgotten.

Tip 100:

If people whom you want to have love you love you, you're a success.

Buffett's Tips from Chapter 16

Buffett Tip 93: Only do with someone else's money what you would do with your own.
Buffett Tip 94: Noble intentions should be checked periodically against results.
Buffett Tip 95: Set objective, measurable performance metrics in advance.
Buffett Tip 96: We should take care of people who've become roadkill because of something beyond their control.
Buffett Tip 97: It's not all about the Benjamins—consider all stakeholders when making important decisions.
Buffett Tip 98: The loss of reputation hurts more than the loss of money. *(Be ruthless in the former behavior and forgiving in the latter.)*
Buffett Tip 99: Leave your kids enough money so they would feel they could do anything but not so much that they could do nothing.
Tip 100: If people whom you want to have love you love you, you're a success.

Appendix

Charitable Lunch Auctions for Warren Buffett, Benefiting Glide Foundation

Year	Winner	Winning Bid
2000	Anonymous	$25,000
2001	Anonymous	$18,000
2002	Anonymous	$25,000
2003	David Einhorn, Greenlight Capital	$250,010
2004	Jason Choo, Singapore	$202,100
2005	Anonymous	$351,100
2006	Yongpin Duan, California	$620,100
2007	Mohnish Pabrai, Guy Spier, Harina Kapoor	$650,100
2008	Zhao Danyang, Pure Heart Asset Management	$2,110,100
2009	Salida Capital, Canada	$1,680,300

Year	Winner	Winning Bid
2010	Ted Weschler	$2,626,311
2011	Ted Weschler	$2,626,411
2012	Anonymous	$3,456,789
2013	Anonymous	$1,000,100
2014	Andy Chua, Singapore	$2,166,766
2015	Zhu Ye, Dalian Zeus Entertainment Co.	$2,345,678
2016	Anonymous	$3,456,789
2017	Anonymous	$2,679,001
2018	Anonymous	$3,300,100
2019	Justin Sun	$4,567,888

Source: Bloomberg.

References

Barrett, William. "America's Top Charities 2019." *Forbes.* Accessed June 18, 2020. https://www.forbes.com/lists/top-charities/.

Belvedere, Matthew. "Warren Buffett, the World's Second Richest Man, Says Eliminating the Estate Tax Would Be a 'Terrible Mistake.'" CNBC, October 3, 2017. https://www.cnbc.com/2017/10/03/warren-buffett-thinks-its-a-mistake-to-eliminate-the-estate-tax.html.

Bishop, Todd. "What Bill and Melinda Gates Are Doing with Warren Buffett's $30 Billion, a Decade after Historic Gift." *GeekWire,* February 14, 2017. https://www.geekwire.com/2017/bill-melinda-gates-warren-buffetts-30-billion-decade-historic-gift/.

Buffett, Warren. "Letter to Shareholders of Berkshire Hathaway Inc." Berkshire Hathaway, Inc., 1978. https://www.berkshirehathaway.com/letters/1978.html.

Buffett, Warren. "Letter to Shareholders of Berkshire Hathaway Inc." Berkshire Hathaway, Inc., 1983. https://www.berkshirehathaway.com/letters/1983.html.

Buffett, Warren. "Letter to Shareholders of Berkshire Hathaway Inc." Berkshire Hathaway, Inc., 1988. https://www.berkshirehathaway.com/letters/1988.html.

Buffett, Warren. "Letter to Shareholders of Berkshire Hathaway Inc." Berkshire Hathaway, Inc., 2005. https://www.berkshirehathaway.com/letters/2005.html.

Buffett, Warren. "Letter to Shareholders of Berkshire Hathaway Inc." Berkshire Hathaway, Inc., 2009. https://www.berkshirehathaway.com/letters/2009.html.

Buffett, Warren. "Letter to Shareholders of Berkshire Hathaway Inc." Berkshire Hathaway, Inc., 2011. https://www.berkshirehathaway.com/letters/2011.html.

Buffett, Warren. "Letter to Shareholders of Berkshire Hathaway Inc." Berkshire Hathaway, Inc., 2014. https://www.berkshirehathaway.com/letters/2014.html.

Carrig, David. "Warren Buffett Gave Away This Much of His Wealth in the Past 10 Years." *USA Today*, July 11, 2017. https://www.usatoday.com/story/money/2017/07/11/warren-buffett-charitable-contributions-bill-melinda-gates-foundation/468837001/.

"Charity Review—Foundation Fighting Blindness." Give.org. Accessed June 18, 2020. https://www.give.org/charity-reviews/national/blind-and-visually-impaired/foundation-fighting-blindness-in-columbia-md-3222.

Chiglinsky, Katherine. "Buffett's Charity Auction Breaks Record With $4.57 Million Bid." *Bloomberg*, May 31, 2019. https://www.bloomberg.com/news/articles/2019-06-01/buffett-s-charity-auction-breaks-record-with-4-57-million-bid.

Clifford, Catherine, and Javier David. "Lunch with Warren Buffett Auctioned off for $3.3 Million." CNBC, June 2, 2018. https://www.cnbc.com/2018/06/02/lunch-with-warren-buffett-auctions-for-3-point-3-million-dollars.html.

Darwin, Charles. *The Origin of Species: By Means of Natural Selection, or the Preservation of Favoured Races in the Struggle for Life*. London: John Murray, 1876.

Gal, Shayanne. "13 Brilliant Quotes from Warren Buffett, the Greatest Investor of All Time." *Business Insider*, August 30, 2018. https://www.businessinsider.com/13-brilliant-quotes-from-warren-buffett-2017-8.

HeilbrunnCenter. "Legacy of Benjamin Graham." YouTube Video, 15:16, February 4, 2013. https://www.youtube.com/watch?v=m1WLoNEqkV4&t=127s.

Henney, Megan. "Berkshire's Buffett Calls Himself a 'Card-Carrying Capitalist.'" Fox Business, May 4, 2019. https://www.foxbusiness.com/business-leaders/berkshires-buffett-calls-himself-a-card-carrying-capitalist.

Lee, Bruce Y. "Muhammad Ali's Greatest Health Achievements." *Forbes*, June 5, 2016. https://www.forbes.com/sites/brucelee/2016/06/05/muhammad-alis-greatest-health-achievements/.

Li, Yun. "Warren Buffett Says the Country Has to Take Care of Poor People Who Have Become 'Roadkill.'" CNBC, March 28, 2019. https://www.cnbc.com/2019/03/28/warren-buffett-says-country-has-to-take-care-of-people-who-have-become-road-kill.html.

Loomis, Carol J. "Warren Buffett's Wild Ride at Salomon (Fortune, 1997)." *Fortune*, October 27, 1997. http://fortune.com/1997/10/27/warren-buffett-salomon/.

Santi, Jenny. "The Secret to Happiness Is Helping Others." *Time*, August 15, 2017. http://time.com/collection/guide-to-happiness/4070299/secret-to-happiness/.

Sellers, Patricia. "How Warren Buffett Learned the Meaning of Success." *Fortune*, May 7, 2013. http://fortune.com/2013/05/07/how-warren-buffett-learned-the-meaning-of-success/.

Singer, Peter. *The Life You Can Save: How to Do Your Part to End World Poverty*. Sydney, AU: The Life You Can Save, 2019.

Todd, Susan. "Graduate Students Spend a Day with Warren Buffett." Rutgers Business School-Newark and New Brunswick, October 17, 2016. https://www.business.rutgers.edu/news/graduate-students-spend-day-warren-buffett.

Udland, Myles. "Warren Buffett: In America, 'Nobody Should Be Roadkill.'" Yahoo! Finance, May 6, 2017. https://finance.yahoo.com/news/warren-buffett-america-nobody-roadkill-224533209.html.

Wootson, Cleve. "A Dairy Queen Owner Unleashed a Racist Tirade against a Customer. He No Longer Has a Business." *Washington Post*, January 9, 2017. https://www.washingtonpost.com/news/post-nation/wp/2017/01/09/a-dairy-queen-owner-unleashed-a-racist-tirade-against-a-customer-he-no-longer-has-a-business/?utm_term=.837d6cb109cf.

Glossary of Financial Terms in "Plain English"

1/N heuristic: A rule of thumb followed by many investors. It states that when given N choices, investors will equally weight each choice. For example, when faced with a menu of 10 investment options, investors subject to the 1/N heuristic bias would place 10% of their capital in each of the 10 investments.

10-K: An annual report required of all publicly traded companies. It is submitted to the Securities Exchange Commission (SEC) and is available to the public. It contains audited financial statements, certified by senior management under the penalty prison if they submitted false information.

10-Q: Quarterly reports required of all publicly traded companies. They are submitted to the Securities Exchange Commission (SEC) and are available to the public. Financial statements in a 10-Q are not required to be audited. 10-Q is easy to remember since the Q stands for quarterly.

401(k): A retirement plan common in large for-profit organizations. Currently, individuals under the age of 50 may contribute $19,500 each year to the plan on a pre-tax basis. Anyone over the age of 50 may contribute an additional $6,500 annually in "catch up" funds.

403(b): The non-profit analog of the 401(k) plan. Currently, individuals under the age of 50 may contribute $19,500 each year to the plan on a pre-tax basis. Anyone over the age of 50 may contribute an additional $6,500 annually in "catch up" funds.

501(c)(3) organization: A type of charitable organization that is subject to stringent record keeping and operational standards. Donations to 501(c)(3) organizations are tax deductible, an extremely important feature for donors.

529 plans: Tax-advantaged investment vehicles used for qualified educational expenses from kindergarten through college years. The name comes from Section 529 of the IRS tax code.

1031 exchange: A provision in the tax code that permits the seller of a home to roll any profit into a new home on a tax-free basis.

1040: The primary personal income tax return completed each year by individuals in the US.

Accounts payable: Money owed by a business to suppliers, due within one year. Payment for a utility bill or for office supplies are two examples of accounts payable. Accounts payable is the flipside of accounts receivable.

Accounts receivable: Money owed to a firm, usually due to a sale based on credit. For example, if a customer buys a laptop at Best Buy with a credit card, it may take a few days for Best Buy to receive the money from the credit card company. Accounts receivable is the flipside of accounts payable.

Accrued interest: Interest earned but not yet paid, between coupon payment dates. For example, if the annual coupon payment of a bond is 2% and six months have passed since the last coupon was paid, the accrued interest would be 1%.

After-hours trading: Trading outside the regular market hours of 9:30 a.m.–4:00 p.m. After-hours trading may occur before the market opens (4:00 a.m.–9:30 a.m. EST) and after it closes (4:00 p.m.–8:00 p.m. EST). It is also known as extended hours trading.

Alpha: A measure of investment performance. It is computed as the difference between the return on a portfolio and the return of a comparable market index. Positive alpha funds have outperformed, while negative alpha funds have underperformed. In an efficient market, the average alpha of all funds is 0, before any fees and transaction costs.

Alternate A (Alt-A) borrowers: Customers with good credit ratings but not the strongest. They fall below prime borrowers and above subprime borrowers in creditworthiness and the corresponding borrowing rates. The typical FICO range for the Alt-A category is 670 to 739.

Amortization: A non-cash expense that accounts for the loss in value of an intangible asset. For example, a patent gradually expires, so the amortization process accounts for its eventual loss of exclusivity.

Amortization schedule: A table that shows the payment of principal and interest of a mortgage or other type of loan. The amortization schedule of most conventional mortgages shows the bulk of the early payments are related to interest expense, while the bulk of the later payments are allocated to principal repayments.

American Banking Association (ABA) routing transit number: A fancy name/number for identifying the bank holding a customer's checking account funds. Some large banks may have more than one ABA routing transit number. For most wire transfers, the ABA number and a second number identifying the customer's specific checking account are required.

American Stock Exchange (AMEX): The previous name for the NYSE American stock exchange, a small stock exchange located in lower Manhattan.

Apprenticeship: A job where someone learns a craft by working side by side with an expert for a period of time, usually several years.

Annual report: A document produced by publicly traded firms that lists their financial statements, risks, and management's commentary on the business. Some firms produce their annual report in a glossy, magazine-type document. Others simply use the dry, required 10-K document that must be filed with the Securities Exchange Commission (SEC).

Assembly line techniques: A manufacturing process where each worker, or robot, is responsible for working on one segment of a product. For example, Henry Ford made his Model-T car more affordable to the public with the aid of assembly line techniques.

Asset: Something of value. In an accounting context, assets are usually classified as either current or long-term. Current assets are cash or something that is expected to be turned into cash within one year, such as a sale on a credit card. Long-term assets may include real estate, machines, stores, website infrastructure, or something intangible, such as a patent or brand name.

Asset-backed securities: Bonds backed by specific items, such as auto loans, student loans, music royalties, or comic book characters.

Associate's degree: A two-year college degree provided by community or junior colleges. Some students choose to begin their career after completing their associate's degree, while others will seek to transfer their course credits to a college or university and pursue a bachelor's degree.

Audited: Verified by an objective third party. For example, the financial statements in a firm's annual report or 10-K are audited by certified public accountants (CPAs).

Automated teller machine (ATM): A machine that dispenses cash and accepts deposits. A debit or credit card is almost always required to access the ATM.

Available funds: The maximum amount of money a customer may use for a check while safely assuming that it will not bounce.

Balance: The unpaid amount on a credit card or loan.

Balance sheet: One of the three primary financial statements of publicly traded firms. Assets are on the left-hand side of the balance sheet, and claims to assets are on the right-hand side. Claims to assets consist of liabilities and equity. The balance sheet is also known as the statement of financial condition or position.

Bank real estate owned (REO): As the name indicates, REO is real estate owned by a bank after it has foreclosed on a property. Banks tend to not want tangible real estate on their balance sheets, so they often sell REOs at a 10% or more discount to market prices.

Bankruptcy: A legal process that may absolve borrowers of some debt or restructure the debt in some manner. Individuals or firms pursuing bankruptcy usually have liabilities that well exceed their assets. It is challenging for both individuals and companies to obtain future credit at reasonable interest rates for several years after a bankruptcy filing.

Baron: A rich businessperson. Synonymous with tycoon.

Barter: To trade products or services without cash changing hands.

Basis points: A measure of unit that is a one hundredth of 1%. That is, 100 basis points equals 1%.

Beating the market: Outperforming the market. For example, if an investor's portfolio is up 12% and the S&P 500 increased 10% over the same period, the investor beat the market by 2%.

Beauty contest / bakeoff: The competition among investment banking firms for taking a firm public or providing some other type of financial service.

Benefit: A non-cash form of compensation provided to employees. For example, health care or life insurance are common benefits. Benefits are informally known as perks.

Benjamin(s): Slang for money, especially when referring to a $100 bill. The name comes from Benjamin Franklin, whose portrait appears on the US $100 bill.

Best ideas approach: An investment philosophy that involves putting the bulk of one's assets in a relatively small number of investments. A best ideas approach results in highly concentrated portfolios, as opposed to a broadly diversified index fund. A best ideas approach is also known as a high conviction approach to investing.

Beta: A measure of market risk that gauges the sensitivity of an asset, such as a stock, to changes in aggregate market prices. For example, Berkshire Hathaway's beta is less than the market average, which by definition is 1; therefore, it generally loses less on down days for the market but also earns less on up days. Many academics believe market risk, or beta, is the main driver of the expected return for any risky asset, but Warren Buffett vehemently disagrees.

Big Four: The four largest certified public accounting firms in the world. The Big Four are Deloitte, Ernst & Young, KPMG, and PricewaterhouseCoopers. They conduct audits for most large publicly traded firms.

Big Board: The nickname for the New York Stock Exchange. Before computers were invented, stock prices were often written on a large chalkboard. Historically, the requirements to be listed on the NYSE were stricter than other exchanges, providing another reason for the nickname.

Bills: Payment due for a purchased product or service. Examples include a phone bill or electric bill.

Bitcoin: The first purely digital currency or cryptocurrency. Bitcoin operates independently of any central bank, and its transactions are recorded in a blockchain, which is a real-time, immutable public ledger of transactions.

Black market: A market outside of governmental control and taxation that is often used for illegal transactions.

Blue chip: The highest quality of a specified asset class. For example, Microsoft is a blue-chip stock. Traditionally, stocks in the Dow Jones Industrial Average are considered blue chip. The name comes from what was historically the highest-valued chip at Monte Carlo casinos.

Board of directors (BOD): The group of individuals that is ultimately in charge of managing a company. The term usually refers to firms that are publicly traded, but it may also apply to private firms. The BOD of publicly traded firms are elected by their stockholders.

Bond: A loan taken out by a company, government, or other institution with the money provided from investors. Bonds usually pay interest and return its face value, or principal, upon maturity.

Bonus: The variable part of a person's compensation, often tied to the profits generated by the individual and/or the firm.

Bounced check: When there is not enough money in the checking account to pay the amount on the check.

Borrower: Someone that takes out a loan, usually from a bank. Institutions sometimes borrow by issuing debt securities.

Bubble: An asset price that is substantially overvalued relative to its true or intrinsic value. For example, real estate prices were likely in a bubble in 2007, and Bitcoin was likely in a bubble near the end of 2018.

Budget: A plan that describes spending and savings over a period of time for a person or institution.

Bullion: Gold bars or gold coins.

Business model: The way a firm tries to make money. For example, most movie theaters make the bulk of their profits from selling concessions.

Business to business (B2B) model: A business that primarily sells to other businesses, as opposed to consumers (B2C). For example, Google's search engine is free for consumers, but businesses pay Google for advertising and search placement services.

Buying long: Purchasing an asset with the expectation that it will increase in the future. The traditional way an investor tries to make money, buying low and selling high, is perhaps the most common way of buying long.

Calendar year: The year spanning from January to December. It may differ from the fiscal year, which is a 12-month time span used for financial reporting purposes.

Capital allocation: Investing money with the goal of achieving high returns. For example, Warren Buffett takes the money earned by Berkshire Hathaway's subsidiary businesses and reinvests it in the areas that have the highest potential for future profits.

Capital Asset Pricing Model (CAPM): A Nobel Prize–winning theory that tries to explain the relationship between expected return and risk. The formula that underlies the CAPM includes the risk-free rate of interest, a measure of market risk (beta), and a factor of market psychology (the market risk premium). CAPM may also be used to compute the discount rate on equity and other risky investments.

Capital gain: The profit earned on an investment, measured as the difference between the total sale price and total purchase price. For example, if an investor buys a stock for $1,000 and eventually sells it for $1,500, the capital gain would be $500.

Capital loss: The loss realized on an investment measured as the difference between the total sale price and total purchase price. For example, if you buy a stock for $1,000 and eventually sell it for $500 the capital loss would be $500.

Capitalism: A set of beliefs related to the optimal way to run an economy, based on the private ownership of resources and pursuit of profit.

Capitalist: A person who believes in capitalism as the best way to generate economic prosperity.

Capitalized cost reduction: A down payment on the purchase of a new vehicle.

Card verification value (CVV) code: A three- or four-digit number, usually on the back of a credit card, that provides an extra level of security for online transactions.

Carpooling: Commuting to and from work with more than one person. Carpooling saves its participants on gas money and provides a traveling companion to make a commute more interesting.

Cash equivalent investments: Cash or very safe, liquid investments. For example, savings accounts, Treasury bill securities, and commercial paper are considered to be cash equivalent investments.

Cash flow from investing activities (CFI): Cash generated by a firm's long-term investments. For example, Berkshire Hathaway's investment in Coca-Cola generates cash whenever Berkshire receives dividends or sells any stock from Coke. Investments in property, plant, and equipment (PP&E) also fall under CFI.

Cash flow from financing activities (CFF): Cash generated or lost due the issuance/payment of debt, stock, or dividends.

Cash flow from operating activities (CFO): Cash generated from the firm's regular course of operations. CFO usually consists of net income plus non-cash expenses (e.g., depreciation, amortization, or depletion) and changes in net working capital.

Cash out: Selling an illiquid asset and turning it into cash. A common example of cashing out is to sell stock in a privately held investment around the time it first goes public.

Central bank: The "banker's bank" for a specific country or region. Well-known central banks include the Federal Reserve (US), European Central Bank (Euro region), People's Bank of China (China), Bank of Japan (Japan), and Bank of England (United Kingdom).

Certificate of deposit (CD): A financial product offered by a bank that usually has a lockup ranging from six months to five years. CDs usually pay higher interest rates than checking and savings accounts.

Certified check: A check where the bank verifies or certifies that the funds are available to cover the amount of the check. Certified checks are usually used for important purchases, such as for the down payment on a home. They eliminate the risk that the check will bounce (except in case of a fraudulent certified check).

Certified pre-owned (CPO) vehicle: Newer used cars or trucks that are in good condition with relatively low mileage. They often come with extended manufacturer warranties, tend to be less than five years old, and have fewer than 50,000 miles.

Certified public accountants (CPAs): The only accountants permitted to conduct audits in the US. CPAs must attain specific educational credentials and pass a series of exams in order to earn the credential.

Chapter 7 bankruptcy: A type of corporate bankruptcy where the firm's assets are sold, creditors are paid with the proceeds, and the firm ceases to exist afterward.

Chapter 11 bankruptcy: A type of corporate bankruptcy that allows the firm to restructure its debt, while still operating. Many well-known companies, such as General Motors, Kodak, and Macy's, have been through the Chapter 11 process.

Chapter 13 bankruptcy: The most common form of bankruptcy for individuals. The individual must submit a reorganization plan to the court, which involves a listing of all assets, liabilities, and repayment plan. Some debts, such as those from credit cards, are usually forgiven.

Charge card: A credit card–type product where payment in full must occur each month for the account to remain in good standing. In contrast, a credit card only requires its holder make a minimum payment each month for the card to remain in good standing.

Charity: The voluntary giving of help, often of an urgent nature (e.g., hurricane relief efforts). Charity also refers to organizations involved in charitable activities, such as the Salvation Army.

Chartered Financial Analyst (CFA): A professional designation for those working in the fields of security analysis and investment management. CFA candidates must pass three detailed exams and have the requisite work experience in order to receive the CFA charter.

Checking account: A savings account with a checkbook attached to it. It may be used to send cash, after the check clearing process, to a person, company, government, or other organization.

Circular: A newspaper or magazine advertisement sent to consumers, usually through the mail. Circulars often include coupons, providing an incentive to shop for a firm's products or services.

Curriculum vitae (CV): An expanded version of a resume often used in the academic profession. CVs often span dozens of pages, unlike resumes, which are often one or two pages.

Classic cars: Vehicles that are generally at least 25 years old *and* also in demand by collectors. Thus, an older Ferrari or Corvette may be considered a classic, but a 25-year-old Camry probably would not be.

Classified (ad): An advertisement designed to sell a product or service. Classified ads originally appeared in newspapers, but they are increasingly found online.

Clearing process: The procedure(s) and amount of time a check or security undergoes in order to be converted to cash. The process may occur virtually instantly in the case of a wire transfer to up to a week for some personal checks.

Closing costs: Expenses incurred on the official sale date of a home. Closing costs include items such as paying for the first month's mortgage, attorney's fees, and property taxes.

Commercial paper: Short-term, investment grade debt issued by companies.

Commission: A fee paid to a salesperson for the sale of a product or service. For example, real estate agents often receive a 6% commission, usually split with their employer and another agent, for the sale of a home they help broker.

Common sizing: A technique to analyze financial statements that enables easier comparisons across firms or for the same firm over time. Items on the income statement are common-sized by dividing by sales. Items on the balance sheet are common-sized by dividing by total assets.

Community college: A post graduate educational institution that offers a two-year degree program, usually called an associate's degree, at a fairly low cost. Also known as junior college, or JUCO.

Comparable firms: Peer firms often used as a basis for comparison, such as in estimating the price of a stock. Often abbreviated as comps.

Conglomerate: A company that is comprised of many unrelated businesses. Berkshire Hathaway is a conglomerate that has business interests in insurance, utilities, railroads, furniture, jewelry, and many other industries.

Consensus estimate: The average estimate of professional securities analysts related to a specific data point. Consensus estimates are commonly generated for earnings estimates, revenue estimates, and price targets of publicly traded stocks.

Consumer Price Index (CPI): A measure of inflation computed by tracking a basket of goods and services purchased by the typical household. In America, the CPI is computed by the Bureau of Labor and Statistics (BLS).

Controlling interest: When one company owns more than 50% of the voting shares of another company.

Cooperative education (co-op): A part-time job for a student while taking courses during the school year, usually resulting in academic course credit. For example, a co-op student may work 20 hours a week at a firm, such as Johnson & Johnson, while carrying a full load of courses during the school year. The student may be awarded 6 credits in a college course (e.g., Co-op 101) for their efforts, as well as payment for their work. As with internships, co-op jobs are often a tryout for permanent, full-time positions.

Co-pay: The partial payment of a bill. For example, a doctor's visit may require a person to pay a $10 co-pay. The remainder of the doctor's bill will be paid by the patient's health insurance provider.

Co-sign: An agreement to pay a loan if the other borrower does not. For example, some parents co-sign a mortgage taken out by children to purchase a home.

Copyright: Legal protection for a work of intellectual property that may only be reproduced with permission of the copyright holder. Examples include books, music, movies, and art.

Correlation: A term that measures how two assets move or don't move together. Mathematically, it's a number that ranges between positive one and negative one. The lower the number, the better the diversification of the portfolio. Similarly, the higher the number, the worse the diversification of the portfolio.

Cost of goods sold (COGS): The cost of producing a product. For example, it costs Apple several hundred dollars to produce an iPhone and Ford tens of thousands of dollars to produce a Ford Mustang.

Coupon: The amount of interest paid on a bond. Most government and corporate bonds pay coupons twice a year, or semi-annually. Decades ago, coupons were attached to bond certificates that were then handed to brokers in order to receive interest payments; hence the name. Outside of the fixed income world, a coupon is a printed or electronic item that provides a discount on a product or service.

Coupon rate: An interest rate calculated as the annual coupon of a bond divided by its face value. For example, if a bond has an annual coupon of $50 and a face value of $1,000, the coupon rate would be 5%.

Cover letter: A letter that often accompanies a resume explaining the applicant's qualifications, fit, and desire for the job.

Crash of 1987: The largest one-day percentage drop in stock prices in US history, which occurred on October 19, 1987, informally known as Black Monday. The Dow Jones Industrial Average fell 22.6% on that *single* day.

Creative destruction: A theory created by Joseph Schumpeter, a Harvard economist during the first half of the 20th century, to explain the tendency of certain new industries to supplant or destroy old industries. For example, the widespread use of the automobile destroyed demand for the horse and carriage" from buggy whip.

Credit card: A financial product that allows its holder purchase things in advance of having the money leave their checking or savings account. It is essentially an advance or loan from the credit card company. At least a partial payment of the amount charged to your credit card, the required minimum payment, is due each month.

Credit score: A quantitative measurement of how responsible a person is when they borrow money or pay bills. The range of a credit score is typically between 300 and 850.

Creditor: A person or institution that is owed money. For example, bondholders are creditors of firms that issue corporate bonds.

Cross-selling: A marketing approach that involves selling the customer another product once they have obtained their current product. For example, most credit cards charge no annual fee, but the banks offering them make money by charging interest to their customers who don't pay their bill in full each month. Banks also hope to sell the customer other financial products, such as checking account, mortgages, and wealth management products.

Cryptocurrency: A digital currency that falls outside the boundaries of any country or monetary authority. Bitcoin was the first popular cryptocurrency.

Current assets: Cash or something that is expected to be turned into cash within one year, such as sales on credit (i.e., accounts receivable), inventory, and marketable securities.

Current liabilities: Money owed for a product or service or other financial obligation that is due within one year. For example, employee payroll, rent, or a bond that is about to mature are current liabilities.

Cyclical firms: Companies with sales and profits that vary widely with the economic cycle. The amplitude or volatility of changes in sales and earnings are higher for cyclical firms than for the average firm. For example, the auto and airline industries historically are considered very cyclical.

Debit cards: A financial product tied to either a savings or checking account that allows its owner to access their money without having to carry around physical cash. Cash from a debit card is usually obtained through an automated teller machine (ATM).

Debtors' prison: A prison for people who cannot pay legal financial obligations. Debtors' prisons were abolished at the US federal level in 1833 but still may occur in some form at the state level.

Deductible: The amount that must be paid before insurance benefits will kick in. For example, if a medical plan had a $2,000 deductible, the employee would have to pay $2,000 in out-of-pocket funds before the health care plan paid for amounts over $2,000.

Default: The missing of a full or partial payment of interest or principal on a bond or other type of loan. Technically, a borrower is in default if they are at least a day late or a penny short with their payment.

Default risk: The chance a borrower doesn't pay on time or in full.

Default rate: The percentage of bonds that default over a specified time period, such as one year.

Deflation: Falling prices; the opposite of inflation.

Demand: The amount wanted for a product or service by consumers.

Demand deposit: A financial account offered by a bank, such as a checking account or savings account. The owner can withdraw or demand the full amount of the account at any time.

Democratization of knowledge: A merit-based economic system, espoused by Andrew Carnegie and others, that suggests someone who works hard and becomes educated has an increased chance of being successful.

Dental insurance plans: A benefit provided to employees related to dental needs. Most plans cover basic maintenance treatment, such as bi-annual cleanings and x-rays. However, they usually result in substantial out-of-pocket expenses for complex procedures, such as a dental crown to repair a chipped tooth.

Dental Plan Organizations (DPO): An insurance plan for dental services. The cost of needed procedures is cheaper to be treated by dentists within the network of the DPO.

Depletion: A non-cash expense for natural resource assets, such as an oil well or gold mine. As the oil is removed from the well or gold from the mine, the value of the remaining well or mine goes down in value. Depletion aims to account for this drop in value. It is analogous to depreciation or amortization expense for firms operating in industries that sell natural resources.

Depreciation: A non-cash expense that accounts for wear and tear on a tangible asset. For example, a new car gradually breaks down, so its price generally falls or depreciates over time.

Deposit: An addition to a bank account or other financial account.

Direct PLUS loans: Student loans for parents and graduate/professional students sponsored by the US government.

Direct subsidized loans: Student loans based strictly on financial need sponsored by the US government.

Direct unsubsidized loans: Student loans not based strictly on financial need sponsored by the US government. Colleges will determine how much students can borrow, based on the cost of attendance and how much other financial aid they are receiving.

Disability insurance: Insurance that pays a portion of an employee's salary if they are unable to complete their work responsibilities due to illness or injury.

Discount bond: A bond with a market price less than its face value (e.g., $900 vs. $1,000). Discount bonds usually exist when the coupon rate is lower than the yield on bonds of similar risk.

Discount rate: The discount rate reduces the value of the future payments by a specified percentage. A dollar received in the future is worth less than a dollar received today due to inflation, risk, and the opportunity to put the dollar in the bank and earn interest. The higher discount rate, the higher the risk of the investment, and vice versa.

Discounted cash flow (DCF): An approach to valuing an asset that involves taking the present value of future cash flows.

Disinflation: An increase in prices but at a decreasing rate. For example, a Consumer Price Index (CPI) of 3% in 2018, 2% in 2019, and 1% in 2020.

Disruptive innovation: A phrase used to describe better, faster, or cheaper products or services that make it likely a firm will overtake the current market leader. For example, the iPhone, the first smartphone, was a product that negatively affected other cell phonemakers on the market.

Distribution: The process of selling a product or service. For example, Coca-Cola distributes its beverages in more than 200 countries. Distribution involves having a relationship with stores, restaurants, websites, and other ways that enable the sale of a company's product(s).

Diversification: An approach to reducing risk that involves spreading one's assets across a number of unrelated securities. It's the application of the expression "Don't put all your eggs in one basket."

Diversified portfolio: A basket of investments, usually spread across several asset classes, such as stocks, bonds, and cash equivalents.

Dividend yield: The annual dividend of a stock divided by its current price. For example, if a firm paid an annual dividend of $1 and has a current price of $20, its dividend yield would be 5%.

Dividend reinvestment programs (DRIPs): A program where a company lets investors automatically reinvest their dividends to purchase more shares of its stock.

Dividends: A cash payment from a firm to stockholders.

Dollar cost averaging: An approach to investing money in stages rather than in one lump sum. For example, with $10,000 to invest, an investor may choose to invest $2,000 a month for the next five months. Dollar cost averaging avoids buying at the peak, but also buying at the low.

Double coincidence of wants: A situation in which both parties want something that the other has, such as in barter transactions.

Double-coupon: Combining discounts from both the manufacturer and retailer. For example, a customer may buy Friendly's ice cream on sale at Stop & Shop and combine it with a manufacturer's coupon from Friendly's.

Double-entry form of bookkeeping: A form of recordkeeping where every entry has an offsetting entry elsewhere in the financial ledger. For example, if a firm issues debt and raises cash, both debt would increase (a credit) and cash would increase (a debit). Double-entry bookkeeping is used in the balance sheet of most publicly traded firms around the world.

Dow Jones Industrial Average (DJIA): The oldest benchmark of US stocks, with a history dating back to 1896. It is a price-weighted average of 30 blue-chip US stocks.

Down payment: A deposit on a home, car, or some other asset that is financed in stages.

Dual mandate: The two primary goals of the Federal Reserve Bank of the US, which are maximum employment and stable prices.

Duplex: A home divided into two apartments or condominiums, with a separate entrance for each.

Early decision: A binding contract that involves applying to a single college or university early (usually in mid to late October of the applicant's senior year of high school). An acceptance, deferment, or rejection letter is usually sent to early decision applicants by mid-December. Earned income tax credit: A federal tax credit that results in less taxes paid for people who work, as opposed to getting a direct cash payment from the government. The tax credits are generally larger for a person with children.

Earnings before interest and taxes (EBIT): The money a firm earns from its regular course of operations, before certain adjustments. Looking at earnings before interest and taxes allows for easier comparisons to other firms since they often differ by their tax rates and debt, which is directly related to interest expense. EBIT is informally known as operating income.

Earnings guidance: Management's estimate for a firm's earnings. They often underpromise and overdeliver, resulting in a positive earnings surprise.

Earnings surprise: The difference between a firm's reported earnings and consensus earnings estimates. For example, if a firm reports earnings of $1.10 a share and the consensus estimate was $1.00, the earnings surprise would be $0.10 or 10%.

Efficient frontier: A graph of all of the possible efficient portfolios.

Efficient market: A market where prices adjust quickly *and* appropriately to new information.

Efficient market hypothesis (EMH): A theory that states asset prices quickly and appropriately react to all information and that it is impossible to *consistently* beat the market.

Efficient portfolio: A portfolio that maximizes expected return, given the risk an investor is willing to take. There are a range of efficient portfolios corresponding to the risk tolerances of the diverse range of investors.

Electronic communication network (ECN): An electronic stock exchange, such as Instinet or NYSE Arca. ECNs have no trading floor.

Electric vehicle tax credit: Tax incentives provided by the government to purchase electric vehicles.

Emergency fund: A financial reserve used to pay for unforeseen circumstances, such as the loss of a job or illness. A rule of thumb is an emergency fund should hold at least Six months of living expenses. Also known as a rainy-day fund.

Emotional intelligence (EQ or EI): A term popularized by author Dan Goleman that measures the ability to recognize, understand, manage, and influence emotions.

Entrepreneur: A person who creates and runs their own business.

Environmental, social, and governance (ESG): An approach to managing a firm that considers all stakeholders (i.e., customers, suppliers, employees, shareholders, community), in contrast to a single-minded focus on maximizing stockholder wealth.

Equilibrium: A state of balance between those demanding a good and those supplying it. This state of balance determines the price of a good or service.

Equity/equities: The formal name for a stock in the singular or plural, respectively. Equity entails an ownership position in a business.

Escrow: Money held by a third party, such as a mortgage servicer, and given to the appropriate firm or person by the due date. For example, a mortgage servicer may hold property taxes in escrow and pay them to the local government on a quarterly basis.

Estate tax: A tax on inherited assets paid before the assets are distributed to heirs.

Exchange traded funds (ETFs): Index-type investment funds that trade intraday like stocks. For example, the SPDR S&P 500 trust (SPY) is a popular ETF that aims to replicate the performance of the S&P 500.

Expansion: The growth phase of an economic cycle. The opposite of contraction.

Extended hours trading: Trading outside the regular market hours of 9:30 a.m.–4:00 p.m. Extended-hours trading may occur before the market opens (4:00 a.m.–9:30 a.m. EST) and after it closes (4:00 p.m.–8:00 p.m. EST). Also known as after-hours trading.

Fair, Isaac and Company: A data analytics firm that computes individual credit scores used by many financial institutions to make credit or loan decisions. Their proprietary model is known as a FICO score.

Face value: The value of a bond at maturity, assuming it doesn't default. Face value is also known as principal or par value.

Federal Deposit Insurance Company (FDIC): A US government insurance program for bank deposits valued up to $250,000 per account.

Federal discount rate: The interest rate charged when banks borrow from the Federal Reserve.

Federal Housing Authority (FHA): A unit of the Department of Housing and Urban Development (HUD) that insures loans made by private lenders. If the borrower fails to pay the loan, the FHA (backed by the credit of the US government) will ensure the loan is paid.

Federal Insurance Contributions Act (FICA): A payroll tax paid by employees and employers used to fund the Social Security and Medicare programs in the US.

Federal Reserve, or "The Fed": The central bank of the US. Its two primary goals are to maximize employment and to stabilize prices. It also supervise and regulate most large banks in the US.

Federal Reserve Board of Governors (BOG): The leadership of the Federal Reserve. The BOG consists of seven members who each serve 14-year terms. The chairperson is appointed to a four-year term and may be reappointed by the current US president several times.

Fellowship: An academic scholarship provided to graduate students. Typically, no work is required for fellows, unlike financial support provided by teaching or research assistantships.

Fiat currency: Money declared by a government or some monetary authority to have value. It is not backed by a physical asset, such as gold.

FICO score: A measure of a person's credit score calculated by **F**air, **I**saac and **Co**mpany, a leading data analytics firm.

Financial ratio: One item on a financial statement divided by another. For example, the current ratio is computed as current assets divided by current liabilities.

Financial statements: Books and records for a firm that are prepared by management and audited by certified public accountants (CPAs). The primary financial statements of a firm are its balance sheet, income statement, and statement of cash flows.

Firm commitment offering: When investment banks guarantee a firm that they will sell a specified amount (e.g., $100 million) of a firm's securities. For example, Goldman Sachs and Morgan Stanley may guarantee Airbnb that they will raise $5 billion for the firm if they take it public though the initial public offering (IPO) process.

Fiscal year: The year corresponding to the financial statements produced by a firm. It does not have to coincide with the calendar year (January–December). For example, some firms may choose to have a July 1–June 30 fiscal year.

Fixed income securities: A formal name for bonds. The name comes from the observation that the amount and timing of the cash or income received from owning most bonds are fixed.

Flea market: A place, often outdoors, where dozens, if not hundreds, of vendors sell goods. Each vendor typically sets up a table and places their items on the table for potential customers to examine.

Flexible Spending Account (FSA): A pre-tax account that may be used for health care and childcare expenses. FSA money is "use it or lose it." For example, if an individual declares they will incur $2,000 in eligible FSA expenses and uses only $1,500 over the calendar year, they will lose the remaining $500.

Flight to quality: The gravitation toward safe securities, such as US government bonds, when fear is prevalent due to some financial crisis or shock to the economic system.

Flipper: Someone who sells an asset over a relatively short period of time hoping to earn a profit. Two common examples include selling stock of a firm shortly after its initial public offering (IPO) date or selling a house after purchasing it at a distressed price.

Float: Money earned on the difference between money received and money owed. For example, Berkshire Hathaway's insurance unit collects and invests insurance premiums but eventually must pay out a least a portion of these funds to cover insurance claims.

For sale by owners (FSBO): Real estate, or some other product, listed for sale by the owner. The owner hopes to save money by avoiding the commission paid to a salesperson.

Foreclosed home: A home taken back by the lender after the prior homeowner stops paying the mortgage.

Form 13-F: A form required to be submitted to the Securities Exchange Commission (SEC) on a quarterly basis by all investment managers that have at least $100 million in assets under management. Form 13-F lists all long stock and option positions of the firm. It must be filed 45 days after the end of each quarter. For example, the form is due approximately February 15, after the end of the fourth quarter (December 31).

Forbes 400: An annual list of the richest people in America published by *Forbes*.

Fractional jet ownership: Partial ownership in a jet or fleet of jets. NetJets, a Berkshire Hathaway company, is one of the largest firms providing fractional jet ownership to its clients. Since the cost of owning an individual jet is extremely expensive, fractional ownership offers the mass affluent customer the opportunity to travel by private jet.

Franchise: An individual or firm authorized to provide a product or service owned by another firm. For example, a McDonald's franchisee may run a McDonald's store. The independent owner, or franchisee, follows the business practices set up by McDonald's and pays McDonald's a percentage of its sales, as well as other fees.

Free application for federal student aid (FAFSA): A form that helps determine student eligibility for financial aid at a college or university.

Free cash flow (FCF): Cash flow after needed (re)investments in a firm. One approximation of FCF equals net income plus non-cash expenses (e.g., depreciation and amortization) minus long-term investments (e.g., capital expenditures) and short-term investments (e.g., changes in net working capital).

Frequent flyer program: A rewards program that provides benefits each time members fly on a specific airline or its affiliates. For example, Delta SkyMiles is the frequent flyer program of Delta Airlines and its affiliates. SkyMiles may be used to obtain free plane tickets, seat upgrades, or to purchase other goods and services.

Fund manager: A person who manages an investment fund, such as a mutual fund, pension fund, or hedge fund.

Future value: A formula that describes the amount at which an investment or loan grows. For a single investment, future value = starting value × $(1 + \text{rate of growth})^T$. T refers to the number of years in the prior equation.

Garage sale: A sale of pre-owned or used items held by a homeowner on their property. Also known as a yard sale.

Generally accepted accounting principles (GAAP): The set of rules that management must follow when preparing financial statements of publicly traded companies listed on US exchanges. GAAP rules are created and modified by the Financial Accounting Standards Board (FASB).

Generic: When a company places its own label on a product manufactured by an outside firm. For example, many Kirkland Signature products sold by Costco are made by third-party firms. Generic items are sometimes referred to as private label.

Giving Pledge: A philanthropic organization set up by Bill Gates and Warren Buffett where signatories agree in a "handshake agreement" to give away at least 50% of their net worth within their lifetimes or shortly after passing. (Website: https://givingpledge.org/.)

Global portfolio: A portfolio consisting of both domestic and international securities.

Gold Reserve Act: A law passed by Congress in 1934, which required that all gold and gold certificates held by the Federal Reserve be surrendered to the US Department of the Treasury in exchange for currency. Individuals were also expected to exchange their gold for currency. Until the Act, currency held by individuals could be exchanged for gold.

Gordon growth model: A stock valuation model that relies on a simplification of the discounted cash flow approach. The model computes the price target of a stock as next year's dividend divided by the difference between its discount rate and perpetual, or steady state, growth rate. Also known as the constant growth dividend discount model (DDM).

Government-sponsored enterprise (GSE): Quasi-governmental, privately held institutions backed directly or indirectly by the US government. For example, Student Loan Marketing Association provides student loans backed by the credit of the US government. The Student Loan Marketing Association is often referred to by its nickname, Sallie Mae.

Grant: Payment for expenses from some type of governmental organization. College grants do not have to be paid back, unlike money received from a student loan.

Great Recession: The recession that occurred in the United States over the December 2007–June 2009 time period. It was one of the most significant recessions in the US since World War II. The initial effect of the Great Recession was on the US real estate and banking industries, but the damage eventually spread to much of the global economy.

Great Depression: The recession that occurred in the United States over the August 1929–March 1933 time period. It was the steepest downturn in recorded US economic history. Gross domestic product (GDP). A measure of the economic output of a country over a period of time, such as one year. GDP consists of the sum of consumption, investment spending, government spending, and net exports.

Gross income: Income before any deductions or taxes are taken out. Mortgage lenders often use gross income as one measure of the ability of a borrower to afford a home.

Gross margin ratio: A measure of a firm's profitability computed as gross profit divided by sales. Ratios allow for easier comparisons across companies or over time for the same firm.

Gross profit: Sales or revenue minus cost of goods sold (COGS).

Growth stock: A stock trading at a premium to the market based on a valuation metric, such as price/book or price/earnings. The market expects these firms to grow quickly, hence the premium valuation.

Health maintenance organization (HMO): A medical insurance group that is part of a health care plan offered by employers that provides limited choices of doctors and hospitals. Normally, the HMO costs less money than traditional plans since the firm negotiates with health care providers, passing along some of the savings to the employee.

Health savings account (HSA): A pre-tax account that may be used to pay for medical expenses. The amount an individual may put in an HSA increases with inflation. It's currently $3,550 annually for individuals and $7,100 for a family. Any unused dollars in the HSA may be rolled over for use in following years, unlike with a flexible spending account.

High conviction approach: An investment philosophy that involves putting the bulk of one's assets in a relatively small number of investments. The high conviction approach results in highly concentrated portfolios, as opposed to a broadly diversified index fund. The high conviction approach is also known as a best ideas approach to investing.

High net worth (HNW) investors: Rich investors. The most common numerical cutoff for HNW investors is that they have a net worth of $1 million or more, excluding their primary residence.

High yield bond: A bond with a high risk of default, typically rated BB+ or below by S&P or some other ratings agency. The informal name for high yield bonds is junk bonds.

Home equity loan: A loan against the difference between the market value of a home and its mortgage (i.e., the home equity). Generally, home equity loans may be possible if there is more than 20% equity in the home. A home equity loan would then result in two mortgage payments for the borrower—the original mortgage and the home equity loan, often called a second mortgage.

Homeowners insurance: Insurance that covers damage to a home, such as by fire, vandalism, lightning, wind, and hail. Most mortgage companies require homeowners to purchase homeowners insurance as a way to protect the value of their loan.

Income: The amount of money someone makes from their job and other sources. For a company, income refers to the amount it earns, after all expenses.

Income statement: One of the required financial statements of publicly traded firms. It measures profit and loss over a specified period of time, such as one quarter or one year. The income statement is also known as the profit and loss (P&L) statement.

Index fund: A portfolio that tries to replicate the performance of a specified index, such as the S&P 500. Index funds tend to charge low fees and are usually very tax efficient.

Indifference curve: A concept from economics that measures the willingness of a person to trade off things, such as money and free time. For example, a person may be willing to earn $2,000 less per year if they had an extra week of vacation. All points on the indifference curve offer equal happiness or satisfaction. In investments, indifference curves are often used to measure a trade-off between risk and return. The prospect of higher returns usually comes with higher levels of risk.

Individual retirement account (IRA): A common type of retirement account for individuals and those working for small businesses. IRAs may also be used as a vehicle to hold other retirement assets "rolled over" when switching jobs. With traditional IRAs taxes are paid upon withdrawal of the funds, usually at age 59 ½ or later, without incurring penalties.

Industry: A group of companies that compete in related business activities and are similarly affected by government regulations and the macroeconomic environment. For example, Visa, Mastercard, Discover, and American Express compete in the credit services industry.

Inflation: A measure of how much prices increase each year. Inflation is usually measured by the Consumer Price Index (CPI).

Initial public offering (IPO): The first time a company's stock trades on a public exchange. Anyone with enough money can buy shares after the IPO occurs.

Inner Scorecard: An approach Warren Buffett follows that involves living one's life on one's terms, according to one's own self-judgment.

Insurance: A financial product that provides payment in the event of an adverse event. For example, life insurance provides a payment to beneficiaries upon the death of the policyholder. Car insurance provides payment in the event of an auto-related accident.

Insurance premium: An insurance bill, such as payment for car insurance.

Intangible assets: Non-physical assets such as intellectual property but also non-protected items such as trade secrets and publicity.

Intellectual property (IP): Non-physical assets, such as patents, trademarks, copyrights, and brand names. IP usually has some form of legal protection attached to it.

Intelligence quotient (IQ): A measure of cognitive ability, or how a person reasons, calculates, comprehends, and solves problems. IQ is usually measured with a standardized test and has an average value of 100 across the population. According to Warren Buffett, a superhigh IQ (e.g., 150) may actually be a detriment to successful investing.

Interest expense: Money a firm pays each accounting period to the lender(s) of its borrowed funds. It equals the coupon rate times the face value of the firm's debt. For example, if the firm has $100 million of debt outstanding with an average coupon rate of 5%, the interest expense for the year would be $5 million.

Interest income: Money a firm earns from its cash and other interest-bearing investments.

Interest rate: The rate at which one's money grows if saving. The term is usually discussed in the context of a bond or bank product. Alternatively, the rate at which one's debt grows borrowing money, often in the form of a loan or credit card balance.

Internal Revenue Service (IRS): A unit of the US Treasury that is responsible for collecting taxes and enforcing the tax code.

International Financial Reporting Standards (IFRS): The set of rules many international publicly traded companies use to produce their financial statements. IFRS differs in some respects from the rules used by companies trading on American stock exchanges (Generally Accepted Accounting Principles).

Internship: A temporary job held by a student that is often a tryout for a permanent position. Internships are commonly held over the summer but may occur at any time.

Intrinsic value: A reasoned measure of what something is worth. It is often computed with the aid of a discounted cash flow or relative valuation financial model, resulting in a price target.

Inventory: Goods or materials a business intends to sell. It may be a finished product or work in progress, such as a partially built Ford F-150 truck.

Investing domestically: Investing within your home country. For example, an American investor would invest in American stocks.

Investing internationally: Investing outside your home country. For example, an American investor may choose to invest in Chinese stocks.

Investment bankers: People that who work for investment banking firms and engage in investment banking–related activities, such as taking firms public, trading securities, and providing advice related to mergers and acquisitions.

Investment banking firms: Financial firms that help institutions raise capital, trade securities, make investments, and engage in mergers and acquisitions.

Investment grade bonds: Bonds issued by firms with a high probability of meeting their promised payments. They are often rated BBB and higher by rating agencies, such as S&P. The opposite of investment grade bonds are high yield, or junk, bonds.

Itemize: The process of listing tax deductible expenses on a tax return.

Jumbo mortgage: A large mortgage of at least $484,850 in value that conforms to standards of government-sponsored housing. Jumbo mortgages may be as high as $726,525 in expensive areas, such as New York, Los Angeles, Miami, and San Francisco.

Junior college (JUCO): A higher educational institution that offers two-year degree programs, usually called an associate's degree, at a fairly low cost. Also known as a community college.

Junk bond: A bond with a high risk of default, typically rated BB+ or below by S&P or some other ratings agency. The formal name for junk bonds is high yield bonds.

Landlord: The owner of a rental property or properties.

Large cap: Stocks with a market capitalization greater than $1 billion.

Lawsuit: A dispute brought to a court of law that usually has financial ramifications for both parties. For example, Samsung was subjected to many lawsuits by consumers when its Galaxy Note 7 phone caught fire in several instances.

Lease obligation: Money owed for the use, but not ownership, of a long-term asset. For example, lease obligations may be incurred by companies operating stores in a mall or for an individual leasing a car.

Legacy admissions: Having a familial relationship when seeking admission at a college or university. The most common legacy example occurs when an applicant has a parent who has graduated from the college or university. The rules vary by school, but legacy may also relate to having grandparents, siblings, or other relatives having attended the college or university. Having a legacy relationship often increases the admissions chances of an applicant.

Lenders mortgage insurance (LMI): Insurance that protects the lender in the event the borrower fails to pay the mortgage. LMI is often required on home purchases where the borrower puts less than a 20% down payment. LMI typically results in an extra expense of 0.5% to 1.0% per year on the amount of the mortgage. Also known as private mortgage insurance (PMI).

Liabilities: A financial obligation, often segmented in two categories on a balance sheet. Current liabilities are financial obligations due within one year. Long-term liabilities are financial obligations due at least one year from now.

Life insurance: A financial product that provides payment to beneficiaries in the event of the death of the policyholder.

LinkedIn: A job-oriented social media website that serves as sort of an online resume. It is also one tool to maintain a formal business network. LinkedIn has been owned by Microsoft since December 2016.

Liquidation: The process of selling assets and turning the proceeds into cash. For example, a liquidation process occurs for firms going through the Chapter 7 bankruptcy process.

Liquid asset: An asset that may be sold quickly *and* at fair market value. For example, a Treasury bill is a liquid asset, while real estate is not.

Litigation: The process of taking legal action against a person or institution.

Loan-to-value ratio (LTV): A calculation often used in real estate transactions that examines the size of a loan relative to the value of the property. For example, a $200,000 mortgage loan on a $250,000 home has an LTV ratio of ($200,000/$250,000 =) 80%.

London Inter-bank Offered Rate (LIBOR): An interest rate used as a benchmark for many floating rate loans. LIBOR is computed as an average of short-term interest rates regularly submitted by a group of banks in London.

Long-term assets: Assets that are expected to last or be held at least one year. Examples of long-term assets on a balance sheet include real estate, land, machines, vehicles, and computer equipment.

Long-term investments: Securities that have at least one year to maturity. For example, a 10-year corporate bond or common stock in Coca-Cola on a firm's balance sheet are considered long-term investments.

Long-term care insurance: Insurance that pays the cost of care after federal insurance for those with chronic conditions. For example, long-term care insurance may pay for the cost of an elderly person, unable to care for themselves, to reside in a nursing home.

Long-term liabilities: Financial obligations due at least one year from today. For example, if a company issues a 10-year corporate bond, the principal repayment and most of the coupon payments are due at least one year from today. In addition, some companies have pension or health care obligations for retired employees, which are long-term liabilities.

Loss: When the expenses of an organization are greater than its revenues. Financial statements typically measure gains and losses quarterly or annually.

Loss leader: A product that a firm leads with (e.g., a free sample of food) that gives it a loss. However, if the customer purchases another item at full cost (e.g., a regular meal), then the business may ultimately turn a profit. In other words, a product that generates a small loss, with the expectation of a larger gain in the future.

Low-cost producer: A firm that produces a product or service at the lowest cost on a per unit basis.

M1: A narrow measure of the money supply, consisting of physical currency, demand deposits, traveler's checks, and other checkable deposits.

Market capitalization: The price of a stock times the number of its shares outstanding. In other words, the market value of all of a company's stock. It is often simplified as market cap.

Market capitalization weighted index: An index where high market value assets have a bigger effect than low market value assets. For example, if Apple has a market capitalization of $1 trillion and Disney has a market capitalization of $200 billion, a 1% move in Apple would have five times the effect on the index than a 1% change in Disney's price. The S&P 500 is perhaps the best-known market capitalization weighted index. Also known as a value weighted index.

Market makers: Traders on an exchange that are always willing to buy or sell shares in a specific stock. Their role ensures that each buyer can find a seller and each seller can find a buyer.

Market risk premium: A measure of investor psychology and risk tolerance. Formally, it is measured as the difference between the expected return on the (stock) market and risk-free rate of interest. Historically, the market risk premium has been in the 6–7% per annum range, but it varies widely during periods of fear and greed in the market.

Market share: The revenues of a firm divided by the total revenues of its product market or industry.

Medicare: The primary health insurance program for the elderly in the US. Most Medicare recipients are age 65 and older, but the program also provides services to some younger people with disabilities.

Mega cap: A stock with a market capitalization greater than $100 billion.

Micro cap: A stock with a market capitalization of less than $100 million.

Mid cap: A stock with a market capitalization between $1 billion and $10 billion.

Moat: A barrier around a business that reduces or eliminates competition. For example, a patent is a legal barrier to competition that may last up to 20 years.

Momentum: A strategy that involves buying what has gone up in the recent past and avoiding, or selling short, what has gone down in the recent past. Some academic studies find that momentum investing strategies outperform the market over short periods of time (e.g., less than one year).

Money factor: A term used in vehicle lease calculators that is related to interest rates. The money factor may be estimated by taking the interest rate applied to the lease and dividing it by 2400. The lower the money factor, the lower the lease payment.

Money orders: A method of sending money if one does not have a checking account. The US post office and Walmart are two places that commonly provide money order services for a small fee.

Money supply: The aggregate amount of money in an economy. There are several measures of the money supply, ranging from something as narrow as cash to cash plus various forms of savings deposits and money market funds, among other assets.

Mortgage: A loan to help buy a home in one of its many forms, including an apartment, condominium, single family home, or multifamily home.

Mortgage servicer: A financial firm that collects and processes a homeowner's monthly mortgage payment.

Mr. Market: A fictional character created by Benjamin Graham to describe the volatile nature of the stock market.

Multiple Listing Service (MLS): The most common database showing real estate for sale used by real estate professionals. Realtor.com, Zillow.com, and Redfin.com are free websites that provide similar information.

Multiple streams of income: Receiving income from several sources, including a full-time job, an investment portfolio, real estate rental income, or other sources.

Municipal bonds (munis): Bonds issued by state and local governments as well as other non-profit institutions, such as schools.

Interest income earned from municipal bonds is generally free of federal income taxes.

Mutual fund: An investment product where investors pool their money together and have it invested by a fund manager. Mutual funds are usually purchased in brokerage accounts or through retirement plans.

Nano cap: A stock with a market capitalization less than $50 million.

National Association of Security Dealers Automated Quotation System (NASDAQ): A stock exchange located in Times Square in Manhattan. Unlike the New York Stock Exchange, there is no physical trading floor at NASDAQ. Trades on NASDAQ are completed via interlinked trading systems around the country.

Natural monopoly: A market where there is one seller of a product and the advantage happened naturally (i.e., through the quality of a company's product(s) and its business acumen) or through powerful economies of scale, as opposed to government regulation. For example, Google isn't the only search engine, but it has roughly 80% market share in the US, resulting in it being close to a natural monopoly in search engines.

Net income: Revenue minus all expenses on an income statement. Sometimes net income is referred to as "the bottom line."

Net receivables: Accounts receivable minus an amount estimated by management that is not likely to be collected. For example, many uninsured individuals that go to the emergency room at a hospital may be unable to afford the services they receive and are unlikely to pay in full.

Net sales: Sales minus returns, discounts, and perhaps other allowances.

Net working capital: The difference between current assets and current liabilities. Net working capital is a measure of a firm's short-term liquidity condition.

Net worth: The amount of money one would have after paying off all debts.

New York Stock Exchange (NYSE): One of the primary stock exchanges in the US, located at 11 Wall Street, in Manhattan.

Normalized earnings: Average earnings over a full business cycle, usually a 5- to 10-year period. Normalizing earnings removes some of its cyclicality, especially for economically sensitive firms.

NYSE American: A small stock exchange located in lower Manhattan, primarily known today as a venue for trading exchange traded funds (ETFs). It was previously known as the American Stock Exchange (AMEX).

Odd lot: A trade of less than 100 shares of a stock. Historically, transaction costs were higher if an investor purchased less than 100 shares, but the threshold is not very meaningful in today's markets dominated by electronic trading.

Odd lot trading desk: The place odd lot orders, those with less than 100 shares, are routed to for trading. Today most trading is done through purely electronic venues, so the distinction is not very meaningful anymore.

Open market operations: A tool of the Federal Reserve that refers to its ability to buy and sell securities, which indirectly influence interest rates across the entire maturity spectrum. Open market operations are usually conducted by the New York branch of the Federal Reserve.

Operating income: The money a firm earns from its regular course of operations, before interest, taxes, and other one-time items. Operating income is more formally known as earnings before interest and taxes (EBIT).

Optimal portfolio: The basket of investments custom-tailored to a specific investor that maximizes the portfolio's risk-adjusted expected return. Mathematically, the optimal portfolio is the point of tangency between the efficient frontier and an investor's indifference curve.

Outer scorecard: An approach discussed by Warren Buffett that involves living one's life concerned to a great extent about what others think about one's actions.

Outsourcing: The process of having an external firm produce a product or service. For example, Apple outsources the production of the iPhone to Foxconn, a multi-national electronics manufacturer.

Overdraft protection: Insurance protection for a checking account that will cover the amount of a bounced check up to a limit, such as $500.

Overhead: An informal name for selling, general, and administrative (SG&A) expenses. Overhead primarily relates to the cost of paying employees and real estate. Overhead, or SG&A, is in contrast to the cost of producing a product, formally known as cost of goods sold (COGS).

Outlet store: Discount stores, at least relative to the full prices charged by the parent's primary store concept. For example, Nordstrom Rack is the outlet brand of Nordstrom, Inc., a luxury department store. The outlet stores frequently offer older items or clearance items in order to keep prices down.

Over the counter (OTC): A decentralized market, in contrast to transactions completed on an exchange with a physical location. Originally, customers would walk up to a counter at a brokerage firm and request a trade; hence the name.

Par bond: A bond with a market price equal to its face value, usually $1,000.

Parent loans: Loans offered to parents from private banks to help their child pay for college. Private student loans are generally more expensive than federally sponsored student loans.

Passbook savings account: A financial product offered by most banks. Historically, a physical book accompanied the account. Today most account information is stored electronically, so they are usually referred to simply as savings accounts.

Patent: A form of intellectual property that prevents competitors from producing the same product or service for a period of time lasting up to 20 years upon issuance. Firms may license their patents for payments, generally known as royalties.

Pawn shop: A place to sell items of value with the option to repurchase them at a higher price within one to four months. Consumers may also buy items at pawn shops without having to sell anything. Consumers who sell items to a pawn shop are essentially taking out a loan, collateralized by the item(s) they sell.

Paying it forward: A concept or belief that involves helping others if one has benefited from someone else's generosity in the past.

Payout ratio: The percentage of earnings paid out each year as dividends. For example, if a firm has earnings of $10 a share and pays a dividend of $4 a share, its payout ratio would be 40%.

P/E relative valuation model: A model that values a firm as the product of its one-year ahead earnings estimate and its industry-adjusted P/E. For example, if AT&T is projected to earn $4 a share next year and the appropriate industry P/E multiple is 10 times earnings, then the P/E relative valuation model would value AT&T at ($4 × 10 =) $40 a share.

Pension plan: A retirement plan for individuals, usually tied to years of service and annual salary shortly before retirement. For example, a policewoman who worked 30 years for a town may receive a fraction (e.g., 70%) of the average of her last three years of annual salaries before retirement. The pension plan is managed by the company, or a representative firm, rather than the individual.

Perk: A benefit provided to employees, usually in the form of non-cash compensation. For example, health insurance and life insurance are two common perks provided to full-time employees. Perk is more formally known as perquisite.

Personal financial literacy: The ability to use knowledge and skills to manage financial resources effectively for a lifetime of financial well-being.

Personal identification number (PIN): A four- to six-digit passcode often tied to a debit or credit card for security reasons. It is often required to access an automated teller machine (ATM).

Philanthropy: Volunteer efforts that usually focus on long-term solutions and active engagement. For example, the Bill and Melinda Gates Foundation is a philanthropic organization.

Plowback ratio: The proportion of earnings a firm retains. For example, if a firm earns $10 a share, retains $6 a share, and pays out $4 a share in dividends, its plowback ratio would be 60%. The plowback ratio is also known as the retention ratio.

Point: A dollar change, or a change in the unit of currency being used. If a stock went up 2 points, in the US it means 2 dollars. In Germany, it would mean 2 euros. In Great Britain, 2 pounds. The term "point" also applies to a market index, such as the Dow Jones Industrial Average (DJIA) or S&P 500.

Poor borrowers: The lowest possible credit rating for an individual. The term "poor borrowers" often applies to individuals with a credit score in the 300 to 580 range. Individuals with poor credit scores usually have missed several payments on prior credit accounts and, in some cases, have previously declared bankruptcy.

Portfolio: A basket of investments.

Preceptor: Usually an upper-class student (i.e., a junior or senior) who acts as a sort of counselor and administrator on a college dormitory floor. The preceptor usually does not have to pay for their housing and sometimes receives some additional pay.

Pre-foreclosure: A property where the current owner has missed payments and one that the lender is likely in the process of taking back.

Preferred provider organization (PPO): A healthcare organization that offers a hybrid plan between a traditional health care plan that permits wide choices among doctors and hospitals and a health maintenance organization (HMO) plan that restricts choices. Costs are lower for staying in the health plan's network, but the flexibility exists to be treated by doctors and hospitals out of network at a higher cost.

Premium bond: A bond with a market price greater than its face value (e.g., $1,100 vs. $1,000). Premium bonds usually exist when the coupon rate on a bond is higher than the yield on bonds of similar risk.

Prescription drug benefit plan: A benefit provided to some employees that allows them to purchase prescription pharmaceutical products at attractive prices. Usually, the plan holder is responsible for a co-pay of $3 to $10 per prescription.

Present value (PV): A formula that describes the amount one would be willing to pay today for receiving a specified amount of money in the future. Present value = Future value / $(1 + \text{rate of growth})^T$. T refers to the number of years the investment is held.

Price target: An estimate of the value of a stock or some other asset.

Price-to-earnings (P/E) ratio: The price of a stock divided by its earnings per share. For example, if a stock is priced at $20 a share and the firm has earnings per share of $2, its P/E ratio would be 10.

Price weighted index: An index where high-price assets have a bigger effect than low-price assets. For example, if Boeing had a price of $150 a share and Coca-Cola had a price of $50 a share, a 1% move in Boeing would have triple the effect on the index than a 1% change in Coke's price. The Dow Jones Industrial Average (DJIA) is perhaps the best-known price weighted index.

Primary market transaction: The sale of securities (e.g., stock or bonds) by a company. The money received from the sale goes into the corporate treasury.

Prime borrowers: Customers that have the best credit ratings according to a FICO score, or some other measure of creditworthiness. The typical FICO range for individuals in the prime category is 740 to the (current) maximum of 850.

Prime rate of interest: The interest rate a bank charges its customers with the strongest credit ratings.

Principal: The face value or par value of a bond that is returned at maturity.

Private label: When a company places its own label on a product manufactured by an outside firm. For example, many Kirkland Signature products sold by Costco are made by third-party firms. Private label items are sometimes referred to as generic.

Private mortgage insurance (PMI): Insurance that protects the lender in the event the borrower does not pay the mortgage. PMI is often required on home purchases where the borrower puts less than a 20% down payment. PMI typically results in an extra expense of 0.5% to 1.0% a year on the amount of the mortgage. Also known as lenders mortgage insurance (LMI).

Private student loans: Loans taken out by a student, typically offered by a bank. They are often co-signed by a parent or another creditworthy individual. Private student loans generally have higher interest rates than those sponsored by federal loan programs.

Progressive tax rates: Tax rates that increase in percentage terms as income increases. For example, the tax rate may be 10% on the first $10,000 earned, then 15% for any amount greater than $10,000 and less than $40,000, and it keeps increasing until the highest tax bracket is reached. In the US there are currently 7 tax brackets at the federal level, with the highest (for a single filer) of 37% at income levels above $510,301.

Profit: The money received from selling a product, service, or asset after any expenses.

Profit and loss (P&L) statement: One of the required financial statements of publicly traded firms. It measures profit and loss over a specified period of time, such as one quarter or one year. The profit and loss statement is also known as the income statement.

Profit margin: A measure of a firm's profitability expressed as a percentage of sales. It is usually computed as net income divided by sales.

Property, plant, and equipment (PP&E): Long-term assets held by the firm related to land (property), buildings (plant), and machines (equipment). For example, Walmart's stores, distribution centers, and trucks all count toward its PP&E.

Property taxes: Taxes paid by a homeowner or institution to a local government. The taxes collected are used to pay for the local government's expenses, such as to support its schools, police department, and fire department.

Publicly traded stocks: Securities that trade on a stock exchange. Anyone with enough money may purchase them through a brokerage account.

Purchasing power: The ability to buy something, often adjusted by inflation.

Quantitative easing (QE): A tool of the Federal Reserve to lower intermediate and long-term interest rates when short-term interest rates are at or close to 0. The Fed aims to accomplish this task by purchasing bonds backed by the US government, such as US Treasuries and government-sponsored mortgage-backed securities.

Quarterly reports: Financial statements that are produced on a quarterly basis by publicly traded companies. The primary reports are the income statement, balance sheet, and statement of cash flows. Private firms usually produce their own financial statements but aren't required to disclose this information to the public.

Quota: A minimum sales hurdle that a salesperson must meet to stay employed in good standing.

Raise: A permanent increase in pay.

Rainy-day fund: Money put aside to pay for unexpected expenses, usually in a safe investment vehicle, such as cash equivalent investments. One rule of thumb for a rainy-day fund is that it should amount to at least six months of living expenses. Also known as an emergency fund.

Random walk hypothesis: A popular name for the efficient market hypothesis (EMH), which states that it is impossible to *consistently* beat the market.

Rating agencies: Firms that measure the ability of a company, or other institution, to meet its debt obligations. In the US, the largest rating agencies are S&P, Moody's, and Fitch.

Ransomware: Software that hijacks someone's computer, typically encrypting files without the owner's permission. The writer of the ransomware often demands payment in Bitcoin or some other difficult-to-trace equivalent.

Recession: An economic downturn in a country often approximated by an economy experiencing two consecutive quarterly drops in its gross domestic product (GDP).

Recovery rate: The amount of money (e.g., 70 cents on the dollar) that bondholders, or other creditors, receive during bankruptcy proceedings.

Rent: Payment for use of a property or land, such as a home, office, or farm.

Refinance: Paying off an old loan and replacing it with a new loan, usually at lower rate. For example, if a homeowner had a mortgage with a 5% interest rate, they would save money if they refinanced the old mortgage and took on a new one with an interest rate of 3.5%. One rule of thumb is that the new interest rate should be at least 1% less than the existing interest rate on the loan for a refinancing transaction to make financial sense, net of fees.

Required minimum payment: The minimum amount that must be paid on a monthly credit card bill to keep it in good standing or "turned on." The required minimum payment varies by credit card company, but typically amounts to 3% to 5% of the credit card balance.

Reserve requirements: The amount of money a bank has to keep in the vault, either literally or electronically, on reserve with the Federal Reserve. The reserve requirement in the US has been 10% in recent years for most banks but was temporarily changed to 0% in the recession that followed the COVID-19 pandemic.

Reverse (stock) split: An accounting transaction where the number of shares owned is reduced, and the price per share goes up. For example, if an investor owned 1000 shares of a stock trading at $1 a share, after a 1-for-10 reverse split, they would own 100 shares of a stock now trading at $10 a share. A reverse split is similar to trading two $5 bills for one $10 bill.

Sometimes companies reverse-split their stock to remain on a stock exchange, which usually has a minimum price requirement of $1 a share.

Research and development (R&D): Funds invested to create new products or services. For example, funds spent by a pharmaceutical firm to develop a vaccine would be counted as part of a firm's R&D.

Resume: A document listing one's qualifications for a job. It often includes sections covering work experience, skills, and educational credentials.

Retail apocalypse: A theory that suggests many traditional brick-and-mortar businesses will not survive after competing with e-commerce giant Amazon.com and large hybrid firms, such as Walmart/Walmart.com, and Costco/Costco.com.

Retained earnings: The sum of the company's profits since it started minus any dividend payments over its history.

Retention ratio: The proportion of earnings a firm keeps. For example, if a firm earns $10 a share, retains $6 a share, and pays out $4 a share in dividends, its retention ratio would be 60%. The retention ratio is also known as the plowback ratio.

Return on investment (ROI): The amount at which one's money grows, or falls when losing money. ROI is often calculated as the difference between the price at which you bought and sold the asset, plus any cash flows received from the investment, all divided by the initial cost of the investment. For example, if you purchase a stock for $10, receive $1 in dividends over the course of the year and then sell it for $12 exactly one year after purchase, the ROI is 30% (= $12 + $1 – $10)/($10). ROI is often annualized to enable easier comparison to other investments.

Reward(s) programs: Programs offered by companies that provide cash back, airline tickets, or some other type of benefit. The more one spends on the company's products and services, the greater the rewards. For example, Dunkin' Donuts' rewards program is called DD Perks and provides its members with free coffee, donuts, and other items. Rewards programs are also widely offered by credit card firms.

Revenue: The amount of money a firm earns over a specified time period, such as a quarter or year. Revenue may also be called sales, or turnover outside the US.

Risk: The possibility of loss or injury.

Roadshow: When an investment banking team takes the senior management of a firm to meet with potential investors, such as before an initial public offering (IPO).

Roth IRA: A type of retirement account for individuals and those working for small businesses. Taxes are paid up front with the Roth IRA and withdrawals are then tax free upon retirement. In contrast, with a traditional IRA, contributions are tax free, but taxes are paid upon withdrawal, usually at age 59½ or later.

Round lot: A trade of 100 shares or more of a stock. Historically, transaction costs were lower if an investor purchased at least 100 shares, but the threshold is not very meaningful in today's markets dominated by electronic trading.

Royalty: Payment to an artist or author for a sale of their work, such as a movie, book, song, or television show. In the business world, royalties may also apply to patents or other forms of intellectual property.

Run on the bank: When a large group of depositors demand to take their money out of the bank, overwhelming its liquidity.

Safe haven: Investments that usually perform well when the stock market or economy are having problems. Common examples of safe haven investments include US Treasury securities, gold, and Swiss government bonds.

Salary: The fixed part of a person's compensation, usually paid biweekly or monthly.

Sales: The amount of money a firm earns over a specified time period, such as a quarter or year. Sales may also be called revenue, or turnover outside the US.

Sales tax: A tax that goes to the government for sales of goods or services. Sales taxes vary widely by state, currently ranging from 0% to more than 11%.

Savings account: A financial account offered by most banks. Savings accounts are considered "demand deposit" instruments, so the customer may withdraw the full balance anytime. Amounts up to $250,000 are usually guaranteed by the Federal Deposit Insurance Company (FDIC).

Scholarship: Payment for college expenses from the college, its alumni, corporations, or nonprofit organizations. Scholarships do not have to be paid back, unlike a student loan.

Secondary or seasoned offering: The sale of securities by a firm that is already publicly traded.

Secondary market transactions: The purchase or sale of securities that were previously issued. For example, a transaction where an investor buys 100 shares of Apple stock on NASDAQ. The firm, Apple in this case, gets no money from these trades. Outside investors are simply exchanging shares for money.

Sector: A way of categorizing investments that comprises a group of industries. For example, the technology sector consists of a number of industries, including software, semiconductor, and information technology services.

Securities Exchange Commission (SEC): A unit of the US Justice Department that is regarded as the watchdog of American financial markets. The SEC requires public companies to produce audited financial statements and pursues allegations of insider trading and market manipulation activities, among its many other responsibilities.

Security market line (SML): The main equation that underlies the Capital Asset Pricing Model (CAPM). It theorizes a straight-line relationship between expected return and risk. The SML includes the risk-free rate of interest, a measure of market risk (beta), and a factor of market psychology (the market risk premium).

Self-employment tax: Tax paid by self-employed individuals to fund Social Security and Medicare. It is analogous to Federal Insurance Contributions Act (FICA) payments from those workers who are not self-employed.

Selling, general, and administrative (SG&A): The costs a firm incurs primarily related to paying employees, use of real estate, utilities, computers, and other items. SG&A is informally known as overhead. SG&A differs from the cost of producing a product, formally known as cost of goods sold (COGS).

Selling short: A way to profit from the decline in the price of an asset, such as a stock. Selling short involves selling *first* and then buying at a later date. For example, if an investor sells short a stock for $100 and it later falls to $70, the investor will have earned a profit of $30 per share if they closed the position.

Sensitivity analysis errors: The wide variation in price targets that often occur due to a small change in the inputs, such as the discount rate or terminal growth rate.

Shareholders: Individuals or institutions that own stock in a business. Also known as stockholders.

Shareholders' equity: Total assets minus total liabilities on a firm's balance sheet. Also known as stockholders' equity, owners' equity, net worth, or book value (of equity).

Shares outstanding: The amount of shares held by all investors in a firm.

Short sale (real estate): The sale of a property for a price less than the current mortgage. Purchasing a short sale property is often a good deal for the buyer. The seller usually needs approval from mortgage company to finalize the sale of the property.

Short squeeze: When an investor is forced to cover a short position by their broker, often against their preference.

Simplified Employee Pension (SEP) or SEP IRA: A common retirement plan used by small businesses. The SEP IRA requires less paperwork than a traditional pension plan. The amount contributed is often tied to the profitability of the business, generally offering higher contribution limits relative to traditional IRAs.

Slumlord: A landlord who spends little money on maintenance and repairs on a rental home and who often rents properties to low-income people.

Small cap stocks: Stocks with a market capitalization less than $1 billion.

Special dividend: A one-time or non-recurring dividend, often paid because of a temporary large gain, or for tax-related reasons.

Stakeholders: Any person or entity affected by the operations of a firm. For example, stakeholders include employees, stockholders, suppliers, and the community at large.

Standard and Poor's 500 (S&P 500): A group of 500 large, high-quality exchange-traded American stocks. The S&P 500 is the most popular US stock benchmark for investment professionals.

Standard deduction: The amount that may be subtracted from gross income for income tax purposes. The current standard deduction for single filers in the US is $12,400. If tax-deductible expenses exceed the standard deduction threshold, then a taxpayer could reduce their tax bill by itemizing their deductions.

Standard deviation: A quantitative measure of dispersion of a variable that is computed as the square root of the variance. Standard deviation is often used as a measure of risk by academics and is more intuitive to work with than variance.

Starter home: A first home often sold at a relatively low price. Over time many people trade up to a nicer home, hence the starter name.

Statement of cash flows: One of the three primary. Claims to assets cons statements of publicly traded firms. It provides a measure of cash that flows into and out of a business. The statement of cash flows has three sections: cash flow from operating activities (CFO), cash flow from investing activities (CFI), and cash flow from financing activities (CFF).

Statement of financial condition: One of the three primary financial statements of publicly traded firms. Assets are on the left-hand side of the statement of financial condition, and claims to assets are on the right-hand side. Claims to assets consist of liabilities and equity. The statement of financial condition is more commonly known as the balance sheet. It is also known as the statement of financial position.

Statement of financial position: One of the three primary financial statements of publicly traded firms. Assets are on the left-hand side of the statement of financial position, and claims to assets are on the right-hand side. Claims to assets consist of liabilities and equity. The statement of financial position is more commonly known as the balance sheet. It is also known as the statement of financial condition.

Stop payment: An attempt to cancel a payment, usually from a check that has been previously sent.

Stock: A financial security that represents part ownership of a business.

Stock split: An accounting transaction that changes the number of shares outstanding, and also the stock price. For example, before a

2-for-1 split, assume a stock is trading at $50 a share and there are 1 million shares outstanding. After the split, there would be 2 million shares outstanding, but the price would initially adjust to $25. A stock split is analogous to changing a $10 bill for two $5 bills. The total amount of money, $10, is still the same.

Stockholders: Individuals or institutions who own stock in a business. Stockholders are also known as shareholders.

Style box: A graphical representation of two dimensions of a stock, its valuation and size. Valuation ranges along the value–growth spectrum, and size is represented by market capitalization.

Subprime borrowers: Customers with weak credit ratings. They fall below Alt-A borrowers in creditworthiness and the corresponding borrowing rates. The typical FICO score for a sub-prime borrower falls under 670, although under some scales, the FICO score is below 620.

Super-prime borrowers: Customers who have the very best credit ratings according to a FICO score, or some other measure of creditworthiness. The typical FICO range for super-prime category is from 780 to the (current) maximum of 850.

Survival of the fittest: A theory proposed by biologist Charles Darwin that attempts to explain how organisms evolve over time. In the context of capitalism, the theory may refer to strong firms gaining market share and, in some cases, putting weaker ones out of business.

Supply: The amount of a product or service created by producers.

SWIFT code: SWIFT is the acronym for the Society for Worldwide Interbank Financial Telecommunication. The SWIFT code is a number that corresponds to select international financial transactions of a bank, such as a wire transfer.

Syndicate: A group of investment banks that combine efforts to sell securities to the public, such as during an initial public offering (IPO).

Tax brackets: Ranges that have different tax rates. For example, the tax rate may be 10% on the first $10,000 earned, then 15% for any amount greater than $10,000 and less than $40,000, and so on until the highest tax bracket is reached. In the US there are currently seven tax brackets at the federal level, with the highest (for a single filer) of 37% at income levels above $510,301. Most states charge additional income taxes as well.

Tax rate: The percentage of income, or sometimes sales, owed to the government. For example, the federal corporate tax rate is 21% at the highest levels, for most large, profitable companies in the US.

Tax tables/schedules: A table that displays the amount of tax owed for specific levels of income. There are often several tax brackets, so computing taxes owed is often more complex than simply multiplying total income by the relevant tax rate; hence the need for the tax table.

Teaser rate: A low, temporary interest rate offered by banks for credit cards or other financial products.

Term loan: Another name for a bank loan, especially when the borrower is an institution. Terms loans are usually paid before corporate bonds, so they tend to be safer from a credit risk perspective for the same issuer.

Term structure of interest rates: A table that shows the relationship between the time to maturity and yield to maturity of a bond. The term structure is often graphed as a yield curve.

***The Wall Street Journal* (WSJ):** The most popular business periodical in the world, with a history dating back to 1889. Dow Jones & Company, publisher of "*The Journal*," also produces the Dow Jones Industrial Average (DJIA), the oldest stock market index in the US.

Thrift shop: A place that sells donated goods. Thrift shops are often run by charitable or nonprofit institutions. Goodwill Industries is one of the largest firms in the thrift shop industry. Thrift shops typically sell many items at low prices, including clothes, shoes, books, toys, sporting goods, electronics, and home furnishings.

Thrifty: Being careful, smart, and not wasteful with one's money. Frugal, but not cheap. Warren Buffett proudly claims to be a thrifty person.

Ticker tape machine: A machine that provided stock quotes before computers became widespread.

Ticker tape parade: A parade where ticker tape is thrown out the window to honor those responsible for a notable accomplishment, such as the New York Yankees winning the World Series. In Manhattan, ticker tape parades often occur down Broadway. Today, ticker tape parades use shredded paper or some other form of confetti.

Title insurance: Insurance designed to protect the buyer in the event that the seller didn't own the home "free and clear" before it was sold.

Tombstone: An advertisement in a business-oriented periodical noting securities that will soon be sold to the public, such as during an initial public offering (IPO).

Top line: A nickname for sales or revenue since it usually the first or top line in a firm's income statement.

Total assets: The sum of the left-hand side of the balance sheet. Total assets equals current assets plus long-term assets. Current assets are cash or something that is expected to be turned into cash within one year, such as a sale on credit. Long-term assets may include real estate, machines, stores, website infrastructure, or something intangible, such as a patent or brand name.

Total capital: The amount of debt plus equity in a firm.

Total liabilities: The sum of a firm's financial obligations on its balance sheet. Total liabilities consists of current liabilities plus long-term liabilities.

Trade or vocational school: A school focused on practical courses and the hands-on learning experience of a specific trade. For example, someone usually learns to become a mechanic at a trade school, rather than at a traditional college or university.

Trademark: A symbol or word(s) used to represent a company or product that has legal protection. For example, the Nike "swoosh" symbol is a trademark of Nike. Other firms are prohibited from creating shoes or athletic apparel with a similar design.

Traditional health care insurance plan: A health care plan provided to employees that allows for wide choices among doctors and hospitals. It is usually the most expensive health care plan offered by employers.

Transmitting money: The process of sending or receiving money, including wire transfers, money orders, checks, traveler's checks, and cryptocurrency. Traveler's checks. A substitute for cash when traveling internationally. The business was popularized by American Express. Traveler's checks are used less today due to the widespread availability of credit cards and other forms of electronic payment.

Treasury Inflation Protected Securities (TIPS): A type of bond issued by the US Treasury. The coupon received by investors increases with the Consumer Price Index (CPI), protecting them from inflation. TIPS are issued with maturities of 5, 10, and 30 years.

Triple-coupon: Combining three coupons in a single purchase. For example, a customer may buy Friendly's ice cream on sale at Stop & Shop and combine it with a manufacturer's coupon from Friendly's, while also submitting a coupon from Stop & Shop that provides $10 off on purchases of $25 or more.

Trust(s): A legal entity designed to protect or transfer assets, often across generations, and minimize taxes.

Tycoon: A rich businessperson. Tycoon is synonymous with baron.

Under the mattress: An expression for storing money in a safe place in one's home, or somewhere else that is readily accessible and perceived as safe. No interest is earned. In the aftermath of the Great Depression, many people lost trust in banks and stored money in their homes, often under their mattress; hence the moniker.

Underwriter: The investment bank that offers to buy shares from a company and sell them to the public. To reduce risk, there is often a group of underwriters with one or more firms acting as the lead underwriter(s).

Unemployment rate: The percentage of people in an economy that are not able to obtain work *and* are looking for a job.

US Department of Housing and Urban Development (HUD): A branch of the federal government that plays a key role in the real estate market, especially in the area of affordable housing.

US Department of Veterans Affairs (VA) Loan: A loan offered to veterans of the US armed forces that may be obtained with as little as nothing down.

US savings bonds: Bonds issued by the US Treasury to individuals. The most common types are Series EE and Series I. The maximum purchase amount each calendar year for a single Social Security number is $10,000. US savings bonds may be purchased at TreasuryDirect.gov.

US Treasury: The branch of the US government that is responsible for managing its finances and collecting taxes.

U.S. Treasury bills (T-bills): Short-term income securities issued by the US government that are often viewed as "cash equivalents." T-bills are safe, liquid investments but usually barely keep up with inflation over time, especially on an after-tax basis. The most common maturities upon issuance are 4, 8, 13, 26, and 52 weeks.

Value weighted index: An index where large market capitalization assets have a bigger effect than small market capitalization assets. For example, if Apple had a market capitalization of $1 trillion and Disney had a market capitalization of $200 billion, a 1% move in Apple would have five times the impact on the index than a 1% change in Disney's price. The S&P 500 is perhaps the best-known market capitalization weighted index. A value-weighted index is also known as a market capitalization weighted index.

Vintage clothing: Pre-owned or used clothing.

Value stock: A stock trading at a discount to the market based on a valuation metric, such as price/book or price/earnings.

Value investing: An investment approach that tries to buy assets at a deep discount to their true prices or intrinsic values. Value investors often buy stocks with low P/E ratios, low price/book values, and high dividend yields.

Variance: A quantitative measure of the dispersion of a variable, such as the rate of return on an investment, from its average. Academics often use it to quantify risk. The square root of the variance is the standard deviation, another widely used measure of risk.

Voided check: A cancelled check. Sometimes a voided check is needed to set up a direct debit from a checking account to pay a bill. Usually the word "void" is written on the check to make the intension clear that it should not be cashed by anyone.

Wall Street: A street in lower Manhattan, but the term usually refers to large firms at the center of the American financial system, regardless of location.

W-2: A tax form that lists annual wages paid to employees and taxes withheld.

W-4: A tax form that provides instructions regarding the amount of money to be withheld from each paycheck.

Warranty: A contract that covers the repair of a product that develops problems within a specified period of time. For example, new cars often come with a warranty that fixes any problems for the first few years of ownership.

Wilshire 5000: A stock market index that aims to track all US publicly traded stocks. Originally, the Wilshire 5000 was comprised of approximately 5,000 stocks. Today, the index tracks roughly 3,500 stocks.

Wire transfer: Payment from one financial account to another where the funds are guaranteed. A wire transfer is often used for important purchases, such as for the down payment on a home. It is extremely difficulty to cancel a wire transfer after it has been sent, in contrast to a traditional check. There is often a fee, typically in the $25 to $50 range, to send a wire transfer.

Withdrawal: The removal of funds from a bank account or other financial account.

Whale: An expression for a very large investor. Warren Buffett is considered a whale investor.

Work study: On-campus jobs provided to a student by the college itself, often as part of a financial aid package. These jobs may include a variety of positions, such as working in a computer lab, library, or student housing.

Yard sale: A sale of pre-owned or used items held by a homeowner on their property. A yard sale is also known as a garage sale.

Yield: The cash flow expected to be received from a security divided by the value of the security. It is expressed as a percentage. For example, if a bond pays a 5% coupon and has a market price of $1,000, the yield would be 5% ($50/$1,000).

Yield curve: A graph of the relationship between the time to maturity and yield to maturity for a series of bonds with the same credit risk. For example, a graph of the yields of all US Treasury debt, ranging from those about to mature to bonds with 30 years until maturity.

Yield to maturity: The discount rate for a bond. It is the market's estimate of the average annual return that comes from holding the bond until it matures.

Index

E

Y

Z